PANZER WARFARE
ON THE
EASTERN FRONT

Hans Schäufler

STACKPOLE
BOOKS

Published by
STACKPOLE BOOKS
5067 Ritter Road
Mechanicsburg, PA 17055
www.stackpolebooks.com

10 9 8 7 6 5 4 3 2 1

Library of Congress Cataloging-in-Publication Data

Schäufler, Hans, 1912–
  [Weg war weit. English.]
  Panzer warfare on the Eastern Front / Hans Schäufler.
      p. cm.
  ISBN 978-0-8117-1079-4
1. Germany. Heer—Armored troops—Biography. 2. World War, 1939–1945—Tank warfare.
3. World War, 1914–1918—Campaigns—Eastern Front—Biography. 4. World War,
1939–1945—Personal narratives, German. I. Title.
  D757.54.S28 2012
  940.54'217—dc23
                                        2012006355

CONTENTS

INTRODUCTION

IT WAS A LONG JOURNEY

From the Vistula in the west to Moscow in the east, and from Leningrad in the north down to the Caucasus in the south, the German armored divisions fought—the tip of the spear in the advance, the backbone of the infantry, always ready to launch an immediate counterattack when superior numbers pressed us.

IT WAS A LONG JOURNEY

Trying to make that journey come to life again in word and picture are a group of men, talented with the pen, from five different armored divisions. The purpose is not to describe strategy or tactics. It is simply to tell things the way they were.

IT WAS A LONG JOURNEY

Hard and onerous—it is still alive in us. But it was also colorful and full of uncommon events. From the safety of time, we can soberly say: Back then, the barely believable was accomplished. And it is important to know what humans such as you or me are capable of when everything depends on us.

IT WAS A LONG JOURNEY

From our own fading diary pages to a complete book, it was difficult—almost an adventure at times—to find the men who experienced the extraordinary back then and who could write down those experiences in an artful manner. Firsthand accounts and pictures had to be discovered. What is special about this book is that everyone tells his own story and uses the correct dates, names, and locations to stay true to what happened and relay the story of those who marched with them through the heat of the sun and the icy cold, through muddy morass and dust devils, through victory and defeat . . . until the very last hope died.

IT WAS A LONG JOURNEY!

Chapter 1

THOUGHTS OF A GENERAL AT THE BEGINNING OF THE WAR WITH RUSSIA

General der Panzertruppen **Walther K. Nehring, commander of the**
18. Panzer-Division[1]

On 21 June 1941, orders arrived for a surprise attack on the Soviet Union at 0315 hours on Sunday, 22 June. An appeal by Hitler to the troops accompanied the orders. So did two ideologically motivated orders concerning the harsh treatment to be given to Soviet troop commissars and the civilian populace. Their execution was prohibited by the German Army High Command to avoid endangerment of the discipline of the German forces.[2]

Thus, the die had been cast for this war. Hitler's decision, after months of deliberation, stood firm. Or was there a chance to change things? Could new suffering for the people on both sides be avoided? There was some optimism whenever one thought back to the use of military pressure in the execution of politics in the fall of 1938, when the occupation of the Sudetenland turned into a "Flower War" instead of leading to the flowing of blood. Hadn't the situation been similar on 25 August 1939, when the start of the war that evening was postponed—if only for a few days—after the approach march of German forces to the Polish frontier.

At that point, the civilian leadership of the state had to decide. The precedence of politics over the military was the basic framework for doing things. Only the leader of the state had access to all of the material necessary to allow far-reaching political determinations.

---

[1] Translator's Note. For each of the armored divisions discussed in detail by the authors in this book, there is an appendix with an abbreviated order of battle and list of commanders for that formation.

[2] Translator's Note. Nehring is referring to the "Guidelines for the Treatment of Political Commissars" (*Richtlinien zur Behandlung politischer Kommissare*), which was issued on 6 June 1941 and rescinded nearly one year later on 6 May 1942.

Nonetheless, the division commander, who felt responsible for the soldiers entrusted to him, was having some serious concerns regarding the decision of the senior man in the state.[3]

The German-Soviet Non-Aggression Pact of 23 August 1939 had been well received at the time of its signing. One perceived it as the end of German-Soviet enmity. In its place, both partners then began the exchange of goods of all types, another well-received initiative. The exchange continued through 21 June 1941 and had benefited Germany significantly, ever since the autumn of 1939, when it had been isolated from the West.

It should also not be forgotten that it was only by means of that agreement—that is to say, Stalin and Molotov—that Hitler was afforded his success over Poland. Or was it possible that those two men only wanted to divert Hitler's attention from their own country?

Finally, one could not forget the solemn declaration of Hitler to the German people in 1938 that Germany had no more territorial claims . . .

Why, then, the expansion of the war to the East, when it had already broken out in the West from the North Pole to Libya?

Moreover, one needs to observe and judge the development of the situation from another perspective. Despite the friendship treaty, political disagreements had arisen between Germany and the Soviet Union. They cannot be overlooked, especially in their far-reaching effects. Following the combined campaign against Poland, Stalin had forcibly incorporated the independent Baltic states into the Soviet Union and, in the following spring, had detached the Romanian province of Bessarabia through massive political pressure. On 30 November 1939, Stalin attacked the small nation of Finland in order to push the Soviet borders considerably westward. Although the Soviets, poorly led and inadequately equipped, had to pay a huge toll in blood, the Soviet political leadership achieved its goals in the end. Coupled with Molotov's visit to Berlin in December 1940 were additional demands that were at odds with German interests, for example, in the Balkans and the Dardanelles. It remained an open question, however, as to what was to be done.

Also troubling to German interests was the strong support the Soviet Union showed Yugoslavia in the spring of 1941, when Hitler was at pains to conclude a treaty with that nation. When Yugoslavia failed to join the Tripartite Pact and was subsequently invaded by German and Italian forces in April 1941, the crisis atmosphere between the German and Soviet governments increased significantly.

The political situation between the two major powers had unfortunately escalated to the danger of war. Russia continuously assembled forces on its western frontier. Germany reacted correspondingly as a security precaution. The Russian actions

---

[3] Translator's Note. As is typical of German writing style, an author often refers to himself in the third person, even though the account is essentially a first-person narrative.

were seen as a temporary measure to tread water while it built up its armaments. If Hitler did not succeed in forcing a clear decision in the West—if England did not relent—then Stalin would finally move into a position of decisive power. The deadly danger of a two-front war loomed over Germany, just as it had in the Great War, and against vastly superior forces, especially since England could count on the support of North America.[4]

Hitler, in his guise as head of state and commander in chief of the German Armed Forces, believed he could and had to avert that threat by quickly eliminating Russia as a potentially decisive ally of England. Correspondingly, he decided to conduct a preemptive war against the Soviet Union after Molotov's crisis-filled visit. It was a war he considered more certain of success than an air and sea war against Great Britain. After the extraordinary successes of the campaigns that had heretofore been conducted, he was convinced that he could do the same thing in Russia. The German Army High Command, as well as other countries, shared that opinion. Within the army, there were differing opinions, of course. There were a number of great difficulties that could not be overlooked: the vast expanse of the Russian territory; the almost inexhaustible supply of trained reserves; the well-developed industrial base, which extended beyond the Urals; the extremely inadequate transportation network; and, as a result, the great sensitivity of motorized formations to weather conditions.

Above all, the relatively limited area of operations that one experienced in the previous fighting was missing. Areas where one could quickly break through the enemy's defenses and his sources of human and material reserves—by means of motorized, mechanized, and armored forces—and encircle them, scatter them, and otherwise render them combat ineffective. In Russia, the situation was different. One ran into the danger of one's own forces being split apart and the great difficulty in providing logistics in an immense area.

It was said the Russians had 96 infantry divisions, 23 cavalry divisions, and 28 mechanized brigades at their disposal. Facing them in the East were 110 German infantry divisions, 20 armored divisions, and 12 motorized infantry divisions. The Germans, it should be noted, had better equipment, better training, better leadership, better organization, and a great deal of combat experience.

---

[4] Translator's Note. When Nehring wrote this some three decades ago, these were assumptions that could not be proven by fact because of the hermetically sealed Soviet archives of the time. Since then, most of these assertions have come to be accepted as true after exhaustive examination of Soviet secret archives by authors such as Viktor Suvorov in his book *Icebreaker: Who Started the Second World War?* (London: Hamish Hamilton, 1990). The matter is far from settled among historians, but the ideas advanced by many senior German generals after the war that the invasion of the Soviet Union was a preemptive strike has gained ground in some circles over the years.

One knew that the Russians had new types of tanks at their disposal, but it was thought they were only in limited numbers. On the German side, many considered the new 5cm main guns and antitank guns to be sufficient to deal with those threats.[5]

The Soviet soldier was considered to be a tough fighter, but company and field-grade officers were incapable of taking the initiative and the senior leadership had been considerably weakened by Stalin's "cleansing" measures. The Soviet air force was considered adequate, but the *Luftwaffe* was considered to be far superior.

In keeping with German leadership principles, the German operations plan relied on sudden surprise, bold maneuver by motorized formations, and the establishment of a main effort.

As far as I, a division commander, knew, three field army groups had been formed—North, Center, and South—which had the objectives of Kiev, Moscow, and Leningrad, respectively. The main effort was apparently in the center, which had two armored groups. *Panzergruppe 2*, under *Generaloberst* Guderian, was deployed to either side of Brest-Litowsk, while *Generaloberst* Hoth's *Panzergruppe 3* was just to the north. Army Group South had *Generaloberst* von Kleist's *Panzergruppe 1* allocated to it, while Army Group North had *Panzergruppe 4* of *Generaloberst* Hoepner.[6]

It was intended to break through the Russian forces with these armored wedges and then advance deep into the enemy's rear area, thus shaking up the entire defensive system through a series of thrusts. The non-motorized field armies were to follow as rapidly as possible, exploiting the successes created by the surprise moves of the motorized forces to complete the victory. The supreme command calculated that six to eight weeks were needed for that—at the latest, until the fall. Measures were not undertaken for a possible winter campaign.

The assigned operational objectives of the field army groups led them in different directions, which contradicted operational principles. Apparently, Hitler was so sure of what he was doing that he could accept that operational disadvantage as part of the bargain in conducting a rapid campaign.

Of course, for the division commander, it was tactical considerations that were of more concern than wide-ranging political and operational questions. It was more a matter of how the troops at the front were to master their missions as Army Group Center moved through Minsk (350 kilometers) and Smolensk (700 kilometers) on its way to Moscow (1,100 kilometers).

Before every large operation there is a great deal of uncertainty. Most of all, there is one big question: How will the new enemy fight? But there are others: Will

---

[5] Translator's Note. The error of that assumption will be borne out in the upcoming accounts.
[6] Translator's Note. For those unfamiliar with German ranks, there is an appendix at the back of the book. A *Panzergruppe* was essentially an "armored" field army, although it was not exclusively or even predominately filled with motorized, mechanized, or armored formations. The *Panzergruppen* were later redesignated as *Panzer-Armeen*.

the desired surprise be achieved despite the extensive build-up? What will be the effect of the poor transportation network on the vehicles that were not designed for it? Can the indispensible supplies of ammunition and fuel be assured? Those and similar questions raced through all leaders at the front on the day before the operation. They were not questions that could be answered in advance.

Every front soldier had done what he could to prepare. Every soldier knew what the new day would bring.

One needed to trust the political and military leadership of Hitler, who had heretofore raced from one success to another—frequently against the advice of his diplomats, generals, and admirals.

What had previously happened seemed like a miracle. The simple soldier did not have an all-encompassing view of things. He had to yield to the primacy of the political leader, who was obligated to weigh the pros and cons of his far-reaching decisions in a responsible manner. He was acting on behalf of the people, who had elected him in an overwhelming majority.

Therefore, the common soldier had no other choice. Tomorrow, on 22 June 1941, he would form up and move out, true to the oath of allegiance he had sworn on the flag to the *Führer* and *Reich* Chancellor, who was also recognized as such by the enemy powers.

THE FIRST STEP ON A LONG JOURNEY

Major **Martin Püschel, battalion commander in** *Schützen-Regiment 33* **of the** *4. Panzer-Division*

An improbably bright midday sun incubated and flickered above the soil of Volhynia.[7] Despite that, the occasional gust of wind caused our bodies to shiver as if under an icy breeze. You could look far across the terrain. Yellow fields of grain, light green pastures, interrupted by the blue-green flecks and strips of treacherous patches of marsh, white sand dunes, black woods, framed by luminous birches—all that gave the landscape its imprint. Despite the bright light, the viewer was unable to suppress the feeling of an inexplicable anxiety. The gigantic village on the horizon—with a church that dominated above the houses like a cathedral—seemed like a *Fata Morgana*. In the foreground were isolated and scattered farmsteads. The squat clay cottages, in a partial state of decline, appeared to have been abandoned by their inhabitants and reminded one of dwellings filled with evil spirits and witches from old legends and fairy tales.

Swarms of larger-than-life crows are the only signs of life. With their funereal appearance and husky crowing, they seemed like harbingers of death, who were announcing an approaching calamity. If we turned our gaze to the east, visibility was

---

[7] Translator's Note. Volhynia is a region of western Ukraine.

limited by a long, flat hill. On its crest was a wide, gray-white ribbon that ran from north to south. That ribbon was one of those infamous roadways that were hard to cross in the summer because larger vehicles sank up to their axles in floury dust and quickly ground to a halt. Whenever there was a rain that lasted for a while, however, they were transformed into a quagmire that made any traffic impossible. Whenever it was dry and the wind swept over them or a poor *panje* cart[8] struggled laboriously to make forward progress, the clouds of dust climbed to the heavens. They would last for minutes at a time in thick clouds. The terrain dropped steeply right behind the hill, transitioning quickly into marshy pastures that were surrounded by sand dunes and individual fields of grain, which bordered the banks of the Bug, which wound through the lowlands in twists and turns.

From where we were standing, the river could not be seen, and the long hill also hid our side from the stealthy and mistrustful gaze of the far bank, where the Russians were sitting. Only the sails of a windmill, which appeared to move day and night over there, appeared in uninterrupted relief above the crest of the hill, like a scout who quickly appears and then, after a fleeting glance into the terrain, throws himself back down into the grass. But we were also curious and mistrustful, since we had every reason to withdraw ourselves from the view of our sinister neighbors. At our location, there were also secrets that were hiding in the dark woods that appeared drunk in magical stillness. Secrets that had established themselves there over the last few nights and which were growing by the day. Secrets: in the form of tanks and artillery, vehicles and soldiers from all arms of the service, which grew in number from night to night. It was during those nights that the ever-quiet woods spoke. You thought you could hear murmurs and whispers. Occasionally, it sounded like a screeching or an involuntary droning, then perhaps a hissing and moaning. Will-o'-the-wisps in the form of white, blue, red, and green colors shot out between the trees.

At night we lay on the banks of the river up front. As a result, we could only hear a distant hubbub to our rear. But from the east bank, the same sounds echoed, stronger and more accentuated. We were thankful for the constant wind from the east, which kept our own noises from the enemy and carried the sounds of his own work on over to us. With our trained ears, we made efforts to interpret all of their variations.

After the short nights around the summer solstice, the first light of day allowed the nighttime apparitions to quickly evaporate. As always, the woods appeared to be the height of quietude, and no eye, even with the help of the strongest of field glasses, could fathom their secrets. When the first rays of the morning sun broke through the dense crowns of the trees, every movement was frozen in place. Nonetheless, overnight, new branches and hedges had sprung out of the ground, where there had been none the previous day. One needed to get quite close to real-

---

[8] Translator's Note. A *panje* cart was a simple horse-drawn wagon, usually with only a single axle and drawn by a small draught horse, known in Russian as a *panje*.

ize that new war machinery had found its way there during the night and, masterfully camouflaged, had denied itself to curious glances, even from above. The soldier, dead tired and bathed in sweat, who was attempting during the day to make up for missed sleep from the previous night, fought and swore in a hopeless battle against bloodthirsty mosquitoes and biting ants of hitherto unknown size and martial spirit. He then longed for the night. But when the ants and the mosquitoes went to sleep, millions of the smallest of flies awoke from the dirty marsh holes and selected eyes, mouth, nose and ears as their attack objectives. There was no weapon against them. The magic of the primeval forest! But that was just a small foreshadowing of the weeks to come.

The first day of summer 1941—21 June—came to a close. The sun sank blood red in the west. Great clouds, not unlike those of fog banks, started to rise, the likes of which we had not seen on any of the previous evenings. But it was not fog. It was the dust from the dry, sandy roads, which was being churned up by endless columns of vehicles. On this day, they were all aiming for the final assembly areas and attack positions. We weren't too thrilled about that drama taking place and looked distrustfully to the east, where the Russians on the other side of the Bug were certainly keeping a sharp eye. In our opinion, those movements could not help but draw their attention.

That night we also had to break camp to occupy our jumping-off points along the river for the attack, positions we had scouted out weeks ago. The storm was to break early tomorrow morning.

As was always the case in such situations, our thoughts raced far ahead of the actual events. We read the attack orders over and over again; looked at the map; visualized the attack sector in front of us; tried to imagine how the initial action would go—crossing the river in assault craft and pontoon boats, which for the most part had long since been hidden in the high reeds and grass along the river bank. We would only have to put a couple of thousand meters behind us that night. It was going to be pitch black. The route was a difficult one and often led across narrow footbridges over numerous stretches of marsh that required our undivided attention. No vehicle could get stuck, no march columns could get intertwined, and utmost calm had to be maintained so as to reach the designated areas in the short amount of allocated time. The intent was to surprise and overrun, if we intended to reach the attack objectives of the first day.

The terrain on the far bank was in no way favorable. After a couple hundred meters of dry ground, we would encounter a two-kilometer-wide stretch of marsh that was not foot trafficable and which offered no cover or concealment of any type. A single broad embankment led across it. On the far edge of the marsh was that thick, dark and foreboding woods. We did not know what kind of secrets it held. Going farther into the rear area, there was one natural obstacle after the other. For the time being, however, the embankment was our main worry. It would only take a few courageous men and a single machine gun to defend it. Correspondingly, we had to cross it at the same time as the fleeing enemy no matter what it cost. Everything else was an afterthought.

All of those thoughts occupied us in the last few minutes before we moved out.

All of a sudden, it turned dark. Silently, the long columns of riflemen snaked their way out of the woods and into the open ground. The ammunition cans and pontoon boats weighed heavily on their shoulders. The orders that remained necessary were whispered. Only an occasional curse word or rattling could be heard. The movement proceeded like clockwork, as if it were the normal routine. And, despite all that, what an effort in work, sweat, and discipline.

The darkness allowed only a few meters of vision. Once again, as in the previous nights, the purring of the engines could be heard—vehicles moving without light at a man's pace. But tonight, they were moving close to the Bug. Would the Russians finally wake up? Once again, there was a cool wind from the east, which dampened the noises. The enemy was still quiet, and the dark woods continued to unveil their secrets. They were still covered by the nighttime darkness, but that was only for another few hours.

Panting, the riflemen march with some effort through the darkness. One could slowly start to see a dim morning light in the east. The stars continued to sparkle in the heavens, however, and nature was still asleep. Only the crickets chirped. At that point, we spied the weakly gleaming, steel-blue band of the river along the bottomland. We would soon be at our objective. The companies deployed and slowly pushed closer to the banks, using folds in the ground and the dense fields of grain.

An unusual rolling sound on the far bank made us listen up. A shrill whistling sound—everyone was flat on their stomachs. Then another long whistle. The rolling sound became a roar. Trailing a powerful shower of sparks, a train was passing the railway crossing guard shack several hundred meters from the east bank of the river along the line that paralleled it. The roar transitioned to a rolling sound and then disappeared gradually in the distance. We breathed a sigh of relief. At that point, we were certain that the Russians did not have a clue of our presence. But speed was also of the essence. The first light was becoming ever more intense. The outlines of hills and woods against the sky a few hundred meters away became sharper by the minute. In half an hour, the signs of life would return.

It turned cold in the vicinity of the river. We were completely drenched in sweat and could barely keep our teeth from chattering. Was it just the cold? Or was it the keyed-up nerves, over which we no longer had any control in the eerie, ashen first light of morning? Was it our own damned weaker self coming to light? We weren't recruits, after all! How often had we had to master similar missions in previous campaigns? It was probably the nightmare of this damned eerie terrain, which never seemed to go away, even on a sunny day, and which never seemed capable of breaking the tight bonds around our chests.

By then, we had reached our concealed positions. A quick cigarette and then get out the entrenching tool. Deeper into the moist earth. The tenseness gradually went away. One after the other, the reports started to come in rapidly from the companies: "Jumping-off position reached; no enemy contact!"

Thank God! A glance at my watch indicated that we were right at ten minutes before H-Hour. At that point, only a few shadowy stragglers and messengers scurried bent over through the tall grass.

We kept nodding off. If only we could sleep! But the morning cold woke us up after a few minutes. Shivering, we pressed together in the hole. A bottle of cognac—one of the last souvenirs from France—made its rounds. The stuff tasted terrible on an empty stomach, but it burned and warmed. Then a few morsels of bread. Who knew when we might be able to do that again?

Morning broke. High in the dark-blue heavens, where the stars were gradually fading, the first larks started to sing.

A slight wind arose and caressed the fields of grain. Otherwise, everything was quiet. We continued to struggle with falling asleep. A couple of snorers were competing with one another. There were still thirty minutes to go; then the fire wizardry was supposed to start. The hands of the watch moved unbelievably slowly. Another twenty-five minutes! "Good God, put the thing away, otherwise you'll go crazy!" The chirping of the crickets was gradually replaced by the buzzing of the mosquitos. In the distance, on the far bank, one pooch was yelping and was holding a dialog with the light barking from another dog in the neighboring farmstead. The cattle were probably being fed there.

There were only eight minutes left to go. Nothing could keep us staying down in the hole. We wanted to take in the deceptive image of peace one more time so as to free our thoughts of everything that was already behind us. Back home they were still lying in warm beds. One last time, my hand worked its way involuntarily up to my breast pocket towards the last letter from home. I hoped no one saw that. Sentimental feelings were out of place at that moment.

One more look at the watch. Another five minutes . . .

The eerie quiet that oppressed us was abruptly torn by a rolling thunder in the distance. Muzzle flashes twitched along the heavens, followed by the bursting crash of the impacts of heavy shells. Everybody jumped up from his half sleep. What did all that mean? It had to be in the sector of the division to the left, farther to the north in the direction of Brest-Litowsk. No, on the contrary, it was a lot closer to us. Were our watches wrong? The flashes twitched again. The thunder rumbled. Once again, the heavy impacts burst. You could also unmistakably hear the hammering reports of the light *Flak* and the rattling of numerous machine guns. Did they screw up or had the Russians beaten us to the punch? Everyone's eyes were directed excitedly to the north, where the racket was continuing. Then there was a singing and a droning above us that did not want to stop. Our aircraft. Pretty high. It wasn't light enough yet to identify them. Only a few position markers could be made out. Put the helmet on quickly . . . tighten the belt some more. You had to be prepared for any eventuality . . .

All at once, there was a long, continuous flash on the horizon behind us, a pulsating sheet of fire that didn't want to end, followed by the dark reports of heavy guns and then the sharp barks of the lighter calibers, whose blasts were reverberated back from the woods. At that point, there was a whistling, a rumbling, and a howling above us like flocks of swooping geese. All of a sudden, we were wide awake. Lances of flame from the impacts twitched on the far bank; we soon saw fountains of earth shoot up. Mushroom clouds of smoke rose skyward. The fireballs of the ricochets formed ugly black specks just above the ground. We heard the old trees burst in the woods. Bright flames struck skyward. A haystack caught fire and illuminated the terrain around it far and wide like a torch.

The cracks of the firing, the sputtering, howling, and whizzing of the rounds, the detonations of the shells, the buzzing and clashing of the shrapnel—all of that was rolled into a powerful storm and the rage of an earthquake, which made the earth shake as if Judgment Day had arrived.

All nervousness was swept away. In the hard faces of the combat-experienced soldiers, the eyes glinted in grim determination. The new soldiers, who were to receive their baptism of fire, pressed themselves to the ground in a somewhat fearful manner. My thoughts were crisp and clear again. All of the soft impulses of the heart had died out. At that point, through the whizzing and hammering of the drumbeat of fire, the explosions of the bombs from the aircraft were overpowering everything.

Thick clouds of black and sulfur-yellow smoke were hanging above the woods on the far side of the marshland. The billowing white smoke from the smoke rounds drifted across the ground and blinded the observation of the enemy.

Once again, we had our watches in our hands, counting the minutes we had left until we jumped off.

We had to shout in one another's ears in order to get individual words. It was still another twenty minutes until the assault. We intended to form up ahead of time, however, so as to get to the far riverbank as quickly as possible, despite the danger of running into our own fire. We wanted to use its protection. We were doing this on our own initiative, even though higher command levels were not in agreement with our intentions.

The rush of battle had us in its grasp. The bonds around our chests had been broken. All heaviness had disappeared. The example set by the unflappable men rallied the hesitant ones. We raced to the riverbank with long strides. The pontoon rafts hit the water with a splash; the engines of the assault craft started their song. Our machine guns fired in continuous bursts against the edge of the railway embankment.

The first of the boats moved to the middle of the river. They were joined by increasing numbers. We had to brace against the streaming water with superhuman strength. A rudder broke apart. We turned in circles. Then we got back on course. We moved forward, meter-by-meter. Just don't break down! "Grab the reeds with your hand and hold tight so we finally get out of here!" And then the guy fell head first into the water! It wasn't deep, though. Others voluntarily jumped in and waded to the shore. The boat was already heading back to get more comrades. We then had solid ground under our feet, the soil of Russia. The bayonets flew onto the carbines; the safety latches were released. Fists grabbed onto the hand grenades more firmly. The hurricane of artillery fire was still racing overhead. The wall of fire caused by the impacts was right in front of us.

The artillery then jumped forward. There was no need for any more commands. Everything raced forward.

Then it was our turn. Forward! The storm burst loose. The door had been kicked in.

THE LEAP ACROSS THE BUG

Gefreiter Hans-Martin Wild, loader in *Artillerie-Regiment 103* of the *4. Panzer-Division*

Bedded down on a few bushels of straw, I got a couple of hours of sleep. A comrade woke me up: "It's time."

It took a while to sink in. I rubbed my eyes and got up. The cannoneers were standing around in small groups, smoking cigarettes and discussing in subdued voices what was to come.

Another fifteen minutes! An unbearable tenseness bore down over the battery. War with Russia! No one wanted to believe it.

Cannoneers were getting the first rounds ready. They handled the familiar, but dangerous shells carefully, like a small child. The hands of the watch moved slowly towards the quarter-hour mark. The crews had assembled around their guns. They stood there silently. Everyone was thinking of his loved ones, who were dozing away a work-free Sunday back home without a worry in the world.

Up front, along the Bug, a shot was heard. Immediately afterwards, a machine gun fired. It was 0313 hours![9] The artillery fell silent. It took a little while, but then all hell broke loose. Hundreds of shells started spewing eastward and filled the air with a thundering and a crashing. I was barely able to hear the commands of the battery officer.

"Fire!" A jerk and the gun shot far to the rear. The first shell started rushing towards the enemy.

The cannoneers showed practiced hands. Shell after shell left the tubes of our 9th Battery. The earth trembled.

Dozens of batteries were nearby: howitzers, cannon, and mortars. All of them were taking the designated targets under fire. The important positions on the far side of the Bug were to be smashed in a deliberate fashion.

---

[9] Translator's Note. German accounts usually use official military time as opposed to local time. In this case, the local time in the Soviet Union was two hours ahead—0513 hours.

The tubes of the guns turned hot. In less than fifty minutes, more than 100 15-centimeter shells left the muzzle. The cannoneers cooled the tube with wet rags and buckets of water. Steam rose skyward.

Then they continued firing.

There was a broad cloud of smoke on the horizon. It was burning in every nook and cranny. It was fiery red looking towards the sky and twitching in the dark of the graying morning. A spooky sight!

The first few aircraft rumbled in the distance, two long-range reconnaissance birds. Right after them, a batch of fighters moved along the Bug to the north.

The prime movers churned their way through the fine dirt towards the avenue of advance. It took hours before the engineer bridge was reached. One column after the other bunched up at the crossing point. Off to the left, where the bottomland of the Bug was flashing silver, it appeared that an engagement was taking place. Cannon and machine guns fired without interruption. It was two Russian bunkers—completely isolated—that defended until the very end.

The roads worsened. We moved ahead very slowly. It was all over by the time we reached the start of the wooded terrain. Truck after truck had to be pulled out by the prime movers. Whole convoys of vehicles waltzed through the knee-deep dirt in that manner. The motorcyclists had an especially difficult time of it. They had to push their heavy machines—and it was brutally hot.

While in the middle of fighting that tiresome fight against the bad roads and the deep sand, we encountered the graves of the first men killed in this war. A peculiar feeling came over us at that location. Shells from German guns had impacted among the ranks of German soldiers. There had been a misunderstanding. The Russians had only offered light resistance and, as a result, our riflemen advanced faster then had been planned. They attacked aggressively into the beaten area of a targeted zone.

Schützen-Regiment 12, which our heavy battalion was supporting, was the flank guard. We stopped outside of Miedna and waited for the arrival of the 1st Battalion. Nearby was the command post of our *4. Panzer-Division*. We saw our commander for the first time, *Generalmajor* von Langermann und Erlenkamp. *Major* Hoffmann, the commander of the 1st Battalion of the rifle regiment, came racing up.

The first batch of prisoners was brought in for questioning. Everyone gathered around and looked at the uniforms and equipment, which were still new to us. All of that was interesting, when you saw it for the first time. I had the dubious pleasure, thanks to my rudimentary knowledge of Russian, of being the translator. After a fashion, I asked the questions *Major* Hoffmann put together. My poor victim took pains to try to understand me. And we actually were able to bring about something tantamount to a conversation. The Russian breathed easier when I assured him that he was not going to be shot—he was a prisoner of war.

The time passed in fits. We were not moving forward. We were still outside of Miedna. Our tanks had been in Kobrin for some time and had reached Avenue of

Advance I.[10] At that point, they were also unable to advance, since they no longer had any fuel. The entire division was literally stuck in the dirt.

We found out that the divisional logistics elements had been rerouted and were heading towards Kobrin via Brest-Litowsk.

The roads worsened. Our prime movers towed an entire medical company through the sandy desert.

Miedna was finally behind us, when it turned evening. We had processed the initial images of destruction. The road became noticeably better. We raced through the night so as not to lose contact. A prime mover crashed into a gigantic bomb crater in the middle of the road due to the poor illumination provided by the night-lights. Fortunately, no one was seriously hurt.

Moving past the traces of the first day of fighting, our long column reached a broad, cobblestone road early on the morning of 23 June. It was Avenue of Advance I. To our left, there was the thunder of heavy artillery. We heard it was coming from the men laying siege to Brest-Litowsk, who were still fighting for the citadel.

A Russian bomber appeared in the glare of the hot summer day. Everyone became agitated and stared skyward. The aircraft launched the craziest maneuvers up in the air so as to avoid the fire from the *Flak*, which was firing like crazy. While diving, it fled the area.

Once beyond the city of Kolbrin, the column got jammed up again. We dismounted. Light Russian tanks were burned out along the road. A Russian lay wounded next to his vehicle.

A German tank with destroyed optics was located somewhat off to the side. An antitank round had hit it right in the vision slot. Moved, we stood next to the freshly dug grave.

Via Triumphalis is what you could have called the avenue of advance. Signs of victory followed the road far into old Russian territory. Vast quantities of light Russian T-26's were shot up or bogged down or abandoned in panic along the roadside. We were stared down by extremely modern artillery, antiaircraft weaponry, prime movers, and antitank guns—tipped over or pushed into the ditch by our tanks. We frequently saw the results of German aerial attacks. Humans, animals, and equipment were mowed over, jumbled together. Dead horses stretched their legs into the air, their stomachs swollen from decomposition. The sweet smell of carrion lingered over the roadway. The trunks of trees—cut down, shredded by bombs—jutted out of the limbs of collapsed crowns.

Onward . . . onward . . . the march continued without interruption into the vast expanse. The German war machinery spread itself out with oppressive superiority

---

[10] Translator's Note. The original German uses the ubiquitous term of *Rollbahn*, which, depending on context, can mean road, avenue of advance, main supply route, or a combination thereof. To avoid any confusion, the term will be translated to match the author's intent.

and waltzed forward in a deliberate fashion. Fighters and reconnaissance aircraft monitored the roads in waves. Dive bombers headed towards the enemy; supply aircraft cruised just a few meters above the treetops, rumbling eastward with fuel for the lead tank elements.

No one had any doubts about a quick victory in this campaign against Russia. The initial misgivings started to slowly disappear.

By night, we reached Bereza-Kartuska. The town was burning. The amount of captured and destroyed Russian war materiel was immense. The area was saturated with rubble far and wide.

It could be seen by what was left behind in the Russian retreat that there was fighting ahead of us. When we moved out the next day to continue the march, one thing was clear: the war was just starting!

THE TANK ENGAGEMENT AT RAZIECHOW

From the diary of *Unteroffizier* **Gustav W. Schrodek, gunner in** *Panzer-Regiment 15* **of the** *11. Panzer-Division*
11. Panzer-Division: Panzer Marsch!

23 June 1941. A knocked-out enemy tank on the road was the only sign that there had been fighting ahead of us. In the haze of a clear summer day, the outlines of a village could be seen on the horizon: Raziechow, our initial objective for the day.

Panzer-Regiment 15 spread out on line. The concentrated power was impressive, especially since it was enhanced by the 8.8-centimeter guns of the *Flak* forces, which had gone into position along a broad front. Behind us, the cannon of the divisional artillery had also pulled up.

What would happen next? We didn't know. We also didn't care. Based on this arsenal of weaponry, we felt stronger than ever before.

Aircraft came into view, a large formation of bombers. Finally, the first German machines we had seen in this campaign. At least that's what we thought in our childlike simplicity. Wrong! We soon saw red stars under the wide wings. Heaven help us, if they dropped their loads on us! Thank God they had already let their bombs go somewhere else.

The lead company on the left moved out. A short while later, the remaining companies of the 1st Battalion followed. Our company, the 5th Company, was still waiting when the husky barks of main guns roughly disrupted the peace of the day. The tank engagement at Raziechow had started!

While we deployed into battle formation and moved up to the village, the sound of fighting was drowned out by the thundering of the tank engines. We then received the first salvo of fire. The first rounds impacted around us with an ear-deafening din. Thank God they did not cause any major damage.

"Halt!" was ordered, as if to grant us a final respite before the battle. We pushed open the hatches and took a look around. No, in fact, there hadn't been any casualties among our ranks.

On the other hand, three Russian tanks were ablaze at the entrance to Raziechow. The terrain in front of us inclined slightly upward. We did not know what was behind the rise. We speculated it might be a military facility. That meant we had to reconnoiter the area in front of the rise. Our platoon leader, *Leutnant* von Renesse, who always liked to stick his nose well forward, volunteered, and nobody took issue with him.[11]

The five vehicles of our 2nd Platoon thundered off after we were given one final bit of information: one of our own tanks was also supposed to be forward as well. Three of the tanks of our platoon had the short 5-centimeter main gun; the other two had the 3.7-centimeter version.

We advanced in a wedge, knowing full well that we were on our own and only connected to our company by means of radio. But was there anything really bad that could happen?

We stopped in front of a road and sent a situation report. There was nothing interesting to report. We felt like we were sightseers, careening around there in no-man's-land. Nothing was seen nor heard from one of our own vehicles.

Suddenly, the sound of an engine could be heard approaching. Pay attention! Over to the right, moving along the road, was a tank approaching over a slight rise. Fifty meters behind it was a second one, then a third and a fourth. We couldn't tell what kind of vehicles they were, since we had to look into the sun. We were convinced, however, that they were friendly vehicles. The idea that they could be enemy tanks never dawned on us.

But what the hell?! Why hadn't someone told us that another platoon had been sent forward to reconnoiter?

As good soldiers, we sent out a friendly inquiry by radio.

The answer—that there were no German tanks in the vicinity except for us— was no longer needed, since we had seen the red stars on the steel monsters in the meantime.

Our hearts were aflutter. Was it the shock, the fear, or perhaps the joy that we would now be able to prove ourselves? Perhaps they had not seen us? Maybe they thought we were Russian tanks? Based on the size, we were about the same. Otherwise? We would have to wait for that.

About the point where we had them about 100 meters in front of our guns, the dance kicked off. Without showing any effect, the lead vehicle, which I had engaged, continued to move on. The same thing happened to the other comrades in my platoon.

---

[11] Translator's Note. Not immediately apparent is the fact that Schrodek is von Renesse's gunner.

What the hell?! Where was the oft-praised superiority we had over the Russian tanks? They had told us over and over again that our main guns would have an easy time with them. But the only thing we achieved with our rapid fire and clear hits was the fact that they quickly turned around and headed back from where they had come.

"2nd Platoon, over!"

"2nd Platoon, over!"

While we sent a few more rounds towards the fleeing Russians, we noticed for the first time that we were being continuously called over the radio.

We reported: "Engaged four enemy tanks. Type not certain, since not listed in the recognition tables. Despite numerous hits, our rounds had no effect. Have the impression our rounds ricocheted. Enemy tanks moved back without engaging. Should we pursue? Over."

We received orders to return to the company. That was fine by us, since we weren't feeling so good about the thought of pursuing an enemy who was able to digest well-placed rounds without any effect.

On the other hand, perhaps we had given him a good beating. It's just that we could not see it. That was our hope, but we didn't believe it.

A little while later, we were back with our regiment. We had to render a long report about our engagement, and we were proud to receive so much attention.

Our tanks were quickly refueled and rearmed. We also had just enough time to choke down a few bites. We then became tired, allowing us to sleep and forget everything. I don't remember how long we dozed. Shouts and a banging on the tank walls brought us back to reality.

We must have slept the sleep of the dead. That's the only way to explain how we slept through an artillery barrage that also managed to damage our left drive sprocket. We quickly changed the track links that were damaged. Then we noticed that there was only a mound of dirt left on the track guard where the rations crate had been stored.

Our division's reconnaissance aircraft, a Fieseler *Storch*, descended and tossed out a report canister. A short while later, orders were issued: "Prepare for combat!"

"Elevated alert status!"

It was said that a large armored formation was headed towards us from behind the hill.

Well, then, let's bring it on!

A quarter of an hour passed before they arrived: 10, 20, 50, 100. The numbers kept increasing.

The first few rounds hissed their way towards us. The impacts were way too short. Since our weapons were most effective at 400 meters, we had to keep our nerve and allow the mass of Russian armor to approach even closer. A depression in front of us removed the first attack wave from our sight. But when they appeared again, we had the best firing positions imaginable. Fireworks of an unbelievable size and scope started up. My first round was a direct hit. My second round tore a chunk of turret away from another enemy tank.

New targets kept surfacing. As if in a drunken rush, we took up our site pictures and knocked them out. The Russians couldn't believe what was happening. More and more tanks kept appearing from out of the depression. They were not successful in penetrating our lines, let alone achieving a breakthrough.

Without suffering a single loss, our tanks knocked out sixty-eight Russian tanks at Raziechow.

It was not possible to determine how many each individual tank knocked out. The main thing, however, was the overall success, to which each of us contributed his part.

As it turned dusk, we continued eastward without enemy resistance.

It was 3 July 1941. A mixed *Kampfgruppe*,[12] about the size of two companies, assumed the lead. *Leutnant* von Renesse would have died of shame, if our 2nd Platoon had not been a part of it. For the first time, we headed to the southeast. We ran into the road leading east from Ostrog and headed east on it.

After a few kilometers, a village came into view. Villages in enemy territory, particularly those along the avenue of advance, merited special attention. We regrouped, and *Leutnant* von Renesse was able to see to it that our vehicle took over the lead.

You have to have experienced it yourself to understand what it means to drive point. All of your senses are stretched to the breaking point. You won't get anywhere without some luck and a certain nose for it. In addition, a very quick reaction time was also a part of it.

Tank 22, with an *Oberfeldwebel* in command, moved to the left of us. In intervals of ten to twenty meters, the other vehicles of the platoon followed behind. Behind them, at a somewhat greater distance, was the mixed *Kampfgruppe* under the command of the company commander of the 6th Company.

We got closer and closer to the village. During a security halt, we heard a few roosters crowing, otherwise complete silence. A suspiciously deceptive quiet—or so it appeared to us.

Then we got to the edge of the village—and we saw them. A few meters in front of us were two nicely camouflaged Russian tanks. I took up a sight picture on the one off to the right of the road. The gun reported—direct hit! Again and again. Tank 22 reported: "Vehicle knocked out!" At that point, the vehicle I had taken under fire started to burn as well. A Russian, probably the only survivor, bailed out. That meant we could also report knocking out a tank.

---

[12] Translator's Note. *Kampfgruppe* = battle group. Unlike U.S. Army usage, no differentiation is made between size. Thus, a *Kampfgruppe* can be a team (company level) or a task force (battalion level) or even larger and can include elements from several different combat arms within it (plus, occasionally, combat service support elements). Usually, such groups were named after the senior commander in the elements, e.g., *Kampfgruppe Peiper*.

That terrible game repeated itself several times. Then we finally made it through to the other side of the village. Tally: Tank 22—five vehicles destroyed; our Tank 21—three more. That's what our report said. In all, nine tanks were counted as having been knocked out. It was really immaterial. It would have been embarrassing, however, if only seven had been counted afterwards. At the end of the village, where we all gathered together, we moved out in line and had a great field of view to the front. The road disappeared into a patch of woods about three kilometers away. In front of it were fields and pastures, which sloped down slightly from the village to the woods. About a kilometer away and about 100 meters off the side of the road was a grouping of peasant huts.

It was a peacetime portrait, lit up by a terrific summer sun. But that didn't last too long. We were rapidly called back to reality.

On the road in front of us, a column of trucks was approaching. As long as it was just trucks, it wasn't so bad. Nonetheless: pay attention!

The closer the twelve trucks approached, the more it became obvious that they thought we were the Russian tanks that we had just dispatched. It was probably their trains.

Whatever the case, they presented themselves as terrific targets, which we carefully divided up among ourselves. But it still wasn't time to open fire.

At that point, however, an unlucky radio operator, in his excitement, pressed down on the release mechanism for his machine gun. We had no other choice but to also let fly. Valuable seconds were lost and three of the trucks were able to turn and flee. It goes without saying that we would have liked to have kicked our own asses. *Leutnant* von Renesse solved the problem in his own fashion. He ordered our platoon to follow them.

And so we moved up, picking up speed as we went. We soon reached the road and figured we would catch up with the trucks, when there were fireworks up ahead. We were taken under fire by guns along the edge of the woods. I then heard that a radio message had come from the company, but I did not understand it. I only heard *Leutnant* von Renesse radio back to the company that he intended to assault and take the artillery position. He yelled to the driver to pull off the road to the left and give it full throttle to the artillery position.

And we sped out. Tank 21, the only one on the open plain. We actually felt the impacting rounds come closer by the second. We swung the vehicle to the left and then to the right. We were flying. I fired at random. We then moved through a cornfield. We turned a bit to the side and rocked along with the tank.

"Bunker!" someone in the vehicle shouted. And then there was a knocking. Lightning flashed; steel shrapnel hissed around. The sounds of pain. Moaning. And the vehicle remained stationary.

"Get out . . . get out now!"

I threw the hatch open, but I had to close it again immediately, since it was covered by a murderous machine-gun fire. I then saw them through the vision slot:

bunkers . . . small ones . . . large ones . . . to the left of me . . . up front. And what was to the right? To the right! For the time being, I was able to see that the loader's hatch was wide open and that my tank commander, the loader, and the radio operator were gone.

Bail out!

Our driver was at my feet, moaning and his shirt covered in blood. He had taken a lot of shrapnel.

And me? What was wrong with me? I didn't appear to be wounded. I wasn't able to find anything initially. Anything else? I still had my wits about me. I slowly started to think. Why don't I just bail out like the others? I was no longer able to do that. For one thing, because I couldn't leave our wounded driver alone. For another . . . they were firing on our vehicle from all sides like crazy. The heavier rounds, however, were sailing past our vehicle. Were the Russians really that bad of shots? Or were they firing at another target?

It wasn't until later that I discovered that the leader of our *Kampfgruppe* had advanced fearlessly close to our vehicle, picking up the dismounted crewmembers. Unfortunately, he did not escape without a scratch. His vehicle was hit, which cost the radio operator his life. That was the reason for the increased amount of firing.

I was still camping out in our tank, however. Following my intuition, I traversed the turret a bit to the left so as to have more of a sloped surface to the front. Should I have just left well enough alone? Probably assuming that the knocked-out vehicle had come back to life, the next few rounds were intended for me. It was enough to drive you crazy!

Then . . . a murderous racket. It took my breath away. A hit on the mantlet. Fortunately for me, it ricocheted—thanks to the positioning of the turret. Then another muffled smack. It shook the tank through and through. The heavy jack on the track guards was no longer there. Old rags that were near me started to smoke. Just don't let the rest of the vehicle start to burn!

All of a sudden, the enemy's fires stopped. Silence surrounded me. What did all that mean? I cannot claim that I was especially comfortable with the thought that I was alone in a knocked-out tank with a badly wounded comrade in the middle of a bunker-spiked line of resistance. The only contact with the company, the radio, was destroyed. Signaling from the open hatch had little chance of success in being seen by my comrades at this distance. It was a different story with the enemy, however. This all meant that I had no opportunity to send out a sign of life.

Afterwards, I discovered that a *Feldwebel* from our platoon had been given orders to keep on eye on us. After a little bit of back and forth, he limited himself to the observation that we must have been dead for some time, since we otherwise would have already drawn notice to ourselves by then.

The "watch dog" of our platoon, an *Unteroffizier*, was not satisfied with that self-serving logic, however. He moved out in his vehicle, Tank 25, and raced out towards our tank from the left at full throttle. I saw him thundering forward and pulled the wounded driver up onto the gunner's seat, hoping I would be able to switch tanks with him. Dear God, I pleaded, please allow 25 to get through to us in one piece! And, in the end, he was actually able to do it, ramming against the left side of the vehicle with a hard blow.

I gave the driver a shove and pushed behind him until he was on the track guard. By the time I was in position to attempt a jump, 25 took off at full steam. In the fireworks that were going off, he had not noticed what had happened.

I remained behind, abandoned and alone.

I had to get away . . . I had to get out of there! I considered the possibilities. I racked my brain. Stupidly, I started thinking about manuals and directives and what they said to do when abandoning a knocked-out tank. According to them, I had to dismount with my gas mask. I slung it around my shoulder. The manuals in the vehicles were also supposed to be taken along. I grabbed them. In addition to my pistol, I also slung the submachine gun on.

I had barely stuck my head outside the hatch when there was hell to pay—machine-gun fire. For the time being, it was all over with any thoughts of bailing out. Besides, the stupid gasmask and the cumbersome submachine gun were hindering me. Off with them, despite the regulations!

I sat there, considered my options, and thought some more. I have no idea how long it was. Then I heard the sound of an engine and saw an enemy tank approaching me from the woods. There was no more time for thinking. I got ready to jump and sprung out of the turret with a mighty leap. I landed in one piece, despite the burst of machine-gun fire intended for me. For a couple of seconds, I played dead. Then I pulled myself with a jerk behind the tank. So . . . at least I was that far. But what was I going to do then? There was open terrain behind me, followed by a barbed-wire entanglement. The cornfield was not until after that; it was the only thing that could offer cover.

Of course . . . the smoke grenades . . . they could help me. With the barrel of my pistol, I freed them from their mounts. Whether they would still ignite? Yes, sir . . . they lit up. Thank heavens! But I no longer had the strength to toss them far. When they started to get hot, I simply let them roll out of my hands. Where was the smoke headed? Instead of towards the Russians, it was drifting towards our lines. By then, I couldn't give a shit. I crouched down to run and gulped down as much air as the smoke would allow. I took heart, geared up, and raced off. At some point in running, I grabbed for an officer's cap, that of my tank commander. I then reached the entanglement, raced through it, and plunged towards the cornfield. I made it to the edge of the field, despite the hail of lead around me. From there, I waved to my comrades and collapsed.

When I regained consciousness, I saw a tank next to me. To be more precise: I saw a gigantic track and didn't know whether it was friend or foe. Finally, I heard the saving words: "Jump up on the rear!" That was easier said than done in my condition. But I finally got up there and someone pulled me through the loader's hatch.

What did I care that the tank was also being heavily engaged? It knocked out the tank I previously mentioned and then put a couple of bunkers out of commission. I had nothing at all to do with what happened.

We moved back slowly. Heavy Russian artillery fire impacted to the right and left. A self-propelled *Flak* that had halted next to us received a direct hit. I was so completely out of my head that I threw open the loader's hatch and jumped out in a panic. Then there was a rushing noise approaching me again. I ran to another tank and rode on it out of the beaten zone.

Finally, finally, I was out of there.

It was *Leutnant* von Seydlitz, a descendent of the famous cavalry general, who had picked me up at the forward edge of the cornfield. For his demonstrated bravery, he received the Iron Cross, First Class. There was no one who congratulated him in a more heartfelt manner than I.

On the following day, the heavily reinforced line of bunkers fell after an appropriate artillery preparation and the employment of our motorized riflemen.

On the afternoon of 4 July, the loader and I recovered the mortally wounded 21. The maintenance section repaired it enough that it could move back to the workshop in Ostrog under its own power. Lacking a driver, I sat myself behind the controls and took it back at a leisurely pace.

A few days later, our 21 was combat-ready again.

✠

It was 21 July 1941. We were marching southeast, in the direction of Uman. Tank 21 had a new driver. *Leutnant* von Renesse, who was leading the platoon from another vehicle in the meantime, switched back to 21.

Four kilometers beyond Nestorowka, we reached a railway line, which led from Uman to Kiev. The point element must have caught a really big fish, since a shot-up freight train, which was loaded with innumerable T-34's, was on the rails. That was the Russian tank, against which our main guns could barely do anything. They, however, were able to shoot us to pieces from 1,000 meters.

There was fighting in front of us. Progress was slow. When we got to the rails, it looked as though we would be staying there for some time. It appeared that they didn't need our tanks up ahead; we were not summoned.

"Hey . . . take a look over there . . . tanks from the 16th Armor!" somebody shouted. There was no denying it: tanks were rolling through the terrain off to our right.

We knew that the *16. Panzer-Division* had been employed to our right, but was their avenue of advance so close to ours? Not likely. But everything is possible in war. Correspondingly, no one was concerned when the tanks started to turn towards us. Maybe they wanted to pay a visit. What was that about paying a visit? The guys started firing at us! No wonder: they were Russian tanks. Shit!

In the blink of an eye, the motorized riflemen on the back deck jumped off the vehicle. Our 5th Company, which consisted of only seven operational tanks at the time, extracted itself from the vehicular column and moved on both sides of the railway embankment in the direction of the enemy. After a short exchange of fire, the Russians fled, as if in a panic. Three knocked-out tanks were left behind.

As a reward for the successful engagement, we did not have to advance any farther. We were left behind as security against any Russians tanks that might break through from the north.

Wonderful—especially since we figured that the Russians wouldn't try anything in our sector any more. Based on the circumstances, we made ourselves comfortable. Fastening a few shelter halves to the track guards, we fashioned half-tents, which allowed us to stretch out our weary bones while sleeping.

Unfortunately, we did not get to indulge in that most favorite of all soldier occupations. And not because the evil enemy put paid to our plans. Oh, no—it was more on the lines of a sudden storm with a downpour of rain, with the result that we preferred to huddle together in the dry narrowness of our tank. It continued to rain through the morning of 22 July. And then the rain stopped as suddenly as it had begun, and there was streaming sunshine all around us. It was a day made for doing nothing.

Among other things the previous day, we had "knocked out" an enemy goose. We put roast goose on our menu for the day. The loader was given the honorable mission of plucking the feathers. In the meantime, we strolled through the area and took a look at the freight train with the T-34's, where some Russian women were tending to the wounded. We then took off a few hundred meters farther towards the woods.

When we finally looked back, we were shocked to discover that we had distanced ourselves impermissibly far from our tanks. We immediately ended our excursion and took a mighty ass chewing from our company commander. We didn't take it too bad; it wasn't the first one and certainly would not be the last one. There was nothing to be seen of the enemy far and wide. Occasionally, a truck or a column surfaced on the avenue of advance towards Uman. Otherwise, there was a peaceful silence.

The goose was already in the bucket and was bubbling away quietly. But it just would not get done.

It turned five in the afternoon. The goose was still as tough as leather, however.

It turned six, and the beast still was not enjoyable. Well, we then wanted to wait until it turned seven. We would devour it then as it was. But then . . . right at the stroke of seven, there was a crash. We were in the midst of fire from Russian tanks. They were coming from that patch of woods where we had taken a stroll a few hours earlier. It took a while before we recovered from the shock. But then we got a fire in our pants. In a flash, we were at our battle stations.

We counted at least nine Russian tanks, and all of them were approaching on the side of the railway embankment where there were only four tanks, most of them armed with only the 3.7-centimeter main gun. Without exception, all of the approaching tanks were T-34's. That promised to be exciting. Good grief! They were already opening fire at great range. We couldn't do anything but hope they didn't hit and wait until they had closed to a good range for us.

The antitank rounds flew past our turrets. I wanted to get out to untie the shelter halves, so that they would not be torn apart during our changes of position. We needed them, after all, since it appeared the war would go on for some time to come.

A headfirst dive and I was out. But no matter how much I pulled and tugged, the shelter halves could not be separated from the tank. Crap! Back into the tank. We had to get out of there; the Russians were starting to get our range.

Finally, it was time I could fire. Round after round left the barrel. Over there, where they were, there was no effect to be seen. "Shit!" *Leutnant* von Renesse yelled at me. But the other vehicles of the platoon weren't having an easy time of it, either. It was enough to make you pull your hair out!

Farthest to the left was Tank 2, followed by Tank 1 of the company commander, and then our 21, the platoon leader's tank for the 2nd Platoon. To the right of us, Tank 24 was fighting. That was our entire armada!

Wham! We took our first hit. It did not cause any damage.

The round in the breech did not want to fire. It was also jammed and could not be extracted. The whole piece of crap was hopelessly stuck. All efforts to clear the jam met with no success. There was no choice left but to move behind the embankment and there try to free up the round from the front. But my tank commander didn't want to hear any of that. His answer: "We'll stay here and lend moral support through our presence. After all, we still have a machine gun!" He couldn't have given me a more stupid answer. A musket against nine T-34's!

"Number 2 is burning!" the driver yelled, putting the tank into reverse.

I looked through my vision port and saw that Number 1 had just received a direct hit; my company commander and another man of the crew were dismounting. A few seconds later and the commander's tank was ablaze.

Now it's our turn! Those were my thoughts. Then there was a hit.

Hatch open—and out! I was out.

My vehicle set back a little bit. *Hauptmann* Zügner, the company commander, who was crouching behind his vehicle, saw me and called out: "For God's sake, go to your vehicle and try to move back."

Fine. I climbed back up on the crate. At the same moment, a hissing sound approached. I threw myself onto the track guard and felt a powerful blow. It shook me powerfully. My ears were already so deaf, I was barely able to hear the detonation.

But I did hear cries from within the vehicle. Horrific cries . . . again and again. It was gruesome.

I finally jumped off the vehicle, looking for cover behind the tank. I found our loader there.

Something exploded in the fighting compartment, and our 21 started to burn. There was only one thing left to do—get away from there as soon as possible before the entire thing went up. But where?

Our last tank, Number 24, turned and pulled back. We took off after it. We had to reach it. It was our last chance. It couldn't get away from us.

We shouted, we waved, we screamed our lungs out. But who was going to hear our thin shouts in the midst of that inferno of exploding vehicles, bursting rounds and thundering engines?

Running through the grain, which had been beaten down by the rain, was sheer torture. But we were getting closer to Number 24. Another shock—it no longer had a turret! Only the driver was still in the vehicle. He was trying to put distance—meter by meter—between himself and the Russians.

Yes—and someone else was taking flight along with the vehicle: the tank commander of Number 24 or, to be more precise, what was left of him. When the turret was shot off, it also took his head and the upper part of his body. The tank commander was the *Feldwebel* who had declined to advance forward to my Number 21 when we were at the Stalin Line.

We pulled ourselves up onto the moving 24, since there was no question of stopping in the hail of fire. All of the fires from the Russian tanks were concentrating on that single vehicle at that point. It took a great effort to hang on. We continued on. 100 meters . . . 200 meters. We reached the avenue of advance. But the hail of fire also continued. That was more than a normal mortal could stand.

So . . . get away from the misfortunate vehicle, which was only a creeping wreck at that point. The loader was in agreement with me, and we jumped off. We ran to the left, crossed the embankment and thought we were finally safe.

Crouched over, we intended to run along the one side of the embankment to the avenue of advance and the rest of the company.

We didn't look back. Fear? You bet, to be quite honest about it. Naked fear bore down on us and drove us on. We didn't want to lose our lives at that spot—not by a long shot. And we certainly did not want to be buried at that god-forsaken place!

Our strength gradually wore out. We were no longer running; it was more like a falling and a tripping. And our goal was still so far away! It seemed we were barely getting closer.

Friendly light artillery was going into position along the avenue of advance. The guns were firing over open sights right towards us. Had those dumb asses gone crazy? We cursed up a storm and prayed they wouldn't hit us. We simply did not understand that they were firing at the Russian tanks behind us.

Angry as hell and with our last bit of strength, we reached the friendly position. We collapsed, exhausted, onto the ground. There wasn't anything more we could do.

The med who was tending to us was horrified: "Both of you are in bad shape. You have to go to the main dressing station immediately." I had a piece of shrapnel in my back, right next to my spine. In the hubbub, I hadn't even noticed it. The loader was in even worse shape.

We were jammed into a motorcycle sidecar and taken to the division aid station, which was just setting up in Nestorowka. After we were treated by the doctors, we fell into the sleep of the dead.

Sometime during the night, there was a pulling and a tugging around me. I jumped up with a start. I was supposed to identify a tanker, who had just died on the operating table.

During the summer, we never wore the complete tanker uniform, just the trousers and the shirt and, perhaps, a turtleneck. The *Soldbuch*,[13] of course, was in the pocket of the tanker jacket.

The dead tanker was dressed in that manner. Despite his bad wound, it was said that he had continued to fire at a T-34 with his pistol. Was that really heroism?

I had a foreboding of who it was in front of me. I looked at him a long time. There could be no doubt: it was my tank commander and platoon leader, *Leutnant* von Renesse.

✠

One of the worst things in war was to get separated from your parent unit. Correspondingly, I resisted the directive to transfer me back to a rear-area field hospital.

One day later, I reported out of the main aid station to head back to my company. Prior to that, I fulfilled a sad duty: I was at the simple grave of my tank commander, when they buried him.

But nothing kept me back after that. A vehicle took me to the trains of the 5th Company. I reported in to *Hauptfeldwebel* Linde: "*Unteroffizier* Schrodek, wounded, reports back to the company from the main dressing station!"

Nothing but silence. The first sergeant was playing cards with two comrades, his back turned to me.

I clicked my heels in a demonstrative manner and started my report all over again: "*Unteroffizier* Schrodek . . ."

The two other comrades looked at me with their jaws dropped.

The *Hauptfeldwebel* interrupted me: "What idiot is pulling my leg? *Unteroffizier* Schrodek has been looking at radishes from the root side for some time now. I personally buried him myself yesterday."

---

[13] Translator's Note. *Soldbuch* = pay book. Each soldier carried this booklet, which not only recorded disbursements of money, but also any special pay, the issuance of equipment and uniform articles, a listing of awards, and other items. It also served as an additional means of identification in case the soldier's identity tags were lost.

All of a sudden, he jerked and turned his head around. He face turned white and his jaw dropped. He attempted to say something, staring intently at me, as if I were a ghost.

"Shit, Schrodek ... you're alive after all!" After a pause: "That can't be true!"

He grabbed me on the arm, pulled me to a truck, pulled out a pine cross, and held it in front of my nose:

Unteroffizier Gustav Schrodek

5. Kompanie / Panzer-Regiment 15

Killed on 22 July 1941

He gave me a friendly jab and said: "Get over to the company clerk, so he can destroy the loss report before it causes all sorts of mischief!"

I read the report over and over again: "*Unteroffizier* G. Schrodek, killed and buried four kilometers south of Nestorowka on the Uman-Kiev rail line on 22 July 1941."

I felt justified in asking how it could be possible that I was reported as having been killed and that I had even been buried. It demanded a plausible explanation. Here it is. Whenever a tank is hit bad enough that it starts to burn, then all of the ammunition in the vehicle explodes as a result of the heat. In addition to the machine-gun ammunition, that could be close to 100 main gun rounds. What then transpires in the fighting compartment is barely imaginable. In any event, what remains of the humans, what was not totally ripped apart by the monstrous detonation, also burns up. That includes the metal identity tags, to say nothing of the pay books. But in order to permit a dignified burial of the comrades who died that way, the remnants of bones, tatters of uniforms, and ashes are distributed among as many ammo cans as the number who perished. In place of the identity tags that were no longer available, sealed bottles with corresponding inscriptions were placed in the ammo cans. There was really no other way to do it back then.

It was therefore understandable that mistakes were made, as was my case, when one did not know who had been able to dismount, especially if the missing had disappeared without a trace.

In war, there is nothing that does not exist, including the situation where a soldier whose comrades consider to be as dead as a mouse is standing at the field mess stuffing his stomach full and then burning his own grave marker.

And that's exactly what I was doing at the time—jarringly alive and glad to be so.

German artillery fires across the Bug River, 22 June 1941.

A one-man bridge has been built for allowing riflemen and motorcycles to cross.

Pionier-Bataillon 79 *(of the 4. Panzer-Division) uses pontoon rafts to carry vehicles across the river.*

While being attacked from above by howling Stukas, deploying Soviets are suddenly confronted on all sides by German tanks. Panic surfaces, and much equipment is simply abandoned.

Simply pushed off the roadway, this Soviet BT-5 light tank will fire no more.

Slusk, destroyed from the air.

Chapter 2

THE ASSAULT OF THE *4. PANZER-DIVISION* FROM GLUCHOW TO OREL

From the diary of *Feldwebel* Hermann Bix, tank commander in the *5./Panzer-Regiment 35*; the daily logs of the *6./Panzer-Regiment 35*; and contributions from Arthur Wollschläger, company commander of the *6./Panzer-Regiment 35*

From Kritschew, we moved deep into the rear of the Red Army towards the south and Lochwiza, where we closed the pocket forming around Kiev from the east. Hundreds of thousands of Russian soldiers surrendered. But we were not allowed to rest on our laurels. Moscow was the big objective. That meant back towards the north!

We prepared to renew the offensive at Gluchow. At 0635 hours on 30 September, *Panzerkampfgruppe Eberbach* moved out to the northeast. The first objective was Ssewsk.

There was a short tank engagement at Esmanij; the advance continued through rain and mud to Ssewsk. Regrouped there and then advanced with gusto, initially towards Dmitrowsk. The 5th Company of our *Panzer-Regiment 35* was in the lead. *Feldwebel* Hermann Bix was a tank commander in that company and has provided his firsthand account.

✠

1 October 1941. Somehow I managed to become the point of the company; other tanks had been disabled.

It was already evening when we stopped just outside of Dmitrowsk. We couldn't allow the fleeing enemy to catch his breath and give him an opportunity to establish himself—that was the watchword. That meant we had to continue at night and "without regard for friendly losses," as it was so nicely put.

We continued to advance and felt our way forward to Dmitrowsk. Our 5th Company was far ahead of the division, and my vehicle was far ahead of the company as the lead tank. The road was horribly bad in that area, and the bridges buckled like crazy. You really had to pay attention at night so that a track did not come off the surface and you wound up sailing into an abyss.

We rolled along behind a Russian column, then pulled around it, going cross-country. In the darkness, Ivan didn't notice that we were from the other side.

Two Russian guards were posted at a narrow wooden bridge. One man guided me in a comradely fashion over the buckling pathway so that I did not deviate from the surface or wind up in the bottomland of the creek with my tank.

I radioed back to the company that no one was to fire at the accommodating Russian. Indeed, they should take advantage of his friendly services. As a result, no one pressed down on a trigger release, and we continued to remain unidentified.

Oberleutnant Lekschat, my company commander, radioed me: "Bix, I was just guided over the bridge by Ivan. Continue to be friendly to the comrades!"

I started to recognize the first houses of the city. It was a peculiar feeling to be the lead tank in the uncertainty of the night and to be advancing into the complete unknown of the enemy's world. Dmitrowsk was most likely a town of about 20,000. In addition to the usual wood buildings, it also had large, massive structures.

When I took a good look, I could see well-camouflaged vehicles all over the place up against the house walls. Most of them were trucks with trailers; in some cases, there were guns. An unbelievable tension was lurking out there in the midst of the eerie quiet. What would happen the next minute?—I only stuck my head out of the cupola as much as was needed to be able to observe. Despite that, they could hit me in the head from any window, if they recognized me. To my advantage was the fact that Ivan thought he was completely secure. The guards took no notice of our tank. This was no time to get nervous and, under no circumstances could I fire. Forward . . . forward . . . gain ground!

We finally reached a large cobblestone square, where I had a bit more observation. The company was following at large intervals, and I radioed that the intervals should be maintained so that no one crashed into another, that other tanks weren't hampered in an engagement, or, worse yet, that they engaged one another. Nothing was impossible at night whenever the fireworks started.

A truck column bumped along in our direction. Sitting on the vehicles—lined up nicely—were Russian infantry, their rifles between their legs, as if on maneuvers. They passed close by, somewhat hesitantly, as it seemed to me. Would everything turn out well? There were lots of Russians standing in the shadows of the houses, getting all jumbled together. I had the feeling that I had been identified, but I asked the company to hold off in opening fire for the time being, since a single tank at night in such situations usually has nothing good to look forward to.

Lekschat recommended that two tanks continue to move forward, while he took the rest of the company around the plaza to screen. He then requested a platoon of motorcycle infantry, which he wanted to move forward with the tanks into the plaza.

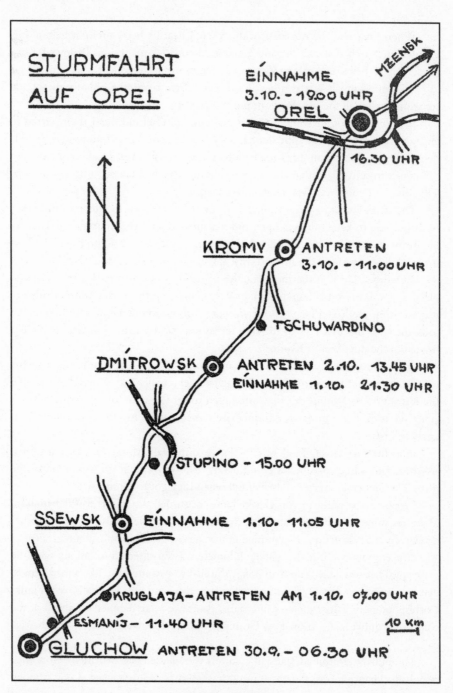

Assault on Orel.

(Antreten = *assemble;* Uhr = *hours;* Einnahme = *capture*)

When I reached the outskirts of the town, I heard a hefty firefight behind me. Pyrotechnics arched skyward; hand grenades detonated; main guns bellowed. I had the feeling all hell was breaking loose. I felt bad things were going to happen.

All around me, it was as quiet as a mouse. Once again, the old saw that it was sometimes safest all the way up front proved true.

In an effort to give some relief to my comrades behind me, I then started to engage every vehicle that approached, since our presence could no longer be hidden. We needed to be on our toes. Ivan had been warned. I had radio contact with the company and heard that the motorcycle infantry had taken a lot of prisoners. The town of Dmitrowsk was firmly in our hands.

The tanks formed a large semicircle in front of the town to screen. It was indescribably hard to keep our eyes open and remain alert after the strain of the day. Taking turns, one man of the crew stood in the turret and stared off into the night. I bit my ten fingers one after the other so that the pain would keep me awake.

2 October. Early in the morning, the company was called back to the marketplace. The motorized riflemen took over screening up front. But another mission was awaiting me. Together with *Oberleutnant* von Gerdtell, we reconnoitered. We took off with the first rays of the sun, remaining hard on the Russians' heels and headed in the direction of Kromy.

After about twenty kilometers, I ran into a Russian fuel dump, right on the road. There were five gigantic tanks. The personnel initially fled. When they saw that there was no one behind me, they attempted to set the tanks on fire with antitank rifles. We took them under fire immediately. A few were hit; the rest sought their safety in flight.

Fuel for our tanks! Fuel was the most important thing for the continued advance. The wheeled vehicles could barely follow in the bottomless mud of the roads. The fuel tanks arrived only half full when they got to Dmitrowsk.

I reported by radio to von Gerdtell. He forwarded the report to the battalion. Measures were immediately taken to safeguard the valuable spoils. We, on the other hand, received instructions to continue hounding the withdrawing enemy.

Our engine gave out after fifteen kilometers. I was directed to link up with the company. That was easier said than done! You had to pay attention like a mad man to make sure your comrades didn't take you out, thinking you were a Russian tank. Correspondingly, I fired green-white signal flares. We were damned far ahead of the company. I didn't really know how far until I saw the following tanks return the signals.

The pursuit continued. Russian columns were passed and disarmed before they even had a chance to fire. Guards at bridges were surprised or tricked. A few wooden bridges were on fire, but they could be put out in time. The large concrete bridge at Kromy was also taken intact by the tanks after a short firefight. The Russians couldn't believe, did not want to believe, that we were already there. One battalion was overwhelmed and disarmed while it was building field fortifications.

On the other hand, the Russian aircraft were constantly over us. They plastered us with bombs and rockets and attacked the march columns like hornets, whose nest had been attacked.

A civilian transit bus, taking its normal route, approached the lead tanks: Halt! Dismount! Final station!

The Russians' surprise in Kromy was so complete that our arrival was not even reported higher, even though all of the telephone lines were running and intact. The regimental translator called the postmaster in Orel. It goes without saying that he told the man he could continued sleeping peacefully, since the bad Germans were nowhere to be seen, far and wide.

We rested, did some sightseeing, and refueled in Kromy. We took the fuel from the Russians, since few of our own vehicles made it as far as the city.

3 October. The tanks moved out in the direction of Orel at 1100 hours. The Russian aerial attacks increased by the hour and by the kilometer. Practically without interruption, the bombers, fighter-bombers, and fighters flew over the columns all the way back to Dmitrowsk. They took off and landed at the airfield in nearby Orel. Friendly *Flak* was ineffective, and there were no German fighters to be seen. As a result, everyone was in a snit: we were taking considerable casualties, since there was no cover and no way to dodge. There was only one answer: forward with twice the effort . . . forward . . . forward!

The tanks moved as fast as their engines would allow; the motorcycle infantry snaked their way forward, avoiding the fighter-bombers with brazen maneuvers. They fled forward, in a manner of speaking, getting close to the enemy and then pouncing. The prime movers of the artillery went cross-country until they got their guns into firing range.

At 1500 hours, the first shells of a 10-centimeter battery of our 103rd Artillery detonated on the landing strip of the airfield at Orel. A dramatic duel developed. The cannoneers, helplessly exposed to the fires of the rockets and weapons of the Russian fighter-bombers, sent shell after shell from the tubes. Whose nerves would fail first . . . whose strength would give up first? Aircraft were destroyed on the ground by the shrapnel. Others were prevented from landing. Many on the airfield were forced to make emergency starts. But the gun crews also suffered heavy losses.

There was no perceptible relief until *Kradschützen-Bataillon 34*, firing from side-cars while rolling forward, assaulted the airfield. Aircraft, both landing and taking off, were destroyed, blowing apart and burning on the landing strip. A portion of the aircraft withdrew in the direction of Tula, where they were then forced to take off and land. And finally the German fighters also arrived—for a few hundred comrades, it was too late.

✠

The forces quickly regrouped. The company commanders were summoned to a commanders' conference. The 6th Company, under the command of *Oberleutnant*

Arthur Wollschläger, a battle-seasoned veteran many times over, assumed the lead. The daily logs of the 6th Company recorded the following:

3 October 1941. The company commander returned from the commanders' conference. After a short orders conference, we moved out as the first ones in the direction of Orel. Russian aircraft greeted us but, thank god, flew past us farther to the rear. They apparently did not think there were German tanks so close to their city. The tanks were ordered to be prepared to engage. A bridge appeared in front of us. Engineers linked up with us in case they were needed in a moment's notice. Individual Russians fled. We stepped on the gas and assaulted in the direction of the bridge. It was prepared for demolition, but the Russians were unable to ignite the charges. Our armored engineers removed the charges with practiced hands. A security group remained behind. But we charged through the thin line of defense; we moved and moved.

We stopped to observe on some high ground. There was a valley in front of us. Then there was a woodline, behind which were houses—the first ones of Orel.

The Russian bombers, fighter-bombers, and fighters droned and roared above us. We could see them take off and land in Orel with our naked eyes. May God have mercy on our comrades farther to the rear!

Moving quickly, we headed downhill and then like wild men across the open space. If there was a defensive belt around Orel, then it could only have been located in the wood line ahead of us. The two lead tanks, including the tank of our company commander, had already reached the first few trees, when fire suddenly rained down on us from all sides. Two tanks received direct hits and started to burn.

Only one thing mattered at that point: find cover and find the enemy! We moved behind a row of houses. We had some cover there and, more importantly, had a field of fire to the front. Our motorcycle infantry made leaps and bounds, nearing the woods. They took out one gun after the other. We supported them and continued to advance. We then encountered our company commander, whom we had all thought dead. In the meantime, he and the old fox Jüppner—it was their tanks that had disappeared into the woods—had assaulted and taken a bridge that was important for our continued advance. We secured it and waited for the battalion, in accordance with our orders. Russian fighter-bombers started attacking us in rolling waves.

At 1600 hours, our artillery started laying down heavy fires on targets ahead of us. At 1615 hours, we moved out again. We continued to be the point of our *4. Panzer-Division.*

We slowly rolled out of the woods. We raced across the open terrain in a long line. We were met by heavy defensive fires from all types of weapons. There was a railway embankment ahead of us; between the embankment and us was a road. It had to be the road from Kromy to Orel. A railway underpass was a reminder to be careful. We pushed our way forward, slowly and deeply echeloned. Like the claws of a monster, the underpass gaped at us. We carefully took a gander into the hole. There was a ridgeline distinguishable behind the railway line. Had the enemy also established a defensive line there?

Who dares, wins! That's what the company commander was probably thinking, as he boldly moved into the semidarkness of the tunnel. He appeared at the other end, unscathed. He immediately issued orders to the company: "Move out!"

Our time had come! The city of Orel was open in front of us. We fired to the left and right, kicked up a ruckus as if we were an entire tank regiment and charged into Orel in a race with the devil.

We received heavy fire from antiaircraft weaponry off to the left, but we disappeared between the rows of houses in the blink of an eye. Large buildings appeared off to the left. Uh oh! It was a military facility. Perplexed soldiers gazed at us. We stormed past them. Let's hope no vehicles become disabled! Gigantic clouds of smoke took away our visibility. We disappeared into it and continued on with unabated speed. Over there, yes, over there . . . a streetcar was still running! Then everything went ass over teakettles. Trucks flipped over. Antiaircraft guns were overrun before they could go into position. We moved along the main street of Orel.

A bridge reared up in front of us. A monstrous structure of steel and concrete. We raced across without stopping. It bore our weight; it did not fly into the air. That was the main thing at that moment. It was not until that point that the city belonged to us!

We advanced as far as the railway station, exploiting the confusion of the Russians. Long columns were assembling there. Everyone was fleeing in the direction of Tula.

We assaulted past the perplexed soldiers in the direction of some high ground. Orel was below us and two kilometers behind us. We were able to take in the entire city. We observed, screened and reported our location by radio.

After half an hour, *Oberfeldwebel* Gabriel with his light platoon and *Leutnant* Küspert with his platoon from the 5th Company linked up with us. We split up our forces in the city and occupied and screened all of the important areas.

The ground fog climbed slowly from the loamy waters of the Oka. Dusk started to envelop the city. The roads and streets were devoid of humans. A few aircraft dropped bombs. Here and there, there was a flash. But a couple of bombs did nothing to change the fact: Orel was ours!

Feldwebel Bix, who had advanced through the city with Küspert's platoon, continues his firsthand narrative:

We were screening on the eastern side of Orel. Suddenly, I heard a freight train departing under heavy steam in the direction of Mzensk. I remembered that a captured Russian had told me before I sent him to the rear that there was a freight train at the rail station, which was loaded with heavy tanks. Due to the great distance, I had no radio contact, and I was unable to relay that information. Besides, I really didn't trust the Russian that much.

But then I saw with my own eyes that the train existed and that it—outside of my firing range—was completely loaded with tanks and was steaming off to the east. By then it was too late!

We would get to meet those tanks in the next few days, however!

6 October. We continued to advance in the direction of Mzensk. When we reached the locality of Woin, we encountered stiff resistance. The tank regiment went into position to the left and right of the road. I was on the left wing of our 2nd Battalion, along with *Leutnant* Böckle. Just to the right of the Orel-Tula rail line.

Oberleutnant Lekschat and *Leutnant* Küspert of our company reported strong enemy fire from up front. Küspert had to pull back in a hurry, because the Russian tanks had bashed up his turret in a bad way. Lekschat also received a hit and had to pull back. Someone identified heavy Russian tanks and reported that he was unable to detect any damage among the steel monsters, even after direct hits with antitank rounds. *Leutnant* Böckle, an old hand at identifying tanks, issued a warning and stated that he thought they might be the new T-34's and KV-I's. It was said they had terrific armor.

I then saw a tank column approaching us as it rolled along the railway line about 600 meters away. The vehicles appeared somewhat nimble and not very large, and I thought, as a result, that they couldn't be all that heavy. Böckle saw them as well and warned me again.

About 300 meters in front of us, they turned to the left and moved across my front across the open terrain like a moving target. This is going to be like a shooting competition, I thought.

But we couldn't believe it—we didn't want to believe it: even the best-placed hits ricocheted off the armor! The crews did not even react when we hit them directly on the turrets. The Russian tanks continued to move unperturbed in the face of our bristling fires. They headed towards our poor comrades on the road, right in front of our noses, until they got to an ideal firing distance.

And then we saw something that we heretofore would not have considered possible: We saw our tanks pull back by the company, turn around and then make haste to disappear over the high ground.

Lekschat also ordered us to pull back, since our losses on the right wing were too heavy. Even at the shortest of ranges, we were unable to take on those beasts, while they were able to take us out at 1,000 meters without breaking a sweat. It was enough to make you cry!

Oberst Eberbach, our regimental commander, recognized the dangerous situation, probably just in the nick of time. He brought 8.8-centimeter *Flak* and 10.5-centimeter cannon forward to prevent the breakthrough of the superior Russian tanks, against which we were completely powerless. An 8.8 knocked out a T-34, but it was then hit. The second gun didn't have any better luck. There was a general feeling of helplessness.

When I pulled back in my tank and took off at full steam, I ran into the Eberbach's command tank on the road. He had also been hit bad. I heard that the regimental signals officer, *Leutnant* Nebel, was badly wounded.[1]

Not too far from the road, a shot-up prime mover of the engineers was burning. A soldier with a shredded leg was lying next to it and screaming in pain and desperation. The flames were threatening to grab hold of a second wounded engineer any moment. There was a whistling and a cracking all around. Should I stop? Somewhat hesitantly, I forced myself out of the turret and jumped down, attempting to at least get the one wounded man out of harm's way of the flames.

Two tankers came running up, bent over. They pitched in without a word, helping me to carry and to find cover. They then grabbed the second engineer, who was screaming in agony, and brought him under cover at the double. I discovered that the prime mover had been loaded with antitank mines and could go up at any minute.

We had just reached a protective ditch with the last wounded man, when there was a brilliant stream of flame heading skyward. The equivalent of a barrage broke loose from the prime mover. The antitank mines detonated. The shards whizzed around for a hundred meters in all directions. The air pressure threatened to burst our lungs, even though we were in a ditch.

I then had the opportunity to take a closer look at the other two, who had helped. They were *Oberst* Eberbach and *Stabsarzt* Dr. Mühlkühner.[2] The doctor started treating the wounded in an expedient manner. He flagged down a vehicle and then the two took off to the main aid station.

The two officers continued running to help wherever help was still needed, since the T-34's had made a mess of things there. It was good that the Russians apparently did not know that there was nothing on our side that could stand up to them. Otherwise, they would have punched through to Orel and left us standing there with our mouths open.

We had to strain our minds the next few days to think of some way to approach the T-34's and KV-I's with our main guns, which had been degraded to the status of doorknockers.

Somewhat embarrassed, I also made a resolution during a quiet moment: To never leave a wounded comrade behind, even if the devil himself was personally chasing me. *Oberst* Eberbach, whom we referred to secretly as *Schnulch*, had personally taught me a lesson.[3]

---

[1] Translator's Note. It was common practice for a formation's signals officer to ride with the commander in his command vehicle.

[2] Translator's Note. The Germans used a different rank system for medical personnel of officer rank. A *Stabsarzt* was the equivalent of a *Hauptmann* (captain).

[3] Translator's Note. An affectionate nickname for which there is no ready English translation.

10 October. We were ten kilometers outside of Mzensk. We had boxed our way forward with some difficulty after overcoming the initial shock of the T-34. We were always careful, using treachery and cunning.

One morning, when I crawled out of our "heroes' basement"—a hole about half a meter deep dug out under our tank between the tracks—I saw that it had snowed for the first time. It was my twenty-seventh birthday.

Together with *Leutnant* Küspert, I received orders to reconnoiter. At a godforsaken hour, I moved cross-country in my tank in the direction of Mzensk.

Without encountering any resistance, we reached the western edges of the city when it turned light. I was all by myself, since Küspert's vehicle had become disabled on the way. Even then, there was an advantage: He was able to relay my radio messages to the company, since the distance was too great for my five-watt transmitter.

I moved through a Russian field position and saw bundled-up Ivans crawling around in their holes, tired and bleary eyed. The waved to me in a friendly fashion, as if they wanted to say: "Nice that tanks are here!" That we were the bad guys was something they could not see on account of the hazy weather. We left them alone in their beliefs. In fact, I even turned my cap around so that they did not get any dumb ideas.[4] After all, I had to hang out of the cupola a bit in order to take a look around.

It appeared that "reveille" had been sounded in Mzensk. Things started to come to life in the village and along its edge. I saw a few tanks behind the house gables, as well as a few infantrymen getting coffee. Mzensk was spread out in front of me like an open book. But I wasn't allowed to fire; I was simply on a reconnaissance mission. It would have been a piece of cake if the other tanks of the battalion had been behind me!

I radioed back my observations, attempted to calm my nerves, and continued to observe conscientiously.

It suddenly occurred to me that we had a steep slope behind us, which hadn't caused any concern when we descended it beforehand. How were we supposed to get back up it fast enough, if we suddenly had to scram? The engine had been turned off for some time. As a security precaution, we turned it over again. Unfortunately, it made a horrific noise. Ivan probably recognized us at that point. I heard a trumpeter's signals coming out of the city and saw everything grow frenzied. The tanks fired up their engines and moved out of their camouflaged positions. It was high time we disappeared.

With some trepidation, we slowly moved back up the slope, our weapons directed forward and ready to fire. It seemed to take an eternity before we were on

---

[4] Translator's Note. At this stage of the war, army tank personnel still wore an overseas cap, which had insignia on the front of it that could identify the wearer as a German. By turning it around, he was depriving the Russian soldiers a glimpse of the insignia, and it looked more like the rather shapeless headgear of the Soviet forces.

the crest. With a sigh of relief, we then turned around and toddled off. No, it was not a flight. We had more than accomplished out reconnaissance mission.

On the radio, I heard that our 2nd Battalion was moving out to attack Mzensk. In the snow flurries that had just started, I saw our tanks, looking like shadows, scurrying over the rise. *Oberleutnant* Wollschläger was once again point with his 6th Company. We integrated ourselves into the ranks of our 5th Company.

✠

Arthur Wollschläger has provided the following firsthand account of the fighting for Mzensk:

Early on the morning of 10 October, there were an orders conference and preparations for attack in Scheino. Another attack on Mzensk, despite the misery there yesterday. I had a small treasure in my possession, a captured Russian map. A smaller bridge was marked on it south of the large Suscha crossing. Our 6th Company was directed to take the lead again. The engineers of the battalion's engineer platoon were directed to mount up on the tanks.

We advanced cross-country in the midst of heavy snow squalls. Overnight there had been a deep snowfall. No tank tracks from the previous day; no paths could be seen. There was nothing to orient on far and wide. On top of that, you couldn't see more than 100 meters. Despite that, I had the excellent Russian map, which showed exact contour intervals and other features; even the smallest of field paths were marked.

I had drilled into my head the exact route we were to take. After leaving the outskirts of Scheino, I only had to follow the ridgeline. According to the map, it led directly to my objective. If the tank started canting to the right, then the driver only had to pull left and vice-versa. The distance to the bridge was known, and the four paths we had to cross could be felt in the tank, whenever the tracks rattled across the frozen ruts in the roadway.

After crossing the fourth path, we turned by plan on an angle of forty-five degrees to the east and ran ... right into the bridge. Since all of *Kampfgruppe Eberbach* was following my tracks, getting "disoriented" would have been disaster. As already mentioned, however, the precise Russian map with the thorough entries helped, as did the fact that the thick snow squalls removed us from the enemy's observation.

The prepared demolitions could be easily seen on the bridge. I saw a hut on the far side of the river, which had bundles of straw on the west side to act as a wind guard. In front of them was a group of bundled-up Russian soldiers, undoubtedly the guards for the bridge, which had been earmarked for demolition.

I waved to the Russians. They were supposed to come over to me. I was right at the river with my tank. Four engineers were shivering behind my turret. About six Russians soldiers approached me hesitantly along the bridge. Our weapons were directed towards the detonators.

The Russians slowly reached the middle of the bridge. Suddenly, there was a hard bang next to my left ear. Despite the headset, it hurt and stung. A Russian collapsed. One of the engineers had lost his nerves and had fired from behind the turret. It was completely unnecessary and in contravention of our proven tactics.

For better or for worse, I had to issue fire commands to my tanks. After a few bursts, the hut was on fire. *Oberfeldwebel* Steger and two men from the engineer platoon sprang across the bridge, which could have gone up at any minute. They went to the main place where the detonators were placed and cut the cords. Others ripped the lines from the charges.

The tanks moved across the swaying bridge slowly and carefully. It creaked and groaned under their weight but, thank God, it held!

Under the command of *Leutnant* Lech, the engineers remained at the bridge to secure it. We raced through the streets of the small town towards the large bridge over the Suscha. We saw heavy tanks there. Nothing we wanted! I reported the situation by radio, and we then broke through a fence into a backyard and played the part of a "shrinking violet."

A group of Russian soldiers came out of the house towards my tank. I fired my pistol at short range. They fled, with a couple of them remaining behind, most likely hit. One man threw himself into the dead angle next to my tank. I needed to act quickly! I was able to get to him by means of a hand grenade.

For the time being, the few tanks of my company remained concealed, and we listened to the sharp sounds of battle coming from the city. We dismounted and, as a precautionary measure, set up the overrun fence again. We waited for our hour to come. Not very dramatic, but stressful and nerve wracking.

After that short break—we did not receive any orders—we moved back towards the bridge. We encountered *Oberst* Eberbach on the way, and he praised our 6th Company.

As part of the viewing audience, we saw how an 8.8 *Flak* knocked out a big boy on the bridge. *Oberleutnant* Ehrenberg and *Oberleutnant* von Gerdtell then succeeded in knocking out two KV-I's at pointblank range. That broke the spell!

Although half a dozen Russian tanks broke through, they were taken under fire by the tanks further to the rear, with one T-34 being set on fire. A friendly tank, which had a stuck round, was hit.

From the northern edge of the city, you could hear the sound of numerous heavy enemy tanks. Additional Russian tanks were reported from the direction of the west bridge. The situation was made more difficult by the fact that the command tank of *Oberstleutnant* Hochbaum, of all people, had damaged the bridge. As a result, a 10-centimeter cannon and an 8.8 *Flak* had to be manhandled carefully across the bridge. The situation grew more threatening by the minute. There was no longer any way back.

A squad of combat engineers laid fifteen mines on the main road. The 10-centimeter cannon finally got into position. Heavy enemy tanks were already attacking from the direction of Tula and from the west. One rumbled onto a mine; another was knocked out by the cannon. That gave us a little breathing room for a while. Then the grenadiers of the 33rd started arriving on foot, with the regimental commander, *Oberst* Grolig, in front. The motorized riflemen were employed directly from the march in the southern part of the city, where the Russians were also attacking with infantry at that point. Screening in the direction of Tula were only a few tanks, a platoon of riflemen and one 8.8 *Flak*.

It was right there that the Russians struck with six heavy tanks and infantry at just the same time as more enemy forces were being reported at the west bridge. The situation turned critical. The 8.8 succeeded in knocking out three heavy Russian tanks. That brought the charging Russian infantry to a standstill. The remaining enemy tanks turned back.

Our little group of tanks had turned even smaller. Towards midnight, we were pulled back. We rolled out of that witches' cauldron, where the motorized riflemen were in the process of digging positions and setting up barricades against the Russian tanks, so that the important crossings over the Suscha bridgehead could be held.

THE DUEL ALONG THE KRASSNAJA METSCHA

Leutnant **Wolfgang Paul, acting company commander in** *Schützen-Regiment* **52 of the** *18. Panzer-Division*
16 November 1941. The summer had driven us into the eastern flatlands, the fall had held us there with its unyielding, unforgettable mud and the winter wanted to drive us out again. It was as though we had stumbled into a world that we would never really get to know.

It seemed everything was cold, inhospitable, and arrayed against us.

In November 1941, we advanced through Orel to the Krassnaja Metscha River, which was part of the tributary system of the upper Don. Our *Schützen-Regiment 52* moved along iced-over roads on German tanks, French trucks, and Russian fire department vehicles. There was a deep layer of snow, and we left tracks on the countryside, tracks in which wolves followed. An enemy was running in front of us, whom we thought capable of doing anything an enemy can do to another human.

During the afternoon, we arrived in a village that was in the vicinity of the river. We were tired, dissipated—as we were every day back then. It was directed for the regiment to cross the river during the night and establish a bridgehead. The engineers were to then build a bridge . . . the tanks would use it . . . the advance allowed for no delays—at least on the general staff maps.

I led a motorized rifle company.

I walked a few steps ahead of the others, who had to go with me that night and who had previously been spared. I walked neither too quickly nor too slowly; there was no special hurry. We had a long November night and time to establish ourselves over there in front of the enemy.

It was quite cold. The field mess had taken care of us. We were full and thought we would get everything over in a hurry. Then we saw the river. There was a village on this side and a village on the far side. A narrow wooden bridge appeared ahead in the darkness. We ran quickly across. It was dark; the sky protected us.

It was not until we were on the other side that the Russians started firing. By then, however, it was already too late; we had already established ourselves on the far side. Like us, the Russians were also freezing and had put out hardly any guards. That's how we surprised them. A few of them were hit immediately, others surrendered, and most of them just got out of there. It was not until morning that we discovered how many there were in front of us.

I established outposts; there were small skirmishes occasionally. I then went to sleep in a hut.

Toward noon, there was a light wind, which allowed us to hear firing from a great distance. We figured that the Russians wanted to retake the bridgehead. Behind us, on the river, the engineers were in the process of building the bridge our tanks were supposed to use. In front of us were a few houses that we had not been able to take the previous night. I decided to also take those houses so that the Russians would be forced out into the open. By doing that, I thought I might be able to drive them away, since it was very cold and no one liked to be out lying in the open.

I took a few men and had our machine guns directed towards worthwhile targets. We then crawled through the snow over to the houses. The Russians soon discovered us, and they did not want to give up their last remaining huts in this area. That's how the engagement started.

We first set the houses on fire though our fires. Only the last hut—the one at the outskirts of the village—did not want to catch fire. Finally, around two in the afternoon, we had closed to within fifteen meters of the house. A few of our number were hit; the medics took care of them.

A soldier practices his craft with playful but deadly earnest, which he needs to learn so as not to take matters too seriously. He often has the impression that he's on a hunt and only has to knock off a few bucks, not other humans. In addition, there was the cold, and we had little desire to delay the matter any longer. I called out the names of a few men who were laying next to me in the snow and who had not yet been shot by the Russians. They were directed to get their hand grenades ready so that we could then jump up to take the house. That they did and, after a few moments and a little bit of hesitation, they called out to me that they were ready. And then something happened to me that I was only able to fathom later.

A few minutes followed my decision to stand up and put an end to the matter. In those minutes, I experienced something extraordinarily important for me. I want to say: In those few moments in the cold countryside along the river with the difficult-to-pronounce name, I succeeded in overlooking that which one calls *war*.

Up to that point, even though I had participated in a few engagements and had also received medals for them, I had only had the feeling in those dangerous matters, which meant life or death, of being *in the middle of them*. But I had not known what it was like when one suddenly *transcends* everything.

The terrain on which we lived and on which there was dying—usually matter-of-factly and without knowing a lot about the death that could come so rapidly—had still remained an unknown quantity to me.

I had no name I could give to this terrain, and I always attempted to accept everything as if it had been put there so that I would perhaps survive. I didn't make any effort to ponder it in some sort of effort to perhaps finally discover where everything was leading.

I think that's the way it was for most back then and, as a result, it also explains our successes.

Determined to put an end to the soldiers in the house, I pulled my left leg up closer to my body, looked around towards the others one more time and was lulled by that false sense of security one has who is dispensing death without any type of human feelings.

At that moment I did not know whether I would get out of there in one piece, but I did know that I had to jump up. In the next moment, it would depend on me, a *Leutnant* in a motorized rifle regiment, as to whether I would be courageous or cowardly.

I jumped up in order to toss my hand grenades. Snow fell from my overcoat. I shook myself and attempted to move my clammy legs forward in order to reach the house. I armed the hand grenade and threw it, standing right across from the door I saw in front of me.

While the hand grenade descended from its high arch towards the door, the door opened and a soldier stood in its threshold. He was someone from the other side, a Russian, who had done the same thing at the same moment as I had done—arm a hand grenade and throw it towards me.

And so we stood across from one another—he over there and I over here—and both of us had the dangerous explosives between us. I saw his cap first and then his face, a pale, unshaven and frozen face, a face like that of my men, no different. I saw rage in this face, also hate and, at the same time, a sureness that comes over someone who is attempting something in order to get out of a dangerous situation. I saw his moist nose and his tight mouth; cheeks that were well nourished and ears under a fur cap.

In his face, I saw the person I would be killing momentarily, and I waited on the explosion of the two hand grenades.

I did not throw myself into the snow so as to possibly survive the explosion. I did not jump to the side so as to get out of the way of the Russian's hand grenade.

I saw how the Russian looked at me, as if he, too, had discovered a different world.

And I saw how he bent his head toward me—as if he wanted to greet me. Then a gray cloud rose from his feet, tore his legs away from his heavy body and tore him in two above the belt.

He died like a tree on which someone had placed demolitions on the trunk, filling his surroundings with a rapid fright and then complete stillness, as if the toppling had been completed.

A few bits of shrapnel from the hand grenade, which he had thrown, burrowed their way into my body and took me out of action.

EVERY MAN FOR HIMSELF

From the diary of *Unteroffizier* **Gustav W. Schrodek, tank commander in** *Panzer-Regiment 15* **of the** *11. Panzer-Division*

Beginning of December 1941, outside of Moscow. The capital of the Soviet Union was our attack objective. Would we reach it?

We crossed the canal, which led from Moscow to Kalinin, to the north of the city. From there, we advanced directly against the Soviet metropolis. We got as far as Kriukowa—indeed, a few kilometers beyond it. But then our attack bogged down, so much so that it simply would not go any more. We were palpably close to the Russian capital. I saw a traffic sign: Moskwa—18.5 kilometers.

We couldn't do it . . . not even another kilometer closer. The Russian resistance was too great. The amount of aerial attacks, artillery fire, Stalin organ[5] salvoes, and armored attacks is simply unimaginable—it was unbearable.

Of course, it came as no surprise that the Russian defensive effort outside of Moscow was enormous. That it would take on such enormous proportions was something that no one could anticipate, however. And all of it hit us full bore.

2 December 1941. It was thanks solely to the attentiveness of our driver that we were not knocked out. He saw a T-34 firing off to the left. He was able to pull the vehicle back a few centimeters so that the round intended for us whizzed just past the turret. But one of the vehicles from the company off to the right was hit. A direct hit on the front of the turret. I saw the tank commander and the driver bail out, before I could traverse the turret and take the enemy tank in sight. By then, it had already pulled back. It wasn't until later that I saw that the tank commander no longer had any legs and the driver was frozen to the track with his bleeding hand.

Our ranks were getting thinner. A couple got hit every day. When would it be our turn?

We had our hands full with our dead as we were barely able to bury them. The ground had frozen as hard as a rock, so much so that we were unable to do anything at all with pickaxes and spades. It was only with hand grenades that we were able to blow out a shallow ditch as a grave.

The trust of the troops in the senior leadership dwindled; the morale had been battered. An order to retreat to the rear to a supposedly well-prepared defensive position did a lot to contribute to that mood. The "heavily fortified winter position,"

---

[5] Translator's Note. Stalin organ was German soldier slang for free-flight rockets launched from mobile launchers, usually modified trucks.

which we passed a few days later under constant heavy pressure from the Russians, did not even have prepared machine-gun positions, let alone lines of bunkers with 8.8 guns.

Given the circumstances, everything went relatively well as far as Wolokolamsk. In and of itself . . . amazing. We had grown accustomed to quite other scenes during the Russian retreats. Was it because this was our first retreat? Possible?

After a long, long time, we finally received mail when we got to Wolokolamsk. We hadn't written. What was the purpose? The mail wasn't being sent, anyway. Moreover, we had other things to worry about at the time. We were being hunted and tracked, and the only thing that matter was saving our skins. It was clear to everyone that we could expect no mercy from the Russians. Ever since 9 December, we had been ordered to conduct a "scorched earth" policy.

"Scorched earth"—a terrible phrase! Even worse was the reality. Ever since Krijukowo, the villages abandoned by us went up in flames. It was a measure of primitive defense or a primitive measure of defense—however you wished to phrase it. It was hated by both friend and foe, but unfortunately necessary in order to prevent the enemy from being able to establish himself, while protected from the cold.

The graves of our dead were supposed to be flattened. Easier said than done. We limited ourselves to taking the grave markers, so as to deceive the Russians about our heavy losses and to keep the troop elements of the dead secret. We hoped to be able to spend a few quiet nights in Wolokolamsk. We set up quarters in whatever was available. Unfortunately, there could be no thought of sleep, since the hovels were crawling with lice. A pipe dream! One *Feldwebel* devised his own method for dealing with the insects. He went after the nesting places in the beam crevices with a blowtorch. The bugs burned up as planned, but the house also went up with them—not as planned. That's all that we needed, since the fire alerted the Russians. Based on their previous experience, they had to believe we were evacuating the village. That meant we needed to get out of there!

But that didn't occur without some dilly-dallying. The end of the story is this: We already had the Ivans at our throats in the middle of preparations for changing positions. Damn it to hell! That's all we needed. At that point, everything went helter-skelter in order to get out of town. Whatever was not operational—unfortunately, that included a few tanks—had to be left behind and blown up. We could only pull back towards the south.

That went pretty well initially. Then, however, a simple ditch became an almost insurmountable obstacle. The first few vehicles were able to make it over. Then the walls of the ditch became so slick with ice that our tanks tracks could not take hold. It was not possible to take the ditch by making a run on it or to go around it. The only way out was to blow up a tank in the hole. By filling it that way, the rest could move across what was left.

When we reached Novo Petrowskoje, a village that had a road leading west out of it, it was burning like a torch. We crossed through it quickly in the direction of

Pokrowskoje. It was only there that we were able to rest. The fuel tanks were almost empty. And there was no fuel available—at least officially. On the sly, I got two cans of fuel. Only a sure thing is a sure thing, or so I thought! But it's a well-known fact that a soldier should not think. He should leave the thinking to horses, since they have the bigger heads.

That old saying came true the next day, 18 December. "Which vehicle is still capable of moving back on its own?" Feeling a bit cocksure, I reported, since it was also the truth. There was one other tank in our company that was not short of fuel.

All of the other combat vehicles were blown up, and the crews did not shed a tear. They were overjoyed, since they were allowed to march back to the passage points immediately and without having to fight. A few of them even rounded up some horses and sleds.

The two of us company riff-raff had to stay behind in Petrowskoje, together with two tanks from another company.

But things would turn even worse. The riflemen providing security were turning back a Russian attack at the time and were crying for tanks. Moving against the Russians was nothing we were looking forward to. But orders were orders! We took off immediately since we were needed urgently.

And so we took up "battle stations" and headed back towards Novo Petrowskoje. After two kilometers, we turned off to the left, where a built-up area could be seen about 1,000 meters away. That's where our riflemen were supposed to be holding out.

The closer we got to the village, the stranger things seemed to be. There wasn't a soul to be seen; that could not be possible! They couldn't be sending us to a regiment that wasn't there!

We then saw a few trucks and a German field mess. A slight amount of smoke was still curling out of the chimney.[6] But where were the men? No guards, no outposts. Nothing. Uncanny. Unbelievable. Finally, a few figures appeared. Damn! They were Russians! Charge into them!

All of a sudden, there were a few German riflemen there as well. They were mixing it up in a big way. I moved with my vehicle further into the village to see what else was going on. It was the same scene in the village proper.

But wait a minute—it was not quite the same film. Heavily armed men stood guard in front of the biggest house. The two guards were Russian. We pushed forward carefully, closer and closer. Although we were barely twenty meters away from them and couldn't be missed, no one took notice of us. The Russians continued to talk to one another without interruption, walking back and forth. When we turned off the engine, we heard them laugh—loudly and with gusto. That was too much. Did they think our vehicle was a Russian tank? If that was the case, then Russian

---

[6] Translator's Note. The so-called *Gulaschkanone*—"goulash cannon"—was a staple of German field kitchens throughout the war. The stove was mounted on a single-axle horse-drawn carriage and featured a prominent smokestack for the oven.

combat vehicles had to be in the vicinity. That meant we had to act quickly. And that's exactly what we did. After a short fire command and a high-explosive round, the Russians guards no longer had anything to laugh about.

Once gone, German soldiers came rushing out of the house. Disregarding any potential danger, they ran towards my tank, mounted up on the rear deck, shook our hands in thanks, and even smothered us in kisses. We were lucky that no one bothered us at that point.

So what had happened?

Around 1100 hours, the Russians had attacked so suddenly that the motorized riflemen had been overrun. The constant staying outdoors in the cold and the lack of rations and sleep had paralyzed alertness and the ability to resist. As a result, they were quickly overpowered and taken prisoner. The fact that we had been able to liberate them made up for a lot. It was also understandable that we then felt responsible for them.

It was clear that Russian tanks were nearby. The icy wind blew snatches of engine noise to our ears. Something had to be done quickly, if the tragedy of the morning was not to be repeated.

But we could not convince the officers in charge of the riflemen to evacuate the village, in spite of the fact that they were in a mousetrap. They had been ordered not to give up the village before 1600 hours, and they wanted to execute their orders as issued.

That meant things could get dicey. It went without saying, however, that we would not leave them to themselves. But holding out for another three hours with our four little tanks and the handful of hastily grouped-together riflemen? I could no longer stand idly by.

But all of the reproaches did nothing to change the situation. My success was limited to getting some of the exhausted men and the wounded out of there on the superfluous vehicles. We deployed our vehicles so that we could keep the withdrawal routes open.

It turned 1400 hours. And then the inevitable happened. The sounds of the enemy tanks drew ever closer. We still couldn't see them, however. Our teeth started to chatter. I will be gracious and say it was due to the cold.

Took a look around—the rifle officers no longer appeared to be so certain of what they were doing. They ran up to us and asked us to move out against the Russian tanks. No way! They still believed in fairy tales and thought that we could scare away the T-34's with our old crates as soon as we appeared. In the meantime, they intended to evacuate the Russian village, since they no longer thought it could be held in the face of a Russian attack.

We were to move forward—give up our good positions—play the role of range targets—allow ourselves to be cut off by the Russians! We weren't about to commit suicide! On the road, we would be knocked out immediately; out in the open, we would have gotten stuck in the snow. All that meant nothing to the Russian

T-34's. They were able to churn through anything. In contrast, we immediately bottomed out.

While we, the tank commanders, were still in the process of explaining all the facts to the riflemen, I received a call from the turret of my tank: "Here they come!" We raced to our combat vehicles, and the rifle officers attempted to reach the positions of their people just as quickly.

Since my gunner had taken my place in order to observe while I was gone, I simply jumped into his seat when I sprang into the vehicle, since I saw a T-34 rapidly approaching us. Unfortunately, it was not the only one.

While I was taking up a sight picture on it, it suddenly came to a stop and fired. My vehicle was not its initial target. I thanked the enemy crew for that with a well-aimed antitank round. But as was so often the case, I didn't do anything to him with my bird gun. On the other hand, the enemy tank came alive. The worst part was that it started to go after me.

It is therefore quite understandable that I devoted my entire attention to the tank opponent in front of me. As a result, I did not notice that the other vehicle from my company was no longer operational and, indeed, had dead on board. I also did not immediately notice that panic had broken out among the riflemen. The rear leaving their cover and attempting to escape across the open, snow-covered fields. Many were shot to pieces.

There was one other thing I did not see: a truck belonging to the riflemen that was approaching my tank, attempting to get past to reach the road. A swarm of rifleman were also climbing up on my tank.

While I was preoccupied with sending round after round over to the T-34, the monstrous truck rammed into my traversed main gun at full speed. The turret was flung to the side. Something broke. The turret could no long be traversed.

Combat ineffective! At that moment, of all times! As the result of such nonsense! No one will think the worst of me, if it didn't matter at all to me at the moment that my main gun batted some of the riflemen in the back and sent them flying in a high arc. God knows, I had other worries.

"Let's get out of here . . . give it some gas!" I yelled to the driver. He immediately caught on to what was at stake.

There was no possibility of moving fast, however, since riflemen were standing in my way, wanting to climb aboard. Using our combined strength, we were able to traverse the main gun to the rear from outside of the turret.

It wasn't until then that I saw the entire drama playing out around me. The riflemen were in wild flight all along the line, hunted by the Russian tanks. The other tank from my company had been knocked out. By then, we were moving past another knocked-out tank. We no longer had any way on our tank to provide aimed fire. There was nothing more to be seen far and wide of the fourth tank. Everywhere you looked there were Russian tanks, which were completely unaffected by our main gun.

Eight riflemen were cowering on the front of my tank. Bunches of them were hanging off the sides. Despite that, more and more were attempting to climb up on the rear deck while we were moving. Many of them had already been wounded by all the shrapnel flying about. But being wounded meant nothing at that point, when you smelled an opportunity to escape the inferno.

Just don't remain behind—that was all that anyone thought!

Trusting blind luck, I let loose an occasional round from my main gun. Of course, I did not hit, and the T-34's drew ever closer. If one of them had halted for a moment in order to engage us with well-aimed fire, then all of our worries would have been over. As round after round sailed past us, we were just hoping to survive the next one.

Looking through the opened gunner's vision port, I saw another rifleman attempting to climb aboard, be he got caught up in the track. I quickly leaned out, grabbed him and freed him from the track. At the same moment, there was a heavy impact next to us and the man was badly hit. He died in my hands.

"Sorry, comrade, but you have to stay here!" I slowly opened my fist and let him slide to the snow on the ground.

At that point, the road was open and we stepped on it. "My" T-34 remained behind. We had escaped death one more time! When we arrived in Pokrowskoje, we saw that two of the riflemen aboard had not escaped that fate. They had been hit by shrapnel on the way and had died of their wounds.

KNOCKED OUT AT FIFTY BELOW

From the diary of *Gefreiter* Robert Poensgen, loader in *Panzer-Regiment 33* of the *9. Panzer-Division*

27 December 1941. We spent the night in a *panje* hut in the vicinity of Tim, not too far east of Kursk. It was horribly cold outside. No one knew exactly how cold it was. Even if we had had a thermometer, it would have been hard to determine, since German thermometers did not work lower than 35 below [-31 Fahrenheit]. Later on, much later on, we discovered that the quicksilver sank to -54 [-65 Fahrenheit] that night. We only felt that it was unbearably cold. We were lying there in our dirty uniforms, wrapped in blankets, which had been reduced to rags, on the clay earth, trying to go to sleep.

The guards outside next to the tanks had to be relieved every half hour so they did not freeze. Every time the door opened, the cold air crashed into the room like a milky white fog. Whenever the guards took off the long driver overcoats, which reached down to the ankles, the coats were so frozen stiff that they simply stood up wherever they were placed, eliminating the need for wardrobe hooks.

When it turned light, we went out to the tanks. We were ordered to prepare to move out. Somewhere, not too far from there, Ivan was coming, and the thin line of riflemen could not hold him up.

Our vehicle, a *Panzer III* with a short 5-centimeter main gun—popularly and properly known as the army doorknocker—was almost covered under by the previous night's snowdrifts. We shoveled and shoveled some more to retrieve it from under the white mountain of snow. We had so many layers of clothes on that we could scarcely move. Over the black uniform, we wore fatigues and a heavy overcoat above that. The head protectors were pulled up so high on our faces that only the eyes peered out. You could not take off one of the layers of clothing for fear of succumbing to the cold.

The turret was frozen in place; the mantlet would not move. We attempted to thaw out the ice with a blowtorch, but everything froze back together again. So we had to scratch and hack with pickaxes and shovels. The breeches of the main gun and the machine guns wouldn't move either. The brown weapons oil was as solid as bee's wax. We took a blowtorch to it, thawed it out and then thinned it with diesel fuel. But the diesel fuel was also as firm as vehicle grease.

The driver lit up a bundle of straw under the oil pan to warm up the oil enough so that the engine could turn over. There was no point in trying it with the starter right away. Although we had placed the batteries next to an open fire during the night, they did not have enough juice to turn the engine over a single time. That meant using the hand crank! Just millimeters at first . . . then, gradually, we could get the inertia starter going faster. We were huffing and puffing. The driver released the clutch. The engine turned over . . . two times . . . three times. We started all over again. We worked nearly half an hour before the engine caught. We let it warm up for ten to fifteen minutes. In the meantime, the weapons had frozen up again. Around 1000 hours we were ordered to move out. In between the singing of the wind and the fine rushing of the snow that was blowing in thick swaths, we heard bursts of fire from machine guns and individual rifle shots, all coming closer. The sun was still low on the horizon. It radiated no heat, not a single bit of warmth.

Even in the fighting compartment, we did not take off our overcoats. As the loader, I was barely able to move. But I had the feeling that without the overcoat I would freeze to death. Our breath formed small ice crystals on the steel walls of the tank. Everything glistened. If you grabbed ahold of anything, your hand stuck to it. There was no way you could work with bare hands.

We deployed in a combat formation. The distance from one vehicle to the next was about 80 meters. We were moving up a slight incline. Everything was a blur of white on white. The cold sun made the ice crystals sparkle.

Information was relayed over the radio: "Prepare to fire . . . high explosive, machine guns . . . no tanks . . . only enemy riflemen in groups!"

We reached the forward lines: A man here, a machine-gun crew there. Infantry in white snow smocks. Then we saw the Russians attack. Always in squad-size elements, eight to ten men at a time.

"Machine guns. Fire at will!"

The radio operator's machine gun under me began to spit. The first belt rattled through in front of my eyes.

"Stoppage!"

Bolt back, a few shots of oil on the belt. It rattled again.

"Stoppage!"

The radio operator cursed at his machine gun and worked feverishly. That damned cold. Nothing worked any more. "No more bets" came to mind. To the left of my shoulder, the felt boots of *Unteroffizier* Frey were stomping. He was trying to keep his feet warm by stamping them. The bursts of fire came at ever-shorter intervals. Our vehicle lurched to the left and then to the right.

The gunner next to me had his eyes glued to the optics. He traversed the turret.

"We're right in the middle of the Ivans. They're taking off!" He yelled over to me.

Another belt was finished. The machine gun was working without practically any stoppages at that point. It was hot enough. Barrel change. Bolt change. And so it went.

We had reached the high ground and stopped there. There was a somewhat deep cut with vegetation in front of us. There were Russian sled columns on the opposite slope, tightly bunched together. I could not see anything myself, but the tank commander and the gunner provided details of the situation.

"Load high explosive!"

The breech slammed shut.

"Up!"

Rrumms!

A biting smoke from the shell casing filled the fighting compartment. In comparison, the little pipe that I clenched between my teeth was harmless, despite the *machorka*[7] mixed in. Besides, it had gone out. Round after round left the barrel. Things were going better. The tank commander issued his fire commands, and the gunner executed them.

Rrumms!

To the right of us, we could also hear tank main guns barking. And then half a belt rattled through my machine gun. The tank commander fidgeted on his small seat.

"Turn off the engine so we don't get such a draft in here!" he bellowed into the intercom.

The engine turned silent. You could only hear the whipping sounds of main-gun fire, the clattering of the Russian machine guns and the rattling of our machine guns.

"This is just like a shooting competition!"

---

[7] Translator's Note. *Machorka* was a low-grade Russian tobacco, which the German soldiers reluctantly used whenever better tobacco was not available.

The tank commander suddenly dropped out of his cupola like a lightning bolt. In the same fraction of a second, there was a terrible hissing sound passing over our heads.

"A tank's firing or an antitank gun . . . fire up the engine and pull back!"

Frey was back in his cupola, spying above the edge. He gave the gunner a target: "It has to be down there in the row of vegetation!"

The starter yelped. Once again, there was a hissing overhead.

"Let's go . . . pull back or he'll get us!"

The gunner had the vegetation in his sights.

"Tanks!" he yelled. "Load antitank rounds!"

"Up!"

Rrumms!

Then there was more firing from the enemy's side. The muzzle flash blazed.

Too short! The bastards were ranging us.

Our round was a bit over. The gunner adjusted. I had already loaded the antitank round, with the next one in my hands.

"Up!"

Rrumms!

"Fifty too short!"

What was going on with our engine? Good God, it wasn't starting! The starter ground and ground. Frey yelled with a cracking voice from his station: "Give it to him! Fire!"

Rrumms!

"Add a hair!"

"Antitank!"

"Up!"

Ivan had also fired again. The impact was so close in front of us that the snow sprayed our vehicle.

"If he fires again, he's got us!"

But we were able to fire first.

"It must have hit!"

But there was no visible effect. Damned peashooter!

Then there was a terrible blow. Everything seemed on fire in front of me . . . next to me . . . fire . . . fire!

A fist struck me on the right shoulder and turned me around in place. A clanging . . . screams. I sank to my knees. Without comprehending, I suddenly saw the sun through a giant hole in the fighting compartment; there was a tangle of steel in front of me. Flames licked all around. The gunpowder from the shell casings, which had been split open by the shrapnel, trickled out, flaming with a hiss. I no longer had any idea what was going on. I squatted among the ruins, and the world no longer made any sense. Slowly . . . very slowly . . . the thought worked its way through my tiny brain: "Knocked out . . . wounded!"

Although I felt no pain, there was a strange dull feeling in my right arm. Suddenly, something short-circuited on me. A strange, alcohol-binge-like idea flashed like lightning: "Hospital . . . nothing to smoke . . . where is my pipe? . . . I need my pipe!" I felt around with my left hand and actually found the pipe bowl. For a few seconds, I was satisfied . . . calm . . . almost happy.

To my right, the hatch was thrown open. The tank commander stuck his head inside and yelled: "What's going on? . . . Why aren't you getting out? . . . Let's go . . . Go!" I gazed at him stupidly. He grasped for me, grabbed me on the shoulder and pulled me up. "Can't you do this by yourself . . . come on!" I pushed my self up with my left hand. Suddenly, I was in the hatch with my upper body, whereupon I fell forward into the deep snow. At that moment, I saw that my overcoat was on fire—blazing. The gunner and the driver were suddenly next to me. They extinguished the flames with snow and yanked me up.

"Man, get away from the tank . . . the fireworks will start shortly!"

They both grabbed me under the arms and dragged me through the snow, which was knee deep. The arm started to really hurt. I stammered: "Careful with my arm . . . something's wrong there!"

"Who gives a shit!" the tank commander gasped. "Just get out of here!"

A Russian submachine gun was rattling behind us; it was atwitter all around us. We pressed ourselves flat to the ground. For the first time I looked at our vehicle. It had just been struck in the turret again; it was ripped off. Pitch-black smoke . . . flames blazing. The machine-gun ammunition went up with a rattle; red tracers were spraying like fireworks.

Were there only four of us? There was the tank commander, the driver, the gunner and me.

"Where's the radio operator?"

"Don't worry about it . . . nothing's bothering him anymore anyway."

They dragged me farther along through the snow. The Russians behind us, whom we had overrun, were using us for target practice. The wing tank was pulling back at an angle, spraying the Russians with machine-gun fire. Impacts from Russian high-explosive and antitank rounds threw up the snow. We kept slogging on. I saw how the clothes were hanging in shreds on the bodies of the other men.

It was only another fifty meters to the wing tank, which was laying down covering fire. In the meantime, all hell had broken out. The main guns of our tanks were firing without a break. There was something being spit at us from Ivan's side every few seconds. Down below, along the valley floor, there were two pitch-black smoky torches. That gave me a little satisfaction.

Finally, we reached the wing tank. *Stabsfeldwebel* Rüdiger climbed out onto the rear deck and helped us up. "Hold tight," he yelled. "We have to pull back . . . we've also been hit."

I lay under blankets on the rear deck and desperately held tight. The engine provided me some warmth. The tank swayed, jolted, and bounced. Every movement went through my entire body like glowing knives. *Unteroffizier* Frey had removed his gloves and was massaging his right hand, which was already pretty white from a lack of blood. "Hang in there!" He comforted me. "We'll be there shortly!"

The damned high ground was behind us. I could no longer hear the sounds of fighting through the din of the engine.

We stopped in front of a *panje* hut, which had a small white flag with a red cross flattering in front of it. My comrades pulled me down from the tank. We all pressed into a small area. A few wounded were already sitting around, applying dressings to one another.

I was placed on a table. *Stabsfeldwebel* Rüdiger, a giant of a man, had carried me in on his arm like a small child. As if looking through a veil, I saw a medic cut open my overcoat with a large knife, peeling off my rags.

The others—*Unteroffizier* Frey, the gunner, and the driver—squatted in the corner and took off their overcoats. Blood, nothing but blood everywhere. I saw the face of the medic over me; he was wearing a pair of gas mask glasses. Somebody must have asked him something. He declined. I then got a shot and was gone.

I came back later and saw a shaft of blue sky. I heard the crunching of sleigh skids and the snorting of a horse. Covered to the nose in previously warmed-up blankets, I was on a sleigh. There was someone else next to me. My comrades were sitting off to the side. They were smoking a cigarette. When they saw that I had opened my eyes, they placed a butt between my lips. That's how we got to the main clearing station—and I knew I had been saved.

...et armored train was destroyed by Schützen-Regiment 12 *(of the* 4. Panzer-
) along the Beresina River, 2 July 1941.

The crew of the train fought to the bitter end, as evidenced by this fallen Soviet officer.

A fuel truck hit by Soviet close air support, 30 June 1941, si.
Beresina.

A Panzer III knocked out by Soviet artillery. The entire superstructure of the vehicle was
ripped off the chassis by the force of the blast.

This aerial scout of the 4. Panzer-Division *was forced down by Soviet Ratas, 3 July 1941.*

The sturdy Rata, one of the first generation of Soviet fighters. It was maneuverable but too slow.

The radio SPW of the brigade commander, Oberst von Saucken. *It was christened the "old hag."*

Most of Stary-Bychow was reduced to rubble.

Artillery forward observers north of Stary Bychow, 10 July 1941.

Chapter 3

WHEN IVAN CAME OUT OF THE COLD

**From the diary of *Leutnant* Karl Burkhardt, liaison officer in the
I./Schützen-Regiment 10 of the *9. Panzer-Division***

Beginning of January 1942. Our *9. Panzer-Division* was employed on the extreme
outer wing of the field army group east of Kursk. The shrunken companies of
Schützen-Regiment 10 established primitive bunkers in the frozen earth under the
most difficult of conditions to protect themselves from the exceptional cold and the
continuously attacking Russians.

18 January 1942. It was Sunday. A radiant winter sun sparkled and blazed over
the ice-stiffened land. The sector of our 1st Battalion seemed endlessly long. The
company bunkers formed the front lines. It was the same for the battalion command
post.

Together with *Major* Gorn, I went to the 3rd Company early in the morning to
discuss a reconnaissance-in-force mission planned for the next day. The 3rd Company was all the way over to the left. As we arrived in the sector of the 2nd Company, the air started whistling around our ears. In between was the sound of
impacting Russian heavy mortar rounds. They left a unique imprint in the previously undisturbed snow: A black fleck in the middle, from which shrapnel left
meter-long trails in the fluffy white.

We were rattling along in our *Kübelwagen*[1] right in the middle of a Russian
attack. The 2nd Company was able to turn back the attack on its own. There were at
least sixty dead Russians in front of our positions.

The Russians had also attacked in the sector of the 3rd Company not much
earlier. The advance bogged down in the minefields. But then they started to come
from the left, the Russians. You could see them advancing with the naked eye, at least

---

[1] Translator's Note. The *Kübelwagen* was the ubiquitous German utility vehicle of the war, not
unlike the American jeep in function, size, and capability. It was manufactured by Volkswagen.

two companies of them. It was almost as if on the parade field. They marched in rank and column in a straight line through the knee-deep snow towards the west, exactly towards the place where our left-hand neighbors were supposed to be in position. The fireworks would be starting shortly.

But nothing happened. It was quiet as a church mouse over there. As a result, the Russians also attacked us frontally. Machine-gun fire came from in front of our positions towards our lines and forced us to take cover. Suddenly, to the rear of us on a piece of high ground, we saw about forty to fifty soldiers marching towards our artillery position. We breathed easier, since we were firmly convinced that they were our own people that the regiment had sent to protect the artillery.

But what we saw in our binoculars took our breath away. We saw that they were Russians, who were only about 300 meters from our guns. Not only we they deep to our rear, they were also doing it at a time that another Russian attack was demanding our full attention. To the left of us, two enemy companies were also marching unimpeded into the hinterland. An almost hopeless situation!

The battery commander, *Hauptmann* Moraw, was compelled to take drastic measures. He had his guns fire over open sights on the advancing Russians. At the very last moment, five tanks and three *SPW's*[2] of the divisional artillery arrived in Uderewka to help. With the combined forces, it was possible to get a little breathing space for the time being.

In the sector of the 3rd Company, Ivan continued to attack from three directions without interruption. When it turned dark, the left wing had to be bent back. The gap between us and the invisible left-hand neighbor grew larger. Highest alert status for the night!

19 January. As was his habit, *Major* Gorn personally led the relief attack that he had ordered of the tracked elements from Uderewka. At the same moment that the tanks and the *SPW's* moved across the slope, a battalion of Russians stormed towards Uderewka from the northeast with their famous *Uräää* battle cry. The tank machine guns rattled, the main guns barked hoarsely and the 2-centimeter *Flak* thundered. From the other side, the automatic weapons of our 8th Company pelted the attacking Russians. The enemy battalion was completely wiped out. About 400 men were left dead in the snow, and 100 men surrendered. And all that was early in the morning, even before the sun had had a chance to shine!

Even though that slaughter had brought some relief, the Russians continued to attack—uninterrupted, from the front, from the left, and from the right. They even attacked with some scattered groups from the west.

A second relief attack that was launched from Uderewka that afternoon bogged down in the face of strong Russian defensive fires. When the twilight of a bitterly

---

[2] Translator's Note. SPW = *Schützenpanzerwagen*—roughly, armored personnel carrier. These were either the light half-track, the *Sonderkraftfahrzeug (Sd.Kfz.) 250*, or the medium half-track, the *Sd.Kfz. 251*.

cold winter night descended, the situation in the battalion sector was still uncertain and extremely threatening.

In Russia, darkness did not equate to a break in the fighting. It was especially in the darkness that the Russians fought with a thousand tricks. We had often experienced the dead coming back to life in the darkness—only feigning death during the daylight hours. But that had to be impossible given the current conditions? Sure, there were some 400 Russian dead in the snow to the rear of us. Granted, the Russians had padded winter breeches and jackets, not to mention felt boots and fur hats. But who could live . . . survive . . . from seven in the morning until the night without moving in -42-degree weather [-44 Fahrenheit], all under our eyes. But there's no thing like a sure thing! A squad received orders to check out the bloody scene of fighting from the early morning. We thought there were 400 lifeless bodies lying in a small area. But that was a grave mistake, just like a lot of things in Russia had already been.

The *Landser*[3] went from man to man, kicking hard against the motionless figures. The dead were frozen solid, but that wasn't all by a long shot. With about every tenth kick, the boots hit a soft, living mass, either waking a dead man to life or keeping a wounded man from most certainly freezing to death. We simply did not want to believe that a few dozen men were marching off to captivity instead of ambushing us unawares in the darkness.

The twentieth of January started with an alert from Uderewka: large Russian formations were swinging east behind our front and attacking our positions from the rear, while there were frontal attacks all along the front at the same time. Even the "fire brigade" ordered to help us—two companies in strength—which the highest command levels had dispatched was unable to provide a lasting change to the threatening situation. Causing the most apprehension was the fact that the only supply route from Uderewka was under the control of the enemy.

Artillery and mortars pounded the positions of the 3rd Company for hours on end. Based on our experience, that meant a larger Russian attack was coming there. The 1st Company had already turned back two company-sized attacks. The situation became so critical, that the men of the battalion headquarters had to be employed as a final reserve on the road to Uderewka. Those were clerks, messengers, cooks, and cobblers and whoever else could be found. Out into the night and fog, without protection, without cover, at forty-two below zero! Oriented to the west! A relief attack by our tanks brought some relief. But security needed to be pulled the whole night through and in all directions of the compass.

Finally, on 21 January, reinforcements arrived. They were formations that had stood in combat with the enemy forces that had broken through to the rear. The

---

[3] Translator's Note. *Landser* is the term given to the common foot soldier of the German Army and is roughly equivalent to "GI Joe" in colloquial American military slang or "Tommy" in British usage.

frontal attacks from the east abated; for the time being, there was only heavy mortar fire on the positions of the 3rd Company.

It was quiet on the front on 23 January, but there was hard fighting to our rear. The night saw a big attack on the positions of the 8th Company; the temperature registered -48 degrees [-54.5 Fahrenheit].

On 23 January, the crisis reached its high point. During the day, the thermometer registered -47 degrees [-52.6 Fahrenheit]. Early in the morning, the 3rd Company had to turn back an attack from the northeast. While that was happening, a reinforced Russian battalion marched through the gap to the left of the 3rd Company, pivoted to the east two kilometers to our rear and then promptly attacked us from the rear. It almost sounds like a fairy tale, but that extremely critical situation was mastered by that last-ditch *ad hoc* band of infantry, supported by two death-defying tanks.

Toward 1530 hours, the numerically superior enemy fled in a panic. Before it turned dark, the gap in the lines between the 3rd Company and the left-hand neighbor was closed. We were hoping for a quiet night, since all of us were in desperate need of sleep. But as was often the case, what we had hoped for was not what we received. The regiment alerted us. It was reported that the Russians were going to attack all along the front. Despite that dire warning, it remained quiet. Early in the morning, the news reached us that the enemy that had broken through to our rear was locked in battle and that the danger to us was growing less by the hour.

When the sun rose on 24 January, we were delighted to discover that it had become "warmer." The thermometer was showing only 30 below [-22 Fahrenheit]. In its place, however, was an icy wind from the east, which was driving the powdery, feather-light snow in front of it. These were the worst types of snowdrifts, which prevented any kind of vehicular traffic. Although we were proud to call ourselves an armored division, we had taken precautions in advance and switched to horse-drawn sleds.

THE WOLVES ARE COMING: A PORTRAIT OF RUSSIA IN WINTER

Oberwachtmeister **Hans Schäufler, platoon leader of the land-line platoon in** *Panzernachrichten-Abteilung 79* **of the** *4. Panzer-Division*
January 1942. "Careful . . . partisan danger . . . road may only be crossed in convoy!" That's what was written in bold strokes on the sign when we, the advance party of the *4. Panzer-Division*, turned off toward Chwastowitschi at Karatschew in order to close a gaping hole in the front.

The instructions didn't mean much to us. What were partisans? We only had a vague idea of what they were. Thus, we didn't pay much attention to the notice and moved on carelessly. Woods and more woods . . . deeply snowed-over woods . . . biting cold . . . snowdrifts that barely let us perceive the route.

We shoveled through the masses of snow. Shoveling was a good thing . . . shoveling made you warm. The thermometer registered 35 to 40 below [-31 to -40 Fahrenheit]. Stop . . . shovel snow . . . move on another hundred meters . . . shovel some more . . . and so we fought our way forward with difficulty. In the end—and at the end of our strength as well—we reached Chwastowitschi toward evening. It was a large village in a clearing in the middle of the immense Brjansk Woods, which appeared to be drowning in snow.

Gray, snow-overcast sky the following day. Together with my landline teams, I was directed to establish a landline network for our forces, who were still fighting in the area of Below and Shisdra. My company commander, *Oberleutnant* Berger, a brand-new man, who had just joined us a few days previously, ordered: "Schäufler, first recon the routes to Lowat and Tubik with your people."

Reconnoitering is good, but what did I have to do it with? The roadways, inasmuch as you could identify them, were covered in areas with up to a meter of snow. There was certainly no way you were going to do it in a motorized vehicle. That meant we had to use a horse-drawn sled. But where were we to get one of those? After a few hours, we located a local Russian police auxiliary and his ragged *panje* pony, which looked like a donkey and had shaggy legs like a bear. With them was a small sled.

But the pony would not have been able to carry more that one additional man through the snow.

There were no further sleds to be found in the locality. "Don't go to your prince, if you are not summoned." So how was I supposed to bother my commander with this? He was new and certainly didn't know any other way. So, that meant the "people" had to remain behind, while Schäufler took a seat on the heaped-up straw behind the Russian, who did not understand a word of German.

He did not awaken a sense of trust, that fellow. You really couldn't see much of his face, regardless. A ragged beard hid everything that the raggedy fur cap covered. A simple overcoat made out of sheepskin, most likely an inheritance from his great-grandfather, made his compact frame appear misshapen. His legs were wrapped with rags and knitwear. His feet bore leather sandals, as was the custom here. I was envious of his fur overcoat, however, since it at least kept him warm, while I was freezing in my quartermaster-procured puny military overcoat.

My men pressed a bottle of vodka into my hands to help keep me warm and two packs of *machorka* just in case.

And then we were off! In the beginning, the pony trotted at a good pace through the snow, following a sled track that had been slightly snowed over. Shivering, I drifted into a half sleep. My coachman, who wore the white armband of a Russian auxiliary policeman, tried to chat with me. But it is a miserable conversation, when one doesn't understand the other language. Lowat and Tubik—those were the only two words that both of us understood. Otherwise, we were relegated to well-understood sign language.

No telephone poles far and wide. Flat land and, in the distance, a snowed-over woods.

We made good progress. I was wrong about the "donkey." In about three hours, we reached Lowat, about fifteen kilometers away. The long village looked sleepy along the woodline. The poor huts were literally groaning under the weight of the snow. An advance party from the 33rd was already there, accounting for the sled tracks.

We continued on to Tubik. That was another ten kilometers. An undisturbed blanket of white stretched out before us. No road, no tracks. The pony had a tough time of it in the deep snow. His flanks glistened with sweat and his breath covered his fur with hoarfrost. His steps grew slower and slower. He fought his way through the pathless snow. The light sled flipped on its side several times. We then walked behind the sled on foot in order to give the poor animal a break. But that wasn't a solution, either. We soon moved into a broad lane in the woods. A couple of crows flapped their wings and took off, carried by the wind. A lone fox crossed our path, curious. Otherwise, the world was empty and quiet.

No, not quite . . . a few dogs followed us at some distance. They walked along in the sled's tracks, their noses just above the snow. Dogs—up to that point, I had hardly seen any in Russia. And here there was a pack of them. My Russian was becoming visibly nervous. He wouldn't stop talking to me. I did not understand a single word. He pointed to the rear and talked and talked. And the pony started to run in a frenzied manner, without a whip, without a tap from the reins. His flanks were trembling and his breath was whistling. The dogs started to come slowly but constantly closer. I was able to count eight of them with the binoculars.

What did they want in this lonely region? There was nothing to be gained here! The Russian yelled at me. He talked with his hands and feet and also started to beat on the poor animal. There wasn't something quite right about the dogs, since my coachman pointed back to them repeatedly in excitement. He was barely able to speak. And they trotted along, monotonously following our sled. By then, they were several hundred meters behind us. If those beasts were exciting the Russian so much, then I needed to chase them off.

I fished out my submachine gun from out under the straw and emptied half a magazine into the air. To my astonishment, that didn't disturb the animals one bit. They only hesitated for a moment, before resuming their trot at a faster pace. I then peered intently at them through my binoculars one more time. It was no longer possible to speak to the Russian. He was beating on the horse, which was already steaming, sweating and snorting.

The dogs looked strange. All of them were the same size; all of them were a yellowish brown with dark hair on their backs, bushy and spikey. Damn it to hell! Those weren't some friendly dogs . . . they were wolves! Eight ravenous wolves.

I stretched out on the sled and aimed as carefully as I could on the bouncing conveyance. I held the submachine gun firmly and squeezed off an entire magazine.

The burst struck in the midst of the animals, but there was no effect. It wasn't quite so simple to hit running wolves from 100 meters on a moving sled.

I had emptied one magazine. I still had three left. I tried firing short bursts in order to save ammunition. I was starting to turn a bit uneasy. I finally hit one, with the result that he went down. A desperate struggle broke out behind us. What did all that mean? We got some distance between us and the pack of scavengers. But not for long. Seven wolves started trotting again. It appeared that they had devoured the hit animal on the spot. A dark spot disappeared slowly in the distance.

I allowed the animals to approach within seventy or eighty meters again. It might have been better to have allowed them to come closer, but I didn't have the nerve for it. Both the Russian and the horse were acting instinctively; they were no longer of sound mind.

After a few bursts, I succeeded in hitting another wolf. The same terrible scene ensued as before: A scuffling bundle and, after a short while, six wolves followed. Only a few clumps of hair and a spot of blood remained behind in the snow.

Dada . . . dada . . . dada . . . the submachine gun fired. But the pack continued to trot along, not bothered in the least. My fingers slowly started to tremble, spurred on by the nervousness of the two others and also because of the cold. I no longer hit any of the beasts. I had only one magazine left. I needed to husband my ammunition.

With practically my last round, I succeeded in finally killing another animal. It then took considerably longer until the wolves started following us again. It appeared that they were gradually getting their fill; their portions were getting larger now that they were down to five. I was almost certain that we were finally rid of them. But no, the pack started trotting along again. There was no house, no Tubik to be seen. Had we taken the right route, the right direction? We must have gotten lost! Damned Russia! And I had really enjoyed the sled ride. This land always came up with new dirty tricks to play on you, new surprises!

I still had sixteen rounds in the pistol. Although I was a good pistol shot and had won several prizes in peacetime, what was I to do with a pistol on a moving sled and aiming at running wolves? How were things going to turn out?

This time, I let them approach to within thirty meters, despite the hysterical cries of the coachman. *Peng . . . peng . . . peng!* No luck. The whole thing was turning serious.

But . . . there were houses ahead and it was no illusion. A few people appeared to be standing in front of them. They were waving and crying out. *Peng . . . peng . . . peng!* One wolf rolled around in the snow, leapt up with a limp and bit into the fur of another wolf. *Peng . . . peng . . . peng!* Empty magazine. I rapidly inserted my reserve magazine.

The Russian jumped off the sled, stumbling in a panic through the snow towards the people, who were still about 200 meters away. The sled turned on its side as a result of his jump. The horse started to gallop. I fell in the snow and grabbed for my empty submachine gun. The pack of wolves stopped. I sent my final rounds headed their way and, in the process, raced up to the houses.

The figures standing there could have been ones to fear. They looked me over with angry eyes. I had the feeling I was the first German soldier they had ever seen. In any case, they didn't have any weapons. At that point it became crystal clear that I was completely defenseless. I no longer had any rounds in either the submachine gun or the pistol. The men stood around me in a tight circle.

An older woman then came out of the house and approached me. In the case of the Russian women, it was difficult to determine their real age. She yelled at the men and gestured to me to enter the house. She spoke broken German, very broken: *"Charascho Pan, charascho!"* She pointed to me with her finger: "You . . . you four wolves *kaputt! Charascho!* " She offered me a cup—no, not quite a cup, but some sort of ill-defined container—with a dark, hot broth. It tasted something like tea. It did me good.

I was only then that I noticed that my knees were trembling. She invited me to take a place next to the oven.

The men also came into the house, including the Russian auxiliary policeman. He no longer had a white armband on his overcoat. Something did not seem right. The sign—Careful! Partisan danger!—popped into my mind. I had jumped from the frying pan into the fire. No German soldier far and wide, and it started to snow and turn dark outside.

As a precaution, I went to the sled and fetched the bottle of vodka and the two packs of tobacco.

I saw the eyes of the Russians stalking me. Perhaps a miracle would happen? I handed the bottle to the first one available and gestured that he should pass it on. It was soon empty. Man, could they drink! Their eyes glistened happily. Then I let each one take a handful of tobacco. They made cones out of newspapers and poured the *machorka* in them. They pinched off the ends and enjoyed their smoke. In return, I received a few warm potatoes from the old woman. I gobbled them down ravenously.

But there was no way I was going to stay there among those dubious figures all by myself. I gave my coachman a sign that we needed to ride back immediately. Based on his reaction, I had to conclude that he thought I was crazy. "*Njet . . . njet!* " he said resolutely. But how was I supposed to survive the night; Tubik was in no-man's-land. But I also had to realize that a return trip by night was impossible. Moreover, I no longer had any ammunition. But the man didn't know that—I hoped to God he didn't find out. I tried to ignore the fact that I was terrified of the upcoming night.

A weak oil stove was burning in the room. I set myself in a corner, the empty submachine gun across my knees, and tried to ward off my tiredness. Just don't fall asleep! Heaven was on my side—because of the lice, there was no temptation to close my eyes. The lice in my shirt also provided some entertainment.

The men cowered in the opposite corner, put their heads together and whispered. They were cooking something up. The old woman went up to them and gave them an earful. I didn't understand what she said, but I thought I picked up that it was her house and I was her guest. She then gave me a worried look, a very worried look.

I jumped up repeatedly, thinking I heard a noise or light footsteps. But nothing transpired. The night was endlessly long. But even it came to an end. It no longer snowed.

Even then, my Russian could not be convinced to take the road back. He indicated to me that he would rather be shot than to have to conduct another race with the wolves. What was I to do? — I would not be able to find my way on foot, since the tracks had been snowed over. I also wouldn't be able to cover the ten kilometers though the breast-high snow. A hopeless situation.

Toward noon, the woman came running excitedly into the house: "*Nemjetzki* soldier! *Nemjetzki* soldier!" She pointed to the window. With a jolt, I was wide-awake and ran to the door.

It was true! I saw three sleds coming through the snow. It was a patrol from *Schützen-Regiment 33*, as I discovered.

"Here you go, everybody! Take my tobacco. Take all of it! Come on, take it!"

I waved and waved and the men of the 33rd came.

The old woman took me to the side, looked at me with happy eyes and made an elaborate cross on my forehead. At first, I didn't know what she meant, but then I felt it: you were lucky, young man, give thanks to God for that!

THE MAJOR SETBACK: ADVANCE TO SIXTY KILOMETERS SOUTH OF MOSCOW

Oberst Heinrich Eberbach, commander of the *5. Panzer-Brigade* and, as of 5 January 1942, acting commander of the *4. Panzer-Division*

On 30 September, our tanks broke through the Russian positions at Gluchow. The heavy enemy combat vehicles there were eliminated by means of fire to the flanks or rear. In an exceptional assault, they raced 200 kilometers by 3 October, when they took the metropolis of Orel against extremely tough Russian attacks from the air and resistance by an enemy airborne regiment.

What fell into the hands of the division in Orel in terms of supplies were enough to last the entire *2. Armee* six weeks. The morale of the men, who had achieved that success, was confident; they were certain of victory.

But from 4 to 7 October, during the advance on Mzensk, our tanks encountered a Russian tank brigade, which was exclusively outfitted with heavy tanks—T-34's and KV-I's. The steel giants were overwhelmingly superior to our *Panzer III's* and *Panzer IV's*. The Russian crews were well trained and well led.

I had to give my soldiers, who were accustomed to victory, the order to pull back twice in order to avoid being destroyed. Friendly casualties were high; morale had sunk. The road network had been softened up by rain; indeed, it seemed bottomless. The snowstorm that immediately followed added even more to an already difficult situation. For the first time, Russian rocket launchers were used in battle.

After slight gains, the attack of the entire *4. Panzer-Division* bogged down on 9 October.

When the division finished reorganizing and another attack on Mzensk was ordered for 10 October, I could see in the eyes of my men that they thought the attack had no chance of success and that their trust in me as their commander was shaken for the first time in the campaign, since I had not refused to carry out the order.

When the city was taken on that same day by the tank brigade, it was only thanks to a desperate attack in a snowstorm. For the next few days, it remained uncertain whether Mzensk and its important bridgehead over the Suscha could be held against the superior Russian numbers. The *4. Panzer-Division* no longer had the combat power to drive the Russians from the dominant high ground north of the city, which featured dug-in tanks in its defenses in some cases.

Despite a success gained through deceiving the enemy, the feeling of superiority over the enemy had been shaken to the core for the first time in the war. How had it been possible for the supreme command not to know about the existence of the new Russian tanks? Why hadn't the tank development plans long since proposed by Guderian been realized? How was the fight to be continued against the T-34's, the KV-I's and the KV-II's with our worn-out crates?

It was not until the entire *2. Panzer-Armee* had been concentrated that the Russian front could be rolled up despite the mud period, assisted effectively by *Stukas* and by bypassing the enemy positions on the high ground. The concentrated armor forces of *Generaloberst* Guderian then struck to the north. The wheeled vehicles, however, remained bogged down in mud up to their axles.

The troops had the feeling that no one in higher headquarters knew anything about the mud period in Russia and no one gave much thought as to what effect it was having. The losses in materiel were large. The city of Tula, which was right on our path, could not be taken, despite all efforts, because the artillery did not have enough tubes up front and not enough ammunition was coming forward as a result of the mud. It was not until there was a freeze that the advance continued, bypassing Tula.

At the beginning of December, despite all of the difficulties, the lead elements of the *2. Panzer-Armee* were outside of Kashira, sixty kilometers south of Moscow. With their last drops of fuel, the remaining tanks of the *4. Panzer-Division* reached the Serpuchow-Tula road. At that point, only fifteen kilometers separated them from the lead elements of the *XXXXIII. Armee-Korps*, which were advancing east to link up with us and finish the encirclement of Tula.

The thermometer registered 40 below. The *XXXXIII. Armee-Korps* never came. Instead, the shrunken *4. Panzer-Division* was ceaselessly attacked from the north by fresh Siberian divisions that had been brought in from the east.

As cold as it was, the tanks would not start; the gun optics fogged over and iced up; the oil in the guns, automatic weapons and engines was as stiff as artificial honey. The recoil mechanisms jammed; the bolts of the machine guns, submachine guns and rifles no longer moved. The troops were exposed to that cold and the knee-deep snow without winter uniforms. The widely extended front, with Tula to the rear, could not be held. Guderian had to issue orders to retreat.

Retreat without fuel? That's impossible! That meant the tanks, the prime movers and the guns all had to be blown up; that the trucks with all of their valuable contents had to be abandoned! The telephones were ringing off the hook. We couldn't pull back. That meant losing all of our heavy equipment! Reply: pull back . . . pull back immediately! Blow up or set immobilized heavy weapons and vehicles on fire!

The officers and men could not comprehend what was happening. Destroy our own tanks . . . guns . . . *Flak*? No, that couldn't be true! That would be a unique triumph for the enemy and a moral catastrophe for us of the first magnitude. And how were we supposed to defend ourselves then? Were our men supposed to stop T-34's with their rifles and pistols? A look at the map had to show the higher officers the absurdity of the order!

Despite all that, the disengagement from the enemy succeeded. There was still enough fuel there for a tank company and for a few prime movers and guns. They provided for a disciplined retreat, together with the riflemen.

The men, who no longer had any vehicles, requisitioned *panje* ponies and sleds. They loaded the machine guns and mortars on them, which they did not want to throw away. It paid dividends that a large portion of the *Panzertruppe* originally came from the cavalry.

We reached the Suscha, in spite of all of the difficulties. The infantry established a defensive position on the hills north of Mzensk. But we knew that the German front line was pulling back everywhere. We knew from bitter experience what that meant at 40 below.

To the north of the *2. Panzer-Armee*, an entire Russian field army had broken through to the west through a gap that emerged as a result of the withdrawal. Portions of a German division had been encircled in Suchinitschi. The Russian forces were advancing far to the rear and deep flanks of our field army. Would the enemy be able to take Brjansk, cut off our supplies and encircle our army? The partisans were already making the woods to our rear treacherous and laying waste to some supply trains.

You had to think about the fate of Napoleon's *Grande Armee*. The conversations of Napoleon with Caulaincourt during the flight from Moscow made the rounds among the officers. We had become all too well acquainted with the Russians. Don't fall into their hands alive! You carried a pistol in your pants pocket. Seven bullets for the Russians and one for yourself!

For the first time, we discovered we were not invincible. For the first time, we saw the supreme command fail us. We were burnt out, exhausted and frozen to the bone.

And it was just at that moment—on 1 January 1942—that the supreme command took away the man who had led us from victory to victory and who enjoyed our complete trust, the commander in chief of the *2. Panzer-Armee*, *Generaloberst* Guderian. Even during the retreat, he had kept our personnel losses to bearable levels thanks to his superior tactics. The man, who had pointed out the mistakes of the supreme command on numerous occasions and who had become a thorn in the side, was relieved and sent away as a scapegoat.

What we did retain, however, was an unprecedented comradeship that permeated the ranks and a loyalty to our company, our regiment and our division, which had become our homeland in enemy territory.

The men did not despair. That was the miracle. They trusted their officers. And whenever they looked into the eyes of their soldiers they knew that they could still rely on them whenever they were prepared—as they always had been up to then—to always and everywhere take care of the men entrusted to them. In plain terms, it meant that the leaders of those little companies had to always come up with something in order to get out of that damnable situation. And for the immediate future, we were still helplessly exposed to the Russian winter.

A new front had to be established. But it was storming and snowing. The temperatures were almost always 30 to 40 below, and even 50 below was no rare reading.

The cold had long since forced us into the *panje* huts, in which the Russian families coexisted with the chickens, the pig, the bugs and the lice in a horrible but nonetheless warm stink. The vermin would not leave us alone. It was only due to the fact that we were completely exhausted that we were able to sleep at all.

We slowly learned that you had to carry the bolts of your machine guns and rifles in your pants pockets and that petroleum instead of grease had to be used. Every company "procured" a number of snow overgarments. The men quickly learned how to protect themselves from frostbite. They checked each other out to make sure ears and noses were not turning white. They saw how the Russians used paper to keep warm and did the same. Some even started wearing Russian sheepskin coats or felt boots.

The dozen tanks that had been saved were whitewashed. But their tracks, much too narrow for the Russian winter, caused them to still bottom out in the snow. The riflemen had to create a path for them. It was not until that was done that they could follow behind like assault guns and give cover. In contrast, the Russian T-34 moved unimpeded through the snow, leaving a white flag of snow spray behind it as it moved.

The trains, which had shrunk in size due to the loss of so many vehicles, were combed for soldiers who were suitable for frontline employment. The men coming from the trains already had experience in Russia, thus providing us with our best replacements.

We learned from the Russians how to emplace mines in the snow. We also discovered that good, old wire provided the most secure and best form of communications in that kind of cold, even if the partisans frequently cut it.

A few excerpts from the surviving daily logs of the *4. Panzer-Division* will shed some light in a sober fashion on our situation:

8 December 1941: Fuel for the continued march to the rear presently available only within *Artillerie-Regiment 103*.

9 December 1941: Due to a lack of fuel, the *II. /[Schützen-Regiment] 33* cannot be rushed to help the *296. Infanterie-Division*. Catastrophic road network conditions.

11 December 1941: The *I. /Artillerie-Regiment 103* has been disbanded in order to plus-up the *II. /Artillerie-Regiment 103*. The road has been cleared of snowdrifts and iced-over portions made trafficable.

12 December 1941: One platoon of tanks—three vehicles—sent to support the *296. Infanterie-Division*.

13 December 1941: Urgent request to the commander of the *296. Infanterie-Division*: Recover stuck tanks under all circumstances.

14 December 1941: *Panzer-Kompanie Wollschläger* (rest of *Panzer-Regiment 35*) has only eight *Panzer III's* operational. Two tanks had to be blown up in the sector of the *296. Infanterie-Division*. Roads and trails completely iced over.

15 December 1941: Heavy snowstorm. Reinforced *Schützen-Regiment 33* establishes a passage point for the *3. Panzer-Division* north of Lapokowo along the Ssolowa River.

16 December 1941: Over the last few days, the number of vehicles has sunk again. If continued marches off the roads are required, then additional considerable losses must be assumed. A large portion of the vehicles still left have to be towed. . . . After extensive combat, the *296. Infanterie-Division* is completely burnt out and apathetic. It is to be assumed that the Russians will break through there.

17 December 1941: Strong enemy forces advancing through a gap in the sector of the *167. Infanterie-Division*. The *II. /[Schützen-Regiment] 33* has been attached to the *112. Infanterie-Division* and is turning back enemy attacks.

20 December 1941: Elements of the [divisional] artillery without transportation constitute 500 men at this point.

21 December 1941: Contagious sicknesses among the Russian populace in numerous localities.

23 December 1941: Screening line south of Orel occupied. Improvement of the positions underway. Snowdrifts. Another company of the *II. /[Schützen-Regiment] 33* disbanded due to low personnel strength.

✠

During the last week of December, strong Russian forces advanced on Kosjolsk. The forces of the *4. Panzer-Division* that were still mobile were directed to Kosjolsk to occupy and hold it. The order could not be executed, because the forces remained stuck in the snow on the way from Belew to Kosjolsk. The men suffered terribly day and night as a result of the cold.

The dismounted elements of the *4. Panzer-Division* had grown to 2,000 men in the meantime. As much as was possible, they were consolidated into sled battalions. *Artillerie-Regiment 103* had only three heavy and six light guns left.

The *4. Panzer-Division* was pulled back to Belew and Bolchow to serve as the "fire brigade" for the *LIII. Armee-Korps.*

A Russian rifle division had crossed the Oka east of Bolchow and was advancing towards it. The road used to supply all of the infantry divisions north of Bolchow was under fire. Our division was directed to throw the enemy back across the Oka. Could it do that with the emaciated forces it still had available?

But *Oberst* von Saucken launched one of his famous pincers attacks with *Schützen-Regiment 12* and *Schützen-Regiment 33.* The Russian division was delivered a devastating blow. A second Russian division suffered the same fate. Their remnants were tossed back across the Oka. *Oberst* von Saucken, who personally led these attacks, was badly wounded in the process. A serious loss for the division!

The spoils of war obtained from the Russian were considerable. Shedding some light on the over-all situation among the individual German divisions is the report of the *4. Panzer-Division* concerning German weapons that were recaptured: four heavy and six light field pieces; one heavy and two light infantry guns; three heavy and two light mortars; and sixteen machine guns. As a result, the division was able to reduce its losses in weaponry considerably.

The losses we suffered did not reflect a tenth of those suffered by the Russians, but they were considerable, considering the shrunken state of our division: 6 officers and 81 enlisted personnel killed; 15 officers and 215 enlisted personnel wounded. Although a battalion of replacements made up the numbers, the fighters with experience in Russia were not so easily replaced.

On 7 January, the *4. Panzer-Division*, whose acting commander I became after the wounding of *Oberst* von Saucken, received the following orders.

Two Russian infantry divisions and a cavalry division are marching from the northeast towards the deep flank of the *2. Panzer-Armee.* Brjansk and even Roslawl, our logistics points, are threatened. The *4. Panzer-Division* will be relieved in place east of Bolchow by the *17. Panzer-Division.*

The motorized elements of the division—consisting of the division headquarters, the *I. /[Schützen-Regiment] 33* (sled battalion), the *II. /[Artillerie-Regiment] 103*, *Panzerpionier-Bataillon 79*, *Panzerjäger-Abteilung 49*, and the 1st Battalion of *Nebelwerfer-Regiment 53*—will move from Karatschew to Chwastowitschi on 8 January.

Employment to the north, initially in the direction of Kzyn, is planned. *Oberst* von Lüttwitz is in charge of bringing up the remaining elements of the division. But these orders were overcome by the continued successes of the Russians and the snowdrifts.

On 10 January, the Russians encircled *Gruppe Gilsa* in Suchinitsci (north of Brjansk). *Oberst* von Lüttwitz, commanding his reinforced *Schützen-Regiment 12*, advanced to free the encircled forces. His regiment, attached to the *18. Panzer-Division* of *Generalmajor* Nehring, advanced from Brjansk to the north. The remaining elements assembled in Brjansk, whose defense was entrusted to the acting divisional commander (Eberbach).

Necessity forced the troop elements to be turned topsy-turvy. Individual battalions and even companies were attached to threatened divisions and remained there for weeks on end. For instance, attached to *Gruppe von Lüttwitz* was the *III./Panzer-Regiment 18* (four tanks and dismounted elements) as well as a company from *Panzer-Aufklärungs-Abteilung 27*.

The first infantry divisions arrived from France, where they had had a relatively warm and comfortable existence. In some cases, they received good winter clothing on their way east. Despite that, the immediate jump into the hard Russian winter hit them mercilessly. They suffered considerably more cases of frostbite that the experienced Russia divisions. Until they had acclimated to fighting in Russia, there were occasional disappointing setbacks. Individual commanders were relieved.

It was imperative to defeat the Russian field army that had advanced north of Brjansk and establish a new front line. Would it be possible to do that in the face of such cold and the increasingly more severe snowstorms?

Gruppe Grolig, the reinforced *Schützen-Regiment 33*, was in Chwastowitschi. On 20 January, the divisional headquarters received orders to move there, assume command of *Gruppe Grolig*, and advance north while securing its own flanks. The *134. Infanterie-Division* was directed to advance along the right, while the *211. Infanterie-Division* was to the left. Attached or in direct support of the *4. Panzer-Division* were:

Bataillon Bradel (consolidated *Panzer-Aufklärungs-Abteilung 7* and *Kradschützen-Bataillon 34*)

Infanterie-Regiment 446 with two batteries in support, a total of 4 guns [*134. Infanterie-Division*]

III./Artillerie-Regiment 103 with an attached rocket-launcher battery

Pionier-Bataillon 41 with two companies and augmented by the *3./Kradschützen-Bataillon 40*

Pionier-Bataillon 10 with two companies

Feldersatz-Bataillon 84 with two companies (140 men)

Panzer-Kompanie Wollschläger with eight *Panzer III's*

Panzer-Kompanie Kestner with two *Panzer IV's*, three *Panzer III's*, and two *Panzer II's*

Because of a blown-up bridge and temperatures of 44 below, the division head-quarters did not reach Chwastowitschi until 21 January. The available forces were spread out around the surrounding villages. The intent was to secure them but also to provide sufficient warm quarters for the men.

The thermometer registered 44 below again on 22 January. The villages of Dudorowskij and Moilowo were reported as enemy occupied by our patrols. *Panzer-Kompanie Wollschläger* advanced toward Dudorowskij and temporarily ejected the Russians from the village.

But a platoon from *Infanterie-Regiment 446* in Jaschinskij, which had not set up sufficient security for itself due to the cold, was overrun by a Russian squadron, reinforced by partisans, and wiped out. Only two wounded men survived. In contrast, a night attack by the Russians on Kzyn, which was turned back, saw eighty Russians and numerous weapons left behind.

On 24 January, the *18. Panzer-Division*, to which our *Gruppe von Lüttwitz* was attached, relieved *Gruppe Gilsa* and a number of wounded and sick in Suchinitschi.

Infanterie-Regiment 446, which was attached to the *4. Panzer-Division*, took the village of Moilowo after hard house-to-house fighting.

On 25 January, the field army ordered the division to quickly take the village of Chatkowo. It was to be assisted by the *I./Infanterie-Regiment 317 [211. Infanterie-Division]*, coming from Debrik. But the infantry battalion was still a great distance away, and the snowstorm barely allowed supplies to be brought forward.

Despite all that, the villages of Brussny and Ssusseja, which were heavily occupied, were taken on 28 January; *Panzer-Kompanie Wollschläger* advanced as far as Chatkowo. As the result of antitank guns and mines, it lost three tanks and was unable to reach Chatkowo, which was also heavily occupied.

On 29 January, heavy snowfall made any larger-scale movements impossible. The division urgently requested the support of a snowplow, since any further advance was unthinkable without it.

On 30 January, the division ordered an attack on Chatkowo for 31 January. It was to be conducted by *Pionier-Bataillon 41*, a sharp battalion, and the 3rd Company of *Kradschützen-Bataillon 40*, all supported by artillery and rocket launchers.

Debrik, located to the west of Chatkowo, was taken, but it had to be evacuated immediately, since the Russians had burned down all the houses. The attack on Chatkowo did not succeed, and the formations suffered two dead and fifteen wounded. A few prisoners were taken, however, and they stated that Chatkowo was occupied by the 1167th Rifle Regiment, which numbered about 2,000 men. The Russian regiment was also supported by heavy weapons.

It was imperative to take the village, which dominated the entire area, if we intended to establish a new front. More forces needed to be employed to that end.

The attack had to take place from several sides and the artillery and other support of the operation had to be considerable. That meant that ammunition had to be brought forward, and all available guns brought into position.

Although Trosna was wrested from the Russians on 1 February, the continuing snowfalls and snowstorms made all of the roads untrafficable. The snow was already a meter high. The snowdrifts reached up to two meters and beyond. Once again, the division sent an urgent request for a snowplow. When would it come? Would it even come?

The attack on Chatkowo was planned down to the last detail and earmarked for 3 February. But the ammunition did not arrive. On 4 February, the snowplow, which had finally arrived, cleared the supply routes. Despite that, the chest-high snow continued to provide the division with concerns.

It was intended for reinforced *Bataillon Bradel* (*Panzeraufklärungs-Abteilung 7* and *Kradschützen-Bataillon 34*) to advance through the woods east of Chatkowo and force its way into the village from there. *Pionier-Bataillon 41*, reinforced by the *2./Pionier-Bataillon 10* and the *3./Kradschützen-Bataillon 40*, was to attack Chatkowo frontally from the south. At the same time, it was intended for *Infanterie-Regiment 317* to move out form Debrik, that is, from the west, to slam into Chatkowo.

The few tanks could only provide fire from the roads. The main effort of the attack was with *Bataillon Bradel*, since it was able to directly attack the first few houses in its part of the village from the woods. The engineers and the infantry, on the other hand, had to work their way forward across open terrain and deep snow.

Another concern was the command and control of the three attack wedges during the attack. Everything had been discussed in detail, but the terrific cold did not allow radio communications, since the batteries would immediately freeze. That meant wire had to be laid. But how often would the lines be shot up and ripped apart?

Under those circumstances, how could we risk such an attack operation? Because the possession of the village of Chatkowo was important. Moreover, we had learned over the previous weeks that the Russians would most likely not hold out against a well-planned pincers operation. Further, a seamlessly executed attack meant the enemy could be ejected without too high of casualties.

The attack, which was supposed to have started at 0800 hours, was delayed for an hour, because the artillery was still not ready to fire because of the high snow. By then, *Bataillon Bradel* had worked its way through the woods and close to the village. Waiting an hour at 35 below must have been a torture for the men. Finally . . . after an eternity, everything was ready. Bradel entered Chatkowo with élan, and our artillery did not husband its ammunition.

The acting division commander moved to the front on skis. He saw that the righthand attack wedge was moving slowly forward. Where were the other attack groups? The sound of heavy fighting could be heard coming from Debrik. That meant that the *I./Infanterie-Regiment 317* was engaged. I hoped that the battalion

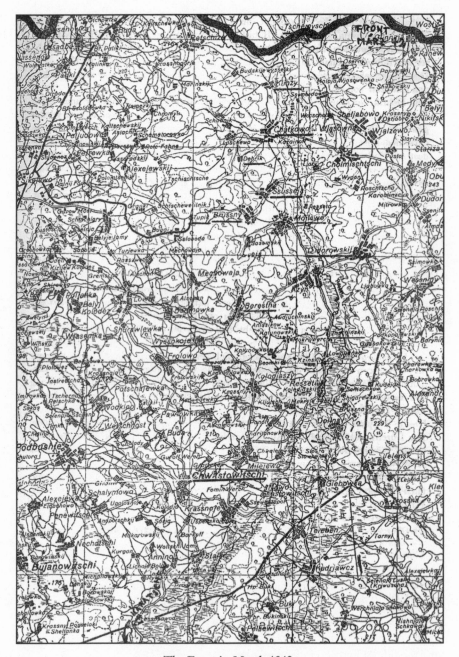

The Front in March 1942.

commander was sending at least one company forward towards Chatkowo to support Bradel. But the landlines to him were broken. Bradel reported that his men were fighting numerically vastly superior enemy forces and that he urgently needed support. Where was the engineer battalion? The acting division commander skied to Ssusseja. The battalion was in readiness there. Through a misunderstanding, it had not moved out. The companies immediately started to move out. Drivers and clerks shoveled the road clear for the four tanks. It was 1100 hours.

There were still sounds of heavy fighting coming from Debrik—and there was still no communications. It was enough to drive you crazy! Finally, the signaleers got it fixed. The battalion had been involved in a merciless woodland fight, which was finally decided in its favor. The acting division commander ordered the battalion commander to finally attack in the direction of Chatkowo with at least some forces so as not to leave the men fighting there in the lurch.

The artillery reported that the Russians were pulling back to the north with at least two of their three battalions and two artillery pieces. Those forces were being effectively engaged by our howitzers. The infantry in Debrik might have been able to interdict those forces.

It was not until 1500 hours that the division could report that the eastern and western portions of Chatkowo had been taken. The central portion of the village was still occupied by weak forces; the northern part was still strongly occupied.

The infantry battalion reached the northwestern edge of the hotly contested locality. All of the battalions cleared the village in a bitter house-to-house struggle. By 1630 hours, Chatkowo was firmly in our hands. *Bataillon Bradel*, which had borne the main burden of the fighting, had lost three officers and sixty men. It was pulled out of the line and sent to Ssusseja. The artillery had fired 1,160 rounds, and it had been effective. The Russian casualties were considerably more than the German ones. The main thing, however, was the fact that the men had learned that they could still advance, even against strong enemy forces.

The possession of Chatkowo paid dividends. It allowed Duderowskij to be recaptured on 11 February with minimal casualties. On 12 February, Wessniny was retaken; Klinzy on the following day. On 23 February, even Tschernytschi was retaken by the *211. Infanterie-Division*, supported by the *4. Panzer-Division*.

Our forces were then able to establish a defensive position along the Resseta. The efforts by the Russians to achieve a breakthrough along the front of the *2. Panzer-Armee* had been thwarted after hard fighting. As a result, the combat troops had won back their combat morale.

The unbelievable had been achieved by a colorful assemblage of *ad hoc* units. The German forces had caught themselves after a severe setback using only the bare necessities in materiel and under terrible weather conditions. Once again, they proved themselves to be superior to a brave and determined enemy.

Whether *Obergefreiter*, *Hauptmann*, or *General*, they had all done their part.

ATTACKING CHATKOWO IN ICE AND SNOW

Unteroffizier **Ulrich Sachse, squad leader in** *Kradschützen-Bataillon*
34/Panzeraufklärungs-Abteilung 7

During the evening of 2 February 1942, *Feldwebel* Franz Oesterreich came into our hovel at the end of the village of Milejewo and brought orders with him stating that our company was to be prepared to move out at 0700 hours tomorrow. "We're attacking," he thought.

I got ready, along with three of my warriors, to relieve the moving machine-gun post. Packaged warmly in overcoats and felt boots, we climbed out over the giant mountains of snow in front of our door and headed out into the frosty evening.

We took over the machine gun from our frozen comrades and told them that they needed to get ready to move out. They then stomped away in the snow. After days and nights of wild snowstorms, the weather had cleared up. A magnificent, starry heaven glittered above us. It had turned colder again; it was already 40 below. It would certainly get colder that night. We walked out into the snowy desert a few hundred meters, past the last hut in the village. At the row of trees, which most likely accompanied a path in the fields over the rise to the next village during the summer, we turned around so as to look between the houses to see whether everything was in order.

All around us, there was nothing but snow, with the exception of the northeast, where there was a line of telegraph poles. A sign with the tactical insignia of one of our motorized rifle battalions provided a miserable set of sled tracks the character of a connecting route, which paralleled the telegraph poles to the next German strongpoint, which had to be somewhere behind the snow-covered rise.

Whenever you took the route of the guard post to the north, that is, from the end of the village towards the row of trees, there was a patch of woods off to the left about a thousand meters away. We gave it our undivided attention, since that was the most likely place the Russians could appear.

The fact that the patch of woods was beyond our strongpoint system didn't mean a whole lot, since there wasn't a front in the conventional sense. Every strongpoint was responsible for defending itself. The many kilometers between the widely dispersed villages were open season. The German and Russian patrols annoyed each other there and played "catch" with one another.

In the rear area, the insidious partisan war was in full bloom. The gangs conducted their mischief along the fifty kilometers of road between Karatschew and here. The fighting with the regular enemy forces centered around the occupation of strongpoints, since the brutal cold made a lengthy stay outside of the localities impossible.

It took a great effort to move through the snow. Where we had just finished stomping through, the biting wind had already filled in our tracks in the blink of an eye. We had to constantly turn our faces away from the wind and thaw out our frozen eyelashes in order to see anything at all. We had to rub our cheeks and noses with snow to keep them from freezing.

Despite all that, the two hours of guard duty went pretty quickly, since we measured it, so to speak, by the short stretch between the edge of the village and the row of trees, which we barely covered in two hours, even though it was not even 800 meters.

Our relief came punctually. It was not until we exchanged overcoats, that we notice how thoroughly frozen we were. My men scurried into their *panje* hut. I ran over to the company command post to make sure a sick soldier from my squad was evacuated in the morning before we departed.

Riders on horseback came riding up the village street. It was the lead elements of the 1st Company, which were already moving out to the tactical assembly area. Like a ghost, they disappeared in the direction of the sled tracks along the telegraph line.

When I scrambled back to our *panje* hut from the company command post, the long column of sleds from the 1st Company was moving through the night-drenched village. The runners of the sleds crunched in the snow, made a racket when crossing the ruts in the road and the drivers growled at the hardheaded panje horses. Good that we were granted a few hours of sleep that night!

But the unrest associated with the move-out disrupted our sleep. The unknown prospect of what was to come had taken hold of us. The attack we had been ordered to conduct worked its way into our short hours of rest. The knowledge that we were going to attack had cultivated the tension that we had already become familiar with from many attacks and with which you never become accustomed. Every soldier adapts to that issue in his own way; he can't solve the problem in advance. Only the attack itself will solve the issue.

As we stood ready to move out the following morning in a long column of sleds, it was already almost light despite the early hour. Under a clear sky, the snow allowed the terrain to be seen for a long distance, and a light on the eastern horizon promised a sunny day.

Our acting company commander gave us the familiar signal to "Start engines!" It was a form of gallows humor to remind us of our formerly proud motorized past. We then shuffled out into the snowy desert in our eighty sleds. The track that the 1st Company had left behind during the night was already so slick that our platoon leader's legs shot out from under him every ten meters, causing him to land on his hindquarters, much to the general amusement of everyone.

The sun climbed above the wintery monotony and made the distant areas very scenic. Destroyers providing escort from the air flew over us. A village signaled us on the far side of the sloping snow. It was palpably near and served as an orientation point for our march. But it took hours until we reached it, since the glittering expanse of snow messed up our ability to estimate and shortened almost all distances for our eyes.

After some hours, the road became better; it actually turned quite comfortable. Scores of Russian prisoners were occupied with snow shovels.

We moved through German strongpoints. The muzzles of antitank guns starred at us threateningly and machine-gun positions on the edges of villages had their barrels trained on us. While our company may have been approaching at that hour, a few hours later a Russian patrol could be there. Who could be sure? A little farther to the right toward the east, the Resseta River accompanied out march route. Behind it was Russian territory, which was contested only by German patrols.

Our attack mission had been borne out of necessity. It was to force the Russians in the north back behind the Resseta and wrest the final locality on this side of the river from them.

We took a lunch break in the village of Kzyn. Our *panje* horses wolfed down their ration of hay with the same fervor we did out noodles and meat, with the exception that they did it outside, while we pressed into the hovels of the village, where we were provided with horror stories by the rocket launcher and artillery personnel, who had settled in there two weeks ago as the strongpoint garrison. The tubes of their guns were pointed in all directions.

We moved on. We greeted a lonely *Panzer III* with a shout as it overtook our column. It was said that our attack was supposed to be supported by *Panzer-Regiment 35*.

"*Heil, Panzerbrigade!* " we yelled out to the tankers, who were sitting on the turret. "*Heil*, foot sloggers," they bandied back. "We're from the *KPD!*" Of course, that did not mean they were communists. In soldier slang, it stood for *kaputte Panzer-Division*.

As it turned twilight, we reached the village of Moilowo, where we took up quarters in a couple of miserable huts on the west side. Even though we were tired, we still had to set up a machine-gun walking guard on the edge of the village.

Before that, however, Emil Müller, a jack-of-all-trades, conjured up some mutton from under the clothes piled on his sled. He started a roaring fire in the oven. Karl Hage, our doctor of agriculture from the Rhön region, proved his mettle by using his homegrown talents to find a hiding place for potatoes. Otto Simon, the assistant machine gunner, prepared the hay on the floor. Adolf Volland, the technical wizard, illuminated our palace by a useful synthesis of an old meat can, some diesel fuel and a wick made out of a cleaning cloth.

While the measures being undertaken to raise our standard of living were underway, I went outside with the rest of the squad to pull the first shift as machine-gun guard. A terrible, bone-chilling cold radiated from the clear heavens. The snow crunched loudly under our footsteps. We circled our sector of the village for two long hours and kept the well-deserved peace of our company.

The deep silence all around us was only broken occasionally by the muffled sounds of artillery harassing fires far to our rear . . . the black darkness lit up from time to time by the muzzle flashes...torn by the report of guns firing and the impact of rounds . . . eerily illuminated by the red stream of fire of a distant rocket battery.

Dead tired, we consumed our portion of Emil's festive meal after we were relieved and then slept like lead until about three in the morning, when we had to pull machine-gun guard again. Once again, the wintery night engulfed us. It turned hazy. The cold, on the other hand, remained barbaric. The skies showed furtively blinking stars, which appeared to be hanging lower on the desert of snow. It turned everything smaller and more muffled.

The vastness of the firmament was gone. It had helped us during our nightly wanderings—despite hunger, cold and tiredness—to remain alert and attentive. Everything seemed close, impenetrable and shapeless.

What was that along the fence? It was no bush, it was no ghost, and it was no Russian. It was Lattke, as we called Ernst Lattner, who had been an assistant machine gunner for three campaigns—in Poland, in France and in Russia from the very beginning. *Obergefreiter* Lattner was having a good laugh. Actually, he was only laughing with his eyes. That said, there was a mischievous sparkle in his eyes. He could laugh better with his eyes than many who laughed with their entire face.

"*Na, Unoffizier*,"[4] he said in an intentionally mischievous manner—*Unteroffizier* was decidedly too long for him and perhaps too impersonal. "*Na, Unoffizier*. It's about time." The old *Obergefreiter* in him always had an earful ready for the young officer candidate. Ever since France it had been part and parcel of my daily routine that Lattke would call me out in his happy-go-lucky manner. The fact that we were more than on time was completely immaterial to him. It was his right as an old warrior to talk crap and harangue—and he did it masterfully.

Of course, I made use of my higher rank, as I always did: "Lattner . . . march, march . . . hit the deck . . . go to the telegraph pole . . . crawl under the fence . . . get in the cooking pot . . . cover it up . . . sing!"

Oh, did I ever intimidate the *Obergefreiter*! Symbolically, of course. Nothing actually happened except that I rattled off my commands and he wagged his butt at me, rolled his eyes and trotted off with an abysmal "Ooooooch."

Behind us, in the village, there was the sound of horse-drawn sleds. Artillery was being brought forward to support our attack. It had been directed that we were to attack early in the morning, but the bad roadways had delayed the approach of the artillery. As a result, the operation had to be pushed back twenty-four hours, that is, to 5 February. At the same time tomorrow morning, we would be waiting for H-Hour in our tactical assembly area or for the opening salvoes of the artillery.

There was something unusual about those twenty-four hours between us and the village up there to the north. Something like "To be continued . . ." in a series in the daily newspaper. The tension dissipated, went away. It was held over for a day, so to speak. It was something like that. The continuum had been broken that had riled up our subconscious from the move-out the previous day, through the sunny day we were experiencing the next, to the anticipated nighttime march, to the

---

[4] Translator's Note. This means, roughly, "Sarge."

tactical assembly area, to the first shots of tomorrow. It all seemed silly to us. We hadn't a clue as to what to do with the extra twenty-four hours that were there all of a sudden.

The blurry scenery of the hovels, the fences, the shrubbery, the trees, and the snowy slopes denied our senses any type of enlivening detail. The attack that had been ordered hid itself behind an abyss of time. And so it was like any of those innumerable nighttime watches: Separated from our selves, our senses lay in wait in the nothingness of night . . . ready to react in a flash to any suspicious something. Our own selves, our individual identities, withdrew from the unreal, shapeless present and, nonetheless, remained ready to move into action at any alert from the senses.

Our selves sought a way to the essential things, even there in the icy Russian winter night. I carried on silent conversations with my young wife and was delighted in my little baby daughter. I thought of my parents and brothers. I spent time with friends doing unforgettable work over long, rich years. Who among those who fought in Russia does not remember those hours of inner peace and renewal?!

And despite that, I can still read off the other tablets of memory—what the alert senses also inscribed on them . . . automatically, but reliably. There was a deathly quiet along the western expense of snow that extended into the unknown beyond the last fence. You could occasionally hear a rustling when loose snow was blowing along the crusted-over snow by a draft of air. The huge barns of the collective farms rose from out of the snow, large and dark.

There was nothing to be heard on the road leading out to the vantage point towards the north, other than the crunching of our footsteps and the occasional sleep snorting of our *panje* horse. The ammo belts sometimes clanked quietly, whenever the machine gunner gingerly shifted the machine gun to his other shoulder.

Our relief arrived. By the time we stumbled into our diggings, it was already starting to turn light. We lay down and dozed.

In the morning, I trotted over to the company command post to poke my nose into things . . . to take a gander at the cards of the strategists. The *Leutnant* would most certainly assemble the platoon in order to dispense last rites prior to the attack, but perhaps he would tell me something ahead of time that was not intend for a broad audience.

Chatkowo was extremely difficult to attack. One battalion had just had its nose bloodied something fierce recently and three tanks of the 35th had also gone up— one through a mine, the other two by antitank/antiaircraft guns. Very little was known about the current enemy situation. Deserters said something about sixty heavy machine guns. Information concerning the size of the force there varied between 200 and 2,000. There were certainly mortars and antitank guns there.

The village was in a large clearing in the woods. The vegetated and broken terrain of the riverbed of the Resseta only got to within 150 meters of the houses in the east. It was only there that an attack could initially be launched. That was where we were to be employed, after we had closed to within 800 meters of the houses by first light and had taken up attack positions in the closest tip of the woods. It was imperative that we remained undetected up to that point.

Three destroyers were supposed to drop hard objects on Ivan at 0700 hours, and the artillery was supposed to start covering the eastern portion of the village at the same time. While all that happy intimidation was going on, we were supposed to be hopping through the vegetated terrain at a pig's gallop and cross the final, completely open stretch.

The moment we reached the edge of the village, the artillery was to be signaled by flares and its blessings immediately directed to the southern part of the village, allowing *Pionier-Bataillon 41* the opportunity to attack from the south across a broad, open, and mined field.

Then the artillery was to be signaled to shift its greetings of love to the northern part of the village, so as to cut off and pin down the Russians until the *I./Infanterie-Regiment 317* had arrived from the west.

"Well, let's drink to that!" *Oberleutnant* Holzheid said after we had conquered Chatkowo on the map. And so we drank a toast to Chatkowo with some terrible stuff that tasted like denatured alcohol and diesel and called itself vodka.

In the meantime, the *Landser* were busy with their weapons and ammunition. Everything was made spick and span. Actually, a lot nicer than during an inspection, since your life depended on it the following day. Hand grenades were picked up and armed. Tracer ammunition added to the belts of ammunition. White coverings for the helmets prepared. Things were hopping, and the hours that had been given to us as a result of the delayed attack were put to good use.

"*Du kannste mal sehen, wie die Weiber sind . . .*" Otto Simon sang.[5] It was his favorite song, even if he only sang it a short while. It was the only music he ever sang. He attempted to disguise his feeling at the time through his artistic expression.

The briefing of the 1st Platoon by the *Leutnant* was short and painless: don't smoke . . . don't cough . . . easy, easy, easy . . . so we can get into the assembly area undetected.

My knowledge of the battle plan was enriched by one additional point. A tank was to move along the road from the south as far as the mine obstacle and was directed to pluck machine-gun nests and similar novelties from the tree of knowledge with its main gun. In simpler terms, it was directed to attempt to identify and eliminate enemy positions from there. So we knew all there was to know. According to Adam Riese, it had to work. But Riese had also suffered frostbite to the feet in Russia, according to reliable sources. We would have to see. We had nothing against it.

We still had time. Chatkowo had to wait. The move-out to the tactical assembly area was set for 0030 hours. All the preparations had been made. We stretched our legs out under the wobbly table and caught lice. I had already account for twenty

---

[5] Translator's Note. This roughly translates, "You can see for yourself sometime how the women folk are . . ."

"kills." Lattke most certainly would have awarded me the Oak Leaves to my dog tag had he been a witness to my success.[6] Emil transformed the remaining mutton into a tasty pot roast. I awaited the results of Emil's culinary skills by playing Karl Hage a game of chess.

I wasn't too well pleased when I was summoned to the Leutnant again. We drank the last of the schnapps. The company commander also showed up later. "If I get killed, please send my things to my wife," he requested. Toward midnight, we split up. I shook my warriors awake in their hay beds. Chatkowo was calling us.

"*Na, Unoffizier*. So we want to go out again," Lattke said. We lined up in the company's column of sleds.

The *Oberleutnant* gave a green light from his flashlight—the signal to "Start engines!" and "Move out!"—and off we went. It was miserably cold. The runners on the sleds crunched. The night march to the assembly area would be fifteen kilometers. The night was clear and filled with stars; you could see some distance.

It was probably about 0200 hours when we took the first break. I was dead tired. Everything around me was blurry. I felt my way through as if in a billowy fog. When I noticed that the sleds were stopping, I took a chance to stretch out for a moment. I told the driver that he should shake me awake before I ran the chance of freezing at 40 below. I had barely wrapped myself in a dozen overcoats, when I lost complete consciousness. A vibration woke me up. Amazing how far deep the senses could alarm you. The sled was moving again. I dug myself out from under the overcoats. I was amazingly refreshed. Like a new born. The complete relaxation had restored my strength. Had I slept forever? "How long was I actually dozing, Ganzke?" I asked my driver. "Perhaps three minutes," Ganzke replied drily.

My feet were tingling. I trotted up front. Ganzke had lent me his felt boots. My feet were quickly warm again.

The sleds started veering off. Only one sled remained with each squad and accompanied it to the assembly area. The last house before entering the woods was the battalion command post. The lead elements halted. "Machine guns remain on the sleds…everything else off!" was whispered down the line. "Riflemen cover left and right! Skiers move forward! Move out!"

Our 1st Company was in the lead. The 2nd and 3rd Companies followed. The 4th Company had broken out its machine guns. *Leutnant* Niedermeier pushed past us on his skis and glided into the clearing, about 100 meters in front of the lead elements of the company. The edges of the wood line on both the right and the left got closer and closer to the road. Occasionally, the skiers stopped and listened intently.

A tank track could be made out along the path, a German tank track. That was somehow comforting. We could not follow the road much longer, since the Russians would be able to observe it after a few more meters. We therefore left it and marched

---

[6] Translator's Note. The narrator is poking fun at the Knight's Cross to the Iron Cross and its subsequent award, the Oak Leaves to the Knight's Cross to the Iron Cross.

off half right into a cut in the woods. We started to feel uneasy. The snow was knee deep, and if you took a step next to the tracks left by the skis, you sank up to your hips.

We went that way about 800 meters and then crossed a trail beaten into the snow, which came out of the vegetation to the right and then had to lead directly into the enemy-occupied village off to the left. It was probably the route taken by a Russian patrol. Let's just hope we don't get fired at now! Our lungs were bursting. It became increasingly difficult to move our legs through the snow. The distances between the sleds and also between the people increased to a dangerous level, since we were all in a column and the tired men could not be passed by those who weren't as tired. The *Oberleutnant* stomped on ahead industriously in his fur coat. He carried his ski poles like one of *Rübezahl's* clubs.[7] It was a puzzle to me how he managed to remain up front after he occasionally broke through the snow and lost the poles.

When was this cut through the woods going to end? We were sweating our-selves to death. The nags in front of the sleds were snorting like crazy and sank into the snow up to their bellies. The moon appeared garish at that point; you could see almost as if it were daylight. Gasping, we tortured ourselves step-by-step forward, weapons at the ready in our hands.

Finally, the cut in the woods came to an end. The woods opened up; there was a clearing in front of us. The lead elements turned off to the left. We had to be suffi-ciently wide east of Chatkowo by then; we started tramping our way west towards the village. We worked our way forward right on the edge of the clearing. Our lungs threatened to stop performing their duty; our legs were as heavy as lead. The clearing transitioned to open vegetated countryside, which was marked by foot trails every-where.

We discovered individual abandoned bunkers, which we carefully searched. We didn't want some Russian telephone operator or listening post to spoil the whole operation. Nothing happened, however, and the Russian telephone operators remained alive, since they were dozing safe and sound in Chatkowo instead of sitting in their holes.

Off to the right, the woods pulled back sharply. We could clearly see the first few houses barely 1,000 meters away. According to the latest intelligence, they had to be occupied. With an uncomfortable twitching at the back of our necks, we waited any second for the blast of firing that would send belts of machine gun rounds whistling our way from over there. But no shots were fired. The skies had already taken on a light color. The pale slice of moon was blurry in a greenish shimmer. Daylight was announcing itself. Visibility was practically unlimited; it was only between the trees that the last vestiges of night lurked in the shadows. We steered more to the left and into the concealment offered by the woodline and made efforts to cover the last stretch to the tactical assembly area through the stands of trees.

---

[7] Translator's Note. *Rübezahl* is the name given to a folklore giant who inhabited the wooded areas between Bohemia and Silesia.

We crossed a path in the woods, which was covered deep in snow. In the middle of it, however, there was a footpath tramped into the snow, which proved that it served as the scene of active Russian patrol traffic. We stopped. At that moment, the commander came forward. With him were a few officers with map boards and in full war paint. *Leutnant* Jakobshagen could not restrain some bantering, which welled out from under his large nose in spite of the delicate situation. Nevertheless, the volume was somewhat diminished. Our commander, *Rittmeister* Bradel, sought to harmonize his native elegance with the horrible road condition which, with the exception of a few unavoidable efforts to maintain his balance, succeeded. He personally possessed an inimitable grandness. His visor cap sat true.

Even in that winter, he refused to comfort himself with ear warmers. The 40 below temperatures had forced him to make a single concession—he had turned up the collar of his fur coat. Weren't his ears freezing off? Bradel must have had different ears than the rest of us foul-smelling *Landser*.

The *Rittmeister* remained standing there with his officers. Damn . . . the edge of the woods were right there. The houses of Chatkowo seemed close enough to reach out and touch through the trees. Not a single Russian was guarding to the east. They were probably sitting stubbornly on the southern edge, straining their ears towards the sound of armor, which was being caused by our single tank.

"Weapons ready!" came whispered back from the front.

The break in the woods—we were standing along its left edge—emptied directly into a large clearing, where Chatkowo was located. The point of the woods, where we were supposed to establish our tactical assembly area, was to the right of us. The woods arched back between it and us. Messengers hastened back to have the 1st and 3rd Companies turn off from the previous march route further back.

We were stuck in the snow where we were, since there was no turning back. Time was pressing. It was already as light as day. We had to risk moving sideways without cover despite the closeness of the enemy. As quickly as was possible, we tramped across the clearing. Chatkowo was to our left. Not a shot was fired; it was very strange.

The long column of the 3rd Company moved ahead of us into the wooded terrain. We were still churning through the deep snow of the open area, our heads turned tensely to the left. When were the Russian machine guns going to start spraying?

"Man," Karl Hage said, "Uli, you know what? The Russians have split. There's not a swinging dick in that village any more."

Chatkowo was peaceful off to our left.

"Hurry up! Hurry up!" came back from the front.

Blue smoke climbed from a group of houses. It was the only sign of life.

There: *pepepepepetsch . . . pepepepepetsch.* A couple of Russian machine guns started rattling, firing in the direction of the clearing . . . excited . . . long, continuous bursts. We realized by the sound that those of us in front were not the intended targets. We churned forward and reached the edge of the woods a few minutes later. Behind us, everyone was on the ground. Whether dead, wounded or only seeking cover could not be ascertained. "Medic!" was also being roared out, however.

We worked our way through the trees to the front, in order to identify the machine guns and eliminate them. The machine guns of the 3rd Company were already replying from the tip of the woods. Lattner's machine gun cut loose.

Looschen's squad was the only one that had completely crossed the clearing. Of my squad, only Simon and Volland had gotten across with their weapons. I placed them between the trees to provide security. They only fired a few rounds blindly, since nothing could be seen from there.

The Russians soon got wind of the tumult in the woods and started firing at us, the bullets pelting the branches. The sprayed the entire edge of the woods.

My second machine gun was not available because Heese, the gunner, had taken a wild nosedive out of fright. The entire barrel was full of snow. I cursed like a drunken sailor, but that didn't change anything. Moreover, all of my ammo bearers were missing. It was enough to drive you crazy! We didn't go crazy, however, we fished a good *Juno*[8] out of a coat pocket and covered ourselves in smoke.

The machine-gun rounds slammed ceaselessly into the vegetated area around us. The ricochets whistled and swirled through the air. Whenever they peppered us in the woods, they had to stop engaging the clearing. That gave the company opportunity to close up to us. My ammo bearers finally came. On the way, they got fat Lecke in the knee with a grazing wound.

We started receiving mortar fire. *Rumms . . . rumms . . . rumms.* The unpleasant stuff started detonating all around us. Now it was time for the shit to hit us. They had identified our assembly area. There was nothing we could do. We had to cover our ears until our artillery engaged. The three destroyers—on whose account the attack could only take place during daylight—mistook us for the enemy. *Rumms . . . rumms.* Their bomblets landed between the trees.

Pepepepepetsch—light Russian machine guns.

Tototototo—heavy Russian machine guns.

We tucked in our heads and tried to hide behind the thickest trees possible. We had to get out of there and release that knot of humanity. A direct hit by a mortar would have done us some serious damage. Besides, it was about time that the Germany artillery started. At that point, it was on to the enemy. We had to advance. But how? The Russians were firing ceaselessly.

Twenty meters into the woods was a depression. No time like the present to get in there! Hell, that was no depression! It was the riverbed of the Resseta. We slid down the steep embankment two, three meters toward the ice. It was brittle under the thick covering of snow. Every once in a while, someone broke through the ice and splashed around in the water with his felt boots. But this at least allowed us to

---

[8] Translator's Note. A type of smoke grenade.

avoid the lead-filled air and move forward. After the river started arching right after a hundred meters, that great respite was over. We crawled back up the slope of snow. Once we got us there, we tripped over a bunch of wounded, who were lying in a depression and being tended by medics. They were still quiet and in control. It still had not sunk in that they might be lying there for hours in the brutal cold. We worked our way further forward. There was the stupid river again. This time, we had to cross it. Franz Arling broke through and literally sank up to his neck. His teeth chattering, he made his way back to the rear.

Looking grim, the *Oberleutnant* came tramping forward, his ski pole in his hand. He was striking in his fur coat. His black armored recon cap sat like a little point on top of a bitterly mad face. You could read it on his face: "I'm not used to this infantry bullshit. This is absolute shit, if I may be permitted to express my self so vulgarly!"

Then, far to our rear and to the left, we heard *bong . . . bong . . . bong*. It never wanted to end. It was the short drumbeats of our artillery. There was a rushing sound that transformed itself into a rushing whistling noise. *Bruch . . . rumms . . . ratsch*. The packages were already there and were exploding among the houses of the village. Oh, boy! That was some magic the artillery boys were sending that way!

The face of the *Oberleutnant* was twitching. He turned around with a backhand and stomped away to the front like *Rübezahl* once did. Didn't he notice how it was whistling all around him? He must have thought he was sitting in an armored car.

The enemy's machine-gun fire slowly abated. The Russians ears were probably ringing. It was time to go forward . . . forward! We had to take advantage of the effect the artillery was having. Once again, we crossed the river, which curved around on itself like an earthworm.

It suddenly crashed above our heads from the far bank. There was a hell of a detonation between the trees in front of us. Branches flew through the air . . . a fountain of dirt and snow sprang high . . . one tree tilted forward and cracked apart . . . shrapnel hurled evilly through the air. What had it been? Was it a 15-centimeter shell that had gone astray? Russian mines of extremely heavy weight? Then there was another gurgling sound approaching us . . . and another one. Once again, the snowed-over Resseta was in front of us. Russian machine guns snapped at us. You can . . . wait, we were in a dead zone!

Our heavy mortars set up. *Plopp . . . plopp . . . plopp*. They were happily passing out their rounds, which they had drug cursing and sweating through the snow, to the Russkis.

There was a wall of snow, from which our machine gun could effectively engage the village in front of us. The heavy machine guns of the 4th Company fired over us, while we jumped over the wall. The defile started there. My men fell back. Only Simon with his machine gun and Volland with two ammo canisters were there. Karl Hage was directed to collect the rest and bring them forward.

To the left of us, I saw portions of the 3rd advance over the open expanse of snow. It was said that the 1st was already engaged in house-to-house fighting along the village street. Our company, which had been deployed along the portion of the village to the right of the road, was still working its way through the defile.

All of a sudden, we were there. Up to the road! Damn, we were out there as if on a dinner platter. We tried to at least get a little concealment behind a wooden outbuilding. The heavy machine guns from the northern part of the village had discovered us and were plastering us. The beams were splintering. Naturally, they offered no protection against small-arms fire.

I saw that we were had strayed into the midst of elements of the 3rd. "Make yourselves thin," *Oberleutnant* Lemke said. "It's pretty dicey here!" He did not apply that insight to himself, however. He sized up the situation while standing upright; he wanted to figure out additional employment options for his company. And as was often the case in such situations: His example outweighed his admonition. The men also remained standing and, after a few seconds, one of them clutched his body and sank groaning to his knees. Another man got his arm shot up. "Get out of here!" the *Oberleutnant* said, shooing us away. I had been on my belly for some time and looked for a way to move while remaining covered. We hopped into some terrain that turned out to be an extended defile. We chased away some Russians with hand grenades and rifle shots; they had also been hanging around the area. We then linked up with our company again. The lead elements, following the course of the defile, were slowly pressing their way towards the northern part of the village.

I was completely exhausted. I sank up to my stomach in the deep snowdrifts of the depression. But at least Simon, Volland, and I had made contact up front again. Looschen, the indestructible soldier, was already providing security at the end of the defile. The *Oberleutnant* needed to get oriented first, before undertaking anything. We couldn't allow ourselves to get bogged down. The terrain was too broken up. As a result of the continuous mortar and machine-gun fire, we were confined to the defiles. For a few seconds, the company commander considered attacking across the open expanse of snow. But that would have been suicide. I lay on the ground among them, at the same spot I had initially dropped down, and devoured snow, since there were no other delicacies available. It was impossible for me to stand up. Every time I tightened my muscles to do that, a cramp from an old wound in the lower thigh shot up my left leg to my hip. Catastrophic!

All of a sudden, there was firing down the length of the defile. Shit! Russians were sitting on our flank. It was a few individual rifle rounds. Impossible to make out the riflemen.

I then saw Lattke drop his machine gun and silently collapse. A rifleman from Meyer's squad screamed out and fell over. My first thought was that we had to get out of there. We had to get at least as far as the next bend around the defile, otherwise the Russians would take us out one-by-one.

I crawled behind the *Leutnant*, who was moving forward into the concealment offered by the defile. I got the poor bastard from Meyer's squad a hundred meters to the rear, where I gave him over to a medic.

When I worked my way back forward again, there was a crack around my legs at almost the same spot on the ground. I quite clearly saw how the bullets were marking their paths in the snow. I soon got the lead-filled spot behind me. Up above, Ernst Lattnew was in a small depression. I quickly ran over to him. There wasn't anything I could do. Our Lattke was dead. Head shot.

Karl Hage, the assistant squad leader, had assembled the men in the meantime and established contact. I sent Gerke, the tall one, who was unable to move forward with his shot-up knee, back to the rear with the wounded.

The defile made an extended bend and ended in the vicinity of the village street. If we were to attack from that point across the snowfield, then we could help the 1st forward, which was only advancing slowly up the village street in heavy house-to-house fighting and was no where near our end of the depression. At that point, we were still fully concealed in the depression. It was imperative to seize the right moment.

"Meddddddddic!" someone yelled out, extending the syllables. "Medddddddic!" It set your teeth on edge. The news was soon passed around: *Oberleutnant* Lemke had been badly wounded. A little while later: "*Oberleutnant* Lemke and the headquarters section leader have been killed."

Russian and German machine guns were yapping at each other over the defile. The snow sprayed up along the edges above our heads, whenever the rounds hit back and forth. We held cigarettes in one hand and devoured snow with the other. We placed our rifles between our knees. We had to constantly move our toes in the footgear, which had frozen as hard as glass. As long as you could do that, no frostbite could be expected. A numb feeling inched its way up from the heels, however.

By then, it had turned noon. We had been attacking for seven hours. Where had the time gone? The German artillery fire was no longer on our part of the village.

"Follow" was ordered. The company commander had discovered a tributary defile, through which we could approach the village concealed. At the very end, we had to jump individually through heavy machine-gun fire. After a sprint of thirty meters, we collapsed, lungs bursting, into a depression, where there were wounded with blank faces. Belly and leg wounds, which did not allow them to be evacuated from there under any circumstances. Once we had caught our breath, we attempted the next leap, which would take us directly into the concealment offered by the houses.

The company assembled there and then rolled up the right-hand side of the street. We combed through yards, animal stalls and houses. The 1st had taken heavy casualties. It was pretty well scattered and was bogged down in house-to-house fighting about 100 meters in front of us. We had to relief it as soon as possible by advancing along the right side of the street. That was very difficult, however, since there was firing from all sides. Our consumption of hand grenades was enormous.

I charged a hand grenade, intending to throw it through the window of a house from which there was firing. I hit the window frame, however, and it bounced back, landing at my feet. Twenty-one . . . twenty-two . . . I looked for it desperately and couldn't find it. I took a mighty leap to the side. *Rumms* . . . it detonated . . . and I received a mighty blast near my butt. I aimed better with the next one. *Rumms* . . . doors and windows blew out. Smoke billowed out of the hollow window openings.

The 4th Company set up behind us with its heavy machine guns. It engaged the northern part of the village and had good fields of fire. The fire from there actually started to abate. We moved forward more rapidly. We got as far as the street crossing, and then it was all over. We had to seek cover as quickly as we could, since a Russian machine gun was engaging us from pointblank range, knocking us for a loop. Fortunately, the guy was a bit excited, and he didn't aim well. Correspondingly, we did not suffer any casualties. But we also could not determine, where he was located. We set the houses across the way on fire. The machine gun rattled on, however, even adding tracer ammo to the mix. In the flash of an eye, the hovel we had sought cover behind was burning like a torch.

The 1st Platoon attempted to cross the connecting street, but it clashed with a batch of Russians. It had to pull back after *Unteroffizier* Meyer was put in bad shape after several hits to the arm and shoulder. The damned Russian machine gun blasted away in between. It had to be in a stone house.

Oberfeldwebel Steinbeißer, an indestructible warrior from Bavaria and normally an armored car section leader, holed up in a pile of hay and took out one Russian after the other with his sniper rifle. The Russian machine gun continued hammering away, however.

We then saw lots of Russians fleeing. It had started getting to them. Horse-drawn sleds raced towards the northern part of the village and disappeared into the woods. Where were the engineers and the infantry? We still couldn't allow ourselves to be seen on the streets.

The Russian resistance stiffened. At that point, *Oberleutnant* Holzheid jumped into our house: "The company will no longer advance. It's to set up for the defense. Sachse, inform *Leutnant* Häusler and *Feldwebel* Gundelmeier."

Karl Hage took off to inform the two platoon leaders. "Two squads under the command of *Unteroffizier* Sachse remain here. *Leutnant* Weidner takes one squad with him. I will try to open up the way to the rear again with the 4th Platoon. The Russians have moved out of the woods and are attacking in the same defile we used to come in here. Communications with the battalion commander have been broken. He's most likely in the woods in a bad situation."

Good God! We had finally taken the street only to wind up in a mousetrap.

Unteroffizier Meyer, a good man, could neither live nor die. I carefully rubbed the fingers of his right hand, which were slowly dying. The arm was bleeding heavily. The cold was really getting to him. We tried to keep him from freezing by bundling him in hay. He was being brave. Nonetheless, he was shivering from the cold and from exhaustion. I fished out a crust of cheese that I had in my trousers pocket and fed him.

Oberleutnant Holzheid came back. Peter Weidner was with him. The 4th Platoon had not made it through. It had gone into position and was screening in the direction of the woods from which we had attacked.

"So, Weidner, we have to see how we're going to get out of this shit," the company commander said. "We don't have any contact with the *Rittmeister*. We have a choice of trying to fight our way back the way we came, or we can try to force our way through the minefield to the south."

"Let me have a messenger, and I'll get through to the *Rittmeister*," *Oberfeldwebel* Steinbeißer said in such a resolute fashion that it was not possible to counter him. He didn't even wait. He disappeared with the man, who had been standing next to him.

It had already started to turn dusk, and the sun was sinking on the horizon. The watch registered 1700 hours. We had been in combat without a break for twelve hours. The machine guns were jamming continuously. The ammunition was practically all expended. It was a really shitty situation. Otto Simon had taken Steinbeißer's place in the observation post above and occasionally let loose with his blunderbuss. Suddenly, he called out: "*Unteroffizier*, what's that over there?"

We were up there with him in a flash. *Feldwebel* Oesterreich got there the same time as I did. Soldiers were moving from left to right in large groups at some distance on the far side of the street crossing. We counted fifty men. All of them wore snow coats and were marching in column.

Over there . . . between the row of poplars in the distance . . . almost to the western side of the village . . . there were even more. A whole company . . . no, several companies. Simon initially thought they were civilians, who were coming out of the woods and back into the village, since the firing had suddenly quit. For a few minutes, there was deathly silence. We struggled to determine through the binoculars who and what they were. Were the Russians heading back to the north? No, only German soldiers marched in column that way. We then saw how they were carrying their machine guns. We saw that they also carried ammunition canisters. We fired a white signal flare for recognition—and they fired back a white signal flare from there.

"Those are the engineers!"

They occupied the northern part of the village; the western part was already in their hands.

Otto Simon sang: "*Du kannste mal sehen, wie die Weiber sind . . .*"

We felt unbelievable relief. The danger of being encircled was over. The terrible machine gun fell silent. They had probably figured out what was going on sooner than we had and had disappeared.

We then had to get *Unteroffizier* Meyer to a medic as quickly as we could! There were about forty wounded in a stone house on the eastern side of the village. Our dead were still outside in the snow.

It turned increasingly dark. Lively machine-gun fire echoed from the woods to the east and from the screening sector of the 4th Platoon. There were also the sounds of fighting to be heard from the southern edge of the village.

We went out into the street and attempted to warm ourselves on the glowing beams from the burnt-out house. There were crusts of bread burned crispy among the rubble. Ravenous, we devoured the seared crusts.

Then came the exhaustion. But we didn't dare to sit down anywhere. The cold was fierce. It had to be more than 40 below.

Who was that coming up the village street? The *Rittmeister*. Elegant as always. He laughed in our direction when we tried to salute him awkwardly. Steinbeißer was with him.

"*Herr Leutnant*," Looschen said. "Lattner's still out there. Can I go get him?"

Looschen fetched him. Better said, he had to rescue him, since scattered Russians were still in the defile area, firing wildly all around them. But Looschen, that remarkable soldier, didn't let anything deter him, even a grazing wound on his hip.

Lattner was then lying there in front of us. His happy sayings had been silenced forever. We placed him on a captured sled in a protected corner. We would not be able to recover our dead until the next day. There were twenty-one in all. For the present, we had our hands full trying to evacuate the fifty-eight wounded. The closest aid station was twenty kilometers to the rear.

I hobbled over to one of the houses, where a pitiful little fire kept the worst of the cold away. *Leutnant* Peter Weidner sat on a crate and slept, his head propped against the wall—the sleep of exhaustion. I had constant cramping in my left leg. Only some warmth could help. With some effort, I pulled off the frozen-like-glass felt boots, ripped the leggings out of the shapeless footgear and hung them up to dry out over the oven. I then stretched out on the floor and immediately fell into a deep and leaden sleep.

Our sleds came two hours later. I can only recall the fifteen-kilometer march back as some sort of dull nightmare. It was more of a stumbling than a walking. Finally, about 0300 hours, we arrived in our quarters in Ssusseja.

Seen here on 10 July 1941, the bridge over the Beresina at Stary-Bychow was blown up by the Soviets after the initial crossing of a platoon of tanks. On the far side, behind the impacting shells, are the five tanks of Oberleutnant von Cossel, which had stormed across the river on 4 July. Cossel and some of his men were able to swim to safety across the river when their positions were no longer tenable.

A typical Soviet peasant: poor but content.

The unfortunate village of Grjasiwez goes up in flames, 15 July 1941. The battle staff of the 4. Schützen-Brigade (of the 4. Panzer-Division) was wiped out there; the command-and-control element was then disbanded.

German antitank guns knocked out this Soviet light armored vehicle in the fighting for the bridges at Propoisk, 15 July 1941.

The division advances into the rear of the Red Army, 22 July 1941. The Kiev Pocket is in the process of being formed.

The night attack on Dmitrowsk is discussed, 1 October 1941. From left to right: Major *von Jungenfeld;* Oberst *Eberbach, the commander of the* 5. Panzer-Brigade; *Oberst* Schneider, *commander of* Artillerie-Regiment 103; *and* Generaloberst *Guderian, the commander in chief of the* 2. Panzer-Armee.

The Germans were not considered the enemy everywhere they went. In the Ukraine, they were often greeted as liberators, as evidenced by the garlanded arch to this village, September 1941.

Chapter 4

TRACKS IN THE SNOW: A STORY OF AN UNFORGETTABLE ENCOUNTER

Oberwachtmeister **Hans Schäufler, leader of the land-line platoon in** *Panzernachrichten-Abteilung 79* **of the** *4. Panzer-Division*

February 1942. We were in Chatkowo, operated the telephone network for the strongpoint and monitored like a hawk our sole connection to the outer world, the telephone line to Ssusseja, about seventeen kilometers in length.

We were the six men of Weiß's land-line section, which had been converted to sleds. "We" also included Wassil, a former Russian soldier, who had been with us since July and was a great comrade to everyone; a bushy-haired *panje* horse by the name of Marusja; some 5,000 lice and a few score bugs; and me, the leader of the entire menagerie. All of that was crammed into a single room of a half shot-up Russian hovel on the northwestern edge of the village.

The field wire had been laid in a broad arc curving out to the north. It was in the same spot as we had laid it during the attack.

From evening dusk to morning dawn, the wooded area around us and all the way to Ssusseja belonged completely to the Russians, since we could not take the chance of venturing out into the night in our thin little overcoats, when the temperature ranged from 30 to 50 below zero. They came in large groups every night, set up dozens of mortars and plastered us in Chatkowo, practically overwhelming us.

During the day, Russian and German patrols romped around in the area. To be more precise: they attempted to avoid each other by means of trickery and deceit. You didn't have to have an encounter here in order to determine where the enemy was, what he was doing and what he was planning. The loose powder of the snow, at least a meter high, told the story like an open photo book of what happened the previous night in the woods, where the Russians had come from and where they had gone, where they had occupied positions, where they had taken a break to observe, where they had taken a smoke break, even where they had had to relieve themselves. After a while, you started to develop a sense for all those details.

Wassil, who had been born in the Taiga, the boreal forest of European Russia, and had grown up there, saw even more than that. He told us how fast they were going, what they were wearing, whether they were tired or still fresh. He was even able to tell how many there were.

He was also the one who first determined whether a Russian patrol was predominantly interested in our field wire. He found a Russian field wire that was next to ours, even though it was buried deep in the snow. That meant that Ivan was eavesdropping on our conversations. That's why the bastards were firing with such precision.

Of course, we had to report that to the division signals officer. The reward: we received orders to follow the line each day half way to Ssusseja as far as the burnt-out and shot-up village of Debrik. That was eight kilometers there and eight kilometers back. With a great deal of sweat and effort, a carrier frequency device was also brought to Chatkowo, which was supposed to make the connection safe from eavesdropping. At least that's what we still believed at the time. It wasn't until much later that we discovered that the Russians could pick out conversations, despite the modulation provided by the device, by means of a regular commercial radio set.

We then starting placing the wire at one place and then another. We also hid it in deep snow. Unfortunately, we could not quite hide our tracks from the Russians. We had to come up with something new each day: Stomping out paths to nowhere; marching with Russian felt boots; moving backwards. It was a real game of cowboys and Indians, despite the biting cold. One party attempted to outsmart the other and to observe from a hidden spot; everyone avoided direct contact, however, and for good reason. It was a rare occasion when shots were exchanged, since everyone knew that even a simple grazing wound could mean certain death. You immediately froze to death if you could not move. Even self-sacrificing comrades couldn't help much there.

Once again, we were churning our way through mountains of snow. We were being careful so as not to traipse on to a mine, which the Russians had just started to place in the tracks that had been worn into the snow. That meant we had to take a new path each time, and that made you tired.

Along the way, we could only conduct a check wherever we had established a testing station. That meant along the woodline, where there was an open bit of marsh land, along the river bottom, which was still not completely frozen under the deep snow, and in Debrik proper, where we had been able to sink the grounding connector in a deep well. It was simply impossible to get a ground out in the open, since the earth was frozen solid for meters on end and was completely isolated. What we didn't try to make contact!

The highest commands had already wrestled with that unfortunate problem—without success.

We tramped our way, step-by-step, to the bottomland, connected our field telephone and . . . no longer had any communication with Chatkowo. Damn it all! Did we need to send everyone back to the edge of the woods? Everything was fine there an hour ago. And then follow the line once again? No! I sent three men on to Debrik, slung the telephone set on my back and went back by myself. What could happen to me, after all? We had just come from there and I would certainly run into line troubleshooters coming form the village. On the other hand, I had been given strict directives that no man was to move through the woods by himself.

As a precautionary measure, I placed my pistol in my overcoat pocket, with my hand right above it. Despite the biting cold, I soon started sweating, since the whole thing was creepy to me, and I was walking faster than I should have. A branch cracked and a handful of snow fell from the tree; a bird took off. All of my senses were on edge. I shouldn't have gone off by myself. But I didn't want to turn around either at that point; I didn't want to be laughed at. I started seeing the clearing through the leafless vegetation. The tree with the testing station was no longer so far away. It was so peaceful in no-man's-land; one could learn to fear.

Wasn't that a cautious step? Wasn't there some crunching of snow up ahead? I chewed myself out. Wait, was there something else again? "Hans. You're going crazy!" I admonished myself. But, nonetheless, something wasn't just quite right. I don't know why I was imaging that. I took my pistol out of my coat pocket and pulled off my right glove. Brrrr! Man that metal was cold. It was sticking to me right away. I was at the oak tree at that point and was in the process of connecting the field telephone. I saw that the wire had been pinched off—no, it had been cut with a saber. In the blink of an eye, I was alert and prepared to defend myself. I had a strange feeling behind my back. I felt . . . I believed . . . I knew beyond all doubt all of a sudden that someone was observing me. I turned around, slowly and carefully and scrutinized everything. No twig, no snowflake escaped my searching eyes.

Then I shuddered, as if I had been struck by a blow. An icy cold and boiling hot feeling ran up and down my back at the same time. I stood there for a moment, as if paralyzed. A Russian soldier in full battle gear was no more than five steps behind me, his submachine gun pointed at me. Initially, I want to throw myself on the ground. That would be a joke, I thought to myself. I ordered myself to get behind the oak tree. Thank God, I did not budge an inch from where I was standing.

The thought that I might be captured almost within eyesight of Chatkowo as a result of my own carelessness . . . my own inattentiveness . . . was unbearable. There had to be a way out.

The film running in front of my eyes was in slow motion. Seconds seemed to expand to hours. How long had I been standing there doing nothing? And nothing occurred to me . . . what a blockhead! Whatever I did could be deadly.

I sized up my opponent, drawing the image into me. Where was there a weak point? Amazed, but also tremendously relieved, I saw that the Russian did not have his finger on the trigger. He had extended it in such an unmistakable manner that I had to see it. I held my pistol cramped in my hand. I painted a picture for myself: How long I would need to take aim; how long the Russian would probably need to crook his finger. Would I still have a small chance, if I were very quick and if I were lucky? I tried to attract the gaze of the one standing across from me. Velvety brown eyes were staring at me—good eyes, somewhat off center in an Asiatic face. It could be the look of a friend. I didn't see any hate. If there had been no war, if that absurdity had not been the law that two men had to kill one another who did not even know one another. Who had never even seen one another before in their lives. Who had never done anything wrong to one another. Who, perhaps, could have been good friends. If only there hadn't been a war.

Should I make a try for it? Should I raise my pistol? No, it may sound absurd, but there was no way in the world that I could aim at those eyes. I felt that with every fiber of my being. At the same time, I also knew that I was not about to go into captivity with him. He would have to shoot me dead first!

Then, suddenly, it occurred to me: that guy could have long since shot me, even before I had seen him. What was he waiting for, that man whom the war had made my archenemy?

We stared at each other without moving; we were literally transfixed. Then, quite slowly, the rigid mask of the Russian started to loosen up. A slight, suppressed smile flitted over the weather-beaten, yellowish face; it remained hidden in his eyes. The whites of his teeth shimmered through the brownish lips. A white breath cloud formed in front of his face. From far, far away it seemed to me that a whispered word fluttered towards me. It hit me like a bolt of lightning. All of my senses, stretched to the breaking point, took it what he was tossing my way: "*Woina*[1]— pfui!" He actually didn't say "pfui." Instead, he spit out to the side with a contempt that came completely from the heart.

You could have knocked me over with a feather. I had anticipated everything but that. Deeply embarrassed, I looked at him and looked back into those warm and good eyes. Eyes that had no hate. Eyes that were not afraid. They were flashing in anger, but the anger was not directed towards me.

I didn't speak his language, and he didn't speak mine. Despite that, I understood him. I knew what his heart was saying. We kept up that silent conversation for a while. We attempted to know one another better. We had so much to say and, at the same time, didn't need a single word.

Never before in my life had I burned the image of a face into my soul so quickly as that of the Russian, who stood within my reach and yet was still a world away from me. His submachine gun was still at the ready, but it was no longer pointed at my breast.

He moved back a few steps while still facing in my direction. He said, "*Woina*," one more time and then spit into the snow off to the side in an unmistakable gesture. It was not in my direction. It was as if he wanted to say: "I don't mean you!" Then he turned around and went back the way he had come, light on his feet and

---

[1] Translator's Note. *Woina* is the transliteration of the Russian for the word "war."

without paying any attention to me. I was still standing there, a pillar of salt. Subconsciously at first, I put the pistol back in my overcoat pocket with clammy hands.

After about fifty meters, he stopped, smiled from his very soul, waved to me like a high-spirited boy, slung his submachine gun around his breast, and disappeared slowly into the underbrush.

I simultaneously felt really lousy and unspeakably happy. My picture of the world had received a little rip in it.

That simple "child of nature," as we, in our arrogance, called those unspoiled people, people who operated outside of the playing rules that we accepted without thinking . . . that philosopher from the woods of Siberia, who was morally vastly superior to us "cultured peoples," had had the courage to vocalize, to demonstrate, and then to act out that which we, in our blindness, no longer wanted to see: "War is the root of all of the suffering in this strange world. Are we supposed to shoot each other dead because of that? I won't think of it! Don't you do the same either!"

At least that's what I took from him. And I am convinced that I understood him correctly, since I had glimpsed into his soul in my hour of mortal danger.

He might have been observing us for days on end and waited longingly for the proper moment to be able to say and demonstrate unpunished to another human, who had to listen to him, what he wanted to fling in the other's face: "*Woina*, pfui!"

WITH THE *9. PANZER-DIVISION* ON THE CENTRAL FRONT

Obergefreiter **Walter Berger,** *Panzergrenadier-Regiment 10, 9. Panzer-Division*
The end of November 1942. Our *9. Panzer-Division*, badly battered by two intense operations in the summer and early fall, was undergoing battlefield reconstitution in the area around Gshatsk along the Wjasma-Moscow road.

Our 5th Company was quartered in Jekaterenino, a village about ten kilometers west of Gshatsk. Jekaterenino was a right proper *panje* village: a loose line of shabby wooden huts along an extended ridgeline, all threaded together by a "road," whose otherwise limitless mud had been turned into a rutted field as hard as stone courtesy of the frost. All around, as far as the eye could see—and it could see immeasurable distances—there was nothing but countryside. The weather suited the landscape: It was a typical early Russian winter weather. The cold was still bearable and there were only occasional snow flurries, but the skies were always covered in a blanket of clouds that were leaden gray, heavy and low hanging. Under those clouds, it rarely turned properly light the entire day. In addition, there was a fine, but penetrating wind from the east.

In order to solve the quartering problem, that is, get places for the soldiers to live, we went about it in the normal fashion. In some cases, the Russians were turned out of their places and put in about half of the houses. They were used to it and, moreover, did not do too badly, since the German soldiers occasionally let something go for the local populace, even though they themselves lived frugally. Although it was not a cordial relationship, it was always polite. The *Maruschkas* washed our clothes for a few boxes of matches. Barter flourished, somewhat along the lines of cigarettes for sauerkraut. We even enjoyed the local sauna—the *banja*—although, as a security precaution, it was not with the locals. You still got lice, but they were not anything you immediately needed to chase down.

The 1st Platoon was quartered at the upper end of the village: a somewhat more presentable house for the noncommissioned officers and the enlisted personnel in two larger houses next door. Those of us in the platoon headquarters, the messengers and the medics, crawled here and there for our places. It was there that the story with the cat took place, a story that offered the company the stuff of conversation and laughter for some time to come.

It should be said in advance that Jekaterenino had its fair share of rats and mice—how could it have been otherwise?—whose activities were sometimes the cause of merriment, sometimes the cause of anger for us. In one of the enlisted quarters, there was also a half-grown cat, gray in color; it was very sociable and spoiled by everyone. I tried to procure it for the noncommissioned officer quarters once, but the effort failed in the face of determined resistance from all of the unwashed masses.

And then there was *Gefreiter* Knödel[2]—I swear that was his real name, hand on heart!—originally a student in a business school in St. Pölten. He was good natured, pretentious, very nervous, not dumb, but also not so smart as he would have liked to have believed. Despite his considerable body mass, he was fearful and uncertain. During the day, I stayed with the noncommissioned officers but went over to the house with Knödel, the cat, and others before going to bed because of a lack of space. So it was on the day of this story.

It was a pitch-black midnight. Despite "total war," everyone was slumbering in total peace. All of a sudden, there was a crashing and banging and shrill cries going through the house. In a broad Austrian accent, we heard: "Help me . . . help me . . . I have him . . . help me . . . help me!"

We jumped up from out of a deep sleep from under our blankets and shelter halves, wide-awake and terrified. What was going on? Russians? Partisans? It only took a few seconds to determine that the situation was not at all that dangerous. The one who was screaming was unmistakably Knödel. But it didn't sound like a death rattle or the cry of a badly wounded man.

"What's up?"

"A huge rat . . . help me so he doesn't get me!"

Flashlights lit up; matches were struck. Knödel became visible, like an apparition. He was sitting on his straw bed . . . hair disheveled . . . dripping sweat . . . bug eyed. Using both hands, he was frantically grabbing the . . . cat! By its throat!

---

[2] Translator's Note: *Knödel* = dumpling.

The little cat hung there, motionless and lifeless. Like a damp rag. For a few seconds, everyone was frozen in place. Then the bomb went off. While one guy started holding his stomach as if he were going to die laughing, the others piled up on poor Knödel and tossed all sorts of abuse his way. That was something he no longer needed. He was already completely destroyed.

We took a look at the cat. It no longer stirred. All efforts to revive it . . . shake it . . . pinch its tail . . . were in vain. Dead! Too bad for the poor thing! But what could you do for it? We tossed the cadaver outside the front door.

The next morning, the dead cat was gone. Probably devoured by a dog. But when I was all alone in the quarters in the morning—as a messenger and a member of the platoon headquarters one sometimes had certain benefits compared to the common folk—there was a scratching outside on the door. It was accompanied by an unspeakably hoarse and pitiful cawing that was supposed to be a meow. I jumped to the door and ripped it open and in walked . . . the dead cat, somewhat worse for the wear but visibly on the road to getting better.

At noon, when the commoners came back from duty and saw our little cat sitting next to the oven, everyone was deliriously happy. Knödel, with his soft heart, was the happiest of them all. That morning, he had all of us swear that we would not tell anyone who did not live in the house about what had happened the previous night. Needless to say, the tale had already reached the other companies in the neighboring villages.

For safety's sake, I decided to kidnap the cat, since who could know what might occur to Knödel—at the very end, he ran amok with his bayonet. Prior to the start of duty the next morning, when everything was in a state of turmoil, it appeared to me that a good opportunity had arisen. I had all of my stuff over in the house where the noncommissioned officers were quartered; in the evening, when I came over, I only had a small bag in which I had a training suit and house shoes. As usual, I put all of that in the bag and, when no one was looking, I grabbed the cat by the neck and stuffed it in as well. Everything went pretty well. The only difficulty was the tail, which, damn it all, didn't want to stay inside. It kept coming our on top by the opening. I had to stuff it back in several times. In addition, there were some suppressed meow sounds as I wound myself out to the door with it. Fortunately, in the hubbub, no one heard anything.

I was able to get into the neighboring house undisturbed with my loot. I then told my comrades that I had brought them something. I placed the bag in the middle of the room and opened it. Everyone stared in expectation in that direction to see what was going to come out. Nothing came out. The cat was on top of the world in the bag with the training suit and the house shoes. It had rolled itself into a purring ball of wool and didn't think twice about voluntarily leaving that warm and soft little bed. I had to vigorously shake all of the contents out to be able to show the others what I had obtained. At that point, everyone was happy and in agreement that the cat was to remain there from then on. Our new female comrade in the house, who had just been promoted from enlisted to noncommissioned officer cat, was even more spoiled than previously. Besides, its life was also safer than before. We soon had other worries, however.

The sleep area had been established on the long side of the room. They were roughly joined frames made out of beams and posts and had straw in them. The individual's house shoes were under each bed. During a Russian winter, whenever you were not on operations, they were among the most important items you had. When *Unteroffizier* Sassik returned from duty the next evening, slightly frozen and tired, and placed his feet into his house shoes, he encountered resistance in the right one. He felt inside and brought a dead mouse to the light of day. It was Sassik, of all people of course. He was already a bit wound up. The audience crowed. After a second of outrage, even Sassik put on a good face to the prank.

On the next day at the same time—at the exact same time. This time, Sassik went off into a rage. The guy who was pulling these pranks needed to think up a new one or find another victim for the old one. It was starting to get old. We looked at each other. Each person looked as innocent as the next.

The following day, return from duty in the evening: Once again a dead mouse in Sassik's house shoes. He was mad. He didn't make a big fuss—that wasn't his style—but he didn't speak a single word to us all evening. We would have been happy ourselves to have known who the prankster was. Once again, everyone looked so convincingly innocent that no one was any the wiser. Finally, we transitioned to the day's business.

The next morning, Leo Zadina and I were alone in the room, mending socks. The cat appeared with a dead mouse in its mouth. Bravo! We expected that it would soon settle down to someplace in the room to enjoy a lovely feast. Mistake! What did our astonished eyes see? The cheeky little thing marched straight across the room to Sassik's house shoes, let the mouse drop into them and then pushed it all the way in with a daintily arched paw. It then stole away on light feet, a satisfied look on its face.

It took a lot of effort to get Sassik to the point where he would believe the actual truth of what had happened. For a long time, he was convinced that Leo and I had placed the mice in the house shoes and only wanted to blame it on the cat.

Such idylls don't last forever, of course. The initial rumors started filtering through during the last few days of November that things stunk at the front. The rumors intensified in the days that followed. And then one morning when I went outside our hut, it could be heard: Indistinct and light at first, but also unmistakable, despite the singing wind—a monotonous, recurring rumbling and wailing. That was something I knew only too well: That was heavy, uninterrupted barrage fire. It might have been about forty or fifty kilometers away from us. But that meant nothing, if things really heated up! At that moment I knew that our rest stay in Jekaterenino would not be of long duration.

The beginning of December 1942. Towardsnoon, we arrived in a village that was located in a shallow depression. It was swarming with soldiers and vehicles, and there was a feverish, foreboding mood. And that, even though you could not only not see anything of the enemy and war, you also couldn't hear anything far and wide, with the exception of the occasional rumbling of artillery.

We spread out among the huts, dismounted, and stood along the village street. What was going on? We also started to be taken up with the general unsettled mood. We engaged in conversation with a few of the people who were standing around and walking back and forth between the houses in a aimless and panicky manner—at least that's the way it seemed to us. From what they told us in choppy and rapidly tossed out sentences, we sort of got a general picture of the situation, even though it was in no way completely clear.

This was it. The Russians had attacked, about a week ago. It was here up front, but not only here. It was also to the left and the right . . . everywhere . . . all along the entire front. Some of them had been interdicted, beaten back and cut off. At other places, however, they had been able to expand their penetrations and deepen them. In any event, the entire front was apparently in turmoil, not to mention that which was behind the front.

It had been directed that the *9. Panzer-Division* assume this sector of the front. It was to do it as it was: Still decimated from the operations along the Shisdra, only just recently receiving some replacements, equipped in a deficient and improvised manner. We were furious.

It appeared that a proper "front" no longer existed. There were a few alert units up front and an infantry regiment, which had already been badly battered. And all sorts of things that were ill defined. No one knew what was going on; no one knew where the Russians were and where we were. In any event, Ivan did not appear to be doing a whole lot in our area at the moment; otherwise, we would have heard something. We started to gain the impression that the Russians had attacked in this sector with forces that weren't especially strong and that, at the moment, they were also lying on their bellies and gasping for air. But in the short or long haul they would receive reinforcements . . . fresh forces. What we would see of that was something we could calculate based on our previous experiences. "A kick in the ass!" *Gefreiter* Ziebert, who hailed from Silesia, bellowed and then spat furiously onto the ground.

The field mess had opened its tin-metal gates, and it least there was something warm to eat. Better and more abundant than we ever had in Jekaterenino. It was the typical gallows meal. Despite that, we didn't let it ruin our appetite. A short while later we were informed to mount up again. The column rolled on towards the east, as it had previously. After a few kilometers, we reached another village. We stopped and there was shouting, and then we moved on again. After a few more kilometers, the following came filtered back to us: "Dismount with your equipment!" It had apparently turned serious. An infantry company was in position there behind a swell in the ground in positions that had been hastily established. Outposts had been sent forward. As much as we could determine, this was the forwardmost element. Somewhere over there was Ivan, but no one knew anything for certain. Consequently, we were directed to feel our way forward, reestablish contact with the enemy but not attack, since everything was still up in the air off to the left and the right.

The company formed up and moved out slowly. Our platoon was in the lead; the 2nd and 3rd Platoons were echeloned in depth off to the left and right. We trundled off silently, tensely and doggedly. It was always the same at the beginning of an operation: The inner turmoil and excitement was so overpowering that you wanted to cry out or do something equally stupid. Things would calm down shortly after that.

The land spread out in front of us under a gloomy gray sky—melancholy, oppressive, and threatening. The gently rolling terrain in which we carefully pushed forward was broad and flat and also completely desolate and empty. Sparse, low vegetation traded places with broad open areas, on which there was only scrawny yellow grass, which was almost chest high sometimes. Perhaps there had been fields there, years ago, when war wasn't being waged here. At this point, however, it was devoid of people and gone to seed. Even the war was silent at this point; there was no sound to be heard far and wide—no firing, no detonations, no engine noise.

In a valley depression, concealed by some brush, was a small group of soldiers providing security. The *Oberleutnant* talked to the men. I stayed close to him and listened in. There were no friendly forces in front of them . . . at the most, a couple of stragglers. An hour previously, a patrol had gone forward and scouted out about one kilometer. The high ground in front of them was also clear of the enemy, as well as the depression behind it. The Russian artillery fired into it occasionally from somewhere off to the left. They must have had some observation into the terrain up front.

We crossed the bottom of the valley and trundled up the gently rising slope on the far side in a loose column. We did it carefully and with skirmishers sent forward, since the uncomfortable terrain there was broken up. You didn't know what the next clump of vegetation might bring. We reached the top of the rise without incident. And then we continued on. There was another shallow depression with a broad base, whose marshy ground was already frozen as hard as a rock. Down below, along the creek bed, in the middle of an open area, was a dead German soldier. He was stretched out on the ground, and there weren't any visible wounds. In the middle of that limitless gray quiet and desolation, the dead man came across as almost unreal, specter-like.

We didn't have any time to worry about him. Once again, we continued on through some vegetation and up a slope. We were already in the middle of completely unreconnoitered no-man's-land. Consequently, the prospects of an unpleasant surprise grew ever greater. The platoon dispersed. In front was the *Oberleutnant* with the safety on his submachine gun off. As a messenger, I was right behind him. The squads followed on line, widely dispersed.

Moving like that, we reached the next crest and remained there a while and observed from under cover. Nothing at all could be seen. In front of us, it continued on, gently sloping down to the next valley floor. There was not a single bush, not a swell in the land all the way to the bottom. It was a scary situation; we were targets being served up on a platter. Oh well, there was nothing you could do about it. If it had gone well so far, it could also turn sour right now!

The *Oberleutnant* stood up and marched off; the platoon set itself in motion behind him. We had gone about fifty meters when we heard it—far off to the left: The reports of guns! *Rummm . . . rummm . . . rummm . . . rummm . . .* a break, then . . . *rummmm . . . rummm . . . rummm.* Then it came howling from over there: *Huiiiii . . . crack . . . crack . . . crack . . . crack.* In front of us and all around us were crashing fountains of fire and iron, dirt and haze. The entire platoon landed on its nose. The fire was still primarily raging in front of us. But that was exactly where we had to go. We couldn't stay lying there forever. Although it wasn't a dense, impenetrable final protective fire, it was bad enough regardless.

The *Oberleutnant* pulled himself together and jumped up: "Follow me . . . let's go . . . let's go!" He raced off into the fireworks with gigantic steps. The men of the platoon likewise rose, but there still was no movement in them. I also got up and started—and felt the turmoil in my stomach and in my heart. It was always the same. When you've been in the shit mill for a week, then you get used to something like that . . . you get hardened . . . at least to a certain degree. But when you see death and destruction in front of you after weeks of peace and tranquility, then the unfathomable horror is back. You lie there or huddle there . . . a pile of misery, with shaking nerves. You feel it take you cold. But the difference between being a coward and a brave man is only a small step...just a narrow boundary. The selfsame man can stay on one side of the border one time and on the other side the next.

Huiiii . . . huiiii . . . crack . . . crack . . . crack. It didn't want to stop. The *Oberleutnant* stopped, turned around and gestured vigorously. And then I made the transition from coward to brave man. All at once—it happened more or less instinctively as opposed to being something considered and conscious. I was behind the *Oberleutnant* again and started marching behind him, albeit with trembling knees and a lump in my throat. But no one noticed it besides me. And, as I turned around for a quick look back, through the whirring shrapnel and the smacking clumps, I saw how the entire platoon was coming down the slope.

In a wild, but deliberate haste—sometimes running, sometimes at double time—we reached the valley floor and disappeared into the vegetated terrain there. Behind us, the howling and the crashing sounds gradually abated. When the *Oberleutnant* counted the heads of his loyal men, he saw that nothing had happened to anyone other than a few harmless scratches. You've got to have luck! We interpreted that as a good omen for the rest of the operation.

We then went up the slope, between the spread-out groups of vegetation, which grew closer and closer together towards the top. We got to the top again and were at the edge of a vegetated area, where we saw another broad slope as flat as a board angling down in front of us, with the exception that this time it ended with thick woods in the valley floor. That was an even shittier situation! We could not believe that the woods in front of us was clear of the enemy. But how could we determine that beyond the shadow of a doubt? To take off marching there across the open plain would have been suicide. If a small patrol had to work its way across, then it had our heartfelt sympathy. To send a patrol off around to the side would have taken too long. Although it was only approaching 3:30, the cloud cover above us was growing ever thicker and it was already looking murky out there.

Everyone lay there rigidly and observed. I didn't need to make any effort, since I didn't see anything anyway. But even the eagle-eyed among us and those possessing binoculars were torturing themselves in vain. To try to make something out—let alone Russians—in the woods a half a kilometers away in that hazy weather was wishful thinking.

While the *Oberleutnant* continued to be undecided and nervously considering things, hushed calls could be heard on the right wing. They sounded more amazed and amused than anything else. And there . . . in the high grass, not too far from us— I didn't believe my eyes—was a fox. The guys over on the right had probably caused him to bolt. Initially, it moved parallel to us in front of our noses. It then swung to the right and then headed off at a trot towards the edge of the woods. It went about fifty meters toward it, when it all of a sudden gave a jerk and stood there rigidly as if rooted to the spot. It tensely eyed the woods with an outstretched neck, whereupon it hooked around and hastened back up the slope towards us. Well, well . . . what was the matter? In about the middle of the area between the woods and us, it halted. Finally, it headed a bit more off to the left, where it then turned back to the woods again. And—fifty meters out—it exhibited the same striking behavior as before. We were already starting to think what might be lurking over there. We continued to observe the fox. He carefully made his way towards the woods over and over again, only to race back in a panic. You could see that the animal was starting to get nervous. Finally, in a wild gallop, it disappeared off to the left.

Well, at that point, we could save ourselves any more feeling our way forward or sending out a patrol. We had no reason to believe the fox was putting on a command performance for us. It appeared the fox hadn't detected a solitary outpost; instead, the entire wood line was massively occupied. The fact that the Ivans had not stirred was no doubt due to the fact that they had observed us for some time but had wanted to let us approach close enough so hat there was no longer any possibility of our getting away.

Since our weak group had only been given the mission to push forward until we had made contact and then remain where we were, we could now take it "easy." Outposts were established to the right and to the left, to the front and to the rear. The remaining men started to dig in. A messenger was sent back, returning a half hour later with an artillery observer. A short while later, our arty peppered the edge of the woods with a few well-aimed salvoes. Things seemed to become pretty damned unsettled over there. We could still see that much in the twilight. We started to understand why our good fox had shown so much respect for the edge of the woods. Our mood relaxed. A "patrol fox" was just the thing to have! Too bad you couldn't raise them for that purpose. They might be able to save you from all sorts of adversity sometimes.

Of course, as a "punishment" for our artillery fire, we then started to receive Russian mortar fire. It was long overdue! But they were firing aimlessly around the area and did not cause us much concern for the time being.

Then things happened the way they usually did. After we had dug in for an hour and a half—with the sweat streaming out of all of our pores—and we had made our foxholes somewhat "domestic," we got our orders: "Platoon assemble with equipment!" An infantry company had arrived and was to take over security in this sector. Thanks to the fact that we were still almost completely motorized, we were earmarked to be the "fire brigade" again. Capable of movement and demonstrating combat power, we were to be committed anywhere it "stank" at the moment.

We trundled our way back in the almost complete darkness, running into our vehicles in a depression, where they had been brought forward. We mounted up and rumbled off cross-country into the darkness.

✠

We rumbled around for a good hour on waves of hard-frozen mud along worn-our roads . . . off to the left . . . off to the right. Once in a while, we stopped here or there for a while. No idea where we were. In the end, the command came form somewhere: Dismount!

It was pitch black around us, only the snow had a dull luminescence. A flat bit of high ground, a shallow ditch, a pair of lonely, spruce, their needles mostly gone. There wasn't anything more to be seen. Our vehicles roared off. We were directed to screen. Against what? In what direction? No one knew anything. Even our *Oberleutnant* was clueless. Very soothing! There was nothing left to do but disperse the company around the area in small groups and drum into everyone's head that he had to keep his ears and eyes peeled in all directions at the same time.

It was an oddly restless night. There was always something to be heard in the distance: A dull rolling sound, the reports of guns, machine-gun fire, engine noise. It was in front of us and behind us; it was to our left and to our right. It appeared that both friend and foe were once again hopelessly entangled and wedged together.

You started to be able to see better gradually in the darkness; to identify things more accurately. Perhaps the moon had risen above the thick cloud cover. Maybe there was a little bit of light penetrating down to us. It was the usual non-descript rolling terrain with individual groups of small patches of wood and vegetation, with ditches and defiles.

There was a rumbling and a rattling. It was far away, then it got closer, only to go further away again. It was off to the left, then in front of us. Then it was all the way over to the right. The tension drove any type of sleep, which was long overdue. Sometimes, you thought you saw something: What was that over there? Up front?

Movement . . . figures. Dark shadows? But all of the patrols the *Oberleutnant* dispatched came back without results.

The engine noise behind us grew louder; it appeared to be coming nearer. Were those our vehicles looking for us? No, those were tracked vehicles. Perhaps they were friendly tanks or the prime movers of the artillery? The rattling seemed to be quite close; then it suddenly stopped. It pushed over to the left and stopped again. Well then, whoever it was, they were on a joyride. They must have had a lot of gas!

The sounds then got closer again; they became more distinct and louder. Over there on the slope right behind us . . . wasn't there something moving there? Certainly . . . you could see something over there! Suddenly, the sound of the tracks fell silent. The dark shadows over there . . . as big as a barn door. Or maybe not, after all? The *Oberleutnant* said: "Berger, why don't you fire a pyrotechnic?!"

I went a few steps forward to the barren crest of the hill, loaded the flare pistol, aimed towards the shadows—a direct-line trajectory—and squeezed the trigger. *Ssssst!* The flare went hissing through the night with a fiery trail. Then . . . *plapp!* The illumination element ignited and the terrain was bathed in a chalk-white magnesium light. There . . . in the middle of the light . . . three Russian tanks . . . T-34's! One was really close, barely 150 meters away. The two others were a little bit behind it. Good gracious! I hit the deck and slid off a bit to the side and the rear, away from the prominent high ground. I wanted to get away quickly before the tanks came up with the brilliant idea of spraying the terrain with a few high-explosive rounds and bursts of machine-gun fire.

"Prepare hollow charges!" the *Oberleutnant* yelled out. Off in the distance, the engines started howling again. The tracks started to rattle. They were coming towards us! Wrong! They were racing away at speed . . . into the depression and somewhere off to the left. Apparently, they were scared even more shitless than we were! It was also possible that they thought my flare was the tracer element of an antitank-gun round. It had to be pretty spooky, after all, to be racing around in the enemy's rear in the darkness and not be able to find a gap to get through to get home. Apparently, those three tanks were the shabby remains of a unit that had broken through but had been wiped out behind the front. Three tanks all by themselves would never break through. Their panicky discomfort was perfectly understandable.

The tension was relieved at our location by a liberating laughter. This is the kind of operation I like, the *Oberleutnant* said. Nothing serious happened, but the "new guys" and the "inexperienced ones" got to experience something of the adventure of war. Fine, if only everything else turned out as well.

Midnight had long since passed. In the course of the long hours, things turned quieter and, in the end, completely still. That meant sleep came as well. The platoon leaders put out guards. The other men then went to find suitable places to sleep, where they would not get frostbite. The temperature had sunk a fair bit below zero, although the cold was not biting so harshly yet. I went with a few of the men to the closest patch of spruce trees. We hacked down some branches and limbs with our shovels and drug some heavy loads to the closest depression. We spread them out into a thick layer so that we did not have to lie on the bare snow. We then layered ourselves, one man close to the next, and covered ourselves, sharing our shelter halves. We didn't have anything else. But it also wasn't so cold, especially since we all pulled our heads under the shelter halves, as was customary in those situations. The warm breath then worked as a sort of "central heating." As a precautionary measure, we also took our weapons with us under the cover.

In fact, we slept really well. Laid there stiff as a board . . . no stirring . . . not to mention no turning over. At the same time, there were all sorts of ill-defined pointy objects in your back and stomach. To learn how to slumber like that—to sleep peacefully and be refreshed—that was something you only learned how to do in the course of a war.

We slept like that for two or three hours, before I started to feel very uncomfortable. Initially, while I was sleeping, then in a fitful half-sleep. Finally, I woke up. Damn it all, I felt like I was suffocating! Air! I pulled the shelter half back and stuck my head out into the open, right into the middle of loose, fine-grained powder snow. It had started to snow after all, and we were covered over by about a quarter of a meter. But the snow had contained our heat and made our sleep that much more pleasant—as long as the snow cover wasn't too thick.

Gradually, everyone started to crawl his way out of the mountain of snow. Helmet . . . rifle . . . shelter half. We stamped our legs, which were still somewhat cold and stiff. And then our vehicles were there again. There was food and hot tea, and the smokers had the cigarettes they had yearned for. We discovered that the Russian penetration in our area had been interdicted. Consequently, the Russians had started attacking to the south again last night. They had already achieved a few penetrations. It was figured that the attacks would increase in the course of the day. That meant we were headed there—at least as a reserve for the time being.

It was still dark when we took off. It was the usual shaking and rattling . . . moving in a zigzag course with the usual halts in between. At that point, when it started to turn morning, the sounds of war came back to life: A droning and a booming, a rumbling and a stomping. It was distant and soft at first; then it drew rapidly nearer and loud. And there, where it was making the most noise, was the direction we were headed. Matted white and fire red lights twitched along the horizon behind gentle snow-covered rises and the black and jagged-edge silhouettes of spruces and destroyed houses.

When it started to turn first light, we entered a village. There were people moving quickly, racing and pressing together along the village street. There were trains vehicles, telephone operators, messengers and wounded. There was artillery fire in front of us, which was growing stronger all the time. But there was also a cracking and a wailing off to the right and the left. We were unloaded on a street at the end of the village that was turned away from the front. We were then chased into the houses with our weapons and equipment. Get away from the street! Consequently, we waited around in the closest *panje* hut and attempted to light a fire in the oven. Then we stretched out on the loam floor; perhaps we would be able to catch up on a little sleep.

Outside, it was rumbling and crashing, almost ceaselessly. *Sssssiiiiuu* . . . *sssssiiiiuu* . . . a few heavy shells passed over the village. They were probably headed for the approach road. *Huuuiiii! Crack!* Damn, that was close! They weren't going to get the bad idea of firing on our village, were they? *Huuuiiii! Crack! Crack! Crack!* I guess they were! The hell with them! The salvo descended a few hundred meters from us. Was it going to get any closer? But what could you do about it anyway? We had already determined that the house did not have a basement. But the powerful concrete block wall would also be able to withstand a lot. As long as we did not get a direct hit, not too much would happen.

Noise outside on the street: calls and shouts; a hustle and a bustle. Tracked vehicles rattled past. Once again: *Huuuiiii! Crack! Crack! Crack!* Damn it! That was a good bit closer. I spied out through the tiny window. I tried to identify something, but there was not too much to see. A twitching red glaring light fell upon the huts across from us. It mixed with the dreary cold gray of the breaking day. It was anything but cozy out there.

There was a crash every two or three minutes. A Russian battery had taken this village as its specialty. And then it came: *Huuuiiii! Crack!* The entire house shook; all of the windows blew out at once. Together with the hail of shattered glass, clumps of ice and dirt came flying in from outside. Mixed up with it all was the plaster from the walls and the displaced window frames. Everything clattered down on us. Once again: A howling and a crashing. The room shook and trembled. There was an impact in the house across from us. The remnants of beams and bushels of straw flew through around. White, dense smoke and biting gunpowder smoke filled the air.

"Everybody out!" The artillery fire had abated somewhat.

"Everyone assemble in the street!"

We jumped up and pressed ourselves with our weapons and equipment through the narrow anteroom leading to the house door, which was filled with rubble and debris. We deployed into combat mode, covering ourselves behind the corners of houses—at least as well as we could. There was a tangle of beams and posts. Debris and straw was on the street; a few dead mixed in, along with a small civilian car, which had been ripped apart by a direct hit.

"Up . . . let's go . . . follow me!"

The *Oberleutnant* was shouting and running in front of us between the houses, past piles of rubble and through trampled vegetable gardens. The impact of heavy artillery could be seen in front of us, about 500 meters, on a piece of domed high ground. There was a constant trembling; gray columns of smoke were tossed up and welled skyward.

There was another hissing sound directly approaching us. Hit the deck! We tossed ourselves down among the clumps of earth as it started impacting: in front, behind us, to the right, to the left. The earth shook and trembled; shrapnel and clumps of things whistled, whirled and smacked around. It's all over now, I thought to myself. And then I was practically amazed to discover that I was lying there as undamaged and alive as I had been before, just a bit stunned. But here and there there was a whimpered and heartrending: "Medic!"

The *Oberleutnant* had hunkered down next to me. He got up and looked around. The third one in our row, *Feldwebel* Krämer, was lying on his face and wasn't moving. We jumped over to him and turned him over. It was all over for him! It seeped out from somewhere within the tattered overcoat—red, sticky, and steaming in the cold air of a winter morning.

"Up . . . let's go!" the *Oberleutnant* yelled. His voice sounded both strangely hoarse and shrill. "We have to go up there. There are bunkers and positions there. We can't stay here."

We jumped up again and gasped our way up the slope. The fire had shifted; it was hitting the area off to the left. It was a rarity for a round to get lost and to land in our vicinity. With bursting lungs and hearts we reached the position half way up the slope. We let ourselves fall into the trenches and holes.

"We lost an officer candidate today . . . the Russians will lose even more!" the *Oberleutnant* said next to me, markedly loudly and firmly. It sounded glib, but perhaps you needed phrases in moments like that. Something you could hold on to without thinking about it.

The artillery fire had abated even more. The *Oberleutnant* walked the company line. Then: "Berger, go to the battalion and report that we have reached the designated position. Thirteen casualties."

I shoved off to take care of my mission. There were still occasional artillery impacts in the village, but you could make your way through after a fashion. When I was on the way back, at the edge of the village, there where we had gotten hit before, I was called to from a bunker next to the road. "Berger, Berger . . . come help us! You've been trained as a medic. Come, it's terrible!"

I stumbled into the low, dark room. A few men were lying next to one another on the floor. In the middle was Ziebert, from Breslau. He lay there and wormed around; he hit into the air and screamed and moaned. Two or three men were trying to keep him quiet.

"What's wrong with him?" I asked.

"That!" said one of the men, throwing back the overcoat. Under the overcoat were his guts—nothing but throbbing guts: kidneys, liver, and entrails. A piece of shrapnel had ripped open his abdominal wall, and everything was oozing out as a bloody, slippery mush. And the poor man cried and whimpered and moaned: "Shoot me dead! . . . Shoot me dead! . . . Don't let me croak like this! . . . Shoot me . . . I beg you!"

And there I was with my nice-sounding "Auxiliary Medical Orderly" training, and I was supposed to help. "Isn't there a doctor anywhere?" I asked.

"We haven't found any, but there's supposed to be one at the battalion."

Clueless looks and a shrugging of shoulders all the way around.

"I'll look for one," I said, getting out of that hole quickly. I just wanted to get out and not have to stand there and listen and watch, not being able to help or alleviate any suffering.

Although there was a clearing station established at the battalion command post, there was no doctor there. I discovered he was said to be somewhere in the rear. But further to the left there was supposed to be a clearing station from a neighboring unit. I raced over there in the midst of artillery fire that was gradually coming back. I wandered about, among houses and ruins, but I didn't find anything. Valuable time was slipping away. In the end, I ran back to our clearing station and gathered up two medics with some difficulty. I led them over to the wounded Ziebert. He had turned somewhat still; he was still alive . . . but for how long? I needed to get going. What else was there left to do?

I decided to drop by the battalion command post again in order to get something. It was cold by then. The wind was blowing sharply and drove prickly, hard ice through the air. It blew into everything—onto your neck and against your throat. The turned-up collar of the overcoat was rubbing terribly. I had previously seen window curtains in the house, where the battalion command post had been set up. They were made of a horrific, poisonous green cotton. They would make for a sharp-looking scarf. Just the right thing for me. *Ripppp!* I tore one down!

While I was still putting it on, it occurred to me how squalid my gloves looked. They were in tatters and crusted over with blood and dirt. My fingers were poking out. But I knew a remedy for that as well. So I jumped on over to the dead *Feldwebel* Krämer. He had terrific, new leather gloves, just my size. Give them to me, comrade! You don't need them any more; your fingers are no longer going to freeze. The feeling I had was a bit strange. But what wasn't strange and macabre everywhere around here? And the gloves were warm and thick and smooth.

By then, I needed to get back to our company. I got there just in time for an alert to move out. Up the hill to the forward positions! The Russians were attacking!

We ran up the hill, jumped into foxholes and trenches, broke into groups and went into position. What was going on? Where did anyone see anything? We weren't seeing anything. The wind was whistling sharply from that direction, sending ice and snow in a biting white veil towards us. It blew into our faces and eyes; it took away your vision and your breath.

But then again—out there in the blowing and driven precipitation—there was something to be seen. Pressing, pushing masses—dark brown. But weren't there also horses under them? Yes, indeed, masses of them, as a matter of fact. It was real cavalry! Did that still exist in 1942?

They were still probably about half a kilometer away, but they were pressing forward slowly. A few rounds cracked next to us from the trench. "Idiots!" someone yelled. "What are you shooting at? You won't hit anything at this distance. Let them get closer!" Yeah, and if our artillery had been there—but where was it?

It appeared that the Russian artillery had also been led somewhat astray. If those guys over there really had something serious planned, then a barrage on our positions was overdue. But nothing of the sort happened. The artillery impacts continued to be somewhere behind us in the village. But the brown masses kept coming closer, veiled and obscured by churned up clouds of snow. Our tension mounted. Riflemen loaded and machine-gun people tinkered with their sprayers to remove the ice that was constantly forming up. There was the rattling of machine-gun belts.

And then the mass of riders set out all at once in an abrupt movement. It approached us, like a tidal wave. A wild clattering and cracking started from our positions. It was a rush, something akin to hunting fever, that had taken hold. The belts rattled through the machine guns. The particles of ice hissed and steamed on the hot barrels. The riflemen took aim on the avalanche of human and animal bodies, fired and jammed in a new magazine. Everyone had turned into a wild automaton, a machine that neither thought nor felt.

What else was to be expected: The cavalry attack, a sheer crazy operation, collapsed a hundred meters in front of our positions. It broke up and fled to the rear. Horses and humans lay scattered in front of us. Some were stiff and still, others thrashed around wildly. Whatever had not been wounded fled and disappeared in the blowing veil of snow.

Artillery and mortar fire commenced and covered us. There was nothing left to do but tuck in our heads and turn small. The almost monotonous routine of daily life at the front had been reestablished.

Thirty-six hours later, we were still in that shi . . . modest position.[3] All hell was breaking loose on the high ground in front of us. There were flashes and bangs. Dull detonations were mixed in, along with the ascent of pyrotechnics and the rattling and barking of machine guns. Figures surfaced in the flickering flames of burning houses. They disappeared again. There were cries and shouts and more banging and clattering. We were down below on the slope, ducking behind mounds of dirt and piles of rubble. We started up, on fire with excitement. No one knew what was actually happening.

The free-for-all up top gradually subsided; only the calling and cries continued, but they also grew softer as time wore Then, from the right, a voice: "1st Platoon . . . up . . . follow me!" We assembled to the right behind the ruins.

"What's going on?"

"What's happening?"

Excited voices; they all swirled together, practically whispered. In bits and pieces, the word got around: the Russian had employed an assault detachment . . . or perhaps a reinforced patrol . . . or something like that . . . to the left of the company command post. It was assumed that the attack had been beaten back; in any event,

---

[3] Translator's Note. The original German is "*besch . . . eidenen Stellung,* in which the ellipsis joins the beginning of *beschissen* ("shitty") with the declined form of *bescheiden* ("modest").

the Russians had apparently pulled back. The whole story was not very clear at all. It was said that a couple of our guys had been hit. Consequently, the 1st Platoon was directed to spend the night to the left and in front of the company command post at the place where there was a gap during the day, so that another mess could be avoided.

A few minutes later we moved out. We went up the hill in deployed for combat. The red flames flickered and twitched in an eerie manner out among the plain of snow in front of us. The action up front had settled down. We pushed past the company command post hunched over and disappeared into the communications trench. Frühauf and Lerner disappeared up front; we cowered in the trench, waiting and observing. We stared off into the darkness and into the mess that was illuminated by fires off to the left.

Frühauf reappeared amongst us: "Follow me, but be on your toes! I have no idea what's actually going on over there . . . Walter, follow right behind. There's supposed to be a few wounded over there!"

We climbed out of the trench and pushed forward in a loose skirmishing line off to the left. There was a narrow open ground in front of us and, ill defined in the shadows, the old, abandoned medic bunker. Next to it, there was a dark body, I it seemed as though I were hearing a slight whimpering. I needed to take a look! I ran towards the bunker. There—*berrrrrrt*—a brilliant flash directly in front of me and a hard cracking sound. A burst of fire for a few seconds. There was a hissing around my ears. I was flat on my face in a flash and disappearing into some sort of shallow depression. That's how fast it went—reflexes at work. You didn't have time to think. And that was a good thing! The next burst of fire—perhaps better aimed—hissed right above me. That had been a close one! Damn it all! I finally had a chance to consider things. It appeared that a Russian patrol had hunkered down in the bunker in front of us. And stupid me ran right in front of the firing port and lit up like a Christmas tree to boot! I heard Frühauf cry out something from off to the right. Of course, I didn't understand a single word.

Wumm! Wumm! What was that? It lit up next to the bunker. Beams slip apart and rubble flew through the air. I then heard Frühauf cry out the German battle cry— Hurrraaaa!—and a few men jump up and advanced toward the bunker. By then, I was also up and running. Frühauf—a hell of a guy—had crawled up on the bunker with a few people in the darkness and had smoked it out with some hand grenades. We saw a black figure run away hunched over and disappear in the darkness. They needed to run!

Burst of machine-gun fire chirped above our heads from somewhere. We needed to get back in the holes; we were nothing but targets where we were. Nothing had happened to any of us. You've got to have luck! I gathered up one of the wounded from before into the trench behind the bunker. He had been shot through the upper thigh. Three of us carried him away down to the clearing station.

We looked around a bit in the battalion area and gathered what we could find: Bread and preserves; medical dressings; some rifle ammunition; and a box of Hindenburg lights.[4] Heavily loaded, we started back "home."

In the meantime, the situation had calmed down some more, at least as much as one would characterize it as "calm." There was some mortar fire every few minutes. It was simply harassing fire, fired in the blind, but they had registered their pieces quite well during the day. There was a bumping each time in an uncomfortably close distance away. In between there was the whistling of bursts of machine-gun fire over the hill. Unfortunately, the trenches had not been established in such a manner that they were good for the current situation. Whether you wanted to go forward or to the rear, you had to always get out and cross open ground. The houses were burning behind us and provided an illuminated flame-red background, with you appearing in front of it as a very nice black shadow. It would have been too much to ask of Ivan that he didn't fire at that. The only thing that helped was to run and zigzag—and hope that the Russian machine gunners continued to aim as poorly as they had before.

In the meantime, the 1st Platoon had hunkered down in the trenches and bunkers and felt out the area in front of it. The light from the flames did not reach that far, since the crest was in between. That had both advantages and disadvantages. We also had contact with the *Flak* off to the left and down below in the depression. That meant that we could get comfortable as long as it was quiet.

At least that's what a layman would think! I was right in the middle of unpacking our loot, when the door to the bunker was thrown open and someone spat out: "Medic!"

"Where . . . what . . . who?"

"Over there at the company command post . . . *Unteroffizier* Gutmann!"

The company command post? It was supposed to have its own medic section. But who knew where it might be after all of the hubbub?

Off I went! Over the crest! *Ffffit—Ffffit—Ffffit—Ffffit!* Kiss my ass! Quick . . . down in the trench! So . . . where was he?

Gutmann was sitting in a bunker. Wound up . . . moaning slightly . . . Not a word out of him. Well, what had happened?

Not a whole lot, when you looked at him more closely: A grazing wound under the shoulder. Of course, things were frazzled and the blood was running, but everything was outside of the chest. No bone was smashed, let alone something else. Playing the role of a badly wounded man as the result of such a trifle was a bit overacting. Especially when Gutmann always liked to put on airs as the dashing, debonair and daring one. Of course, a few heartless remarks in that vein were incapable of changing his mood.

---

[4] Translator's Note. A field candle named after the commander in chief of German forces in World War I, *Generalfeldmarschall* Paul von Hindenburg. It was a shallow candle, somewhat reminiscent of a Sterno heat tab.

I tended to his wound, put his uniform back over it as well as I could and started to take my leave.

"But . . . but . . . I can't stay here like this . . . oooch!"

"Of course not, *Herr Unteroffizier,* go as quickly as possible down below to the battalion aid station."

"Go . . . I can't walk . . . I'm much too weak!"

In an effort to help out, someone offered him a shot of Schnapps, but Gutmann turned it down with a moan.

"Give it to me . . . I could use one. Otherwise I might turn out weak in the end as well . . . Aaahhh! . . . What's the matter? . . . Of course, you can stay up here if you want to and wait until you get your strength back. But it's not too cozy up here!"

"No . . . no . . . I'm not staying here under any circumstances. But I'm not going down there by myself. Berger, you have to lead me down there. You have to . . ."

That didn't sound anywhere nearly as weak as it should have coming from that limp dick of an *Unteroffizier.* But I wasn't so stupid, either, that I was going to run next to that shit-scared bastard as another target. I tried to make it clear to him that one man could get through fire a lot better than two figures next to one another, especially when one all by himself can run a whole lot faster. It was the type of conversation that started with *Sie* and *Herr Unteroffizier* and ended with "you schmuck."[5] But nothing worked. Gutmann was acting like a small child. The others sitting with him in the bunker also talked me into schlepping him down the high ground, since they just wanted to get rid of him. In the end, I could have cared less, whether they got me at that point or the next day. The chances of getting me were hundred fold. Whether you escaped, one way or the other, was just a matter of luck.

"Off we go, *Herr Unteroffizier,* let's go!"

Sounding doleful, he whimpered his way through the trench with me behind him. Then we jumped out. *Ffffit—Ffffit—Ffffit!*

"Run, damn it! Your hams are still fine!"

"Don't leave me alone, Berger! . . . Berger, come here, stay with me!"

He was standing there, shaking, in the middle of the light from the fire. A big bullseye at the firing range.

I jumped over to him, hooked my arm under his and pulled him forward. There was a hissing and a whistling all around us. We tramped off. Then—a shrill cry—the man next to me jack knifed and turned as heavy as lead on my arm. He collapsed and fell forward. I threw myself down next to him. It was whistling just a hair above our heads. I grabbed Gutmann and shook him. He didn't stir. I flipped him on his

---

[5] Translator's Note. German uses both a formal and informal "you" when addressing someone. The formal "you," or *Sie,* would normally be used by a subordinate rank when addressing a superior. In this case, the author indicates the relationship has deteriorated to the point where the informal you, or *du,* is used.

back and looked into the blank eyes of a dead man. I could scream at that point! Had it really been that necessary for you?

They would certainly get me shortly. My entire body was shaking. Was it excitement or terror or anger? Perhaps all three mixed into one? I carefully low crawled down the hill and into the cover afforded by the next mound of dirt. Then off to the side and out of the light of the fire. Taking a long detour, I went as quickly as I could back to the position. I had had all I could take for the time being!

Twelve hours later. We were still in the "leaden" corner. I climbed out of the trench and pulled the wounded man up. I grabbed him around the body and he hung around my neck; we then stumbled off. There was still heavy mortar fire all along the slope. With that type of load, you couldn't simply toss yourself to the ground and seek cover whenever it came hissing towards you. The only thing you could do was to stubbornly steer a course straight ahead. If only everything would go faster! The poor devil moaned and whimpered with every step, but I pulled him along mercilessly. To show consideration out of sympathy at that point was sheer suicide. Every second longer that we spent wavering in that circus of fire could cost us our lives. The artillery was also starting to drop rounds in between. About half way up the slope, they had just got a couple of infantrymen. A black crater in the snow yawned wide in the middle of our route. Right next to it were four lifeless forms. Well, nothing was going to hurt them anymore. If you get the blast so close, then no amount of dressing will help. One of them was just a bloody clump. If you didn't see a few pieces of uniform, you had no idea what was the front and what was the rear. Why did those infantrymen also act so dumb and run around together like sheep? Of course, the round always landed in the middle of them, and there was half a dozen dead all at once.

Of all the times for it to happen, the artillery impacts were landing below in the depression in the vicinity of the medic bunker, where we had to go. But that didn't matter much, if we stayed here and waited until it had quieted down there, since they would then get us here on top. That meant keep going! And we succeeded in getting the last bit behind us. Relieved, we showed up at the entryway. Once again, we had been lucky! How many times already? How many times to go?

My "patient" fell like a sack in a corner, and I allowed myself a short break. It was packed in there, with everyone stepping on each other's toes. If things continued that way, then all three companies would be assembled there shortly. Theoretically, at least, they were still holding the positions at Nikinowo. If an artillery round ever landed here as a direct hit, then it would all be over!

I stuck my head out the door. Outside, the barrage fire rumbled and seethed with a regularity that could practically lull you to sleep. It didn't seem to be in our area, though. That meant it was time to get up and go! The slope in front of me was not being fired on. I trotted up the slope. *Huuuiiii! Crash!* I was just able to save myself behind the remnants of a wall. The shrapnel rapped against the brickwork. I had counted my blessing too early! It was artillery fire on top of everything else! The hell with all of them! *Huuuiiii! Crash!* That time I got a hail of hard-frozen clumps of dreck on my back and on my helmet. Well, then. My hat seemed to hold up well! My skull wasn't about to withstand that stuff without some armor, but it would be better to get out of there.

It seemed to be quieter. Time to get up and move out! Let's run another short bit. As I went past the crater with the four infantrymen, it looked to me as if one of them was moving. I had to be imagining things. That guy could no longer be alive the way he looked! No one would be surprised, if you slowly started to go crazy. And there certainly had to be a few topside that needed me. So . . . I couldn't allow myself to be held up.

I arrived at the bunker up top without any more artillery salvoes. Two meters from the piled-up dirt from the trench, near the entrance, there was someone on his face. I would be able to quickly pull him into the bunker. But when I turned him over and saw glassy, turned-up eyes, I knew that I was no longer responsible for him. I needed to at least look for his dog tag, however. But then there was an incoming hissing sound—shrill, cutting, and hostile. Just fractions of a second. Jumping head first, I reached the trench leading to the entrance in time. At that point, the world turned topsy-turvy with a crashing, flames, black smoke and a hail of dreck and iron. After a few seconds, I could see some things again, but I was not overwhelmed with curiosity. I pulled myself up, hit the door of the bunker and stumbled in.

I initially had to get used to the semi-darkness that prevailed there. Whenever you came in from outside, you didn't see anything at all. Moreover, the "oven" made out of a fruit can smoked so much that it took your breath away. Then I had to wipe away the ice that had formed on my glasses, ice that formed immediately upon entering the dank room from the cold outside. It wasn't until those preparatory measures had been taken that I could take a look around.

Scheurer was sitting next to the oven; he was someone from my platoon. In the rear, whenever we were drilling, he always stood out like a sore thumb. He was holding his helmet with both hands in front of him, and it looked like a strainer. They must have sent something his way that exploded right in front of him. His head was a mass of blood, but he was completely conscious and was cursing like a drunken sailor. He would make it, but I had no idea where to start with dressing him. I fetched a couple of field dressings from the large first-aid kit and tried to wrap Scheurer systematically—round and around—until only his eyes and his mouth were visible. I then intended to carefully take him down to the medic bunker. But he said no. He wanted me to stand by for bad cases; he said he would get there by himself. Then he shook my hand so hard that I went down on a knee. With the portion of his face still visible, he attempted a grin. Then he pushed himself out the door and ran off. He was a hell of a fellow, even though he always stuck out like a sore thumb whenever we were drilling in the rear area. Or perhaps because of it?

The next one was an infantryman with some shrapnel in his hand. I didn't take care of anything like that there. I showed the man where the battalion clearing station was and sent him off in that direction. The guys down below needed something to do as well. Two were sitting at the rear of the bunker on the makeshift bunk.

"What's up with you?"

Nothing at all, they said, they only wanted to warm themselves up.

That was fine by me. I would send them out in fifteen minutes. I had the feeling it was always the same two who came to warm up. I had not seen Frühauf and Lehrner the entire day in the bunker, although they weren't but ten meters away from the bunker in position. It certainly wasn't any warmer there.

It was not until then that I noticed through the haze and the smoke that another guy was sitting in the corner. He was another infantryman. He then came forward. His left pants leg was shredded and there was some red dropping out—not a lot. I cut open his pants and underwear and saw that it was only a small bit of shrapnel, a flesh wound. It was rapidly dressed. He could make his way below without any problems. When I told him that, he turned paler than before. His eyes welled up out of their sockets in dismay and he struggled for words. Man, the guy was afraid! Good God! I certainly had no great desire to get some shrapnel in my back on account of such a wimp, and I told him that in unmistakable terms. I told him how fast this "wounded transport" was going to go. But that was not necessary at all. The guy could run like the devil, despite the shrapnel in his hams.

We raced past the four infantrymen and I had a fright—the one guy really was alive. He was a really young rascal. He raised his head a bit and looked at me with his eyes horribly wide open. His lips were moving, but the words could not be heard. I'll get you shortly! Down below, I pushed the guy with me into the bunker. I didn't go in myself; I only called through the door. Two or three men needed to come out to evacuate a badly wounded man, who was only a few steps away from the bunker on the slope. I only heard an indistinct and murmured *Jawohl*. I hastened back and threw myself next to the guy. Boy, was he a pretty sight! Blood was trickling from his forehead; it was steaming. The lower part of his right arm was a mass of hacked up flesh. Blood was seeping through his overcoat, and he had another hole in his upper thigh. And then they started peppering us with precision again. *Sssssttt—Wummmmm! Sssssttt—Wummmmm! Sssssttt—Wummmmm!*

Did those guys like me so much that they had to fire wherever I was? Or was I only imagining that because I no longer took notice of the impacting rounds that weren't landing close by? *Sssssttt—Wummmmm! Sssssttt—Wummmmm! Sssssttt—Wummmmm!* How long was that going to last? And, of course, there was no cover here . . . no ditch . . . nothing at all. I grabbed the wounded man under the shoulder and drug him a bit into the shallow crater. But it was so small and so shallow that it offered hardly any protection at all. *Sssssttt—Wummmmm!* Good God! Stop right now or at least let us have a direct hit on our backs! It just couldn't be taken any more. I pressed myself flat over the wounded man and tried to make myself as small as possible. *Sssssttt—Wummmmm!* That one went into the snow right behind us. The powdery ice was sifted into the area between my coat collar and the helmet. Finally, the fire shifted a bit. Thank God!

I looked at my patient again and wondered how he was still alive. Assault pack, ammunition cans, reserve barrel, carbine, gas mask, bread bag—everything was still hanging off of him. The half-dozen straps had conglomerated into a Gordian knot. Trying to untangle them was out of the question. Get the stuff off! I tried to make my way to my pocketknife. But it was not so simple to find my way through the different coats and blouses to my pants pocket with my frozen and torn-up fingers. Finally, I had the folding knife. It was a miracle that I had not lost it in the mess. Of course, I could not get the blade out right away with my trembling fingers. Finally, I did it. And then I had that wonderful moment when I was allowed to destroy military property without being punished. Sweet revenge against all the nastiness handed out by NCO's in charge of the supply rooms and the arms rooms. Cut after cut, one strap after the other. I even cut the belt in half, because the jammed buckle would not budge. At least I had uncovered the poor guy. But I could apply dressing at that location. Where were the others? It was wonderfully quiet at that point; they could at least come. I straightened up and looked in the direction of the medic bunker. But there was nothing stirring there. What kind of limp dicks were they? I couldn't haul this guy back by myself. But if I were to wait until they came up, peace would break out. I decided to fetch a couple of the lame bastards myself!

I ran back to the bunker and pressed inside through the door. You could barely move any more in there. They were all infantry people, but apparently nothing but simple cases. I couldn't see anything serious with anybody. One or the other could help me without any problem.

"Come . . . please . . . two or three of you! One of your comrades . . . about a hundred meters away . . . he's badly wounded!"

Icy silence. A few eyeballed, some dully, others with animosity; most of them, however, looked away and pretended as though they had not heard me. My blood slowly started to boil.

"Good God, people. Don't be so stubborn and so cowardly. Is that guy out there supposed to croak? I can't drag him in here by myself. He tore up pretty bad."

Nothing. Finally, two figures pressed forward from the back. Of course, it was people from my company. It was Hadamla from my platoon. I had dressed his wound in the morning. It was wrapped thicker at that point, and he was carrying it in a sling. The other guy, with a bloody bandage around his head, was from the 2nd Platoon. I could depend on those two. Let's go!

Of course, with all the stupid talking, we no longer had a break in the fires. Once again, there was hell to pay. Right outside the bunker, we had to crawl into the ruins. They were really thrashing away. But then we jumped up between the whistling shrapnel and the pelting clumps of dreck and raced to the crater, where the wounded man was. I grabbed him on the upper body, and the other two each took a foot.

We then shoved off. The fire had abated somewhat, and we were able to get to the medic bunker without incident. We couldn't get inside, however. We had to place the wounded man on the snow-covered entryway. Hadamla and the man with the bandaged head stayed with him.

I squeezed myself into the squirming mass; I needed to take a look. It just wasn't right to me. How they looked at me again.

"What kind of wound do you have?" I asked the first one sharply, as I grabbed him by the coat collar. "No . . . no . . . nothing!" I heard, astonished.

"And what's wrong with you?" I yelled at a teeth-chattering pitiful creature, who happened to be standing right in front of me. The guy actually started to howl: "Oooohhhh . . . I feel so bad . . . the shooting and . . . the dead!"

"I also get ill when I see a shit figure like you!" What kind of sorry creatures were in this pigsty! Not everyone in our company was a hero, either, but this type of behavior would have been unthinkable. The one guy, crying, pointed at me, turned away and whimpered: "Oh, look at all the blood!"

I looked down on myself. It was true. I didn't look all that appealing. My one-time snow-white camo cover was a single sheet of blood from top to bottom. A butcher on shiftwork couldn't even compete. I continued my "interrogation." The next few didn't even provide an answer. Another one only wanted to warm himself; another get rested up. One man wanted to wait until the fire abated. He had been waiting three hours already. I had seen him sitting there that morning; he probably still had a long time to wait.

I had had the inner rage for some time. It then boiled over. I hit the closest guy in the stomach; the next one I struck in the back, causing him to fly out the door just as he was. I then started to yell just like on the parade field. I fumbled around with my pistol and said something about shooting on the spot, if space wasn't made immediately for the wounded man. There was a violent wave of movement, with a pushing and a pressing towards the door. Everyone wanted out, but no one wanted to be the first one. I hoped they didn't step on my patient out in the entryway. After a minute, the hovel was cleared out, except for the truly wounded. An old *Obergefreiter* came out of the corner, reported to me as a medic and asked whether he might be of service to the *Herr Assistenzarzt*.[6] He could not see what kind of rank badge was hidden under my butcher's apron. It was one other sign of proof to me that you only get authority in the army by yelling. It was too bad that I was always yelling at the wrong spot! I tapped my comrade on the shoulder in a friendly manner and said: "Idiot, I'm also only an *Obergefreiter!*" He looked at me, disconcerted. Then, however, I noticed that he now had more respect for the *Obergefreiter* than he previously had for the *Assistenzarzt*.

In the meantime, they had drug in the wounded man. I got to work with the old *Obergefreiter*. The lower right arm looked terrible. The bones were probably shattered in a dozen places, with some of them sticking out of the wounds at attention. It was

---

[6] Translator's Note. An *Assistenzarzt* is an intern.

probably all over for the arm. As a precaution, however, we decided to splint it. There was no materiel in the bunker. That meant out into the light once again. I didn't have to look very long. The hut next door must have received a good dozen direct hits. The shredded roof beams were scattered around the area in abundance. I fished a couple of usable ones from out of the rubble and then went inside again. After we splinted his arm, we took a look at his other wounds. The hole in his upper thigh was only a flesh wound, albeit very deep. On the right side of the chest, his skin was shredded and torn open, but the wound was not any deeper than that. The head wound was also harmless. Even in his misfortune, the guy had been very lucky. After half an hour, we were finished with our work.

The poor devil's entire body started to shake from the cold. That wasn't surprising with the amount of blood he had lost. Besides, whatever he still had on his body was dripping wet with blood. If we left him lying there like that, he would eventually freeze. I talked to a couple of lightly wounded men, who were lying in the straw towards the back and got a blanket from them. Then we bedded the guy down on a layer of straw and wrapped him in the blanket. Outside, in front of the bunker, was a dead man. I removed his overcoat and spread it out on top of our problem child. He then received a big gulp of coffee, although it was unfortunately ice cold.

"So . . . stay lying here for a while . . . nothing more can happen to you . . . and your wounds are not life threatening. We transport you to the rear with the next vehicle and then you'll be off to home. Your mom is certainly waiting for you."

He didn't say anything for a while. Then he felt around with his good left hand and found mine. Then, he quietly said: "You are a good comrade."

It turned very quiet, and those five words remained in the stillness. All at once, I felt wonderfully at peace and happy.

"You are a good comrade." It was said modestly, but it was perhaps the nicest award I received the entire war.

✠

I then allowed myself a short break. I fished out a hunk of bread from my bread bag and chewed on it for a while. The particles of ice were ground up softly between my teeth; perhaps they were also bits of clay. It was a hard thing to tell exactly. It was also immaterial to me at the moment. One of the wounded offered me the luxury of a cigarette. Too bad I was a non-smoker; otherwise, a cigarette would have most certainly done me good. Unfortunately, no one offered me schnapps, because no one had any.

After a quarter of an hour, I got up, shook my stiff arms and legs and took off on my journey again. It was eerily quiet outside at the time. The way to the positions on top was practically a walk in the park. Even the weather was nicer than the previous day. The sun shone; despite that, the skies were not clear. Instead, they seemed to be overcast with a fine, veil-like milky mist. That produced a simultaneously strangely mild and yet at the same time unpleasantly blinding light. The wind drove the crystal-like snow powder in sparkling and flitting veils up the slope. It formed small dunes, only to whisk them away again. It wasn't enough, however, to cover all of the craters nor the dead and the rubble and the carbonized beams, which imprinted the stamp of war on the peaceful countryside.

Bursts of machine-gun fire were chirping along the crest. As a precautionary measure, I hit the deck and crawled forward, as the regulations required. In my forward aid station, there were already a couple of guys sitting there, and they greeted me with happy amazement. I had already been gone for more than an hour, and those up front had already made the sign of the cross for me. Leo Zadina was especially cordial in greeting me. Blood was running out of his left ear. A piece of shrapnel had gotten him. It was puffed up quite a bit. I hoped that he didn't lose his eardrum or that something else in the interior had been ruined! We'd find out soon enough. I softly whispered into the clot of blood: "Are you a nut cake?"

"No more than you," he replied in a thick Bavarian accent.

Thank God! His ear was working. I wrapped Leo's head confidently and wanted to send him off. But he would hear none of it. He said he wasn't going to take off for that kind of scratch, especially now that everyone was needed like a piece of bread. Later on . . . when the relief came . . . he said he didn't feel a thing.

It was not until I held a long anatomy lecture on how dangerous a sitting piece of shrapnel was at that place and all that could happen that he listened and bent to my scientific authority. But he insisted that he also take another wounded man with him. I was able to grant him that wish. So . . . send the next one to me. He had shrapnel in his shoulder and his back; nothing serious. I dressed him and turned him over to Leo. He shook my hand again and disappeared. I hoped that both of them made it through unscathed. There was already some rumbling outside again. At the moment, I was unemployed.

Correspondingly, I decided to go forward into the trenches to see what the others were doing. Frühauf and Lehrner greeted me enthusiastically. In their minds' eyes, they had already envisioned me laying dead somewhere in the rear. Frühauf had been at the battalion command post in the morning and said that life up front in the trenches was almost peaceful and safe compared to that which was going on 500 meters to the rear. To contradict his claim, a round impacted right behind us almost as soon as he had said that. Half of the trench wall collapsed upon us. It was good that the ground was frozen so solidly; otherwise, the entire trench system would have been collapsed by then.

I raced back to my bunker, sat in a corner and listened. *Wummm—wummm—wummm—wummmm!* It came down at regular intervals, like the workings of a clock. And it continued to *wummm* the rest of the day. It seemed like the guys on the other side of the lines had unlimited amounts of ammunition. Whenever one of our mortars fired, it was answered a hundred fold. And even if they were lousy and couldn't aim at all, they had to hit somewhere sometime. *Wummm!* That seemed to be almost right on the bunker again. Dreck rained down from between the roof timbers each time. A hundred mortar rounds on the roof would have been fine. Just as long as they didn't think of sending us a direct hit by artillery, the bunker would hold out.

Everyone was still in an uproar from excitement when I got forward to the trenches. Among the dead was also *Unteroffizier* Sassik, as I discovered. He was lying over there! But I did not look at him; I was already choking up enough. Poor bastard! You were always teased and ribbed by us, because you were always an easy touch with your earnestness. You were such a good guy!

I took off to get back to Frühauf and Lehrner. Reported to them what had happened. Strange, how we could all discuss those things so soberly. Then . . . silence . . . skulking . . . waiting. Weren't we tired to the point of falling over? Weren't we sleepy . . . hungry? Who still knew . . . who still felt it . . . who even thought about it?

In the midst of that monotonous artillery rumbling there was a cry, off to the left, where the machine gun was positioned. Bent over, I raced to that location when a break set in. In front, along the cover, it was still smoking. There was a small cloud above the freshly churned up soil. It went in there. Gunner I, the small Janisch, was flat on his face, motionless. Gunner II was moaning next to him. I grasped Janisch on the shoulder and spun him over; his helmet was like a sieve and his head hacked up. Blood and more blood. Dead!

The other guy had a few bits in his shoulder, perhaps something elsewhere, but God only knew where. He was unapproachable. My teeth clattering and grinding, I went back to work. How many times had that been? And how many times to come? I was barely able to get my aid packets out of my pockets with my clammy fingers. I would have long since run out of supplies, if the abandoned medic bunker next to me hadn't offered unending reserves. Good God! If only I weren't so clumsy . . . so trembly and stiff! *Sssst—wummmm!* They were firing again! It was barely perceptible in my consciousness any more.

And then there was the hard crash of an impact right behind me. A hot, sharp blow jerked through my right leg and deep into my lower thigh. Damn it to hell! No, it really did get me. There was no pain, even though I was waiting for it. On the other hand, my leg suddenly turned strangely heavy . The blood was oozing and steaming through the hole in my tattered trouser leg. For a moment, I froze. Then I tried to pull myself together. Strange: It worked. Yes: I can still move my leg, practically without effort!

I was back at Frühauf's location in a single bound.

"They got me this time! Down below!"

"Jesus! Can you walk? For God's sake, get out of here! Before it's too late! None of us can help you!"

I knew that much. I only had one option left: To try to get back on my own. If the Russians ever got there, then everyone laying around here wounded would get a shot to the back of the head. We all knew that from personal experience.

A final handshake. Frühauf pushed and lifted me up over the edge of the trench. Then down and no delay. Down the slope! How many had I already dragged down there. Now I was the last one to go. The word "dragging" is a bit too dramatic. I was once again amazed: I certainly wasn't too elegant, but it was going reasonably well. Once below, there was the long village street, or what used to pass for the village street: a hellish picture of fire-scarred ruins, rubble, craters, smashed equipment, and the dead—a burned out *Schützenpanzerwagen* with two completely carbonized corpses hanging down from the sides—and more rubble and dead, burnt framework from houses.

I hastened, stumbled, staggered down the street. Just keep going . . . keep going! There hadn't been an aid station in the village for some time. To try to crawl off and hide somewhere would have been suicide. It was imperative for me to reach the next village further to the rear, about three or four kilometers away.

The rolling terrain, white under a leaden-gray sky, spread out in a seemingly limitless and oppressive vastness. Running through the middle of it was the dark ribbon of road. Even there, there were impacts, rubble, an occasional shot-up vehicle, a dead man, a couple of foxholes along the edge of the road and more opened-up and shredded earth. It appeared as if everything had died out. A couple of wounded men with bandaged heads and arms hastened past me towards the rear; once there was a small contingent of perhaps a dozen men headed towards the front. Keep going . . . just keep going! Damn it! My leg was getting heavier and heavier. A dull, icy, crippling feeling started to climb higher, from my knee into my hip. Every step became more difficult. I was distancing myself ever more slowly from the spot I had been in. If only you could just see the neighboring village! It had to be behind the ridgeline. But, man, how the road could twist on its way there! My heart was pumping; sweat was pouring down. Despite that, my teeth were chattering. Cold? Exhaustion? Excitement? Or even fear? Now, when I was defenseless. I was feeling how everything was collapsing in me that had held me together the past week.

I was just passing a couple of disabled vehicles when I suddenly heard the swelling sound of aircraft above me. Two Russian fighters jumped out of the cloud cover, raced along the road and made a straight course for the wrecked vehicles, presumably not seeing that they weren't worth the gunpowder any more. Impacting rounds to the left and right. Of all places, they had to catch me there!

Fortune in misfortune: Right next to me on the edge of the road was a deep foxhole. Get in! I made myself as small as I could. Just disappear . . . hole up!

Then the aircraft disappeared. Get out—keep going! But, all of sudden, nothing worked any more. I was unable to get up. My leg wouldn't cooperate; my entire body gave up. I clawed into the earth, pulling and pulling. My teeth were grinding, my pulse throbbed. Every muscle was cramped. I was in need of help, but I was unable to get out of the hole. Gasping, I laid back on the clumps of frozen earth. There were red and black shapes dancing and fluttering in front of my eyes. I was both hot and cold. I would have cried out—I could have cried—if I had had the strength. Give up! Stay where you are! Freeze in the ditch! Let yourself be shot! I could care less about everything—whether I got further to the rear or farther toward the front. One way or the other, it really didn't matter any more!

My thoughts were jumbled and memory traveled in circles like a nightmare.

I didn't stay there, and I didn't freeze. Somebody came by, pulled me out of the hole, and helped me out. There were always comrades somewhere; one poor dog helped another. Somehow, I got to the village. There was a forward aid station there; it was filled to the brim with wounded and dead, with blood and dreck.

I disappeared into the masses of wounded, strength and desire gone. Incapable of feeling and thinking. Not much different than the others outside in the mass grave.

And so that's the way it was in Nikinowo in December 1942, three weeks before Christmas. At the moment I was wounded, the company still had a "combat strength" of fourteen men, at least as far as all that allowed itself to be reconstructed. When it pulled back from the position in accordance with its orders at the end of the day, there were only seven men left! Frühauf and Lehrner were also wounded. In fact, Lehrner was badly wounded; his left foot had to be amputated.

But while all that was happening, a German counterattack was underway far off to our right with freshly introduced forces. It paralyzed the Russian offensive, and brought the entire situation in the Gshatsk area back in order. Our Nikinowo and the many other Nikinowos to the right and left of us had not been in vain.

At the end of our company's sacrifice, there was a small, but symbolic incident. I didn't hear about it until much later.

We had a career *Feldwebel* in our company—let's call him Dietrich—who was a much hated and despised man. In neither case was it unjustified. Sometimes he appeared to be a character that might have been personally invented by E. M. Remarque[7]: capricious, quick-tempered, malicious, a hazer and harasser, intemperate with both wine and women. But he wasn't cowardly; that much you had to give him. And sometimes, in shitty situations, there were moments where you could appreciate him. But all that would soon be over.

In Nikinowo he was one of the last ones remaining. In the end, he led what one still referred to as a "company." When the last few men were evacuating the position, with the Russians pressing in from all sides, *Feldwebel* Dietrich was shot through both upper thighs, with a bone being shattered. His little group of men was clueless. Evacuating him was out of the question. Leave him behind? Everyone knew what that would mean.

At that point, Dietrich said, ice cold: "Leave the position immediately . . . go . . . go . . . leave me here!"

When his people started to hesitate, he yelled: "Disappear . . . right now! That is an order! I'll personally shoot anyone who does not follow it!"

Dietrich was officially listed as "missing." But his fate was never in doubt to any of us.

Legends emerged in long-forgotten times from those sorts of events—heroic legends.

---

[7] Translator's Note. Remarque was the author of *All Quiet on the Western Front.*

A prime mover from Artillerie-Regiment 103 (mot.) *(of the* 4. Panzer-Division*) brings forward a 10.5-centimeter howitzer to assist in the preparation for the assault.*

By evening, the preparations have been made. The tanks of Panzer-Regiment 35 *(of the* 4. Panzer-Division*) are on the outskirts of the metropolis on the Oka River.*

Orel was defended in a heroic manner. Even wounded personnel from the officer academy fought to the bitter end.

Orel, 3 October 1941. Stuka formations, engaged by Soviet antiaircraft fire, attack the focal point of the enemy's defenses, the airfield.

Soviet paratroopers, committed in the final round of fighting, were killed in this trench line.

Enemy antitank guns attempted to hold up the advance into the city. They were wiped out before they could even unlimber.

Mzensk also proved tough to take. The first snow fell as well, a warning that winter was coming. It melted, but the mud remained. Pictured here is the "road" from Orel to Mzensk. Supplies could be delivered only by air.

The defensive ring around Mzensk was finally blown open. Soviet dead remained behind in the positions surrounding the city, 25 October 1941.

A 10-centimeter cannon knocked out this T-34 along the main street of Mzensk.

On to Moscow! Tanks with mounted infantry during the assault on Tschern.

Chapter 5

A GLANCE BACK IN POETRY

Obergefreiter **Walter Berger,** *Panzergrenadier-Regiment 10, 9. Panzer-Division*

It lies deep in the ocean of time,
Almost like a legend, as old as man's fate, —
But it suddenly takes on life and form
And reaches towards us from infinity.
And it enters our dreams nightly and cries
And shows faces, stiff and pale and cold,
And things long forgotten take hold
Of our sleepy daily routine.
And voices rise from the depths; surge
Into our ears as a pressing command,
To talk for them and to bear witness, loudly.
So that you know how men once stood
For you in ice and fire, night and death,
For you as a wall, built out of flesh and blood.

WE WERE IN THE WAR

For those of us who felt the icy breath of strange worlds,
We will never completely return to you.
A piece of us remains behind with our dead,
wherever our army restlessly ranged the land.
In our dreams we still breath in the ice-laced
crystal air; in our glance is still
The white broadness, where fate abruptly
Matured half boys into men.
And it's always as if time

Suddenly turned: — shots in the distance, —
We creep through enemy territory as a patrol.
And dark shadows stand in the walls of fog,
Causing the sinews to tense, and the hands
To clench tightly around invisible weapons.

A SOLDIER'S HAND

You, my hand
On the wall of the trench! —
Caked, smudged,
Clawed into the soil and animal like, —
Like ghostly figures
The creases and folds, —
Stiff from weapon oil, clay and soot,
From chunks of soil, from rounds fired! —
And you dream of treasures that have long been denied:
You play with blossoms, with colorful crystals; —
All by yourself among all the others
You still continue to dream. —
You, my hand
On the wall of the trench! —
Covered by cracks and crevices
Scabbed-over wounds
and scars,
Bloodstained, —
How are you so rough and coarse and hard,
Did you bury this one or that one tonight! —
And yet still dream of miracles, of things special:
As if you were lying on dark silky hair, —
You've been dreaming it for years, —
How many more?

RUSSIAN WINTER

Road, fences, carts disappear in the snow,
The sky and the countryside drown in the snow,
Blood and steel and fire disappear in the snow,
The listening, the peering, the waiting drown in the snow.
The sneaking, silent snow ghosts fool you:
The fox hole, the stretch of trench disappeared;
Where there had been someone next to me the day before,

Who fell—I didn't need to bury anyone.
The entire gray army sinks into the snow,
And the hard whiteness swells without banks
With its merciless star-like glittering.
The world is cold and hopeless and empty;
Just the bullet that is looking for me is hot,
And only death is gentle and warm and dark.

OCHOTSCHEWKA

The icy wind grovels around the corners of the houses
And chases the snow into spraying white banners
Along the hard-frozen gray rutted routes and
Along the village and over fence and hedge.
The guards, freezing, attempt to cover themselves
And pull in their shelter halves tighter.
Aren't those voices outside? — Partisans? —
What can be hiding in these white drifts?
In disrepair, a house cowers at the edge of the village;
The straw roof rustles, black from old smoke,
And its dead windows glare threateningly
Out into the frost frozen empty countryside. —
Now lurking behind huts, tree and bush
Of the cold countryside are greedy ghosts.

SHISDRA 1942

A hole, churned up in clay-like yellowy soil
And half filled from the last downpour,
And vegetation and a tepid river up front,
Which washes up against the bank, sleepily gurgling.
The dew has cooled my hot forehead
And the smoking bolt on my rifle. —
Still twitching in my heart, shot upon shot,
Death, which I felt a hundred times today.
Oh, how the gunpowder smoke stung! —
I still feel how I ran, jumped and crawled
Solitary through blood and fire along my path. —
A thin blade in God's broad mountain pasture. —
A bit of luck that in the same hole next to me
There is a second one squatting now—a comrade!

OUTSIDE OF OREL, AUGUST 1942

"Defensive Fighting in the East"
Was printed in the Wehrmacht Daily Report back then.
Endless days and nights; —
But you don't know any of that.
The Shisdra, a loamy water,
Brush and morass and sand; —
And like an insatiable glutton
Death devoured its way through the countryside.
We over here—and the Reds over there —
Sinking our claws into furrows and roots; —
And between us were the dead lying
In the Kolodesny Woods.
We squatted in dreck-filled holes
And chewed moldy bread,
And rain poured down all around us;
Death was monotonous and gray.
The descent of the artillery shells was monotonous; —
The Russians did not aim well, —
But even after hundreds of flashes
The next one sends your blood racing.
The position remained unbroken; —
Ivan attacks daily. —
When relief came after five weeks
We were but seventeen men.
We went back and reported; —
They hung something on our chests. —
Back then, we were all heroes
And didn't even know it ourselves.
We weren't rewarded with the rush of victory;
The front in the east had frozen up! —
I don't know how many are lying there,
Buried under in collapsed trenches.
I don't know—the ones who fell there —
Are they to be considered today as idiots or heroes? —
If every one of us were to stand like that,
Then the world would be harder—and better.

FIELD BURIAL

The rain was cold and the sky was gray,
We brought him there; carried
Through trenches and craters and wire entanglements,
Wrapped in a bloody shelter half.
The ground was black and the earth was heavy,
And the clods of earth stuck to the shovels.
The water dripped from helmet and rifle
On rounds and hand grenades.
No psalms and no prayers, no pious hymns,
No murmuring chorus and no blessing.
Only the organ-like sound of muffled rounds in the distance
And the monotonously rushing rain.
A foxhole, water in the clay shaft.
We sank him silently into the depths.
From up front, the battle grumbled and growled,
As if its voice were calling out:
The voice of the God of fire and steel,
Who created the worlds in wrath. —
The sky was dead and the earth was barren, —
And we hastened silently back forward.

LATE FALL 1943

The world has turned endlessly wide and gray,
No ray of sunshine lies on our path;
The puddles in the ruts glisten palely,
And the great frost beckons threateningly from the north.
The wild murdering of humans is becoming monotonous,
And the dull agony presses ever more;
The blazing sign of our belief
In our martial order has sunk to ashes.
We stand stubbornly at long lost outposts,
Clammy fingers on the trigger,
Our perpetual gaze directed eastward.
A hundred thousand mounds in the countryside in front of us,
On which the helmets rust, row upon row,
The crosses rot and the birches take a beating.

WE OLD SOLDIERS

We old soldiers stand closer to
Death and the dark powers,
Have become harder and more tenacious
In God knows how many battles.
We are familiar with the choking dread
Of a thousand hammered-apart hours
Of bodies, shredded and chopped up,
And gaping, twitching wounds.
We no longer consider ourselves heroes
And do not dream blessedly of victories;
No Wehrmacht Daily report needs to announce,
Where we lie, dead and living.
We have nothing but callouses and claws
From shooting and hauling and shoveling
And damn it all, we'll fall
Without a "Hurra" on our lips.
We curse and binge and swear:
"They've sold us down the river and betrayed us!" —
We stand at lost outpost's
And know in blazing fires:
At some time, out of decay and rust, the world will
Regenerate itself in a soldier!

THE FINAL FIGHTING OF THE *16. PANZER-DIVISION* IN THE STALINGRAD POCKET

Oberstleutnant i.G.[1] **Hubert Menzel, operations officer of the *16. Panzer-Division***

The daily logs of the *16. Panzer-Division*, which covered the fighting of the formation in the Stalingrad Pocket from December 1942 to January 1943, were destroyed shortly before the end of the fighting to prevent them from falling into enemy hands.

With great difficulty but while still fresh in their memory, the officers who had come out of the pocket alive helped to reconstruct it while in captivity. The results, sewn into the sole of a shoe, accompanied me until I was sent to a Ministry of the Interior Prison at the beginning of 1950. It then had to be destroyed, since it was impossible to get it through an examination by the prison specialists.

This represents the third effort to retain something for posterity concerning the final fighting of the *16. Panzer-Division*. After thirteen years as a prisoner of war, it

---

[1] Translator's Note. *i.G.* = *im Generalstab* = "in the General Staff." General staff officers up to the rank of general officer appended this suffix after their rank as an honorific.

has been created primarily from memory. It is therefore possible that small errors, particularly concerning chronology and the operations of individual forces, have crept in. It is impossible to do justice to all the deeds and suffering of everyone, especially for *Panzer-Regiment 2*, which fought for more than a month outside the framework of the division. What the men of all of the units of the division accomplished in the Stalingrad Pocket is worthy of being recorded in history. The story of their end is recorded here.

General Situation of the *6. Armee* in the Middle of November 1942

Toward the beginning of October 1942, when the fighting for the possession of the city abated in the wake of exhaustion on both sides, the *6. Armee* was in a difficult position. Jutting to the northeast, the field army was in the operationally most exposed position in the outermost corner of the southern front. It had been bled white of personnel; it was in need of materiel reconstitution; it was not stockpiled for the winter; it had only a single-track railway for its logistical lines of communications, a railway that could not cover the continuing combat needs of the many divisions, let alone a stockpiling of logistics.

As a result of a lack of forces, the broad Kirghiz Steppes to the south could only be screened by weak Rumanian forces.

Rumanian, Italian and Hungarian field armies adjoined the German field army to the northwest, extending as far as the area south of Woronesh. Their combat power was weak. Both of the weak positions on both sides of the *6. Armee* had to tempt the enemy to carve out the bulwark of the front, Stalingrad, by enveloping to both sides.

That danger had been recognized by all of the higher command levels for some time, with German motorized ready reserves brought up behind the threatened sectors of the front. Despite that, the lack of forces prevented a true deployment in depth and the earmarking of strong operational reserves. In addition, the *6. Armee* was forced by the poor terrain of the steppes to leave the majority of its depots at the end of the railhead west of the Don, to send its horses to inhabited areas along the Don for the winter, and to prepare reconstitution areas for the majority of its motorized elements in the Don Valley.

✠

On 17 November 1942, the expected Russian offensive was started. The defensive capabilities of the Rumanians had been seriously overestimated; their antitank capabilities insufficient. In their first true stress test, their front collapsed and drew the German ready reserves into the whirlpool of flight. Thick fog negated the German antitank capabilities.

By 21 November, the pincers of the northwest and southeast Russian breakthroughs closed at the bridge at Kalatsch. The field army was encircled.

In order not to be rolled up from the rear, the field army was forced to pull both of its wings back and formed a southern and western front.

In order to win time to do that, the *16. Panzer-Division* was alerted on 21 November in Rynok, where it had executed a difficult operation without decisive success, and sent west. Its mission was to bring the Russian forces that had broken through west of the Don to a halt by means of a counterattack. As a minimum, it was to keep the crossings over the Don open for the divisions of the field army that were west of it.

Although it was not possible to prevent the collapse of the Rumanians in difficult fighting west of the Don, the bridgehead at Pestkowatka could be held until the main bodies of the *44. Infanterie-Division*, the *384. Infanterie-Division*, and the Rumanian 1st Cavalry Division could cross the Don to the east and then establish a defensive front oriented west. Under heavy enemy pressure, elements of the *16. Panzer-Division* disengaged from the bridgehead and were sent back to the northern blocking position to establish defensive positions oriented north.

Since the field army anticipated orders to break out of the pocket to the southwest, it had the majority of its armored forces concentrated there. Despite considerable concern for its own combat power, the division dispatched its *Panzer-Regiment 2* and an *ad hoc* group, *Kampfgruppe Strack*, to that location.

The main body of the division rolled to the northeast to its new area of operations in the northern blocking position on the morning of 27 November. The men of the maintenance battalion and the replacement parts section underwent their baptism of fire during that period in brave defensive fighting against Russian tanks and infantry that had broken through in and around Kalatsch. From there, they were forced back to the south out of the pocket.

The *16. Panzer-Division*, minus its *Panzer-Regiment 2*, was then attached to the *XI. Armee-Korps* for operations in the northern blocking position. It received orders to insert itself into the gap between the *24. Panzer-Division* (right) and the *60. Infanterie-Division (mot.)* (left) and establish defensive positions. The *3. Infanterie-Division (mot.)* had previously held that sector, but it had been withdrawn and inserted into the southwest corner of the pocket that was forming. The gap had been provisionally closed by elements of the *60. Infanterie-Division (mot.)* and a construction battalion. They had not been able to prevent the Russians from pressing forward, however, and taking possession of the established winter positions in the main line of resistance.

That gap remained the festering sore of the north front during the entire pocket battle. Once they had infiltrated, the Russians pressed on almost continuously. While in their old positions on the flanks, the friendly forces were barely attacked, the *16. Panzer-Division* had to bear the entire brunt of the defense there. That there was never a breakthrough is thanks to the unbending toughness of the soldiers of the division.

The dominant high ground was not in our hands. To take back the former main line of resistance would have required intensive preparation, strong forces, and much ammunition.

Since it was anticipated that a breakout attempt to the southwest would be started soon, the division decided not to continue the attack and to establish a new main line of resistance in the line that had been won.

On 28, 29, and 30 November, the *Kampfgruppen* organized in their sectors, turned back enemy advances, some of which were accompanied by tanks, and started the initial improvements to their positions.

The positions were not heartening. The squads were positioned on barren, flat pieces of high ground in the steppe. There were no prepared positions, just a few bunkers in the defiles. In the entire division sector there were no trees, no wood for the construction of positions and no materials for burning.

The cold weather, which had let up a bit from 25 to 27 November and had transformed the surface to slush, started to return. At night, it was between 15 and 20 degrees below zero [between 5 and -4 Fahrenheit]. During the day, the Russians prevented any type of movement within the positions by means of harassing fires. Digging in and the construction of positions were made exceedingly difficult.

Panzer-Regiment 2, under the command of *Oberst* Sieckenius, had been taken from the division. All of the armored forces of the field army had been concentrated in the southern portion of the pocket. On the march there, elements of the tank regiment got mixed up in the confusing situation around Kalatsch; new passage lines had to be established.

The 3rd Battalion of *Hauptmann* Warmbold provided some breathing space, wherever it could. Initially, it reported directly to the *XIV. Panzer-Korps* as its ready reserve. The 1st and 2nd Battalions were consolidated and placed under the command of Hauptmann Baron Freytag von Loringhoven.

From 29 November until 2 December, the two battalions were constantly employed in Dimitrejewka and Nowo-Axelandrovski as fire brigades. The hard-pressed *44. Infanterie-Division* was especially thankful for the help of the tanks, which were on hand again and again to close gaps in the lines, seal off penetrations and retake and hold lost positions by means of immediate counterattacks.

Kampfgruppe Strack established itself in a defile near Dubininski, where it was on call as the ready reserve for the western portion of the pocket. Thanks to ceaseless operations, the division rations section under *Oberzahlmeister* Rossberg was able to evacuate all of its stocks from endangered Marinowka and relocate them to Dubininski, where it established a new rations point. As a result, sixty-six truckloads of rations and uniform articles were saved for the division. That was able to keep our heads above water for some time. The rations headcount for the division was around 7,000 men; the trench strength was around 1,000. On 25 November, the field army ordered that rations be cut in half and the daily bread ration reduced to 200 grams.

Defensive Fighting from 1 to 7 December

In the meantime—and against the recommendations of all command levels of the army—the *Führer* made his decision: "Stalingrad will not be given up; the field army remains in the pocket and will be supplied from the air."

The field army submitted despite new and ever-more-serious reservations, but it also had to assume that the promise concerning aerial resupply would be kept. Sufficiently supplied, it would have been able to hold out for a long time.

It goes without saying that the first recommendation of the field army—to break out as soon as possible—was the proper one. A portion of the forces of the field army would have certainly established contact with the *4. Panzer-Armee* in the south.

At the same time, it cannot be denied that a breakout attempt would have been a very difficult and risky operation. The division itself had experienced the fact that it had not been possible on 26 November to bring up enough fuel to get the entire division across the Don and into the pocket.

The *6. Armee* would have had to advance to the south across the barren Kalmuck Steppes with limited fuel supplies. Most of the heavy weapons and vehicles would have had to been left behind; moreover, thousands of wounded soldiers would have been left for the Russians. That was very difficult for the soldiers.

The *6. Armee* had submitted and obeyed in a military fashion and perished fighting as a result. In the end, everything was lost.

But one thing remains undisputed: With its sacrifice, the field army had tied up some seventy-five large Russian formations for two months, thus preventing the torn-open Eastern front from collapsing in 1943, with millions of comrades suffering our fate. Despite that, the war was still lost. But in 1942, we still believed there would be a good end to things.

Based on Hitler's decision, the division had to also make new decisions. The positions in the north, which had previously been considered only temporary in nature, then had to held for a longer period of time. The main concern at that point was the improvement of the positions. There was no materiel in the division sector with which to accomplish that. It had to be fetched from the rubble of Stalingrad along with the all-important firewood. Fuel was only allocated in limited quantities, however. All travel had to be analyzed numerous times. It was only for the evacuation of wounded to the airfield that fuel was always made available. The division surgeon, *Oberfeldarzt* Dr. Gerlach, organized the evacuations.

The winter uniform items that had been saved by the rations section was rapidly handed out. Only the combat forces received a complete issue. But they also grew ever smaller by the day. As a result, the winter clothing had to be removed from the dead and taken from the wounded at the airfield in order to be brought back to the companies.

The unequal balance between ration headcount and combat strength was apparent. By 1 December, it was ordered that all vehicles were to be parked and all non-essential drivers to be incorporated into the fighting forces.

Despite that, the infantry needed to man the wide division sector was insufficient. Since the artillery was only provisionally operational due to the lack of ammunition, artillerymen had to had to be employed on the line with carbines and machine guns.

In Reinisch's sector, especially in the western portion, there was almost ceaseless combat activity. The Russians advanced against Hill 147.6 again and again with company-size assault detachments and tanks. The main line of resistance was penetrated twice; it was sealed off and cleared twice by means of immediate counterattacks. The heaviest fighting was on 4 and 5 December. The constant barrages by artillery, mortars, and rockets had heavy casualties as a consequence.

It was somewhat quieter in the two other sectors, but there were constant casualties there as well due to frequent barrages and raids.

On 6 and 7 December, the Russians were observed across the entire sector making preparations for an attack. The enemy's fires increased.

Our hands were tied due to the lack of ammunition. There were no heavy artillery shells at all; lighter artillery ammunition was only flown in in limited supply. The division had to limit the batteries to a consumption rate of sixteen rounds a day. For the heavy infantry guns, there were only two rounds a day available. The cutbacks were analogous in the case of other heavy weapons. Great thriftiness even had to be directed in the case of infantry weapons.

The engineer battalion of *Hauptmann* Immig was held back as the division reserve. Night after night, it went forward to the positions to lay mines and emplace obstacles.

Kampfgruppe Strack had one of its most difficult days on 6 December. It had been in the vicinity of the Pitomnik airfield ever since 1 December, serving along with a few tanks from the *24. Panzer-Division* as the immediate counterattack reserve for the western portion of the pocket. Immediate counterattacks were repeatedly conducted successfully with SPW's and tanks. The Russians were ejected from their gains and the German riflemen brought back to their old positions.

On 6 December, the fuel ran out. The *Kampfgruppe* moved on foot to take back the high ground near Baburkin. It was rapidly taken. The *Kampfgruppe* was then suddenly attacked from a defile by a superior Russian force with heavy tanks. Since neither antitank or artillery covering fire was available, the *Kampfgruppe* had to pull back. Everyone ran for his life. *Oberleutnant* von Mutius and *Leutnant* Wupper were killed. Half of the *Kampfgruppe* was wiped out. *Oberfeldwebel* Wallrawe assumed command of the remnants of the company.

Despite being considerably weakened, the *Kampfgruppe* remained the ready reserve of the western sector, along with a few tanks of the *24. Panzer-Division*. It was eventually wiped out in continued hard fighting. On 1 January 1943, it was officially dissolved.

Panzer-Regiment 2 remained employed and divided into two groups along the western and southwestern sectors of the pocket. The 3rd Battalion of the tank regiment continued to report directly to the corps. The fighting seemed to never end. The tanks were the backbone of the western sector, which had no positions or focal points in the hard-frozen steppe. The cold—usually between 20 to 30 degrees below zero [-4 to -22 Fahrenheit]—was a heavy burden for both men and materiel. Each tank battalion had an average of ten tanks operational. The capable tank mechanics made the impossible possible. Without support from the maintenance company, which was outside of the pocket, the battle damaged or mechanically disabled tanks were put back together again. Replacement parts were taken from the tanks that had been completely knocked out.

Despite superhuman performance, the front lines of the infantry divisions became ever more brittle as a result of the heavy losses, the deprivations and the shortfall of everything. Day and night, the tanks had to clear up penetrations, close gaps and serve as the backbone of the defense. Friendly losses increasingly became a cause for concern as well.

8 to 24 December: Heavy Defensive Fighting in the Northern Blocking Position; Preparations for a Breakout; Christmas

On 8 December, the anticipated attack started along the entire division sector after extensive artillery preparation. Shortly after the attack started, two Russians crossed over to our lines and betrayed the attack plans and times.

In Reinisch's sector, the attack collapsed in front of the main line of resistance. A major crisis developed in the middle sector. The Russian main effort took place there. Russian tanks broke into the positions of the motorcycle infantry and eliminated foxhole after foxhole. The men fought to the last round. Despite heavy losses, Russian infantry followed in several waves. The Russians took most of Hill 145.1 in their possession, but then their attack bogged down in the defensive fires. The *5./Artillerie-Regiment 65* was practically wiped out. The *2./Panzer-Artillerie-Regiment 16* took heavy losses. Both had been employed as infantry.

The enemy expanded his penetration to the west. In Dörnemann's sector, the Russians put down a barrage fire. They then attacked into the flank of *Panzer-Grenadier-Regiment 64* from the point of penetration. They were forced back after heavy fighting.

The infantry strength and the ammunition reserves of the divisions were too small to assure the success of a major attack by day. Therefore, the attack was shifted to the night. In a nighttime immediate counterattack, *Kampfgruppe Dörnemann* was able to clean up the situation in its sector by itself.

In Dormann's sector, a deliberate nighttime attack was planned. In Reinisch's sector, the *1./Panzer-Grenadier-Regiment 79* advanced across the railway up the southern slope of Hill 145.1. A tank company from the *24. Panzer-Division* and a few *SPW's* were brought forward. *Generalmajor* Angern, the division commander, led the attack personally in his command vehicle. *Bataillon Axe* and a platoon from *Panzer-Pionier-Bataillon 16* conducted a nighttime counterattack, eliminating the

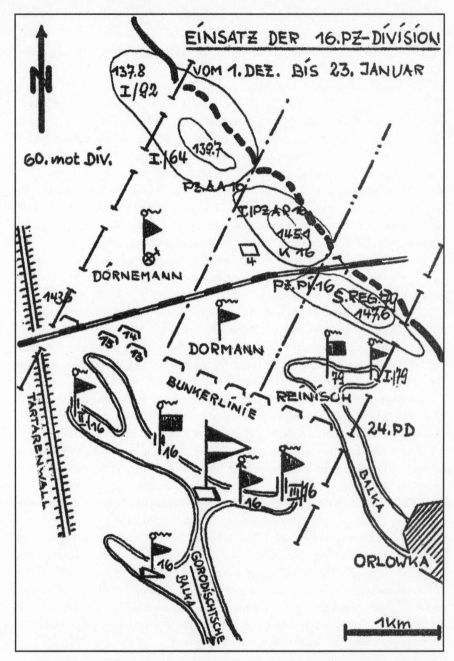

Operations of the 16. Panzer-Division, 1 December 1941–23 January 1942.

(Tatarenwall = *Tartar wall*; Bunkerlinie = *bunker line. Boundary formations:* 60. Mot Div = 60. Infanterie-Division (mot.)*; 24.PD = 24. Panzer-Division. *Sector formations: all 16. Panzer-Division, except* I./92, *which is the* I./Infanterie-Regiment 92 (mot.) *of the* 60. Infanterie-Division (mot.). I./64 = I./Schützen-Regiment 64. Pz.AA16 = Panzer-Aufklärungs-Abteilung 16. I./Pz.AR16 = I./Panzer-Artillerie-Regiment 16. K16 = Kradschützen-Bataillon 16. Pz.Pi16 = Panzer-Pionier-Bataillon 16. S.Reg79. = Schützen-Regiment 79) enemy and restoring the main line of resistance on the hill, albeit suffering heavy casualties.

The artillerymen passed their baptism of fire as infantry in a magnificent manner.

On 9, 10, and 11 December, the heavy fighting in the middle sector continued. Despite a few crises, the high ground remained in our hands.

In Reinisch's sector, there was a deep enemy penetration on the left wing on 9 December. Once again, the situation was cleaned up by means of a nighttime counterattack. The intense enemy attacks with strong artillery preparation lasted until 12 December, but they were all turned back with heavy losses for the enemy. The friendly forces were exhausted, however. The lack of rations was making itself noticeable. Valuable ammunition and equipment were lost during the enemy penetrations, since the riflemen were no longer in a position to take them with them in the deep snow as a result of their emaciation. Prisoners were taken. A piece of bread captured from them or a daily ration captured in a counterattack was the greatest victory booty of all.

The heavy Russian artillery fires along the entire front of the division lasted until 17 December. On 14 and 17 December, there were additional enemy attacks with tanks in Reinisch's sector. They collapsed in front of the positions of *Panzer-Grenadier-Regiment 79*, with heavy losses for the enemy. The attacks abated on 18 December, with the artillery fire becoming weaker.

At that point, the first concern of the division was getting replacements for the bled-white forces. A Rumanian company of about platoon strength was brought in. It was employed in Reinisch's sector as the contact forces with the *24. Panzer-Division*. After a few days, the company was no longer there. The personnel went looking for food. Additional Rumanian units were brought in; they were divided along the front and proved themselves well as ammunition runners and guards. The most important thing, however, was the fact that the Rumanians brought horses with them. They rapidly wound up in the field messes.

The division received considerable reinforcement as a result of the dissolving of the *94. Infanterie-Division*, from which our division received the remnants of two regiments. *Infanterie-Regiment 276* was reorganized and was attached to Reinisch's forces, effectively becoming the *II./Panzer-Grenadier-Regiment 79*. In a similar manner, *Infanterie-Regiment 267* was reorganized and went to *Kampfgruppe Dörnemann* as the *II./Panzer-Grenadier-Regiment 64*. A hearty comradeship was soon formed with the brave men from the Sudetenland and the Vogtland.[2]

Despite the heavy casualties, the deprivations and the intense cold, against which there was frequently no protection other than lying behind a wall of snow,

---

[2] Translator's Note. While the Sudetenland is well known, the Vogtland remains obscure, primarily because it was not a bone of contention prior to the start of World War II. The Vogtland is an ethnic region of southern and southeastern Germany (Bavaria, Saxony, and Thuringia) and portions of Bohemia in the former Czechoslovakia.

the discipline and morale of the forces was firm and determined. All of them were convinced that their liberators had already fought their way close to the pocket. Rumors permeated the air.

That almost was the case. On 13 December, the *LVII. Panzer-Korps* had moved out from the south to relieve Stalingrad and had fought its way to within sixty kilometers of the *6. Armee* by 19 December. All of the preparations had been made in the pocket for the breakout attempt, as soon as the relief force had come closer. The amount of fuel was measured again and again. It was sufficient for fifteen kilometers, perhaps thirty for the armored vehicles.

All of the armored forces of the field army had been concentrated in the south, including our *Panzer-Regiment 2*. It was intended for the northern sector to form the rearguard during the breakout attempt and follow the main body, pulling back to the south, sector-by-sector. The *16. Panzer-Division* was to continue to remain between the *24. Panzer-Division* and the *60. Infanterie-Division (mot.)*.

It was clear to the division that this would be a suicide mission. Despite that, all necessary preparations were made. Freedom was calling, even though the chances for us were small and getting smaller. Preparations were made for issuing fuel. The new units were divided among the vehicles that were still operational, and the delay lines as far as the southern edge of the pocket were established and reconnoitered. The orders for Operation *Donnerschlag* ("Thunderclap") were named after the days of the week. The remaining elements of the division, which were in the Marijinskaja-Losnoje area along the Don under the command of *Major* von Burgdorff, radioed that twenty-six trucks with rations, fuel, and replacement parts were standing by to push through to the division as soon as the first hole had been created. Unfortunately, they never reached us.

Starting on 18 December, it started to turn quieter in the north. The combat elements were able to breath a bit. Preparations were made for Christmas. The division rations point was able to distribute ten cigarettes and three cigars to each man from stocks of comfort items; the *Kampfgruppen* were allocated some spirits and 200 liters of red wine.

The field army authorized a complete ration for one day for each man of the battle groups and a complete loaf of bread for each wounded. What that meant for those who were there can only be understood by those who experienced it. The weakened men cut the bread, slice-by-slice, in an almost reverential manner.

That was the last time many felt full for many years—in most cases, forever.

The twenty-fourth of December was a sunny but cold day. It was completely quiet in the division sector. Not a round was fired. What did that portend? The units passed Christmas Eve in a happy and introspective mood. The division commander visited the men in the strongpoints. Toward 2200 hours, when the division commander and the operations officer returned from the troops, the Christmas celebration also started in the division headquarters.

25 December 1942 to 5 January 1943: New Offensives

During the night, the weather turned. Christmas morning started with gusting snow. The sound of Russian artillery, the bark of mortars and the penetrating howl of Stalin organs suddenly started booming in the middle of the storm at 0500 hours. The deep-frozen earth trembled under the impacts. We immediately knew that today signaled the start of the anticipated Russian offensive.

It slowly turned to day. In the middle of the snowstorm, you could barely see ten meters. From out of the drizzle, tank after tank suddenly appeared, among them were truckloads of Russian infantry.

The defenders fired as long as they had ammunition. The men manning the bunkers defended desperately. The casualties and losses were horrific, however; the onslaught of the enemy seemed to have no end. Whoever remained alive finally attempted to reach the infantry-gun positions somewhat to the rear.

In Dörnemann's sector, there was an 8.8-centimeter gun right up front. Even though the riflemen that had been given the mission of guarding the gun were either dead or wounded, the gun crew held out and destroyed thirteen enemy tanks in short order. The gun was blown up with its final round.

A little bit farther to the right was a platoon of the 10th Company (Air Defense). It forced the Russians to ground as a result of its rapid and well-aimed fires from its 2-centimeter guns. When one gun after the other was silenced as a result of a lack of ammunition, a bitter struggle ensued between the gun crews and the enemy infantry. The men defended to the end with their small arms. The enemy dead lay piled up in front of the guns. But in the end, the superior numbers prevailed. The last men of the *Flak* platoon fell in close combat. The time they had bought, however, was enough to enable a blocking position to be established in the infantry-gun positions. Suffering heavy casualties, the enemy forces were finally brought to a standstill there.

The Russians had also penetrated into the left-hand portion of Dörnemann's positions. The sector reserve, a few motorcycle infantry from *Kradschützen-Bataillon 16* and a company from *Artillerie-Bataillon Axe* jumped into *SPW's* and conducted an immediate counterattack. They were received by violent fires, but the attack rolled on and the Russians finally ran. The artillerymen dismounted their vehicles and were in the trenches in a few strides. Hand grenades cracked. Seventy prisoners were taken. The *Flak* position was regained. But the Russians were on Hill 139.7 in the main line of resistance and forced the riflemen into the snow as a result of their heavy defensive fires. An immediate Russian counterattack ensued; it collapsed while taking heavy fire. Both sides became entangled. Casualties mounted. It was bitterly cold. The men had been lying in the snow for hours. They had not eaten anything since early in the morning. It slowly turned dark.

At daybreak, the division brought forward whatever there was that could be brought forward. Despite that, it was clear that the friendly forces were insufficient to retake the important high ground.

The *60. Infanterie-Division (mot)* fired artillery on Hill 139.7; the *24. Panzer-Division* sent a company of tanks. The field army placed a battalion of infantry, the *III./Infanterie-Regiment 544* of the *384. Infanterie-Division* at the division's disposal. Unfortunately, it was in terrible shape. An *SPW* company came from Reinisch's sector.

Once again, because of the shortage of ammunition, the counterattack had to be postponed until the night. *Major* Dörnemann, who knew the terrain best, led. The division commander was up front. The commanding general[3] was in the division sector.

The attack started at 0200 hours on 26 December. On the right, *Leutnant* Baukenkrott inspired his men forward for the nighttime attack. It was bitterly cold and the heavens were clear. A hurricane of fire descended on and around Hill 139.7. The Russians were prepared for the attack this time. Our men's attack bogged down under the disciplined defensive fires. *Leutnant* Baukenkrott was killed. The attack by elements of the *384. Infanterie-Division* did not make any progress, either. The infantrymen were not well practiced in working with armor. Despite all the bravery, Hill 139.7 remained in Russian hands.

Morning dawned. The attack had to be called off. For the first time, the division was unable to reclaim the main line of resistance. After the loss of the bunkers, the men lay in the snow 150 meters in front of the enemy. The casualties were very heavy. Within the 2nd Battery of *Artillerie-Regiment 16*, only three *Unteroffiziere* and four *Obergefreite* were left. There were hardly any more men left in *Kradschützen-Bataillon 16* and the *I./Panzer-Grenadier-Regiment 64*. The *III./Infanterie-Regiment 544* was then employed in a defensive role in Dörnemann's sector. Once again, the watchword was building bunkers; given the temperatures, it was a matter of life or death.

Over the next few days, there was little combat activity. On the other hand, the continuous artillery fire caused additional casualties. Every night, construction parties from the signals battalion and the division headquarters went up front to help their comrades. Once again, the remaining engineers were between the lines laying mines and emplacing obstacles. For the division, it was imperative to build a reserve again. The antitank battalion, which had lost all of its guns with the exception of one 5-centimeter antitank gun, consolidated its 1st and 3rd Companies. Fifty men from the division support elements were sent forward and formed a company under the leadership of *Oberleutnant* Holtkamp. A trains company was formed out of the trains and given quick training.

On the insistence of the division, *Panzer-Regiment 2* was returned. It had already had additional heavy fighting behind it on the southern and southwestern sectors of the pocket. The tanks were sent from one operation to the other as final reserves.

The enemy air attacks became increasingly bothersome. Friendly fighter protection was missing. The *Flak* had hardly any ammunition left. But the casualty-intensive

---

[3] Translator's Note: That is, the corps commander.

fighting was borne with an eye to the great mission that had been given to the tank regiment: It was intended for it to lead the breakout wedge to the south under *Oberst* Sieckenius. Intensive preparations had been made. It had become a difficult mission: With insufficient ammunition and fuel, the approximately 100 operational tanks of the field army had to drive a fifty-kilometer-deep wedge into the superior enemy forces.

But a tanker always prefers to take on the most difficult and risky attack whenever the alternative is to crawl into the ground, be slowly chewed up by hunger, shortages and enemy artillery fire and not be able to defend yourself.

By Christmas day, the relief forces had been able to fight their way forward another few kilometers by dint of untold effort and against a powerfully numerically superior force. They were still fifty kilometers away, however.

Given those circumstances, the High Command of the Armed Forces had forbidden the breakout attempt. The field army submitted. Operation *Donnerschlag* was called off. The tanks were no longer so essential in the south. The great hope, almost realized, had to be buried. Despite all that, the forces in the field did not lose their confidence. They bore the deprivations and suffering with an admirable attitude in hopes that things would turn out all right.

Although the divisions in the southern and western sectors had been pushed back in long and difficult fighting, they had held up the enemy again and again in every position, despite the sharp cold and the lack of fuel and ammunition. They had held out heroically against the foe. But the pocket was becoming increasingly smaller. Strength was waning; cases of death through exhaustion and freezing increased.

But as long as the airfield at Pitomnik was in our hands, the heart of the field army continued to beat and there was still a glimmer of hope of surviving.

Ever since 15 December, the *Luftwaffe* could only fly at night due to the extremely heavy antiaircraft fire. The amount of logistics that came in, which had previously not even been one half of the requirement, sunk to less than a quarter. Hard words were said against the Luftwaffe, but its personnel did as much as they could. The close-by airfields had long since been lost after the collapse of the Don Front.

In the wake of the heavy losses suffered on 6 December, *Kampfgruppe Strack*, together with tanks of the *24. Panzer-Division*, had participated in additional difficult operations in the southwestern corner of the pocket. There was only a small group left, and it was disbanded on 1 January. From that point forward, *Hauptmann* Strack assumed responsibility for the infantry training of all personnel in the rear-area services. His men remained with the battle group of the *24. Panzer-Division* in the southwest.

The final days of the year had transpired in the division sector without large-scale combat operations. By means of loudspeaker propaganda, the Russians continuously tried to rob the defenders of their courage and convince them to defect. No one responded.

Russian side from east to west and into our sector. We observed it but were unable to prevent it.

Ever since the start of the year, the bread ration of 200 grams daily could only be maintained for the front-line fighters. Everyone else received only 100 grams.

Every dead horse was dug out of the snow and consumed. But there was no flour left in order to thicken the horseflesh broth. In Dörnemann's sector a few strands of wheat and sorghum that had not been harvested jutted out of the snow. They were collected and cooked. Despite that, the decline of the men's strength could no longer be stopped. The continuing casualties were a cause for concern. The division surgeon, *Oberarzt* Dr. Gerlach, tirelessly attempted to evacuate the wounded to the airfield and, through personal effort, to get them loaded on a machine. We were happy for everyone who got a "life ticket."

The division was aware of the danger that it faced. While both of the neighboring divisions were in well-established winter positions and were hardly ever attacked, the Russians had concentrated from four to five assault divisions in front of the sector of the *16. Panzer-Division*. They were attempting to force a breakthrough through from the north and press on with all means available. There was no continuous series of positions there, and the defenders were exhausted. If the casualties remained as high as they had been, then it was only a matter of time before the infantry defensive capabilities of the division would be exhausted, the lines along the high ground lost and the Russians broke through and achieved the desired splitting of the pocket from north to south.

The few days of lessened combat activity were used to improve all heavy weapons positions, bunkers and other facilities to all-round defensive positions, in order to achieve a certain depth to the defensive system.

Approximately 1,500 to 2,000 meters behind the main line of resistance throughout the division sector was a prepared bunker line. In its effectiveness, it could not be compared with the high ground to its front, but it was a backstop. Ever since Christmas, two Rumanian companies had been employed there with the mission of improving the position under the direction of the engineers and hold the line as a security force in order to prevent surprises.

Major Dormann reconnoitered in the area in between to find a blocking position along the railway in the event that that main line of resistance was lost and a pull back to the bunker position was forced. A platoon of medium antitank guns was attached to the division from the corps and formed the backbone of the antitank defense.

10 to 23 January 1943: Ultimatum and Crisis

On 9 January, the Russians had sent emissaries to the *6. Armee* with an ultimatum: "Capitulate by 1000 hours on 10 January!"

The field army turned down the offer by order of the High Command of the Armed Forces. The division discovered this chain of events after the fact. It did not

On New Year's Eve, we heard a lot of engine noise coming from tl
lines. Everyone was put on high alert. On the morning of 1 January, the dar
up again. This time, it was on the right in Reinisch's sector. Hill 147.6 disap
the haze of artillery impacts. The division was worried whether the exhau
of *Panzer-Grenadier-Regiment 79* would be able to withstand the storm. In
the attack was beaten back. *Major* Wota, the brave commander of the 1st Ba
the regiment, was the soul of the resistance.

The Russians attacked again, but again without success. In the process,
fered very high casualties. The attacks and artillery barrages continued on 2
They were turned back on that day as well.

During the night of 2–3 January, a large Russian raiding party moving
railway line penetrated into the bunkers along the boundary between Rein
Dörnemann's forces. An immediate counterattack conducted by the *3.*
Grenadier-Regiment 79 bogged down in the defensive fires. At that point
struggle for the bunkers began, which lasted three days. During the night of
uary, the bunkers were retaken, only to be lost again the following night. Tl
and the ammunition were no longer sufficient. The bunkers had to be aban
the enemy. It was the second penetration that caused a major concern. The
threat that the division could be split in two.

On 6 January, there was another dangerous penetration on Hill 147.6.
nant Günther Korte rallied his men forward and was killed at the head of hi
the penetration area. Nonetheless, the penetration was sealed off and cleaned

At that point, the combat activates died down somewhat. The 1st Com
trains and supply personnel under Holtkamp was sent forward to the ble
Kampfgruppe Reinisch. Once again, the divisional reserves that had just been
had to be committed.

The *II./Panzer-Artillerie-Regiment 16* received orders to park its remaining
ment and start reorganizing and training as an infantry formation. A 2nd Com
trains personnel was formed, this time primarily from the trains of the tank re
That was probably the last personnel that could be combed out of those forn
The men approached their coming assignment with understanding and insight

Panzer-Regiment 2 had only four operational tanks left. Since the allocat
was only sufficient for one to two kilometers, the tanks were employed as
armored pillboxes behind the high ground in the center of the sector, whi
especially threatened. The fuel basically lasted only long enough to warm
engines.

The rest of the tank regiment was consolidated under *Major* Warmbold.
reorganized and trained as infantry. For the division, it was a source of reassu
that it could form a small reserve for the time being out of those co
experienced and brave men.

Ammunition became scarcer and scarcer. Ever since 8 January, the Volg
frozen over. A never-ending stream of men and materiel crossed openly fro

bother us too much. The prospects of surviving Russian captivity were slim to the point of none at all. The division had made that discovery all too frequently. Who was going to believe the Russians? As long as there was a small chance of surviving through fighting, that was all that mattered.

Two minutes after the ultimatum expired on 10 January, all sectors of the pocket were lit up with a hurricane of fire from the Russians. In the northern sector of the pocket, the fires once again were concentrated on the sector of the *16. Panzer-Division.*

The Russians moved out to attack with five divisions; the attack was turned back. Renewed artillery preparatory fires. Once again, the attack bogged down just outside out positions thanks to the defensive fires of the infantry and the good support offered by *Major* Zinkel's *III. /Panzer-Artillerie-Regiment 16*. But the friendly losses were very heavy. The main effort of the fires was once again on the sector of *Kampfgruppe Reinisch.* The *II. /Panzer-Artillerie-Regiment 16* prepared to be employed as infantry, sending elements forward to fill the holes. *Hauptmann* Jahnke was badly wounded. *Hauptmann* Strack assumed command of the antitank forces.

The heavy artillery fires and attacks continued throughout 11 January. The enemy continued to work his way forward towards the main line of resistance and started to infiltrate into dugouts that had been emptied through fires. He continued those tactics on 12 January. There were hardly any men left up front who could prevent the breakthrough. They were tired, exhausted and half frozen; they only had submachine guns and rifles. Machine-gun ammunition was getting extremely low. The high ground could no longer be held. The division ordered a pull back to the blocking position along the rail line during the night.

The disengagement succeeded. On 13 January, a few men from *Kampfgruppe Dormann* and *Kampfgruppe Dörnemann* held out along the railway line and at the old command post for *Kampfgruppe Dörnemann.* The bunker position was occupied by elements form the *II. /Panzer-Artillerie-Regiment 16*, *Panzer-Regiment 2*, and the 2nd Trains Company. The Russians only followed hesitantly; the high ground in the left-hand portion of the division sector was in enemy hands.

Oberst Reinisch and his men continued to hold out on Hill 147.6. The hesitancy of the Russians was our salvation. A single German regiment with equivalent tank and artillery support such as the Russian divisions had would have long since wiped out the exhausted men of the *16. Panzer-Division.*

The field army placed a company composed of field army rear-area services personnel at its disposal. It was brought forward during the night of 9–10 January behind the railway embankment to screen the disengagement from the enemy up front. The men held out for a night up front, then a day and the start of another night. The men had run around in circles behind walls of snow in order to stay warm. They lost their nerves when hit by artillery. A panic broke out. The acting company commander appeared at a dead run near the field kitchen at the division headquarters. What kind of example was to be set here? What was being demanded here went well beyond what was humanly bearable. That which was accomplished by the men of the division can only be characterized by one word, a word that soldiers do not like to use: Heroism! The trains personnel of the *6. Armee* were in no position to do that. It was the only case of a human breakdown in the area of the *16. Panzer-Division*.

On 15 January, the new positions in the bunker line were occupied and ready for defense. *Kampfgruppe Reinisch* had also pulled back to there by then.

The cannoneers of the *II./Panzer-Artillerie-Regiment 16* had emplaced their guns behind walls of snow in the forward lines, right next to the dugouts. There were three to four rounds available for each one. Whenever the Russians came or a tank presented itself, two gunners ran to the gun and engaged over open sights.

After the loss of Hill 147.6, the crossroads southwest of Orlowka, over which the supply route of the division ran, was under direct fire. A new, more difficult route through the defile to Gorodischte was reconnoitered by the engineers and improved.

During the night of 15–16 January, the division commander, *Generalmajor* Angern, and the operations officer, *Oberstleutnant i.G.* Menzel, sat together to discuss the situation. The western and southern portions of the pocket had collapsed; the western wing of the neighboring division had already been practically bypassed. The powerful superiority of the Russians irresistibly pressed the small group of defenders to the east and into the ruins of Stalingrad.

On that day, the airfield at Pitomnik finally fell into Russian hands. Although the small airfield at Gumrak was still available, it was already being threatened.

The division was also at the end of its strength. Our fate was sealed. There were no more reasonable chances for survival. Should the division capitulate?

The thought was rejected. Nothing would be bettered by that. We would only pull our neighbors into the whirlpool of destruction. A capitulation could only be ordered from above as long as the division could maintain a cohesive front. Suicide? That could not be expected on moral grounds and also not ordered. Suicide presumed feelings of guilt or fear of what was to come. There could be no talk of that in the first case, and we could bear whatever was to come.

Captivity? It stood there as a slow death in front of us. Continue to pull back? That would expose the northern sector to being split up and destroyed. That could only be ordered for the entire northern blocking position. Where would we go anyway? It was only a matter of hours before the enemy was in our rear. Additional help from the corps or the field army was not to be expected.

There was little chance that individuals could make their way back to the main front. We were unaware of the big picture, but we did know that that the Caucasus Front was at least 100 kilometers away and it was continuing to pull back.

Nothing was left but to do our duty and hope for a quick end to it all. The division decided to remain where it was and not pull back any further. All of the leaders were to remain with their units. Everyone would fight from his position until the end.

The sixteenth of January brought new worries. The Russians pressed forward and put pressure against the dominant left wing of the bunker position with strong forces and tanks. The trains company was employed in Bunker 15 there. It turned back the attacks. During the night, the Russians attacked once again with strong forces. In man-to-man combat, Bunkers 13, 14, and 15 were lost.

At first light, the trains company and portions of *Kampfgruppe Dörnemann* launched an immediate counterattack. Paymasters led. The Russians were ejected. All of the bunkers were occupied again.

On 17 January, the Russians attacked again. The three bunkers were lost again. Once again, the men moved out in an immediate counterattack. Bunkers 13 and 14 could be retaken. The Russians could not be forced out of Bunker 15, the most important bunker, however. The strength of the trains company was also at an end at that point. It had performed admirably.

On 18 January, *Major* Dörnemann was badly wounded. He was almost shot blind and was driven to the airfield. We had little hope that he would be able to get out. With him we lost one of the main bulwarks of the defense.

On 19 January, the smaller bunkers, Bunkers 13 and 14, were also lost. The remnants of the trains company hunkered down along the edge of the defile to the south of Bunker 15.

On 20 and 21 January, the crisis reached a boiling point. If the Russians moved out, there would be no way to stop a breakthrough. But they did not exploit their advantage. The division continued to hold for another two days in a position that had grown desperately untenable.

The *60. Infanterie-Division (mot.)* to our left was also withdrawn even with us. At least that meant contact to the left was reestablished.

The Russians attempted to soften up the defenders by frequent and heavy artillery barrages. No large-scale attacks were initiated. Apparently, the Russians were also exhausted. Their losses must have been very heavy. Numerous attempts to penetrate the bunker line with raiding parties collapsed in the face of the defensive fires.

In the southwestern portion of the pocket, men of the division—remnants of the former *Kampfgruppe Strack*—continued to fight with personnel of the *24. Panzer-Division*, *Luftwaffe* companies, and platoons of Cossacks. They had been employed west of Karpowka ever since 2 January. They were forced back to the village in daily heavy fighting that resulted in heavy casualties. There had not been any positions available for some time. During a large attack on 10 January, Karpowka was taken from the rear. All of the vehicles, including the attached *SPW's*, were lost.

Starting on 11 January, the men no longer had any warming bunkers, any warm food and any rest. They continued to defend but they were forced back from one blocking position to the next in the direction of Stalingrad. On 14 January, they were still able to turn back a large-scale Russian attack.

Oberfeldwebel Wallrawe of *Panzer-Grenadier-Regiment 64*, the leader of those elements [detached from the division], was badly wounded, shot through the stomach.

Two of his men drug him back, placed him in a truck and then went back to the front. The truck ran out of gas. Wallrewe crawled three kilometers to the airfield. He was flown out.

He had not eaten anything for several days, and that was what saved him. Life's games were strange sometimes!

The remaining men of the *Kampfgruppe* were wiped out and lost in the ruins of Stalingrad. We heard nothing more from them.

On 23 January, a surprise order came from the corps directing all divisions along the northern sector to pull back immediately through Gorodischtsche to the western outskirts of Stalingrad. Only movement corridors were specified.

Delay lines could no longer be assigned, since the entire western and southwestern sectors had collapsed in the wake of extremely intensive enemy attacks and were fleeing back to Stalingrad. That meant a new situation. Actions needed to be taken immediately; resignation and a wrangling over our fate did not help anything. Warning orders were dispatched as soon as possible. It was only a short while until the onset of darkness. Preparations needed to be made for the destruction of all inoperable vehicles and weapons, as well as the quarters.

We were happy that we had previously reconnoitered and marked the route along the defile to Gorodischtsche. Engineers were sent forward to difficult spots. A rearguard under *Major* Dormann had to remain in contact with the enemy. It was important to deceive the enemy. If he slammed into the withdrawal before we had infiltrated into the defile, it would result in a catastrophe.

Would the troops, who had lost practically all of their experienced leaders, be able to do it? After the onset of darkness, the *Kampfgruppen* disengaged from the enemy. There was the occasional rattling of a machine gun and the occasional sound of an engine but otherwise there were no sounds and no light. We were walking on hot coals. Didn't the Russians notice anything?

Our greatest concern was the badly wounded men, who could not be transported. Ever since the airfield was lost, the field army no longer accepted them from us. They had to remain behind. Good night, comrades! May God ensure that everything happens quickly! We'll be following you shortly!

The first elements started entering the defile. The improbable happened. Maintaining magnificent discipline, the troops disengaged from the enemy without being noticed. The engineers set up booby traps in the abandoned bunkers.

It was amazing how many vehicles could suddenly move. Most of the drivers had hidden a canister of fuel in some corner or the other for the direst of emergencies. That was good, but it tossed all calculations for the traffic flow out the window. By midnight, everyone had filtered in and rolled or marched along the route in the defile towards Gorodischtsche. To the front, the rearguard continued to fire and bounded back to the southeast prior to daybreak.

We arrived in Gorodischtsche early in the morning. For the first time, the combat forces exhibited signs of dissolution. Leaderless units and scattered forces fled to the east; vehicles got jammed up; and wounded asked to be taken aboard vehicles. The route to Stalingrad was a single massed column. You could only join in and roll along. The division was in no position to lead there. The units had their objectives; the headquarters moved ahead.

New orders from the corps awaited us in Stalingrad. We were to establish a new line of resistance along the defile about one kilometer west of the city's outskirts. Once again, the division was to position itself between the *24. Panzer-Division* and the *60. Infanterie-Division (mot.)*.

The division command post was set up in the basement of a silicate factory on the western edge of the city. On 24 January, the division was once again capable of working.

The field replacement battalion of the *305. Infanterie-Division* was already in the division's sector. We were happy to accept it among our ranks. We also received a medical company form the *389. Infanterie-Division*. It was employed to our left.

The elements of the division arrived, were passed through the lines and, for the most part, placed in the right portion of the sector at the fork in the defile under the command of *Oberst* Reinisch. They had contact with the *24. Panzer-Division*. Contact was also reestablished with the *60. Infanterie-Division (mot.)* through insertion of elements of *Panzer-Regiment 2* under *Hauptmann* von Cramon.

On 25 January, a new front was established on the western edge of Stalingrad. Portions of all of the divisional elements were located. *Major* Zinkel was actually able to bring along three guns of his *III./Panzer-Artillerie-Regiment 16*. His was the only battalion of the divisional artillery that could still be employed as artillery. Two tanks were also on hand, albeit completely immobile.

Major Dormann arrived with his small and exhausted band from the rearguard. They had trundled their way for three days and nights without rations or sleep through the pathless snow. They had also brought their weapons. For the time being, the enemy was only following hesitantly.

In Reinisch's sector and in the sector of *Feld-Ersatz-Bataillon 305*, enemy thrusts were turned back. At that point, the focal point of the fighting was in the center and southern portion of the pocket.

On 23 January, the last airfield at Stalingradski had been lost.

On 24 January, the Russians punched through to the Volga for the first time from the west. By doing so, they separated the northern pocket from the main body of the *6. Armee*. The supply situation became catastrophic. Starting on 25 January, the front-line troops received only 100 grams of bread daily. Everyone else received only 50 grams.

From that point forward, the only rations received were by means of aerial canisters dropped at night. Despite keeping a sharp eye on them, it was unavoidable that starving men would pounce on them and start to devour the contents. We were out of ammunition. There was no resupply. The division formed search parties that occasionally found additional ammunition in the ruins of former positions.

On 26 January, a Rumanian regiment that was inserted into the front defected en masse to the Russians. The front collapsed in that sector.

On 27 January, the pocket was split again, this time into a center and southern portion. It would not be much longer at that point. The men's strength rapidly dwindled. In many cases, the hunger initiated apathy.

Starting on 28 January, artillery and mortar fire recommenced in our sector. The Russians attacked with tanks and infantry and were turned back. New artillery preparations; new attacks.

Once again, the *16. Panzer-Division* and the elements attached to it successfully defended. In immediate counterattacks conducted at night, the Russians, who had penetrated into the positions in some cases with tanks, were ejected. Even we did not know where we were drawing our strength from to be able to do that. In the end, it was only the instinctual feeling of not leaving the comrade next to you in the lurch. But the bloody losses soon let the number of fighting soldiers sink to an absolute minimum.

Despite the sacrifices of the doctors, the fate of the wounded was horrific. They could barely be fed. The "binder building," an apartment complex of large and still somewhat intact units in our vicinity was packed to the rafters with wounded and sick. It started receiving extremely heavy artillery fire. There were no other quarters available.

The scattered forces also had a heavy burden to bear. *Luftwaffe* elements reported to us, willing to fight as long as we provided them with something to eat. We could not give that to them, so they continued on in desperation. All of the foxholes were full of wounded, exhausted and broken men. No one could provide any help any more. The division's bunker was filled with wounded. The staff was forced into a small anteroom.

The enemy strolled in front of our positions a kilometer away and installed his weapons without interruption behind snow walls. We were able to watch everything in great detail and were unable to do a thing about it.

On 30 January, heavy artillery fire commenced. The troops bore it in stoic quiet. There wasn't enough strength left to get mad. What would have been the purpose; it was soon to be all over with anyway. The only thing that held us together still, that made life worth something was comradeship. Whoever gave that up or lost it was abandoned to nothingness.

That evening, we heard Göring's speech about our heroic demise. A bitter feeling arose in us. Our mood was anything but heroic. We did what we had to do—that was all. And dying is not as simple as the speaker would lead you to believe. It takes a while before you've come to terms with the fact that it's over. Then, however, there's a strange feeling of freedom and detachedness until you finally discover a glimmer of hope and desire to live again somewhere in the corner of your heart.

On 31 January, *Generalfeldmarschall* Paulus surrendered on the Red Square in the southern part of Stalingrad. The *16. Panzer-Division* continued to fight in the northern pocket.

On 1 February, the hour had also come for our division. Once again, there were heavy fighting and artillery fires. The division turned back enemy attacks along its front one more time. It was almost a miracle.

To the left of us, the *60. Infanterie-Division (mot.)* was overrun in the course of the day and ceased to exist by evening. There was no more outside contact. A patrol sent out reported that the Russians were involved with taking the remnants of the *60. Infanterie-Division (mot.)* prisoner. They were practically all wounded.

The Russians had achieved a deep penetration into the *24. Panzer-Division* to the right of us. There was still fighting at the tractor works. Our *Kampfgruppen* up front reported heavy losses, with no more contact to either the right or the left. The last ammunition report for the entire division listed: "In all, two crates of infantry ammunition (found); two impact fuses for light howitzers."

It was clear to all of us that things were coming to a close. But the will to live raised its head one more time. The position up front could no longer be held by evening. It was pulled back to the houses in front of the silicate factory. The operation succeeded. *Hauptmann* Schmitz and *Oberleutnant* Brendgen from *Panzer-Grenadier-Regiment 79* were on the go the entire night to direct the remnants of the regiment—barely a company—into positions. The entire northern pocket had been reduced to about 400 to 500 meters in width. There was nothing off to the left of us any more.

During the night, the Russians to the left of us pressed far into the rear area behind us. The remaining survivors of *Panzer-Nachrichten-Abteilung 16* and the division staff attempted a relief effort of sorts, inasmuch as they advanced into the former sector of the *60. Infanterie-Division (mot.)* in order to gain some breathing room. The men were scattered.

Shortly before daybreak, *Major* Dormann and some wounded put up resistance against efforts to encircle the division from the left rear. It was pointless. He only advanced into groups of wounded men and prisoners, who were being assembled by the Russians and were standing around between the Russian combat forces. He was the only one to return.

At daybreak on 2 February, the fate of the division was finally sealed. The Russians had apparently identified the focal point of the division's resistance and rolled up the remaining elements of the *Kampfgruppen* and the group around the division command post from the rear and the southwest with tanks and infantry. The last act of the drama took place at great speed. The two crates of infantry ammunition had long since been expended; the last gun had fired its last round. All of a sudden, the Russians were on top of us from two sides in the morning twilight. After a short fight, it was all over. There was no capitulation. A few powerless figures were assembled. The division had done its duty to the utmost to the very end.

By chance, the division commander, *Generalmajor* Angern, was able to make his way out through a gap on the right to the rear. He tried to make his way to the tractor works with *Oberleutnant* Brendgen, whom he ran into, since the sound of occasional firing could still be heard there. The effort did not succeed. He sent

Oberleutnant Brendgen back and decided to make his way back to the south by crossing the Volga. He was accompanied by his loyal enlisted aide. Brendgen saw him disappear behind a hill of snow.

The Russians reported on 5 February that they found the corpse of a German general while clearing the combat zone around Stalingrad. It was most likely the commander of the *16. Panzer-Division*.

It was quiet around Stalingrad. The fate of our wounded and sick men was sealed. Practically unattended by the Russians, there were hardly any who survived the next few days.

The prisoners were hauled away from the battlefield in a long column. Inadequately supplied and housed, almost half died over the next few weeks in the collection point at Beketowka and elsewhere.

In tortuous marches, another portion of the prisoners were driven through the steppes—first to the west and then to the east—without quarters in the cutting cold. The crack of a Russian submachine gun, whenever someone remained behind, was something that we grew accustomed to.

After four weeks, the remnants of that group reached the rubble of Stalingrad.

It is good that we did not know at the time what was to face us. Only about four percent of the prisoners survived the long, bitter years in Russia. The last ones did not see their homeland until thirteen years later.

General Winter. 6 December 1941: retreat at 40 below zero.

Laying cable in deep snow.

One of the fallen, frozen solid in the snow.

Attack on Chatkowo: an infantry gun mounted on a sled, 5 May 1942.

Winter along the Reseta River. At night, it dropped to 50 below (-58 Fahrenheit).

Chapter 6

HANNES, A DRIVER

Leutnant **Walter Ziehm, regimental signals officer in** *Panzergrenadier-*
Regiment 12, 4. Panzer-Division

Someone might say that a tank or an armored personnel carrier was just a machine, a device that only needed to be serviced properly so that it functioned. No . . . no . . . an armored vehicle is a living creature that, behind a rough skin, has the capacity for joy and pain. Every vehicle is different despite the same exterior dress. No man who drives it is like any other. According to his rank, he is either a *Gefreiter* or an *Obergefreiter*. Normally, he's just referred to as a driver. In reality, however, he is like a husband, who feels united with his companion in love and who has all of his attention.

When the engine growls and rumbles, the steel body of the tank trembles like a thoroughbred before a race. The hand of the driver lovingly strokes the cold steel or the rounded curves of the steering wheel. It is the secret expression of inner connectedness and spiritual kinship.

If words are spoken, then they sound like this: We're off again and the two of us . . . well, we understand one another. To the inattentive observer it could be that it only sounds like a loud cursing. That's also a part of it: Not only as a release for the tremendous tension, but also to hide it.

As with all things, there are good times and bad times for the driver. The good times are those where man and machine are on the march, in the darkness of the night, through dirt and mud or even through snow and ice and, not least of all, in deadly combat, where neither one may fail and where the concept of comradeship takes on its actual meaning. The bad times are those where everything is quiet, the front has stabilized and only short skirmishes remind one that there is still a war going on.

Drivers have abundant faces and very unique ones when they are behind the wheel. They also have chagrined ones when they also have to pull guard during quiet times.

One of those in the fraternity was Hannes. His former life back home, where he earned his daily bread as a craftsman, only seemed like a distant dream any more. At this point, the war was providing him his nourishment in accordance with much tougher rules. But that did not bother Hannes much; he did his duty and that which was demanded of him and in general behaved in accordance with the tried-and-true axiom of not standing out.

But he did stand out—as a reliable, safe driver and a tireless maintainer of his vehicle. For that reason, he was transferred to the 1st Company and took over the *SPW* of the company commander. That meant that his destiny was to always be out front.

In the summer and fall of 1942, there were no major events in the center sector, where *Panzer-Grenadier-Regiment 12* was employed, but at the beginning of 1943, the Russians once again attacked in masses in the center sector of the front. It was around the time that the drama around far-off Stalingrad was coming to a close. But we also had our share of names that would go into the history books: Kursk and Orel.

Our regiment had been reconstituted with men and materiel. It had once again become what it once was: the fire brigade at the hot spots of the battlefield. The drivers and their vehicles had a special role to play. Depending on the changing situation, the regiment would attack and give hard-pressed units some breathing room until night came and offered the opportunity to reestablish contact with neighboring forces. Under the cover of night, the regiment disappeared and moved to another assembly area, from whence it would roll out the next morning into new fighting. That meant no chance to fully rest for the drivers; they could never get forty winks.

Hannes drove point. The engine roared and the tracks rattled outside. He knew that a long snake of vehicles was following him, and he also knew that it was all up to him. The men crouched inside the vehicle with their backs turned to the direction of travel. Their heads were tucked deeply into their chests in an effort to protect themselves from the icy snowstorm. The shaking and the jogging did not prevent them from sleeping like bears, however. They would need all of their strength later. They could rest easy, since they knew they were in good hands.

In a raging snowstorm, it was an almost inhuman task to drive. Hannes held the wheel until his hands were practically paralyzed. He stared through the vision port. The snow collected around the tiny slot and robbed him of his vision. He had to open his hatch. He was then able to see the path three meters ahead of him. It was silhouetted in the honeycombed flecks of snow that hit him in the face.

His eyes burned from the strain, and the flakes of snow melted on his cheeks from the warmth that climbed up from below from the engine compartment. It was roaring with a well-mannered strength as if it wanted to say: Just go slowly, I can handle it.

Snow and sweat glistened on Hannes's face, and it almost appeared that there was a bit of joy there and the certainty that he would do it. He felt his way forward, slowly and in a measured way. He was prepared to turn the wheel around at any second, if an obstacle surfaced in the wilderness of snow. Hour after hour slipped into the night.

Hannes did not perceive any of that. He was in another world, in his world. When it started to turn light, he had covered eighty kilometers, but Hannes knew nothing of that. Once at the objective, he only stretched his stiff limbs for a moment before turning his entire attention to his companion. He knocked against the tracks and listened to the engine, ready to help like a doctor, who is checking to see whether a heart is healthy.

Ivan had penetrated into the eastern portion of Kursk and had already shot past to the north and south. In the face of the threatening encirclement, *General* Schneider had ordered the city be evacuated. Things were going according to plan. There was still a rearguard screening at the train station. Hannes was with it.

He was no longer driving an *SPW*. Instead, he was in a captured T-34, since he had once been in *Panzer-Regiment 35*. There was a howling and a cracking from the east; it was no less violent in all the other directions as well. It was time to disappear, before the last bridge—the one that led from Kursk to the west—flew into the air.

A paymaster came running up and said that there were still seven freight cars in the freight yard in the direction of the enemy that were loaded with comfort items: cigarettes, cigars, schnapps, wine, and a thousand other treats.

The phrase "comfort items" electrified the men of the rearguard. That was some sort of precious booty! But what was to be done? There was no locomotive to be seen far and wide. Moreover, the firing was getting dangerously close. There was only one thing to do Hannes drove onto the tracks with his T-34, turned onto the proper track and trotted along in reverse across the bumpy ties in the direction of the seven freight cars. He reached them, coupled them to his tank in the flash of an eye and slowly rolled west with the precious cargo.

The rearguard performed its duties with vigor and held the last bridge until the strange freight train had crossed it—and the Russians were firing with everything they had. But the seven freight cars were a terrific shield against shrapnel. Since Ivan followed vigorously and did not allow the withdrawing forces any breathing room, the bumpy ride on the ties had to be continued more than thirty-five kilometers.

It goes without saying that Hannes was massively celebrated after his Hussar raid and also received more than his share of the precious cargo.

PARTISANS: A STORY OF COEXISTENCE

Leutnant **Hans Schäufler, platoon leader in** *Panzernachrichten–Abteilung 79,* *4. Panzer-Division*

May 1943. We encountered large-scale Russian partisan formations for the first time in the large tracts of woods around Trubschewsk. In the middle of that dirty war, I received the mission of picking up five half-tracked vehicles in Brobruisk with fourteen men, a radio center and a *Kübelwagen*.[1] They had been earmarked for our signals company.

In the rear-area city on the Beresina, I reported as required with my assembled group to the military administration. After the hard winter war and all of the hulla-baloo, I had the understandable desire in my heart to spend a couple of days taking it easy at the military movie theater and the rest center.

"That's great . . . you also have a comms center with you!" the heavyset rear-area *Oberst* noticed while going through my marching orders. "I have a great place for you to set up!"

So much for the dream of having it pretty cushy. It was over before it even started. My men, who were really in need of some rest, and I were sent into a village in the middle of the woods. It was something that ended in "—witschi." Apparently, the place was swarming with partisans. It was to protect the supply route, according to the "King of the Rear." The comrades there emplaced mines nightly, blew up bridges and ambushed smaller groups of troops. They weren't going to grant these poor frontline troops a few days of rest, even though the city on the Beresina was practically bursting at the seams with rear-area soldiers.

And so we went to our —witschi[2] with a burning anger in the pit of our stom-achs. In our naiveté, we thought we could get by there at night with a simple two-man guard mount. That was a bad assumption, unfortunately. There were stirrings at night all around our houses. The guards were engaged from ambush positions. A wet-behind-the-ears *Gefreiter* found out the hard way. He was taken down with a round through the lungs.

We didn't even have a medic with us. Thus we had to evacuate the poor bastard by night through the partisans and mined roads to Brobruisk, fifteen kilometers away.

Rummms! We had rattled along about 500 meters when we ran over one of those damned mines, and we had another badly wounded man. There were figures sneaking through the vegetation everywhere. We tried a second time with a *panje* cart that we "procured," wrangled our way cross-country, bearing a grudge and the wish that the "comrades" would at least fight us openly. But they didn't do us the favor.

When we returned in the middle of the day, we saw an occasional civilian, who greeted us with spiteful grins. We would barely get another 200 meters, when we would receive fire from the rear. We simply couldn't grab the bastards; we didn't want to punish the non-guilty with the guilty. Were there, in fact, non-guilty parties

---

[1] Translator's Note. The *Kübelwagen* was the German equivalent of the American jeep and was made by Volkswagen.

[2] Translator's Note. Although the author never identifies the village, it is more than likely that he still remembered the name and did not want to have it published for fear of reprisals by Soviet authorities on the local populace, based on the events of his narrative.

here? We were beginning to doubt it. But I did not have the desire to win doubtful laurels in a fight with partisans. I only wanted to get the men entrusted to me back safe and sound from this mess.

Correspondingly, we set up three guard posts with two men each during the night in the village. They pulled guard every two hours. That meant two hours of being wide alert and two hours of leaden sleep—and then again another two hours of guard. Those kinds of nights were long.

But the few hours of sleep also came to a halt a few days later, since there was a young woman in labor in our hut. She bawled at intervals as if on a spit—one entire night, followed by one entire day. Initially, we had no sympathy for her; we even thought it was a part of the war of nerves being directed against us. Gradually, however, we grew to see that the poor woman must have been in unbelievable pain. She looked at us, silently and pleading. Should we look for another set of quarters? There was someone akin to a midwife with her. There was no Russian doctor far and wide. But we couldn't let the poor woman die like an animal!

I remembered that the doctor who had attended our two wounded in Brobruisk was a gynecologist and obstetrician in civilian life. Could we take her to Brobruisk? When I spoke with my comrades about that possibility, a few of them categorically rejected that idea: "Are we supposed to take the wife of a partisan to the doctor and then get blown up in thanks?"—"The bastards fire at us in ambush and shoot our comrades down like rabbits, and we're supposed to take their womenfolk through the woods to the city to a German doctor so they can bring more partisans into the world!"

By God, who could blame them? So I waited another little bit; the Russians didn't do anything to indicate they were going to try something. She's going to die, they said laconically. That would put an end to it, they thought.

"Who's going with me?" I asked my soldiers. Otto, my driver, spontaneously said he was willing. The father of the young woman got a *panje* cart and we set off. As we started to head cross-country, he indicated decisively that there was no danger for us along the road. All of the scoundrels had hidden themselves under a blanket!

We reached the city without incident. Only the military police caused us some problems. But, as an officer, I was able to have my way in the end; I was given a spiteful grin. I took it in stride; since it was not a daily event to see a young German *Leutnant* swinging through the countryside with a Russian woman, who was in labor. The doctor was very nice. Without any type of formalities, he promised to help. We trotted back through the partisan territory, toward —witschi.

Our vehicles still had not arrived in Brobruisk, when the young mother was brought back into the village with a robust little baby boy about a week later. The partisan war slowly melted away. Although we had been observed in our every move in the intervening time, nothing had been undertaken against us. We were given vodka and food. From that point forward, a simple two-man guard mount was sufficient.

My unit kept on radioing: where are the vehicles? No matter how much we wanted to, we were unable to pick them up at the train station, since no vehicles had come.

A new problem then surfaced. The young mother was unable to breastfeed her baby. The child needed milk, and there was no longer a single cow in the village. Rear-area German facilities and partisans had drug away all of the cows. Thus, two soldiers set out one night to a neighboring village where there was a German logistics unit in order to "procure" a milk cow so that "our" baby got something in his stomach.

The next day, a paymaster showed up with a section of military police to search for the cow, which had been stolen from the local military command headquarters, of all places. The tracks led to precisely our village, they claimed. Further, the cow had been marked with red paint, so it was easy to identify.

So I had to keep the persistent people at bay until my soldiers had hidden the mark of shame with gasoline and a lot of patience.

The milk cow had been saved! We slowly started to understand the Russian resistance. Of course, the poor people did not have a whole lot beforehand, but under the German occupation they had nothing at all.

The vehicles just did not seem to come. We were not very upset about that, since life in—witschi started to become quite comfortable. Without exception, the locals were very friendly to us. A lively trade started blooming. We traded salt for eggs and tobacco for chickens.

One night—Otto was on guard—I slept alone in the hut. Something shook me a bit, and I thought I saw light. I mechanically grabbed under my overcoat, which served as more than a pillow, for my pistol. The excited voice of Lola, the approximately fourteen-year-old daughter of our host, whispered to me: "*Leutnant* not shoot . . . man wants to speak." Something just didn't seem right. A quick glance at my wristwatch indicated that Otto would not get off of guard for another hour.

From out of the darkness, I heard a male voice that spoke Russian. And Lola translated in her broken German: "You help our people. Your soldiers not our enemy. We not your enemy. Your cars tomorrow in Brobruisk and you go. Thank you for everything! I chief of the partisans."

A cold shiver went down my spine. I tried to make it clear to him that his war and that of his men was a rotten one. He had Lola say: "We fight with the weapons we have." Was I supposed to get excited and make a fool of myself?

When he shook my hand to say good-bye, he had Lola blow out the candle ahead of time, so that I could not see his face. A piece of paper with a note on it was thrust into my hand: "If you encounter partisans sometime or get captured, note well: the watchwords are *Moskwa dwa! Moskwa dwa!*"

Suddenly, the squalid room was empty. As silently as he had come, so silently he left, my eerie nighttime guest. But I also had the note in my hand. I was unable to read the writing. I also never showed it to anyone. In any event, it had a signature, even a stamp.

What I did not want to believe then happened. The locals of the village took their leave of us in a very friendly manner. Then the radio message came that our vehicles had arrived in the rail station at Brobruisk.

The people of —witschi stood outside of their houses, as we prepared to depart. I was allowed, no, I had to take "our" son once more into my arms. We took off over the mined road, past the local military administration and the train station to our company, which was then in Narischkino near Orel. We had become somewhat richer in terms of life experiences and knowledge. The word "partisan" no longer had the severe tone in our ears.

Ten months later, we fought in the area around Baranowitschi. During a courier run at night, I was caught in a bad position by some partisans. My driver, Otto, was wounded on the other side of the road. Whenever I tried to come to his aid, bursts of sub-machine-gun fire whipped down the road. The partisans were pressing in from all sides. I might have been able to make off in the darkness by myself, but Otto desperately needed my help.

It suddenly occurred to me that I had once been given a partisan password. Although ten months had passed in the meantime and the village was a few hundred kilometers to the east, I did not want to leave anything untried in that difficult situation. I kneeled behind a bush and cried out into the night:

"Watchword: *Moskwa dwa!* Watchword: *Moskwa dwa!* "

A practically unbearable silence ensured. A figure surfaced about ten meters in front of me on the road but did not approach any closer. I also stood up hesitantly.

"Watchword: *Moskwa dwa! Charascho!* " the figure answered calmly on the road.

I carefully made my way forward a few steps, my pistol at the ready. Everything remained quiet. No rustling in the vegetation. I hastened across the road to Otto. He had a flesh wound in his back. He was able to move on his own, albeit with some difficulty. I supported him as far as the vehicle. I wanted to continue driving, but the figure signaled not to. A tire had been shot up. I had to change the wheel in the darkness. There was a deathly silence all around me. I turned the vehicle around on the road. The eerie quiet unnerved me. I then drove back without anyone taking notice of me. Otto looked at me with a horrified expression and said: "The comrades must have suddenly lost their senses." That night, on that unique night, I gained back some of my belief in mankind.

THE UNLUCKY ONES: AN INGLORIOUS TANK STORY

Gefreiter **Robert Poensgen, loader in** *Panzer-Regiment 33, 9. Panzer-Division*
This crew really existed; only the names have been changed. I no longer remember the real names; perhaps that is just as good, since the story that I relate here does not exactly belong to the hall of fame for tanking.

It was somewhere between Orel and Brjansk in the late spring of 1943. *Panzer-Regiment 33*, which bore the Viennese statue of Prinz Eugen, the noble knight, as its coat of arms, had been thoroughly reconstituted after its employment along the Shisdra in early March—both in personnel and equipment. Once again, each company had its seventeen tanks, and a 4th Company had been added to each of the two battalions, with the result that the regiment had the impressive inventory of 140 fighting vehicles, including the respective command-and-control vehicles.

That armada had to train, train, and train yet again. With the exception of the higher headquarters, not a single soul was aware of Operation *Zitadelle*, the code-name for the large-scale operation in the center sector of the front, which was intended to bring about the breakthrough to Kursk. But everyone knew and felt it in his bones that something big was afoot.

The infantry and weapons training of the good old days was replaced by crew-level tank training, the "Combat Crew Drills," as well as maintenance and combat training at platoon and company level. The drivers' training course spit out new drivers by the dozens, and the radio operators were drilled in communications procedures.

All of the trains were combed through in the search for young soldiers and personnel of more senior rank capable of combat service, who still lacked front-line experience.

And so it came to pass that *Stabsfeldwebel* Hornig, who, it seems, had always been the leader of the rations point, suddenly had to reactivate and refresh the tank training he had enjoyed in peacetime. They gave him *Unteroffizier* Schindlmair as a gunner, who, up to that point, had been the driver of a prime mover in the recovery section. It was intended for him to take *Oberschütze* Berges under his wing as far as technical training was concerned. Berges was a nineteen-year-old "newbie." Just like Baumeister, the loader, neither of them had heard a main gun fired before. Only the radio operator, *Unteroffizier* Jahn, had been in a tank previously. His downfall was more of the human kind. He was viewed from within the entire company as a self-opinionated troublemaker, which explains why he was gladly handed off to form a new crew.

That elite force took over an old *Panzer III* with a 5-centimeter main gun. From the battalion commander on down to the platoon leader, all were in agreement that initially nothing great was to be expected from this combination. It was decided at the very beginning to have Hornig and his crew move with the third wave and send them back to the trains whenever an experienced crew lost its vehicle to a mechanical problem or through enemy action.

Up to that point, Hornig's crew did everything in its power to make a name for itself within the regiment. From a technical standpoint, everything looked good thanks to the tireless efforts and drills of the gunner. Otherwise, however . . . the *Stabsfeldwebel* was not only lacking in experience, he was also lacking in mental capacity. And because his radio operator soon figured that out and did not bother to hide the fact, the work environment, as one would say today, was extremely miserable.

Whenever the platoon was supposed to swing right, it was a sure bet that Hornig would head left. If there were a spot of marshy ground somewhere, the driver would find it with deadly accuracy and drive right into it. Whenever going into position along a reverse slope, Hornig would either pull up too short, so that the gunner would have pulverized the mound of dirt in front of his nose, or pull up too far, so that he stood out like a barn door in the countryside.

The day approached where the entire regiment was supposed to demonstrate what it had learned in front of the demanding eyes of the division commander: Attack by the regiment with the two battalions on a frontage of about 1,000 meters each.

All of the details were discussed exactingly; every tank commander had to know what he was doing in his sleep: Front man; wing man right; wing man left; distance from the lead man; direction of attack; intervals to the neighboring tanks; firing halts; and everything else that was part and parcel of it.

"Make sure you once again make the point clearly to all crews," the regimental commander reminded emphatically at the last commander's conference, "that the attack terrain increasingly slopes downward after crossing Hill 211 and finally ends in a steep cut off to a creek. The slope is to be negotiated only in first gear. You will turn off to the left at the waterway and follow it along the banks of the river. The division commander will follow the attack from his radio *SPW* and observe the negotiation of the regiment across the difficult steep slope from the far bank."

The company commanders passed on those instructions and a few of their own as well. *Leutnant* Stängl buttonholed his *Stabsfeldwebel* separately: "Guide on the people in front of you! I will inform you by radio when it is time to shift down!"

The regiment offered a magnificent picture when the attack exercise took off. Tank after tank, as far as you could see. Wave after wave rolled over the unending pastureland, widely dispersed. It moved forward through fields of sunflowers and across ditches.

The fire mission came on the hilltop. Move, halt, fire, move. Small practice demolitions detonated between the tanks. It was the perfect representation of a battle. And in the middle was Hornig's tank. No rounds left his main gun, since his breechblock had jammed once more. The gunner, loader and radio operator worked together to clear the jam until the sweat was rolling down their foreheads.

Hornig dropped up and down in the turret as if on an elevator: Sometimes down below to take a look around in the fighting compartment and sometimes above to orient himself within the formation. He was completely beside himself, since his platoon leader had to have noticed for some time that something was not quite right on board once again.

Barges received no order to take a firing halt and, as a result, gradually landed up among the vehicles of the 2nd Company moving in front. He careened around restlessly and tirelessly in the middle of the combat formation. He moved in front of the right-hand tank so that it had to turn away in order to be able to fire at all.

Leutnant Stängl bellowed for all he was worth, but it was all in vain. It had to be all in vain, since the frantic Hornig had long since ripped the plug of his headphones and throat microphone out of the connector. Correspondingly, he could neither hear nor make himself understood.

In his excitement, he had also let his company get completely out of his sight and imagined he was hanging way back. He then reached the hill with the first wave.

Finally, the main gun fired again, and Hornig's tank then started firing the practice ammunition for all it was worth. The order that had been issued some time back to cease firing did not reach him, after all.

The driver thought it was terrific to be able to race ahead and bet his prestige on being able to push his way to the front. That was not too difficult, since the other vehicles had already shifted down in accordance with their orders and were moving down the steep slope very slowly.

It occurred to the *Stabsfeldwebel* in the turret—much too late, but he did think of it nonetheless—what he had been lectured about. "Slower . . . slower . . . downshift . . ." he kept yelling into his dead microphone. All of hell's curses were poured onto the driver. But he did not hear anything, since the intercom system had also been interrupted. The tank commander kicked the gunner who, in turn, kicked the driver, but it only had the effect of him speeding things up.

And then the critical juncture arrived. The slope suddenly seemed to disappear for *Obergefreiter* Berges. Far, far below, he saw the creek. On the far side of it was an extended village. Desperate, he stepped on the brake and attempted to shift down but was unable to get the gear engaged. And then things took off! The speed continued to increase, the tank swayed, the gearbox howled and the crew braced itself with its arms and legs. The empty casings, along with everything else that wasn't nailed down, danced and rolled through the fighting compartment.

Hornig's crew was the first one to reach the valley floor, well ahead of the rest of the regiment. It was practically a miracle that the tank did not do a headstand. It slammed into the road in front of it at full speed. The shock absorbers blew out and two torsion bars broke. The crew tumbled around in the fighting compartment.

That was followed by the river embankment! A mighty leap and, for a few seconds, twenty-four tons of Krupp steel flew through the air before the waves of water slapped together over Hornig's tank. But the water was not too deep. There was a crashing impact. The fighting vehicle plowed through the river like a fast boat, propelled by its own momentum. It reached the far bank and was tossed onto land, like Poseidon in his day, and covered the invited guests and the uninvited gawkers with brown water and gray muck. It was exactly the spot where the division commander and his staff had taken up position.

The unfortunate tank then plowed through the collection of vehicles and between the terrified and scattering villagers and into a garden, where it rammed the corner of the house behind it. It turned right with a jolt and then entered the kitchen without knocking. The cloud of dust that arose from the clay ovens, which received a direct hit, looked like the impact of a 15-centimeter shell. It was not until then that the enormous momentum was used up and Hornig's tank, dripping water, remained stationary, covered with dirt and pieces of wood, at the foot of the opposite embankment. A single roadwheel came spinning along behind it. The remnants of the turret stowage bin and two bundles of shelter halves swam in the creek.

Embarrassed, bleeding, and lacerated from a number of places, black and blue . . . the crew crawled out the various hatches and staggered towards the medics racing up.

The tank silently disappeared the next day to the maintenance facility. I cannot say whether it was ever possible to restore it to a combat-ready condition.

By the skin of his teeth, *Stabsfeldwebel* Hornig escaped a court-martial and soon found himself back at his rations point. The remaining men of that glorious crew survived their wounds. After a while, they were distributed among other crews back at the trains. Later on, without exception, they proved themselves.

One thing did stay with them for almost as long as there was a *Panzer-Regiment 33*. If one of them did something even a little bit out of the ordinary, then someone would point a finger at him and someone would say maliciously: "Man, there's one of those unlucky bastards . . . you know . . . the guys who . . ."

And so it came to pass that the story of the unlucky ones came to pass and remained unforgotten, unforgotten to this very day.

OPERATION CITADEL AS EXPERIENCED FROM HILL 238.1

Leutnant **Hans Schäufler, platoon leader in** *Panzer-Nachrichten-Abteilung 79,* *4. Panzer-Division*

Unternehmen Zitadelle. That was the magic formula that people had been whispering behind cupped hands into ears for weeks at the various headquarters. When they did that, their eyes also rolled.

Unternehmen Zitadelle. The forces in the field discovered at the beginning of July that that was the code word for the major pincers attack against the lead elements of the Red Army that had pressed forward from Woronesch through Kursk during the winter fighting from out of the area around Stalingrad.

"Victory at Kursk must send a signal to the entire world," according to Hitler's Operations Order No. 6.

Unternehmen Zitadelle started with the delivery of new weapons that were to be introduced into operations for the first time. On the one hand, there were the ninety *Ferdinand* tank destroyers of *Oberstleutnant* von Jungenfeld, who originally hailed from our regiment. They were giant tanks with a weight of seventy-two tons and with a tree of a gun—8.8 centimeters. It also actually had twenty centimeters of frontal armor. Then there were rumors of a remotely controlled midget tank with the witty name of *Goliath*. It was designed to create gaps in Russian minefields by means of a powerful demolition charge. In addition, there was talk of a miracle tank, the *Tiger*, which was fielded by *schwere Panzer-Abteilung 505*. It was also outfitted with an 8.8-centimeter main gun. There were also assault tanks with 15-centimeter howitzers on the chassis of *Panzer IV's*.

Unternehmen Zitadelle was the concentration of a German tank armada in a very small area; the largest the world had ever seen. It was said that there were some 900 tanks and assault guns in our sector alone.

Standing ready south of Orel for the assault was the *2. Panzer-Division*, the *9. Panzer-Division*, the *18. Panzer-Division*, and the *20. Panzer-Division*. In reserve were our *4. Panzer-Division*, the *12. Panzer-Division*, and the *10. Panzergrenadier-Division*. In addition, thee were a large number of proven infantry divisions, including the *78. Sturm-Division*.

In the area around Bjelgorod there was another strong armored force assembled for an advance to the north. It was said that there were 1,200 tanks, including a brigade of the new *Panthers*.

Unternehmen Zitadelle was intended to be the decisive battle on the Eastern front for 1943. It had been carefully planned for a long time, although it had been postponed several times. The dice would be tossed at Kursk. Based on the concentrated strength that we had, no one doubted that they would fall in our favor!

The fireworks started on 5 July. It was intended for the infantry divisions, working together with the assault gun battalions, the *Ferdinand* regiment, which included *Sturmpanzer-Abteilung 216*, *schwere Panzer-Abteilung 505*, and the remote-control companies (that is, the *Goliath* companies), to clear a path through the deeply echeloned Russian defensive system for the tanks, which would follow.

But the operation stood under an unlucky star from the very beginning. The Russians had been bombing our assembly areas for some time. According to the German Armed Forces Daily Report, 162 Russian aircraft were shot down on the first day alone. It is not too difficult to estimate the numbers of Russian bombers employed to unnerve our forces.

The engineer forces of all of the divisions were consolidated in order to create lanes through the mines, since the *Goliaths* were unable to spread fear into the hearts of the Russians.

On 6 July, the *2. Panzer-Division* and *schwere Panzer-Abteilung 505* moved out to attack. They broke through the first, second and third defensive lines, but they did not succeed in achieving the intended breakthrough to Kaschara. The Russians had apparently expected our attack at that point and at that time. After all, they had worked for months in excruciating detail to transform each meter, twenty-five kilometers in depth. Position after position had been built; antitank position after antitank position; tank after tank had been dug in on commanding high ground by the hundreds. It was also there that he had established his ready reserves, large tank formations. On a sector fifteen kilometers wide, a tank battle ensued for which there had never been an equal. It was hard and merciless.

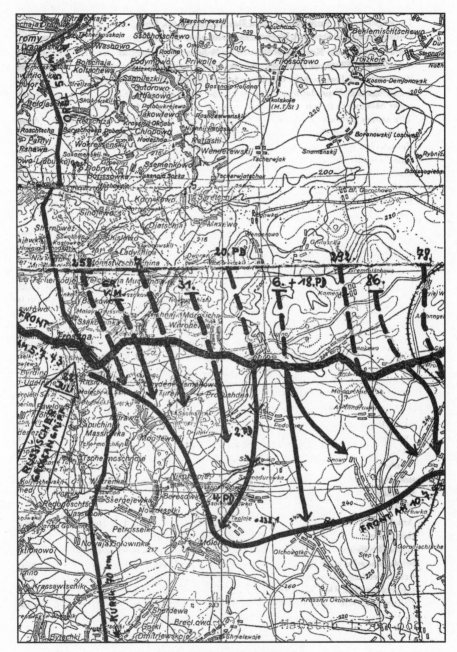

Operation Citadel (North).

(Russischer Gegenangriff = *Soviet counterattack*)

On 8 July, our *Panzer-Regiment 35* joined in the seesaw battle. Reinhard Peters participated in the attack as a young Leutnant and platoon leader and provided the following firsthand account:

0230 Hours, 8 July 1943. We received orders to move out. Teploje. Wing after wing of the *Luftwaffe* thundered above us in that direction—bombers, *Stukas*, bombers, *Stukas*. It went on for hours. All of them dropped their cargoes on the hill. The *Stukas* also attacked individual targets, the dug-in T-34's and KV-I's on the forward slope of the hill. We felt confident that nothing could go wrong after that.

Geoghi's company took the lead initially. When our tanks appeared from out of the defiles around Ssamodurowka, they were greeted by bitter tank and antitank-gun fire. We had not expected that after the gigantic employment of bombers. The first attack wave started to waver. After the next tank company also bogged down in its attack, we were up next. *Oberleutnant* Prast gave the order to attack, but he was knocked out after a couple of hundred meters. *Leutnant* Beck, the senior platoon leader, assumed command. But that was only of short duration as well. After a few minutes, his tank was also hit. Then it was my turn. I ordered: *Panzer marsch!*

But there weren't a whole lot of us; only a few vehicles were rolling next to me. *Oberfeldwebel* Allgaier identified a dug-in KV-I, one of many. With typical Swabian composure and calmness, he took up a sight picture. But the distance was still too great; the 7.5-centimter rounds ricocheted. He then fired with high-explosive rounds in front of them, so that the churned-up dust and dirt would rob the enemy of his visibility. He then used the time to get closer. He repeated the same game several times. Then he was at the spot he needed to be. With an antitank round in the breech, he waited in ambush. The dust blew away and revealed the target. Round on the way! Direct hit! It was masterful.

As a result of the hours-long bomber sorties, there was a dome of haze above us composed of dust and gunpowder and other smoke. It was as if the skies had a veil over them. My gut feeling said it must be the afternoon, but the hands on my watch barely registered 0900 hours.

By then, Petrelli's company had reached the houses in the village of Teploje at the base of the hill. Our attack had started to waver again. For the first time, we experienced the employment of the *Goliaths*, small, remotely controlled tracked vehicles with a mine charge. But it didn't work out so well. They became disabled due to mechanical problems, or they were knocked out. In any event, they did not bring success with them. We breathed easier, when *schwere Panzer-Abteilung 505* pulled up. We needed some relief and reinforcement. Just as I started observing over the commander's cupola with my binoculars, a monstrous concussion along with an ear-deafening crash knocked me off the commander's seat. They got us, I thought to myself. But all of us were in one piece, as was out tank. An explanation was quickly found. A *Tiger* had sought cover behind my *Panzer IV*. When it fired, its muzzle was barely a meter away from my open hatch. That wasn't what we had had in mind, when we knew the *Tigers* were going to be employed.

The afternoon saw an immediate counterattack by the Russians. We pulled back to the edge of the defile and waited for them. A Russian tank unit rolled about 1,000 meters away from us and off to the left. We could take it under effective flanking fire; the rest of them were taken care of by the *Tigers*. But Russian infantry also attacked at the same time. It was swarming with them in front of us. The earth-brown figures approached us through the cornfields with a stoic calm. We let them approach to within 300 meters before we gave permission to fire with machine guns and high-explosive rounds. The attack was turned back with heavy casualties.

During the night, a portion of Petrelli's company was able to get on the prized Hill 240. But the tanks had to be pulled back at first light. The enemy's key position could not be taken. It was a black day for the battalion. There were a lot of entries in the record books of the maintenance sergeants: "Total Loss: 8 July 1943, Teploje."

✠

Unternehmen Zitadelle. It meant death . . . it meant blood . . . it drove us to despair! We were running against a wall of fire and steel . . . against a forest of anti-tank guns . . . a gauntlet of artillery . . . a defensive bulwark of enemy tanks.

Unternehmen Zitadelle. It gave us a sense of dread.

The fighting between Soborowka and Ponyri raged back and forth. There were about 1,000 tanks fighting on each side. *Generalfeldmarschall* Model[3] ordered an attack with all means available.

On 10 July, our *4. Panzer-Division* rolled forward *en masse*. The division commander, *General* von Saucken, accompanied the attack in the first wave in his command-and-control vehicle, *DO 1*. He always led from the front and rallied his tankers and infantrymen to follow him. It was possible to penetrate into Teploje. During an advance, the general's vehicle collapsed the span of a bridge. It was unable to either back up or move forward. The signals officer, my friend *Leutnant* Simon, was badly wounded while looking for a way to recover the vehicle, and he remained lying out in front of the friendly lines. *Leutnant* Lecius, the division commander's aide, wanted to help him and was mortally wounded in the head in the process.

---

[3] Translator's Note. Model was the commander in chief of the northern arm of the pincers, the *9. Armee*.

By field-expedient means—a fragile voice radio connection—the division commander led his division from that exposed position. On top of the other bad luck, the division operations officer, *Oberstleutnant* Lutz, was also badly wounded at nearly the same time at the division command post. The commander of *Panzer-Aufklärungs-Abteilung 4* was killed.

That was the situation when I received the mission to establish a landline with my wire teams from the division command post near Bobrik over Hill 238.1 to the division commander in the village of Teploje. Truly a suicide mission! But the connection needed to be established, no matter the cost. Some of the heavily engaged troop elements of the division were hanging in the air.

It went relatively quickly and well as far as Hill 238.1. It goes without saying, it was on foot. A vehicle could not allow itself to be seen, since the Russians peppered everything that showed up from their commanding high ground. But there were also constant *Stuka* attacks that forced Ivan to all duck his head. Whenever that happened, we took off in a full gallop.

We found an abandoned bunker, but the gentlemen on the hill started to register on it. The battlefield switchboard had barely been set up, when they started firing with everything they had. And there was no doubt that everything was meant for us. We needed to quickly find another dwelling in the wide-ranging Russian defensive system, without being observed from above. The field wire was buried whenever that was possible.

From there, the terrain sloped gently down towards Teploje. We needed to go there with our lines. It was not too far, but it was as if we were on a silver platter. We were without cover and had to move directly to the feet of the Russians.

Out of the haze behind the houses, dark like a gigantic log, was the ridgeline where the Russians were positioned and could observe the flat-as-a-board terrain and dominate it with their weapons. They were firing at every individual man.

There was absolutely no way to take the direct route. And if it were indeed possible to get the line through unscathed, then it would be clearly impossible to maintain it. It would be interrupted all the time—shot to pieces or chewed up by tank tracks—and no line troubleshooter would get through unscathed during the day.

A Russian trench line ran along the ridgeline about a hundred meters behind us. It was filled with dead men. We crawled along on our backs with the field wire over the bloated corpses and forced our way through the collapsed trenches. Just don't raise your head above the edge of the trench, because it would start blazing from up above—and they didn't always miss their mark.

We even had some luck with our tiresome exercise under the blazingly hot July sun: We ran into a well-laid Russian wire—shot up here and there, to be sure—but basically running in our direction. We worked our way forward, meter-by-meter. It was already evening by the time we reached Teploje and the command post of *Panzergrenadier-Regiment 33*. In a defile on the slope was also the armored reconnaissance battalion, which we also connected.

While crawling back, we buried the wire in the loose dirt so as to avoid as many disruptions as possible. The landline connection with Teploje functioned, and they were happy with us for a while, even if they could only reach *Panzergrenadier-Regiment 33* via its 2nd Battalion.

I crawled into a foxhole and slept. But it wasn't long before I was nudged and someone was tugging on my sleeve. The driver of the general's vehicle in Teploje reported to me. He wanted to spend the night with us in his *DO 1*. The crew had had a horrific day; you could see it in them. Two men of the crew had been killed in the morning, *Leutnant* Simon and *Leutnant* Lecius. They had spent about six hours in front of our own lines stuck at the bridge.

"Drive off before daybreak, otherwise the Russians will shoot us to bits," I asked the driver. He promised he would. But he was back again after twenty minutes and woke me from my leaden sleep: "*Herr Leutnant*, have you seen our section leader? He disappeared all of a sudden."

I could only answer in the negative and attempt to go back to sleep.

At first light, a strange, oppressive feeling awakened me. I awoke with a start and looked around. The driver of the command vehicle cowered in front of me, starring at me. He was lost in thought; as pale as a corpse. What was wrong? "The *Unteroffizier* is dead. Yesterday, when he was guiding us in, we ran over him with our vehicle. The vehicle was on him the entire night. That's why we could never find him, even though we had looked everywhere."

I jolted upright. He was lying there, blue in the face. No visible injury. He had suffocated, since he was laying face down in the dirt. For the crew, that was the third man they had lost within fifteen hours.

"At least get out of here before it turns completely daylight!" And that's what they did, the remaining two men.

And then the circus started up again: Fighter-bombers, Stalin organs and mortar fire to wake you in the morning. The line was out! Check it out!

All of a sudden, something sprang over the earthen wall and laughed at me in a friendly manner:

"*Unteroffizier* Zöller reports back from home leave!"

"Man, Oswald, how was it at home?"

"We got married; my wife sends her greetings!"

I congratulated him heartily, since I knew his wife, Hanna, from Opladen ever since 1940, when we were stationed at Bergheim. A nice girl, who was a good match for him, the wood carver and author from Dorfprozelten am Main. He was practically bubbling over with joy: "It was great to be a human again! The world can be a really beautiful place! Damn war!" he whispered in my ear.

"But how in the world did you get back to this hellhole, Oswald?"

"I have been assigned to you," he said, reverting to the more formal form of address, since we were no longer alone, "as a troubleshooter, and we're in a bomb crater fifty meters behind you."

Would Oswald Zöller master the steep curve from a quiet vacation existence to hard front-line combat in time? That was going through my head over and over again. I initially decided not to employ him right away. We had known each other since 1938, when he arrived at our unit as a reservist. There had barely been a day since then when we hadn't seen or spoken to one another.

Around 0800 hours, I received orders from my company commander, Hauptmann Berger, to establish a direct line to *Panzergrenadier-Regiment 33* across downward-sloping open field towards Teploje. I knew it was insane, but orders were orders! We therefore loaded the necessary wire on the wire truck and intended to start laying it. But Ivan took us under aimed fire fro up on the high ground, with the result that we had to make ourselves small and uninviting. *Unteroffizier* Helmut Scheuermann muttered something to himself and Heiner Klippel cursed bitterly in the dirt.

We tried it one more time; this time starting out in a run. The fireworks intensified. We still didn't have any casualties. But if that was what we were already receiving, what would it be like when we got close to the village? And then once the line was in? It wouldn't remain intact any longer than five minutes. And then try to troubleshoot the line while being served up on a platter. That was craziness!

I rang up *Hauptmann* Berger one more time. I pressed upon him the observations I had just made and my conclusions, and I attempted to divert the crazy operation. But apparently they didn't see it that way in the rear. The orders were repeated back to me in a very sharp tone.

We made another attempt. Result: our switchboard was covered with such intense mortar fire that we had to set it up elsewhere, since all of the lines, including the very low router, had been shot to pieces.

"What's going on with the line?" my company commander inquired when the line going back to the rear had been reestablished.

"This is all nuts. Why don't you take a look at this place yourself!" I shouted indignantly into the receiver.

"That's exactly what I'm going to do, and I'll be there right away!" was his brusque response.

It didn't take too long before I heard a motorcycle come rattling up. It was parked behind the high ground in the defile. And who was it that came marching towards me, upright, and without any particular hurry—with no Russian firing at the 1.9-meter figure—my company commander, Berger!

Those Russians were dirty bastards! They had plastered us the entire day whenever we poked a hand out of the trench. My company commander, that guy, however, he was allowed to walk upright and casually across the open terrain. No doubt to curse us cowardly dogs afterward.

And I was right: "What kind of nonsense are you spewing, Schäufler? Everything is quiet at this location." He spit out the words maliciously.

"Just wait . . ." I threatened. So we waited. But there was only an occasional shell, so that we did not fall asleep. Otherwise, nothing stirred.

It ticked us off to no end that Ivan had chosen that moment not to fire. But I was able to partially bring my company commander over to my side in light of the completely open and coverless terrain. And I was firmly determined not to lay that line, since I was convinced that none of my men would be alive after a day—and for nothing, nothing at all.

Completely unscathed, Berger took rattled off with his motorcycle. He had left his cigarettes with us—not a bad sign.

He had barely disappeared behind the high ground, when the fireworks started up again: *Ratsch—bummm, ratsch—bummm, uiii, uiii, uiii, crack, crack, crack . . .*

The line to the rear and the line going forward were all gone.

Naumann, from Zöller's section, came running forward. I thought he might ask what line they had to troubleshoot. But he sputtered: "*Unteroffizier* Zöller has been badly wounded. Shrapnel in the upper thigh . . . in the groin."

I wanted to race over to my friend. Naumann held me back by the sleeve. They were already on the way to the main clearing station with him. An *SPW* in the defile had taken Zöller immediately.

I was very depressed. I was no longer able to do anything for him. Of all people, it had to be Oswald during his very first operation at the front after returning from home leave. I had to get to him.

The wire mission at Teploje was called off. The front was pulled back a bit; the attack called off. I was able to get away for a few hours and received permission from my company commander to go to the main clearing station.

The directional sign pointed towards a patch of woods. At the edge of the woods, I saw a large burial field. I wanted to take a quick look to see who had gotten it whom I had known. The first grave I approached: "*Unteroffizier* Oswald Zöller. Killed 11 July 1943."

I stood there at the mound as if struck dead. I heard him whisper one more time: "Shitty war!"

I picked some flowers and placed a large wreath on his grave.

Deep in thought, I went from cross to cross. Everywhere: "Killed on 10 or 11 July 1943 at Teploje." There were hundreds of fresh graves, all from our combat units: *Panzer-Regiment 35, Panzergrenadier-Regiment 33, Panzerjäger-Abteilung 49, Panzer-Pionier-Bataillon 79, Panzernachrichten-Abteilung 79, Panzer-Artillerie-Regiment 103*, and *Panzer-Aufklärungs-Abteilung 4*.

On the way back, I stopped for a short while at the company command post, reported to Hauptmann Berger, and stated that Zöller had died at the main clearing station. My company commander took my hand, without saying a word. He knew that I was very close to Oswald Zöller: "Hannes, write his wife right away . . . you know her, after all."

That letter was damned hard, since I had not yet come to terms with Oswald's death myself. How was I supposed to say the inconceivable to an unsuspecting young wife?

A distraught letter from *Frau* Hanna Zöller reached me after three weeks. Her world had collapsed. She also made bitter accusations against me, because I had left her husband, my friend Oswald, die alone.

I tried to console her as well as I could in a lengthy letter. But the comfort seemed a bit tawdry, when you were still alive. Moreover, I could have spared myself the effort. After a few weeks, the letter came back, unopened, with a notice: "*Frau* Hanne Zöller was killed in a bombing raid on Cologne."

Ski patrol in no-man's-land, March 1942.

As pleased as punch—tankers on sleds, February 1942.

Ruling the roost at night was this obsolete Soviet biplane, which conducted nuisance raids over the German front lines and rear areas, summer 1942. The Landser had a number of names for it, including "sewing machine," "road yodeler," "night owl," and "duty NCO."

Outside of Mzensk again, fall 1942. The Soviets approach at first light. Everything depends on the nameless foot soldier in the trench.

Panzergrenadier-Regiment 12 *(of the* 4. Panzer-Division*) turned back more than one assault.*

Chapter 7

ENCIRCLED

***Obergefreiter* Walter Berger, squad leader in *Panzergrenadier-Regiment 10,*
*9. Panzer-Division***

Late summer 1943, near Orel. Every experienced frontline soldier is familiar with
the oppressive feeling that comes whenever it becomes clear, whether officially
announced or unofficially making its way through the rumor mill: We're encircled.

A mood sinks in from one heart to the next like that of a poor sinner on his
way to the gallows. The knees turn weak and your guts start to rebel. It crawls high
from the belly, turns the stomach on its ear and ties up the throat.

When we were advancing, it wasn't so bad. We could still count on someone
hacking us out as long as we held out long enough.

At that point, however, when we started withdrawing, being encircled meant
something else: Remaining where you were, hopelessly lost, in front of your own
lines, which were growing ever more distant.

The Russians made a decisive psychological mistake in those instances, which
no doubt cost them a lot of time and blood. Without restraint, they took out their
pent-up rage on the German, who fell into their hands.

The chances of surviving if taken prisoner were, therefore, slim. Even if you
weren't finished off right away with a bullet to the back of the skull—because you
were unable to march due to a wound or the Russians had just received an order to
that effect from above or they just wanted to have a little fun—you at least faced years
of existence as a slave and the hardest form of drudgery with the underlying thought
that could not be suppressed: Who knew whether you would be able to hold out?

For that reason, even the thought of being taken prisoner was something that
could not be entertained for any of us. Even in the most hopeless situation, you
would rather face any risk than to surrender yourself to death and perdition at the
hands of the Russians.

But being "encircled" was not quite the same as being taken "captive." Some
troop elements gained considerable practice over the course of time in being

encircled and then breaking out or exfiltrating. But you never knew with certainty from one mousetrap to the next, whether there was once again going to be a whole large enough to escape through.

There were too many Stalingrads, where there was no way to slide out any more, where all the experience in the world was to no avail. That knowledge had also started to make the rounds.

At the end of August 1943, we found ourselves in that situation again. The large-scale German offensive at Kursk and Orel had been turned around. At that point, the Russians were attacking with all of their vast superiority in numbers, and our forces had to pull back, step-by-step.

When we had been attacking, we had reached a line on a ridgeline. We had bogged down there and had clawed our way into the earth. We had established provisional positions, set up communications trenches and dugouts, which we improved over the course of time and aspired to reinforce. We were there for three or four weeks under very uneasy conditions.

After the heavy losses of the past few weeks, our company consisted primarily of wet-behind-the-ears youths—kids from Thuringia and the Rhineland, from Austria and Upper Silesia, a motley crew—who had only been sent to us recently from the replacement depot. They were inadequately trained and without combat experience. Most of them didn't know what to do and lost their heads at every opportunity.

At the same time, the thinned-out ranks of noncommissioned officers had been filled up with gray-templed *Stabsfeldwebel*, who had been combed out of some rear-area duty station.

Correspondingly, they may have been masters of supply and administration, but they didn't understand anything at all about combat leadership. There was a terrific lack of noncommissioned officers with frontline experience, which led to the fact that the couple of "old warriors"—*Unteroffiziere* and *Obergefreite*—had to lead patrols almost nightly along with the couple of reliable personnel that we still had.

In that situation, the Russians were of less concern to us than our own men, who, trembling with excitement, fired at everything that crawled around in front, even after they had been informed a good ten times that it was a friendly patrol.

My "colleague" from the 2nd Platoon, who had been sent out the same night I had been, was killed in such a manner when he returned—shot through the heart—while we, 300 meters farther to the left, had our noses in the muck and had to practice taking full cover while taking fire from our own trenches.

But it was not only in the dark of night that we experienced those happy events. They also occurred in broad daylight. One time, it occurred to the Russians to attack our positions with tanks and no infantry support. Their fires were landing somewhere in the area, but not in our positions, in any event. No need to get excited. Despite that, a right proper panic broke out among our green troops. They wanted nothing more than to climb out of their trenches and run away across the open, coverless terrain—and into certain death.

I apparently did the only proper thing, which they also understood: I started to scream and rage, pounding them with my fist and kicking them with my feet on their shoulders, backs, and asses. The result was that the herd of rabbits was apparently more afraid of a raging old *Obergefreiter* than a dozen T-34's. They curled up small and inconspicuously in the bottoms of the trenches and allowed the rattling wave of tanks roll past them.

A hot reception was prepared for the red tanks further to the rear by the antitank guns and *Flak*. Just three or four of them returned in a panic towards the evening hours. So there you go! But nerves also took a certain type of combat leadership!

One long-range round reached a tank in the middle of no-man's-land in front of us. It burned out.

Each night, the Russians established a nest in the blackened-red steel ruins with snipers, turning our life in the trenches miserable. All efforts during the day to blow the tank apart from rearward positions failed. The nest was empty each time. Finally, orders arrived: Engineers would blow up the tank; Berger's squad would provide security.

We set up around the tank, but not too far from it, since no one knew for sure where Ivan was running around in the middle of darkest night. Whenever everything was prepared and ready to blow, we would be informed in time. That's what we were told. That's what we also believed.

We lay there and waited in a night devoid of stars and a moon. We couldn't see anything at all. Behind us, around the tank ruins, there was the occasional sound of ill-define work noises. They gradually grew lighter and then disappeared. So . . . that meant we would be relieved shortly. We waited. They must have been working on the firing charge. Nothing could be heard. Man, they were taking a long time! Why was it taking so long? Just don't become impatient! Listen up! Don't just listen to the rear. Listen to the front, as well. Over there, where Ivan had to be . . . suddenly, a volcanic eruption behind us. A thunderclap, as if the earth were about to burst. Lightning and heat and a blast wave! And then nothing but a hail of steel remnants raining down, from the size of a walnut to the size of a desk. So . . . that had been the demolition! There was a lot of demo, in any event.

The upshot: one dead man and a number of slightly wounded. I myself got away with a few scuffs and bruises.

The explanation: After having prepared the tank for demolition, the engineers had run into one of my "men" while tapping around in the darkness and informed him that everything was ready. At that point, the engineers scrambled to get out of there. I could have screamed! But what purpose would it have served if I had had the bastard brought before a court-martial? The poor guy hadn't had a clue what he was causing. The dead man would not have been brought back to life, and the others would not have been any better off either.

And then one terrible day, it happened: we were encircled! That on top of everything else. And with the personnel we had! The "old hands" had already had an inkling of that for several days. It had become fairly quiet in front of our sector, while the sounds of heavy fighting could be heard off to the right and left of us, sounds which gradually moved more and more into the deep flank. Very suspicious! We didn't talk about it with our men or with our *Stabsfeldwebel* superiors, but we did think it. And then everyone knew what we had already guessed.

One day of stomach aches but otherwise it was amazingly—or suspiciously—quiet. Then, toward evening: All platoon and squad leaders to the company commander!

We discovered that the Russians were not only sitting behind us to the left in Staroiwanowskoje and off to the right in Malakonstantinowka, but also in between! Our *Kampfgruppe*—the battalion and attachments—was to snake its way through there that night in column formation. All security measures were to be followed—et cetera, so forth and so on. The rearguard was to be our company and our platoon, the 3rd Platoon, within the company! That meant that from the onset of darkness until midnight my squad—ten men, or what one was calling a "man" at the time—had to "hold" or "screen" a sector of at least 700 meters.

Perhaps Ivan wouldn't attack, but he could be allowed to get any bad thoughts or to observe anything. That meant fire, fire some more and then fire even more after that! I hammered it into each one of my little men. Fire with everything you had. There was enough ammunition there, more than enough. Whatever we fired off didn't have to be taken back.

We would fire and then run back and forth like madmen, so that there were muzzle flashes and the sounds of gunfire at the same volume all over the place. I grabbed a machine gun for myself.

And then the circus started: Three or four short bursts into the fog in the direction of the enemy, then shoulder the spray gun and take off at a pig's trot a hundred meters to the left. Then: *rrrrt—rrrrt—rrrrt*. Off to the right. More fireworks and then run. In between, my little men fired unaimed individual rounds in the raven-black night. They had become courageous through the commotion I had caused.

The intent was for Ivan to gradually come to the conclusion that a battle-hungry battalion of slightly crazed Teutons was getting ready for the final victory at that location!

On occasion, the fire was returned. Gradually, it grew longer and more frequent. But the enemy's fire was also fired in the blind, most likely out of nervousness and for demonstrative purposes. Russian mortars also joined in, but thanks to the wide dispersion of our one and a half men, there was little chance of getting hit. Occasionally, they covered a trench position with concentrated fire, where the machine gun had just finished rattling. It was at exactly at that spot that there was no one to be seen far and wide.

Doing something like that was actually enjoyable and raised one's spirits and self-confidence. In the end, despite the unenviable position, we were almost in a sporty mood.

It soon turned midnight, and the order came for us to also pull back. While my men slipped past me, I rattled out some more fire with what I had left. Then, I also toddled off.

We marched for the rest of the night: Silently, on our toes, beating hearts, straining not to lose sight of the man in front of us. Just don't lose contact; make as few sounds as possible. And none of that was very easy, since the night was as dark as a raven and the terrain under our probing feet full of surprises.

Occasionally, there was the sound of engines, tracked vehicles and distant shouts off to the left or right of us. Much further away was firing and signal flares. We hunched over and crept along, past black rows of bushes. Keep on going, always keep on going. Once in a while, there was a short halt and strained listening. Whispered orders . . . and then off we went again.

Finally, hours later, with the sun already edging up on the horizon behind us, there were outposts. They were from another unit. They addressed us quietly and directed us where to go.

At that point we knew: we had been lucky one more time—we were through!

WITH THE *4. PANZER-DIVISION* FROM THE OKA TO THE BERESINA

Leutnant **Hans Schäufler, platoon leader in** *Panzernachrichten-Abteilung 79,* *4. Panzer-Division*

19 July 1943. The Russians had turned the tables. On 12 July and then again on 15 July, they launched successful offensives from the northeast and east in the direction of the Orel salient. *Unternehmen Zitadelle* was called off without fanfare. One of the propaganda statements issued was that Karatschew was already under the fire of Russian tanks.

Our *Panzer-Aufklärungs-Abteilung 4* was pulled out of the line and sent there as expeditiously as possible. The remaining combat elements of the *4. Panzer-Division* were moved during the night of 17–18 July into the area around Gostoml and prepared for offensive operations.

Ivan had broken through there along the Trossna–Kromy road in the direction of Orel. His intent was to sew the sack shut. The highest state of alert was ordered. *Major* von Cossel's tank battalion was already heavily engaged and had sealed off the point of penetration to a certain extent. It was directed that we throw the enemy forces that had penetrated back to the south.

I received orders to establish a wire network in the assembly area, set up a switchboard at a suitable location, connect the tank battalion, *Panzergrenadier-Regiment 33* and *Panzergrenadier-Regiment 12*, and organize troubleshooting parties for the entire area.[1] That sounds so simple and uncomplicated.

---

[1] Translator's Note. The signals officer was often used to locate the sites for the command posts, especially since he would best recognize the optimum locations for maintaining radio traffic.

When we got over the hill south of Gostoml, the air started to get filled with lead. There was a crashing and a howling to the right and left of us. The cross-country vehicle zoomed off at speed toward the valley floor. We tried to "hide" the wire nice and neatly in the roadside ditch, since there would otherwise be hell to pay when troubleshooting. The Russians were firing at every individual man. They were sitting on the hill across from us and had a great view.

Some good soul had taken good care of us. Not too far from the road, we found foxholes at regular intervals, in which we set up testing stations for the troubleshooters. The poor devils could catch their breath there, whenever the fireworks started.

We got to a built-up area that wasn't printed on my map. It consisted of five squalid straw huts. But we also found an ideal bunker there, a magnificent edifice—many thanks to whoever it was who once built such a durable structure. It was in a fruit orchard between the row of houses and the edge of the woods. Thank God, the line also worked. We just couldn't keep the vehicle there. Ivan would have made short work of it. We unloaded the equipment and the spools of wire and sent the vehicle back with our good wishes across the crest of the hill that was drawing so much enemy fire. The driver made a running start and disappeared in a cloud of dust.

We knew the larger villages in the area from 1941: Kromy, Ssewsk, Dmitrowsk. A dignified military cemetery at the end of the fruit orchard reminded us of the fighting from back then.

I reconnoitered the command posts of the 12th and the 33rd there on the valley floor and one for the tank battalion at the fruit orchard right on the road on the opposite slope. We quickly laid the wires. They were not too long.

In the case of mortar fire, you quickly learned how to run, even in blistering heat. The steel helmet always slammed maliciously into the bridge of your nose and then back on your neck. The field telephone you had slung around you bounced against the small of your back whenever you had to hit the deck. Sweat and dust glued your eyes shut. Despite that, we were happy when *Oberst* von der Damerau, *Oberst* Dr. Mauss and *Major* von Cossel were able to report back to the division: "Assembly area occupied!"

Dog-tired, we slipped across the terrain back to the switchboard and memorized all of the lines for the units. When we finally collapsed exhausted in the bunker, the bewitched line to the division command post was interrupted. It was no wonder, since the Russians were firing continuously on the damned crest behind us. The troubleshooters raced along the road, cursing. The line to the rear was barely sparking, when one to the front was interrupted. The operations officer was no longer able to get through to the command posts, and he chewed my ass royally. All of my people were constantly on the go. Despite that, it was only a matter of minutes before another line was down. Wherever the Russian mortars spared our lines, it was torn up by tanks, antitank elements and the *SPW's* of the mechanized infantry. It was enough to make you despair!

20 July. We set up redundant lines to the front, but we had more work as a result, since both lines had to be maintained. Whenever the Russians started a barrage fire, all of the lines were destroyed at the same time anyway—and that was the spot where they were needed the most. We trotted here and there, but the Russians fired and fired and fired at the spots were our wires were laid.

My company commander, *Hauptmann* Berger, was apparently being hard pressed by the new operations officer, *Oberstleutnant* Kühnlein, since he was constantly on my case. Finally, I had an idea: the line was destroyed some 100 meters from the division communications center. Consequently, my troubleshooters had to run back eight kilometers, with the result that they were missing up front for four hours. I used the situation to cut a deal: Troubleshooting in the rear would go as far forward as the damned crest of the hill. I was successful.

"You need to take a look at the fireworks up here some time," I lashed out in my excitement to my company commander. He was willing to do it, apparently, to get out of the line of fire of the operations officer.

"If he does come," *Unteroffizier* Kordes said, "then the Russians won't fire a shot. That guy's always got the luck!"

Ivan launched another immediate counterattack and sprayed the entire area with mortar fire and Stalin organs.

All of a sudden, there was a rattling at the entrance to the bunker. It was turning dark. Someone was fumbling around out there. An endlessly long frame fell through the curtain, gasping for air: "Hannes, I'll be damned!"

Hard to believe, but it was actually *Hauptmann* Berger, the high-bred one, the well-groomed one. At that point, he was encrusted in dirt and dust. His uniform was drenched in sweat and in tatters. His helmet was pushed back to the nape of his neck. He struggled for air and for words. We quickly patted him down. He was in one piece and not wounded. Slowly, his wits came back to him.

"Man!" was all he would say as he straightened out his limbs. No accusations, no ass chewing, just a gradual catching of breath. And the Russians peppered the fruit orchard monotonously. We grinned to one another.

"I threw the motorcycle in the ditch along the road topside," he reported. One man went out silently and brought it back after half an hour.

"That was the revenge of the Russians for Teploje. You had also come forward to us there. It was at that moment, though, that the Russians barely fired a round, and you said gloatingly: What's going on with you? It's quiet in your sector!" I couldn't restrain myself. I had to say it to him. He looked somewhat crestfallen, our company commander. Generally, he was a great guy!

A few hours later, the road leading to the rear was only released for combat vehicles during the day. Things went better for our lines at that point, since the Russians only had infrequent reason to fire on the road.

22 July 1943. A blood-red sky announced the rise of the sun. Thick banks of fog crawled out of the valley floor. Here and there, a lonely machine gun bellowed. The

hills in front of us had changed hands several times over the last few days. There were muzzle flashes at short intervals over the crest. Rounds howled and thundered across our valley on their way out and burst somewhere to our rear. Our artillery responded from the rear. The cannon duel started. High in the air, a reconnaissance aircraft swam in silvery tones.

A clearing station had been established in a bunker along the road. The wounded could no longer be brought back in ambulances during the day along the road that could be observed by the enemy. It was intended for *SPW's* to do that. They lined up like a funeral procession along the roads and next to the houses. If Russian aircraft saw them, then so help us God!

Acting to calm things down, both regiments reported: "No serious incidents." *Major* von Cossel reported: "Twenty-seven tanks operational."

Orders came from the division: "Take the last hill occupied by the Russians!" Artillery and aerial support were promised.

Our guns started to fire: *Uiii—uiii—uiii. Crack—crack—crack*. The fountains of earth rose skyward up top on the hill. A few *Stukas* dove like vultures. We could openly see the Russians run. The grenadiers worked their way to the crest, slowly but steadily. "The attack is moving swiftly forward," *Oberst* von Damerau reported.

0910 hours. Von Damerau had hardly said that, when it started to rumble mightily over in the Russian sector: *Blub—blub—blub blub blub blub blub*. A terrific wave of fire descended into the creek bed in front of us and along the slope, right in the middle of the attacking grenadiers. A grayish yellow cloud arose in front of us, as if created by a hurricane. Heavy rounds whistled overhead and crashed into the artillery positions behind us. It sounded like a frog concert, except with a lot of horrible tones. Shrapnel, tree limbs and clumps of earth hissed through our fruit orchard. Wounded cried out in a way that went to the marrow of your bones: "Meddicccc!" During all of this, we were only on the outskirts, better said, we were between two storms of iron and gunpowder.

The remnants of our lines were hanging up above in the crowns of the trees. We involuntarily tucked in our heads in the corner of the bunker. Dirt tickled in through the cracks in the bunker ceiling and clumps of dirt sprang out of the bunker walls. We were primarily receiving mortar fire in the fruit orchard.

The Russian mortar fire raged for more than thirty minutes along the valley floor. It was like . . . well, there was no comparison. We had never experienced anything like it. There certainly couldn't be anything left alive.

Then . . . just a sporadic *crack—crack—crack* and the entire spookiness was over in an instant. The troubleshooters wanted to crawl out on their backs with a roll of wire. I saw it in their eyes: They would gladly do it, just to get away from there . . . to have something to do . . . just not to have to sit there idly.

"Listen up . . . stay here . . . something's going to happen, otherwise the Russians would not have put on the fireworks!"

I only had the lines going to the rear be fixed, since there was at least a foxhole every couple of hundred meters. After ten minutes, they reported: "Fifteen patches . . . we're continuing to look!"

At that point, there was a familiar rattle and clatter over the woods and, high in the air, a metallic singing. Our hearts literally sank, since our nerves were not exactly steady at that moment. Russian fighter-bombers, Il-2's, jumped over the treetops. That would not have been so bad, but there were condensation trails high in the sky—bombers, some thirty, sixty, ninety of them before we stopped counting, since the monsters were headed directly for us. They silently opened their bomb bays, and the bombs came tumbling out. Thousands of them. Directly down towards us. It was no wonder, given the collection of vehicles along the road and next to the huts! Ice-cold chills ran down our backs. There was a howling and a hissing in the air—it hissed for a damned long time. Were the bombs passing by us? Then there was a crash, as if the entire world was collapsing. The bunker shook as if in the middle of an earthquake. Some bombs must have fallen extremely close by. But where were the remaining thousand? We risked a look through the entryway. Outside, a mighty cloud of smoke and dust rose to the heavens above the road. It was swiftly borne away by a wind from the east. That can't be true! There was another wave coming. Once again, there was another couple of thousand bombs hanging in the air above us. They landed in the monster cloud of smoke and dust, and they landed in the open field, where there was not a single soul. Five, maybe six waves dropped their loads. All of them tossed their destructive cargo into the gigantic cloud, which was growing higher and larger and which was being driven away from us by the wind. Only a few "strays" fell in the vicinity of the built-up area.

You need luck in a war—or an enemy who aims poorly. In our relief, we almost forgot that there were still Russian fighter-bombers and fighters. We were quickly reminded of them, when the tree limbs started flying around our ears and the strafing churned up the earth around us. The Il-2's came back to take a look at their colleague's efforts. Cannons bellowed and rockets hissed from the wings. The rockets life a trail of fire in the churned-up air and detonated all around us. Here and there, there was the hoarse cry: "Medddiccc!"

Soldiers ran around, bent over, to help their comrades, whom they pulled under cover. We hastened over to the clearing station. Like a miracle, nothing happened to anyone. But they begged us to get them out of that hell. We helped place them in the vehicles that were standing by, since a whole lot more capacity would be needed there soon. They were being drug in from all sides, the torn-up bodies.

The division signaled us. Despite everything, the troubleshooters had fixed the line. The tank battalion was desperately needed. I almost said: Don't make me laugh!

"*Leutnant* Schäufler, remain on the phone. The ops officer wants to talk to you." I prepared myself for an ass-chewing.

But he only gave me a mission that made my blood run cold: "There was a radio message that just arrived from the 35th that said that *Major* von Cossel had been killed. Check to see whether that's true!"

I rushed out and down into the valley floor and then up the hill to the command post of the 35th. It was whistling on all sides. The earth-brown figures of the Russians were pressing down from the hill here and there and our few soldiers pulled back. Scattered soldiers stood around, leaderless. There were dead by the dozens in the creek bottomland and half way up the hill. Wounded were bent over and moaning, mutually helping ne another. They asked for the location of the clearing station and were carried or drug by comrades.

I stumbled over fresh shell craters and fell into bomb craters. I caught my breath in a hole that was still smoking and ran until my lungs were bursting. Everywhere I turned, it looked like a horrific natural catastrophe.

Distraught faces gazed at me accusingly. I could not, was not allowed to help. I had to go on. When I got to the first tank, I asked for *Major* von Cossel. A *Panzerschütze* pointed forward, wordlessly. A combat vehicle was burning there. I found Stabsarzt Dr. Schulz-Merkel, the "tank doctor," in conversation with *Oberleutnant* Burkhardt. I wanted to ask where I could see the commander, but I dropped it when I saw the serious but determined look on the two men. I then looked at the burnt-out command vehicle.

"Is he dead?" Just a nod of the head.

Major von Cossel—as a young *Oberleutnant*, he had already received the Knight's Cross—was considered a blessed one within the division. His courage, his calmness, and his manner of leading—all of that was something special with him. He had been there from the beginning—as a tank commander, as a platoon leader, as a company commander and, finally, as a battalion commander. In 1941, when the bridges over the Dnjepr went up in the air under his advancing tanks and he had been reported as dead, he held out with a few of his men for days on end right under the firing ports of the Russian bunkers. Only slightly worse for wear, he then returned to his company under the eyes of the nonplussed Russians by swimming across the Dnjepr. And he did it as if nothing at all had happened.

At that point, when he was no longer there, everyone seemed a bit flustered. I took in a few bits of conversation. No company commander wanted to, could leave his company in the lurch in that situation. They were also all men, who had been with their bunch since their days as recruits. Their men trusted them. It was at moments like those that they really felt their obligations as soldiers. Perhaps that was the secret of our "bear battalion," of its exemplary comradeship and the unrestrained recognition of its successes.

To those not in the know, it might appear odd that the company commanders asked the "tank doctor," as those in the 35th called him, to assume command of the battalion. He did not whine. He did not say much. He mounted the command tank of the battalion adjutant and rushed out front, ahead of his tankers.

The combat vehicles moved to a reverse-slope position so as to interdict the attack of the Russians, which also appeared to be leaderless at the moment. I ran back, since the firing started up again and grew stronger.

The line to the rear was intact. I could send my report: "*Major* von Cossel dead. *Stabsarzt* Dr. Schulz-Merkel is leading the tank battalion." *Oberstleutnant* Kühnlein probably didn't believe his ears, since he had only been with the *4. Panzer-Division* for a week. I had to repeat my report.

We set up a new line to the 12th. There was basically nothing left of the original two. The report that went through was bad news: "The regimental commander, *Oberst* von Damerau, was killed by a direct hit from a mortar round. The battalion command posts were overrun by the Russians. A large portion of the company commanders and platoon leaders have been wounded or killed. The forces are scattered and, in many cases, without leaders."

It couldn't get any worse!

The Russians were attacking along the entire division sector. They were already pressing into the valley floor along the creek bottomland to the east of our switchboard. If the Russians did not encounter appreciable resistance in the next few minutes, the way to Orel would be open for them.

We then saw the first T-34's coming. They pushed along on both sides of the road and down the hill farther to the west in large groups. What were we to do at that point? The Russians tanks had already bypassed us on the right and were engaging the artillery positions to our rear, which were desperately defending themselves. There didn't appear to be anything in front of us any more. The last wounded men raced off in the *SPW's*, already taking tank fire.

Then Russian bombers came back. That's all we had been missing up to that point. This time, they would not miss their targets. In addition, there was rifle fire coming from the woods nearby to the east of us.

I don't know who came up with the idea, but we ran into the cornfield, which was as tall as a man, in the direction of the woods occupied by the Russians. We assumed that the bombers would not drop their loads so close to their own people. Although the Russian riflemen took us under fire, they could not see or hit us in the cornfield. We hoped they didn't come up with the brilliant idea of attacking us from out of the woods. In any event, we looked for a covered escape route, since we were not going to put up much of a defense with our little pistols.

At that point, the Russian tanks helped us, since they apparently thought the fire coming from the woods was intended for them. In any event, they took the edge of the woods under main-gun fire.

Schulz-Merkel's tanks then pressed in from the right. The Russians were so busy with the woods, that they neither saw nor heard anything. *Rumms—rumms.* Two T-34's were burning. *Rumms—rumms.* Another one went up. The tanks moved back along the road at full speed and left another one burning behind. We couldn't believe our luck, and we crawled back to our switchboard bunker. It was pretty exciting there. A hit from a bomb had wiped out the wire hub. The fruit orchard had been churned up by the bombs and looked like it was in fallow. Most of the trees had been snapped in two. The bunker proper had half collapsed.

While we patched together some of the lines and completely replaced the others, we saw a lurid spectacle in front of us in the bottomland. One T-34 after the other flamed up. The tanks of Schulz-Merkel were cleaning up. They were positioned so well behind a swell in the ground, that they Russians could not return fire. They raced up the slope as if the devil himself was behind them.

As we started to get our heads above water, we ground our way through the valley and patched lines together with fingers that were still jittery. The tanks had torn them up with their tracks. Further off in the distance, the antitank forces also appeared to be cleaning up.

The first reports of success started to come through our lines. The 33rd reported that *Panzerjäger-Abteilung 49* had knocked out sixteen enemy tanks, ten of them to the gun crew of a single *Feldwebel*. Our tank battalion reported: "Sixty-two T-34's knocked out to one complete loss of our own."

Ivan had missed his golden opportunity. The latch on the door to Orel had been bolted shut again. By and large, the old positions had been retaken. Here and there, there was still fighting. A gigantic cloud of haze, smoke and dust hung over the valley floor, arching its way from slope to slope and from friend to foe.

The sun hung over the woods like a blood-red ball of fire and disappeared into the grayish yellow cloud to the west. A difficult day was slowly coming to an end, a day on which the decision stood on razor's edge a few times. The onset of night was accompanied by fires all around us. It slowly turned quiet on the slopes in front of us.

Wassil and Ivan: Two *Hiwis* Work Their Way through the Russian Lines
25 July 1943. I can't swear with certainty whether the date is correct; my calendar got terribly messed up in the flurry of events.

All of a sudden, things were hot everywhere at the same time in the center sector of the Eastern Front. The rumor mill stated that the Russians intended on reducing the Orel salient. In any event, it was an absolute certainty that the Russians were marching west to the south of us. And there wasn't a soul there that could slow them up.

Because of that, we were directed that night to disengage head over heels from the enemy, even though the front was holding in our sector, despite heavy losses and fighting. To the west of us, however, the Russians had overrun the 7. *Infanterie-Division* and were pressing in the direction of Kromy. There was heavy firing from the high ground around Trossna, because they wanted the major road to Kromy, no matter what it took, in order to bring their heavy weapons forward.

Our telephone lines were constantly shot up. Everyone who had a set of legs was out patching lines, since orders needed to be issued for the upcoming nighttime operation. Reports from the front concerning the current enemy situation chased one another. I soon had my ass chewed by the operations officer; then I was screamed at by the leaders of the rearguards. With the fireworks going on, the lines only lasted a matter of minutes.

The first units were already pulling back in accordance with their orders. The Russians immediately pursued. In the vicinity of our switchboard, the Russian machine guns were already rattling. Patrols were already firing to our rear. You could unmistakably hear the unpleasant clatter of Russian submachine guns. Correspondingly, we received orders from the company commander to close shop immediately and pull back to the forward communications center for the division at the ridgeline south of Gostoml.

It was then my main concern to notify and intercept the troubleshooters, who were still racing through the night. If only they would report in! I was sitting on hot coals. At the same time, we had to screen in the direction of the edge of the woods, since Ivan was already on line with us about 150 meters away. At the moment, he didn't feel confident enough to come closer, because the mechanized infantry were pulling back along the main road. But it wouldn't last too long, before we would be all by ourselves on the valley floor.

Hauptmann Berger pressed and pressed: "Hannes, get out of there . . . now . . . hurry up!"

But two men were still on the line to the 33rd. Who were they? *Unteroffizier* Theo Kordes thought it over: "Wassil and . . . and Ivan." Those were two volunteers, that is, former soldiers of the Red Army, who were now serving voluntarily with our armored signals battalion and were called, in a somewhat deprecating manner, *Hiwis*. It had always been our wont that a German soldier was to accompany a *Hiwi*. In the confusion, both of them had rushed out without orders, since there was otherwise no one available.

Wassil was the longest serving of our Russians. He had been with us since July 1941. He came from darkest Siberia. I personally took him prisoner along the Dnjepr, and he categorically declared at the time: I remain, chief! And he did. He sort of wrote the rulebook, since his type of service had not been foreseen in the military regulations. Even when the battalion commander gave him an order, he would reply in his casual way: "I ask *Leutnant, charascho?*"

I only needed to wink to him with my eyes and he took off. But not before that happened. The *Unteroffiziere* and the all-powerful *Obergefreite* vented their spleen on him, since he showed them no respect. That didn't bother him in the least. I was for him his friend and not his superior, because if had not sent him to the prisoner-of-war camp, and he felt himself not to be the subordinate of anybody. He had no thoughts about either Hitler or Stalin. The only thing that counted to him was his Siberian homeland and his *mamuschka*. Politics and war were *schisko jedno*. In other words: he couldn't give a shit.

Ivan, who had been with the company since December 1941, was a Ukrainian from Kiev. He was uncomplicated and Wassil's vassal. Ivan loved a well-filled mess tin and a full bottle of vodka. He also could care less about war and politics.

In a nutshell, both of them were fine fellows who felt at ease in our company, despite occasional friction.

Both of them were off alone in the night, and no one could say to them that we were pulling back. They were wandering though the hail of lead, probably already in the middle of the pursuing Russians, since it there was already firing coming danger-ously close from the valley floor up to us. Damn it to hell!

"Let's go . . . right now!" my company commander thundered to me through the landline. We fired white signal flares. Nothing stirred. Just a pair of Russian mor-tars diverted their attention to us in a very unfriendly manner.

"The two Russians have long since scrammed, otherwise they'd be crazy," Karl Möhler said. He was probably right. Despite that, I had the line to the 33rd be trans-ferred to the new switchboard. We couldn't retrieve the wire anyway, since the vehicle had long since disappeared.

We worked our way back through ripe cornfields to the north along the line. We patched it, wherever the tanks had torn it up or it had been shot up, even though Heiner Klippel secretly thought I was a crazy man—I could see it in his eyes.

Toward 0200 hours, we collapsed dog tired in the communications center on the rise outside of the village of Gostoml. We could get a few hours of sleep. But I was unable to rest. Nothing had been heard from Wassil and Ivan there, either.

I simply did not want to believe that the two of them had disappeared without a trace, even though they would have been stupid not to exploit the favorable opportunity. For that reason, I remained sitting at the field telephone, even though my eyes were closing due to over exhaustion, and waited. I was waiting for a miracle, despite my best instincts.

Occasionally, I listened into the line. All of a sudden, the phone rang, very slightly, almost shyly. It only rang a tiny bit. I put the receiver to my ear: "Wassil?"

"*Ja*. Here Wassil, *Leutnant!*"

"Where are you?"

"At the old switchboard."

"Man alive! You're far behind the Russian lines."

"I know, *Leutnant*. Where are we supposed to come?"

Although I was pleased as punch, what was I supposed to tell him? Should I defy logic and tell the two of them to race towards a miserable death and advise them to fight their way through the Russian lines? The Russian soldiers would draw and quarter them if the two of them fell into their hands in German uniforms. In the end, I was also responsible for their lives. Perhaps not to the army command, but at least to their mothers. Wassil had always blindly trusted me up to that point.

The chances of getting through the tightly held lines were pretty slim, in my opinion. Wassil waited patiently. I could only think it; I couldn't say it: Get Russian uniforms as quickly as possible. There are so many dead around there. Remain where you are. You'll be able to come up with a convincing cover story!

Wassil probably had an inkling of what I was thinking. He spoke hesitantly, but resolutely: "We not here remain. We to our company come back!"

"Run along the line. Run, but be careful, Wassil! We are ion the high ground two hours away from you. We are waiting for you! *Charascho?*"

And then the line went dead. Down in the bottomland, between Wassil and me, I heard T-34's rumbling.

"My company," Wassil had said proudly. My company? We were an assortment of colorfully assembled men after four years of war, sorted by chance and constantly being reorganized due to death and wounds. A miserable, ill-disciplined group, if you went by bourgeois viewpoints. Half-finished theology students and prisoners paroled for service at the front; young teachers and hard-bitten truck drivers; and Red Army men who, preferred to remain with us as volunteers to going to a prisoner-of-war camp. There were also a couple of war-weary *Obergefreite* left who did not like the *Hiwis*, because they did not understand what they didn't want to understand. But, strangely enough, they all stayed together, despite the differing backgrounds and despite the unavoidable friction. The wounded forewent hospitals and homeland so as not to lose the company. The convalescents at the replacement depot had only one wish: To return to this company. What was the secret of those bonds formed in war? That question bore down on me again and again that night. A peacetime garrison *Unteroffizier* would be shocked to be in our company. Wassil, the Russian, said it full of pride a few kilometers behind the Russian lines: "My company!" And he, the former Red Army man, was willing to put his life on the line and the life of his comrade to find his way back to a bunch of Germans. Besides those of us who were at the front, who would ever be able to understand that?

I could only have an inkling of the answer. I certainly couldn't give one. Moreover, I could no longer stay upright on my legs. I let myself collapse and slept the sleep of exhaustion into what would certainly be another difficult day.

Toward 0500 hours, something poked and prodded at me. I only perceived it in my subconscious initially. But then it continued persistently. Sleepy eyed and hesitantly, I tried to gather my wits about me. I forced myself to open my eyes. Then I jumped up with a shock.

Filthy and with sprays of blood on his face, Wassil was standing in front of me. Right behind him was Ivan. I first thought I was dreaming. Wassil's eyes were beaming from out of his broad face. He came to attention, something that had never before been part of his ritual: "Wassil and Ivan back from troubleshooting!"

Despite all military tradition, I had to hug him for a short time. It could not have been otherwise: "Man, Wassil . . . great, Ivan!"

I could see that both of them had a Russian automatic rifle with a scope, even though they were otherwise always unarmed—for understandable reasons. I didn't ask them, however, how they had made it through the lines, so as not to embarrass them. I also saw how Wassil quickly wiped his eyes with the back of his hand.

The order arrived to pull back in anticipation of new operations, further to the west. And I was noticeably proud of "my company" and of the undisciplined horde, as our top sergeant, Walter Schubery, the super-Prussian guard soldier from Saxony, called it.

I knew that he loved these men in his own reserved way and that he only called them that so that no one would notice.

I also knew that we would not offer a pretty picture on the parade ground with our band of brothers, formed by fate and infused with comradeship. It was a band that was ruled by other laws, in which the leaders were formed, hard and inexorably, from the enlisted personnel, in which the influence of a superior is only accepted in combat by example.

Across the Dessna by the Skin of Our Teeth

Beginning of September 1943. We simply were unable to bring the Russian forces, which had moved out of the Kursk salient to the south of us to attack west, to a standstill. They had moved primarily in pathless terrain outside of the area of operations of our field army. Our *4. Panzer-Division* was employed on the extreme outer wing of Army Group Center. It was soon helping out in the sectors of the *7. Infanterie-Division*, the *31. Infanterie-Division*, the *102. Infanterie-Division*, and the *258. Infanterie-Division*. The advance of the Russians to the south inevitably led to a slow but constant pulling back of the front in the Orel salient. Brjansk, Karatschew, Orel, Kromy, and Dmitrowsk were lost. At the moment, we were fighting for Nowgorod Ssewersk.

We prayed daily: "Dear God, please don't let the sun shine!" The constant marches on completely jammed roads were an invitation to the numerically superior Russian air force to strafe and bomb to the point where it was more than humans could bear.

Whenever we saw that the sun was rising in a clear, cloudless sky, we knew we were done. It was especially the poor devils in the signals units who had to travel back and forth day-in and day-out on those goddamned roads that the Russian fighter-bombers owned. The fact that we also had an air force was something that we had long forgotten.

I solved that problem in my own way.

In the course of the withdrawal movements from one line of defense to the next and the racing around from one hot spot to the next, certain "rearguard specialists" had gradually emerged. I inherited that with my landline section within *Panzer-nachrichten-Abteilung 79*.

Generally, we had to establish a telephone contact point for the nighttime disengagement of our combat elements. It had to be maintained until the last combat vehicle had passed. Then, at first light, we worked our way through on the byways, along with the rearguards of the grenadiers, the engineers and *Panzer-Aufklärungs-Abteilung 4*. It goes without saying, that there were occasional clashes with Russian advance guards and patrols. At times, the Russians attempted to cut us off. The biggest danger was of losing your way in the darkness. Damage to a vehicle could also be deadly.

My signaleers and I preferred those dangers to sitting around on stopped-up roads and having to wait until a Russian bomb fell on our heads or an Il-2 turned us into sieves. Maybe I just had a phobia against aircraft ever since Trossna.

Over the course of time, we developed a special technique. We established our switchboard a little bit off to the side of the main stream of traffic. That ensured that the combat vehicles would not tear up the wire and that the damned aircraft wound not be on top of us. Initially, we selected the bottom of deep defiles for that purpose. The area we were in was filled with them. But then we were stuck. Rainfall during the night made it impossible even for tracked vehicles to go up the sides. The Russians knew that as well, and they cut off our route, since they could count on the fingers of one hand, where we had to come out. Moreover, at the bottom of a deep defile, you had no way you could observe.

We then stuck our switchboard like a swallow's nest high up on the slope. If possible, on the east side. Before the Russian flyers could see us, they had already raced past us. The shrapnel from the bombs that fell in the bottom of the defile did not reach us up top. Whenever things got hot, we could immediately take off.

The rearguards of the other troop elements liked linking up with us, since they knew that the signals people were generally well informed about the situation and the platoon leader of the telephone troop had to know the best way to the rear based on the laying of the wire, which made it easier to find in the darkness. Up to that point, I had not disappointed my combat comrades in the rearguard. As a result, we had become quite the crew during the many days of withdrawals and had our own rules and customs. No one left anyone else in a bind.

Based on my calculations, it had to be 7 September. I wouldn't swear to it, however. Any sense of the calendar had been lost during that hard defensive fighting and the race against death and captivity.

I had the mission of laying wire to Leskii from the forward divisional communications center. Once there, I was to establish a switchboard and hook up troop elements that arrived there. Leskii is an extended village that is not too far from the Dessna but on the eastern side. A thick, marshy patch of woods extended between the village and the river to the north and the west.

We placed the wire very properly along the edge of the woods, high in the branches, so that we would be spared unnecessary wire patching. We allowed ourselves time.

We set up our switchboard in a relatively nicely maintained house, somewhat away from the village. It was in the woods, surrounded by huge sunflower plants. The line was working, and the clarity outstanding. What else could we want? No aircraft, no Russians, no sounds of fighting far and wide—but also no German forces to be found anywhere.

For that reason, we went through the village. I was only able to pick out an armored-car section from *Panzer-Aufklärungs-Abteilung 4* and a few military police. The leader of the bunch was *Feldwebel* Limmer, whom I had known forever. He was from Munich. A fellow full of life and with a somewhat rough sense of humor. That said, he was a great comrade, and someone you could depend on. We were in the motorized rifle brigade headquarters together in 1941.

There was not a single civilian in the village: no woman, no child, not even a chicken. Although that seemed a bit strange to us, it didn't bother us in the least. The deathly quiet was something we liked after all of the hubbub.

It turned noon. We allowed ourselves a pan full of fried potatoes. It turned afternoon. *Panzer-Grenadier-Regiment 33* did not appear; *Panzer-Aufklärungs-Abteilung 4* did not cross our path. The forward division communications center had nothing to say in that regard. No one had shown up there either yet.

I went to see Limmer in the middle of the village. He had been directed to pass and direct the fighting forces. He didn't have the foggiest idea, either. He adamantly promised to let us know immediately, if anything should happen.

It continued to be completely peaceful around us. We hadn't experienced a day like that for a long time. But something just didn't seem right to me. Something just didn't add up.

Only the wire connected us with the rest of the world. But no one was checking in there, either. Two linemen waddled off in the direction of the wood line. When they were about 300 meters from the village, they started receiving heavy rifle fire from the woods. Things could get interesting!

At the same time, *Feldwebel* Limmer raced into the yard, standing on an armored car: "Call up the division immediately! The Russians are moving on the village and towards the Dessna!"

"Damn! There's nothing on the line . . . it's dead!"

"Then we need to move back right away. There's no getting out going forward." Wimmer said, in his youthful naiveté.

"Back . . . to the north? Something's not right there. Listen for yourself? That can't be kept quiet."

The armored car moved in the direction of the linemen, who were still lying on their stomachs, and took the edge of the woods under fire with his automatic weapons. The two men jumped back across the meadow.

I took a hard look at the map with my old friend Limmer. There was no getting through to the north. We could forget about that. The Russians were approaching

Leskii and the Dessna from the east via the village of Ssobitsch. There were throngs of them. There wasn't any way for us to get out any more!

"We need to get to the river before the Russians!" I yelled at Limmer in an epiphany. He nodded deliberately.

We threw the switchboard, the field telephones and the small stuff into our *Muli*, an Opel *Blitz* with tracks.[2] The armored car came racing up with the two linemen. Limmer tossed them out and packed his military police inside. And off we went, like the fire department. Every second was more precious than gold. That was crystal clear to everyone.

While en route, we picked up the other armored car. The Russians had already reached the first houses as we were leaving the village. We had to literally clear our path with fire. The two armored cars fired with everything they had. In exemplary comradeship, Limmer covered our unarmored vehicle with his armored plate. The fire started coming from behind. As a result, I went forward. The hellish journey continued. The vehicles disappeared in a gigantic cloud of dust.

The Russian trucks were already a good bit ahead of us on a parallel route. They moved towards the river very carefully, however. We could therefore assume that the crossing point was still in German hands. My driver got everything he could out of the vehicle. The field trail was piss poor. I was tossed from one corner of the vehicle to the next. The telephone operators were on the vehicle floor, looking for cover behind the toolboxes, since we were also receiving fire from the south. The two armored cars fired in support. They probably could not hit much in the bumpy ride, but the firing calmed our nerves and it apparently unsettled the Russians considerably, since they jumped out of their trucks and went into position. Damn! They were firing at us with antitank rifles. I heard the smacking against the running gear quite clearly. Just as long as they didn't fire higher!

"Quicker . . . quicker!"

Ivan slowly started to lag behind us. A bridge appeared at the end of our path. Hurra! We had not expected to be so lucky. The Russians usually made do on smaller roads with fords.

We shifted up and move forward to the rear as fast as we could! We then started receiving fire from the bridge. It came directly towards us, with tracers.

"Oh, you dumb bastards!"

I fired a white signal flare for recognition. The firing increased, but it did not hit us. Had the Russians already occupied the west bank of the Dessna? That would be the crowning moment of this goat screw! No . . . there were white signal flares coming from there. But why were the dummies firing at us? Well, right past us? They were then joined in by antitank guns. And more and more white signal flares, which

---

[2] Editor's Note. The *Maultier* ("mule") was a half-track conversion of the standard three-ton supply truck and used extensively on the Eastern Front. The load capacity was reduced to two tons.

were visibly aimed towards the north. That could not be missed. That had to mean something?

A concerto of antitank guns kicked in. The fire trails went from the far bank to the south and into a cloud of dust. Damn it to hell! T-34's were rumbling up. That's the only thing we had been missing! At that point, they were about 800 meters from us. An ice-cold chill ran down my spine and sweat was dripping out of all of my pores up front.

No matter what it took, we needed to find the shortest route to the bridge, which was about 300 meters in front of us, if some of us wanted to have the chance to make it to the other side in one piece. But our comrades over there apparently wanted to block that route with their fire, even though they had to have realized that we were also German and in dire straits. What was the meaning of the circus?

Mad as hell, I moved off the road and into a field, since our friends were firing red signal flares along the road and white ones—over and over again—toward the north. I decided to swing out wide, until those guys were happy. Thank God that the pastureland had firm ground underneath so that the eight-wheeled armored cars did not bottom out. I could literally see the face of Limmer behind the vision slot and how he called me an idiot, because I did not see the road to the bridge. The two armored cars had not been firing for some time, since our comrades at the bridge had assumed that duty.

The pastureland started turning difficult, however. I turned back towards the bridge to the south. On the other side, they apparently no longer had anything against that tactic. Just keep your nerves until the end! Another 200 meters! Another 100 meters. The three T-34's were also dangerously close by then, but they were fighting it out with the antitank guns.

We then just had to get past the roadside ditch. Following that, we raced across the bumpy bridge surface. The T-34's were also storming towards the bridge. We churned our way through the sand on the far bank and up the slope. Then there was a horrible cracking sound behind us . . . once . . . twice . . . three times. Then there was a jolt that lifted us off of our seats. But the vehicle was still intact. Beams, boards and stones flew into the air in a black cloud.

We looked to take cover behind a group of German soldiers to catch our breath. Damn! That was close! They all looked at us stupidly, or so it seemed to us. We certainly didn't have much to offer them, either.

"Well, well, well," *Unteroffizier* Kordes said. "I believe I need schnapps." He fished around in his secret bag for the "emergency rations" and conjured up a well-preserved bottle of real French cognac.

"No, don't open it up. *Feldwebel* Limmer needs to get it. He got us out of there," Small Reinhardt said. He grabbed the bottle and went to the armored car, all of us following. But he had all of his hatches closed. I banged on the armor plating with my fist. The turret hatch opened.

"Limmer gets this," I said. I wanted to hand up the bottle, but no one would take it from me. I looked into the fighting compartment. *Feldwebel* Limmer was stretched out on the floor. Blood was flowing from his mouth. I then saw two small holes in the armor. Antitank rifle rounds that had penetrated! Limmer didn't need schnapps any more.

"He was killed immediately," the *Unteroffizier* said with a voice that was cracking a bit. "Give your bottle to the comrades on the bridge. They earned it."

Bridge, right! There was no longer any bridge. And then we found out exactly what had happened.

The Russians had broken through all of a sudden. The operations of our division towards the south had to be called off. *Panzergrenadier-Regiment 12* had to move as rapidly as possible, swinging out wide to the north, to be committed on the west bank of the Dessna, so as to prevent the Russian forces that had raced forward from taking the Dessna bridge in a *coup de main*. It was directed that all of the crossing points were to be blown up and the approach routes mined. Minutes before they wanted to set the charges, they saw us racing towards them like crazy men, directly towards the minefield. That's why they attempted with all the means at their disposal to divert us from moving straight ahead. They used signal flares . . . they used tracers . . . they even used antitank guns. They delayed the approach of the three T-34's; otherwise, the guys would have been to the bridge before us and would have been more than happy to blow us to smithereens from there.

As had been intended, two of the T-34's than ran over mines. The third one went up in the air with the bridge.

"Many thanks . . . many thanks . . . you guys really deserve the bottle of schnapps."

We then shoveled a grave for our comrade Limmer in the soft sand of the banks of the Dessna and decorated it profusely with an armful of yellow sunflowers.

We moved slowly back to the division command post, which was said to be in Nowgorod-Ssewersk.

The game went on: Forward comrades . . . march to the rear . . . march!"

Dry Bread in the Wet Triangle

Beginning of October 1943. Along the southern flank of Field Army Group Center, far to our rear in the so-called "wet triangle," a marshy area formed by the confluence of the Pripjet and the Dnjepr, the Russians were attempting with all means available to form a bridgehead on the west bank.

Correspondingly, our *4. Panzer-Division* was pulled out of the line and ordered there as expeditiously as possible. The reconnaissance battalion raced ahead, our tanks rumbled on behind it and the *SPW* battalions of the mechanized infantry followed.

We encountered the Russians in a movement to contact. We hardly saw any German soldiers. The reconnaissance battalion screened to the north. On the first attempt, the tanks of *Hauptmann* Fritz Rudolf Schulz, together with the 1st Battalion of *Panzergrenadier-Regiment 12*, took Karpilowka and Kopatschi. Ivan fled back across the Pripjet and left weapons and equipment lying about. He also left behind several hundred dug-in mines. Many prisoners were taken.

I received the mission of laying wire from Karpilowka to Kopatschi, hooking up all of the troop elements, establishing a combat switchboard and continuing to follow the attack.

When we arrived in Kopatschi, Schulz's *Kampfgruppe* had already turned north and was attacking the village of Nagorzy. We found the perfect example of a bunker, which *Organization Todt*[3] had probably built once at its leisure. Uh oh! There were still Russians in it. They looked at us mystified and surrendered without resistance. We disarmed them.

We set up a switchboard and established contact with the 2nd Battalion of the 12th. At the time, we could not take the three prisoners back, so they remained with us at the switchboard.

Red signal flares announced that Ivan was pressing across the Pripjet with strong forces to the north of us. That was why the 2nd Battalion had been employed against Nagorzy. Only weak forces remained in Kopatschi, when we received orders to extend our lines to the edge of Nagorzy.

Just as we started to work on the extension, our first sergeant, *Hauptwachtmeister* Walter Schubert, brought us rations: Cans of meat, sausage and fish and army bread. Although we were as hungry as bears, we had neither the time or desire to eat at that point. We therefore left the food for the entire platoon at the switchboard in Kopatschi.

Russian machine-gun fire was rattling from the dunes along the banks. We tossed down the wire from the rear of the moving *SPW* and quickly reached the southern edge of Nagorzy. All hell had broken out there. There was the sound of heavy fighting coming from the village. The Russians were covering us with artillery and mortar fire. Even though all of the advance elements of the division were committed there, the attack did not make any progress. Ivan kept sending new forces across the river.

All of a sudden, there was wild firing to our rear. Red signal flares rose in the fall skies, which were filled with gray smoke, and announced that the Russians were coming across the Pripjet at Kopatschi again. The switchboard there excitedly notified me that Russian soldiers were already in the village and the few men there were pulling back to Karpilowka. I was only able to tell the three signaleers to spike the lines and then pull back, when the line went dead. I did not know what was going on and was very worried.

---

[3] Translator's Note. A paramilitary organization that was responsible for a wide range of civil and military engineering projects. It was named after its founder, Fritz Todt, who died in an aircraft crash in 1942.

A few tanks and an *SPW* company from the 12th raced out of burning Nagorzy and went to the assistance of the hard-pressed defenders of Kopatschi. We set up a communications point at the location of the 1st Battalion of the 12th at the outskirts of the village, but it did not have any contact to the rear. We joined up with the *Kampfgruppe* with our radio *SPW* so as to look after the men and the lines in Kopatschi.

Without putting up a lot of resistance, Ivan pulled back across the Pripjet. I intercepted my three signaleers at the outskirts of the village and we reoccupied our communications bunker.

But then I had an unpleasant surprise. Our three prisoners were still sitting there placidly. They had not allowed themselves to be freed by their comrades, they had not gone back with them, they had not fetched their weapons . . . no, instead they were devouring meat and sausage and fish from the rations cans with their bare fingers, a look of satisfaction on their faces. They stared at us with full cheeks.

"Enjoy your meal, comrades!" *Unteroffizier* Willi Dierl yelled at them. They raised their arms high and looked out into the light. I took a can out of the hands of one of them, but it was already too late. With the exception of a few dry pieces of army bread, there was nothing left. The piggy little bastards had eaten up the entire day's ration for the entire platoon in that short amount of time. And we were so hungry that our eyes were bugging out of our heads.

When we then choked down the dry bread, they looked at us somewhat embarrassed. One of them could speak a little German, and he told us that they belonged to a Russian penal battalion and they had been told that if they were hungry, they needed to fetch food from the Germans.

One of the three, Ivan, remained with our company until the very end as a volunteer. Whenever the rations were tight, he would poke me with his elbow and smile impishly: "*Leutnant*, enjoy your meal, comrades!"

Taking a Peek at the Russians' Cards

Middle of November 1943. All of the Eastern Front was shaky. Our *4. Panzer-Division* was withdrawn from the "wet triangle" and committed to the area around Turowitschi.

The Russians had succeeded in crossing the Dnjepr at Retschiza. Their tank packs were advancing west across a broad front. It was directed for our decimated bunch to launch an immediate counterattack against them by moving through the Pripjet Marshes to the east in the direction of Retschiza. *General* von Saucken railed against the army corps, since he saw no sense in that action. But it was nevertheless still ordered; we formed up, never losing sight of the threat to the flanks.

We knew that a strong Russian force, vastly superior, was operating to the northwest of us. It was already to our rear. It could have cut us off at any moment. We also knew that we were at the completely at the mercy of a single road that went through the marshy terrain from west to east. We knew we had to keep our eyes and ears wide open.

Since the situation to the north was completely unknown, radio intercepts were employed. Our tank battalion augmented us with a veteran command-and-control vehicle, the *IN 2*. I was the "fortunate one," who was entrusted with this operation. I was given a wire section and two translators. The Russians did us the favor of doing a lot of transmitting in the clear. I was connected directly to the operations officer and intelligence officer of the division staff through a landline.

Our tank armada, under the leadership of the regimental physician, Dr. Schulz-Merkel, had shrunk to a small bunch. Moreover, it was also engaged in heavy defensive fighting in Karawotitschi.

A chance occurrence came to our aid. The command vehicle of the Russian brigade commander bogged down in the marshland, which was only frozen on top. He was careless enough to radio his location and misfortune in the clear.

Two tanks that had been held in reserve were sent racing to his location, where they knocked him out, before his comrades could come to his rescue. One of the two tank commanders secured the Russian radio operating instructions and took them at top speed to the intelligence officer at his behest.

General von Saucken immediately realized his big opportunity and took one of his unusual ways. We were directed to assume the radio traffic of the eliminated Russian command vehicle, directed by the operations officer and the intelligence officer. Frequencies, code names, tactical shorthand, even the names of all of the tank commanders had been involuntarily provided to us by the Russians. We would be able to observe their customs and peculiarities for twenty-four hours. We just had to get closer to the Russian tanks, so that we could be heard with the same loudness. So . . . we snuck up to the vicinity of the knocked-out brigade vehicle and positioned ourselves along a woodline next to a solitary barn.

Initially, we only eavesdropped on the excited Russian radio traffic. We heard the report one more time that the brigade vehicle had bogged down and probably received a hit. That was our invitation. "We" received orders from a higher command—it was really more of a bawling out—that Tank Brigade "Volga" was to immediately attack the Germans. We acknowledged the radio orders in the format we had monitored, and it was confirmed. Having grown more confident, we reported up and down the chain of command, that the radio operator had been wounded, which was also the complete truth. That made the new voice believable. That was also confirmed from the reception station. In order to tell the complete truth, that was not my idea. We were receiving instructions from the operations officer. I was responsible for the technical side of things.

We then ordered three T-34's to the location of the deposed brigade commander's vehicle. They also quickly bogged down and were knocked out by our *Panzer IV's*, which had been in ambush positions. The remainder of the Russian tank battalion—twenty-two vehicles—was directed to another suitable marshy spot and bogged down according to plan. Naturally, we had to report our "misfortune" to the superior Russian headquarters. "We" earned an ass chewing for that, which left nothing to the imagination. There was talk of saboteurs, leadership failure, and being held account-able. It was fairly difficult for us to feign contriteness. In its place, we received unre-served praise from the operations officer. The initial danger had been eliminated.

A new Russian tank formation was sent out against the evil Germans. Our "command authority" was over for the time being. We only eavesdropped on the radio traffic and passed on the information on the landline. As a result, the location, time and strength of the Russian tank attack were known well in advance.

Our attack on Karawotitschi was called off. Schulz-Merkel's tanks were to be used against the Russian tanks that were due to come out of the woods shortly. Unfortunately, the positioning of the tanks was delayed somewhat. There was almost a screw-up. As a result, we disrupted the Russian radio traffic so as to win some time, since the T-34's were already along the woodline ready to attack and our tanks were still engaged in the village. We were sitting on hot coals and sweating blood. If the Russian tanks succeeded in reaching Karawotitschi, then we would be cut off with our wonderful fake main gun constructed out of aluminum.[4]

Correspondingly, I ran over to two assault guns from another unit that were screening to the east along the road.

"Knock the bastards out yourself" was the coarse answer I received. How—with our fake main gun? They didn't want to understand me. There was always a cross to bear with other units.

But, at that point, the tanks of our "tank doctor" came streaming out of the smoking village at full speed. The assault guns also received orders to go into reverse-slope positions in the direction of the woods. There was a hissing, a cracking and a whistling 500 meters behind us. Our landline was shot. The tanks were dragging the wire behind them.

While we were considering what we should do at that point, a T-34 approached our barn. Unfortunately, we saw it too late, because we were attentively observing the tank engagement behind us—a punishable offense. The Russians set up on the other side of the barn, without having seen us. We stayed under cover. The monster started sneaking up to our side. We snuck off towards the wooded side. We switched our radios to Schulz-Merkel's—as a precautionary measure. But there was nothing to be gotten there, since they were in the middle of attack frenzy and were knocking out one enemy tank after the other.

We didn't let our Ivan out of our eyes. He was separated from us only by the barn and was only five meters away. Damn it! Our tanks were getting even farther away from us! There was little help to be expected from them.

The T-34, which must have gotten our scent, moved to the front of the barn. We moved to the backside. We didn't have a *Panzerfaust* or even a hollow charge, just a damned machine gun—and the Russians seemed to be hunting us at that point.

---

[4] Editor's Note. The command vehicle was probably a *Panzerbefehlswagen III, Ausführung H*, a converted *Panzer III* with a dummy main gun and additional radio sets.

We went around the barn five times. Up to that point, we had been lucky, since the Russian tank was following us very, very carefully. It also appeared not to have noticed that we only had a tin gun to use against it. We disrupted the Russian radio traffic; without directives, we couldn't do anything else. Two men observed the monster, until our nerves didn't want to participate any more.

We heard a lot of activity on the other side of the barn. The Russians appeared to be turning to get at us from the other side. That appeared to be a good moment to us to scram. We crawled into the turret, got a little wind and hurried past the corner of the barn. *Crash!* We had rammed the T-34 right in the corner. It practically threw me out of the turret. The two tanks were caught up in one another. After a second of terror, two of us jumped out of the turret and onto the rear deck of the Russian tank with a tanker's bar in order to jam the turret. But . . . it didn't have a turret either! I almost wanted to shout with joy. It was also a command vehicle! It had made itself scarce, since it thought we were a combat tank. Hand grenades! At that point, the hatch opened and two hands appeared. The crew surrendered.

It was a captain and his crew. He was the commander of the Russian tank battalion that was being taken apart outside the woods at that moment by our tanks. We put the four men on our rear deck, poured a can of fuel over the T-34 and threw a couple of hand grenades into the fighting compartment. That's all it took. I could have hugged the Russian captain.

Dr. Schulz-Merkel radioed a report: "Fifteen enemy tanks knocked out without any losses."

I corrected his report: "Sixteen tanks, including a command vehicle."

Ivan reported the loss of twenty-two tanks. Ooops! We hadn't counted correctly.

We dropped off "our" Russians at *Hauptmann* Götz's location. In departing, I gave them a bottle of vodka. I didn't have the heart to tell them that they had surrendered to a tin gun.

Following the successful breakout from the pocket at Saschtschebje and *IN 2* reporting back to *Hauptmann Grohe*—Dr. Schulz-Merkel had been wounded—the driver pointed out the "kill" ring on the tin gun of the old tank. Grohe laughed heartily and said: "Is this some sort of joke?"

"*Nein, Herr Hauptmann!* " the driver replied, his feelings hurt. "The 'kill' rings just put in the wrong place. It actually belongs on the tracks."

The Baptism of Fire of Our Youngest Soldier

21 November 1943. We had just come back from our successful radio intercept mission. We were exhausted, dog-tired, starving, and frozen through and through. The situation had become life threatening for our *4. Panzer-Division.* The Russians had broken through to the north with large armored formations and was a good twenty kilometers to our rear. The Pripjet Marshes extended to the south, roadless and trackless. They were also dominated by strong partisan bands. There was only one improved road that led to the rear for us. But it was in the hands of the Russians. We

had not been resupplied for days. The wounded from the heavy fighting of the last few days—there were hundreds—could not be evacuated to rearward hospitals. We were as good as encircled, and Ivan continued westward, unstoppable.

I knew that all too well, since I had spent several days with a specially formed platoon eavesdropping on the Russian radio traffic.

Just as I tried to lay down to sleep for a while, I was summoned by the division commander, *General* von Saucken. It had to be something special when a *Leutnant* was ordered to see the General. Still drunk with sleep, I reported to him in Saschtschebje, which was under Russian artillery fire.

His face was earnest, very earnest. He was never a bubbly personality to begin with. His face was gray and the scar on his forehead was visibly red. The *General*, who was normally the soul of calmness, could no longer hide the grave worries he had for our *4. Panzer-Division*. He talked to me in a soft voice that was almost hoarse. There was an unmistakable urgency to it. He spoke deliberately, as if it were difficult for him to say what he was about to say:

"As you know and can see, the division is set up for an all-round defense around Saschtschebje. We now have to attempt to breakthrough the enemy to our rear. Elements of the 5. Panzer-Division have been directed to support that effort by means of a counterattack launched from the southwest.

"As a result of the large gap in the front, which the enemy created between the *2. Armee* and *9. Armee*, the enemy's lead attack elements are headed westward, without encountering any appreciable resistance.

"It is therefore imperative that our division rips open the current envelopment in order to gain freedom of movement.

"It would be good for accomplishing this difficult mission, if we could take back an intact German ammo dump that the enemy captured. That would mean that our artillery would not have to husband its resources.

"The fact that the division has only a single road available to it to break out to the west with its heavy weapons, vehicles and wounded is very disadvantageous to us.

"If our intent were not to succeed, then we would be forced to destroy our heavy combat equipment and snake our way on foot through the almost impassable area of the Pripjet Marshes at night.

"In order to accomplish our mission, a landline connection with the elements of the *5. Panzer-Division*, which are conducting the counterattack, of great importance.

"Your mission is to establish that line."

I repeated my mission in so many words, assumed the position and zoomed off.

For special missions like that, I had a special group. Not because it was any better than any other, but because I had known every individual man for years and from many operations.

I conferred with *Unteroffizier* Willi Dierl and organized reinforcements in the form of the small connection section under Scheuermann, which would have to assume maintenance of the line, if we succeeded in breaking out of the pocket.

We then took off at a run. It appeared that luck was on our side that day, since we found completely intact transmission line poles on the road. We bundled the wires to a single line and were at the edge of the wood exactly half an hour later. The 33rd and the armored engineers were the last outposts there. Schulz-Merkel's tank battalion had also been directed to assemble for the breakout effort there.

Heading to the west, the line poles were completely shot up. Poles and lines were tangled together. We cut those connections.

Major von Gaudecker from *Panzergrenadier-Regiment 33* went up to the edge of the woods to reconnoiter on site for the breakout attempt. We set up a telephone line to him.

At that very moment, the Russians attacked from out of the woods to the north. They put down a barrage fire that took your breath away. They pressed forward with their battle cry of "Uurräää!" Hand grenades detonated all around us. The line to the rear was shot up. The engineers determinedly turned back the attack. We linked up with our line 200 meters farther back and put a line in to the edge of the woods, where there was still heavy fighting.

Right in the thick of things, I intercepted a young signaleer who was hopping about panic stricken in the midst of the hail of lead. I had never seen the fellow before, but discovered that he had been assigned to Dierl's section that morning as a replacement. I didn't know what the man's name was and, since I didn't know him, I somewhat sarcastically called him "Benjamin."[5]

He was still a school boy, probably no older than seventeen, although he only looked about fourteen. He lay next to me, eyes wide open with fear. When it started cracking all around and the calls of "Meddddiccc!" could be heard, he wanted to run away. I pushed his head into the muck of the roadside ditch and pulled his butt down from the road. In the process, I noticed his entire body was shaking and the cold sweat of fear dripped out of every pore. I had a harsh word ready on my tongue, when it occurred to me in time that we hadn't looked any better at the start of the war at Mokra in Poland. Back then, we were already grown men. The trembling milk face in front of me was that of a child, who most certainly felt all by himself, without a friend, without a comrade. The youth needed someone at that point to take him under his wing. I had the feeling he would soon be bawling for "mommy" otherwise.

Major von Gaudecker was speaking at the moment on the telephone with the *General.*

What Benjamin heard there was not exactly encouraging, even if the regimental commander was the picture of calm. A messenger got hit two meters away from us. I pressed my hand into the small of Benjamin's back, so that he would not get any dumb ideas. That I tried to calm him, even though I wasn't exactly feeling calm myself at the moment. He looked at me with thanks in his eyes. During a break in the fire, I sent him back to troubleshoot lines, even though the wire was intact.

---

[5] Translator's Note. A biblical reference. Benjamin was the youngest of Jacob's twelve sons.

There was an open area in front of us, about a kilometer in width. Then some low vegetation started up. The road embankment led straight as an arrow across the clearing. There was a tank burning on it, giving off a black cloud of smoke. Ammunition detonated. We had to lay our wire along that road.

About 300 meters farther to the north, parallel to the road, was a threatening looking woodline, which extended out in the direction of the road. It was apparently thickly held by the Russians, since there was firing coming from it without interruption. Between the edge of the woods and the cobblestone road, in the middle of the moor, were a few groups of bushes, apparently on some sort of dune. Russian antitank guns and mortars banged away from there in salvoes. The "moor fortifications" were only about 100 meters from the road. They dominated the road completely. It was not possible to get past them from there. The road itself was elevated. The terrain south of the road did not seem to be occupied by the enemy. In that area, the woods pulled back at least 500 meters. I committed every detail of the terrain to my memory.

If what the *General* had said was true, then the tanks of the *5. Panzer-Division* had to approach from somewhere off back there along the road. I was unable to identify anything with binoculars, however, even though the road embankment led straight west, as if laid out by a ruler. I could see a good three kilometers. But there were no sounds of fighting coming from there. I saw no obstacles. I also saw no Russians.

For the time being, there was to be no advancing in this sector, since there was no relief advance from the rear. But we needed to get through with our line. Should we try it all by ourselves?

I held a council of war with my old hands: "Take a good look at it, since we have to get through, and immediately, if possible. I can't tell you for certain whether we'll meet up with any German soldiers on the other side. Up to this point, no one's gotten through. But no one's tried it yet, either. Who's going with me?"

"It doesn't matter to us. The situation is shit everywhere!"

And so we got ready: Willi Dierl, the *Unteroffizier* and section leader, the son of a hotel manager in Marienbad; Poldi, a waiter from Lübeck; Konrad, also known as Peronnje, who spoke a horrible-sounding German but a useful Russian, a handyman from Upper Silesia; and Wassil, the former Russian warrior, who always accompanied me like a shadow.

Everyone placed a backpack spool carrier with a kilometer of wire in the small of his back and put on some equipment. They then took their carbines in their hand.

Benjamin must have misunderstood me, since he was also carrying a back rack.

"You're staying here, you little pipsqueak!"

"Can't I go with you?"

It's not going to be too nice out there," I said, somewhat hesitantly. I left the question open, however. I was unable to give a strict no, because he looked at me with such trust, even though I really didn't want him along. He persevered and kept the back rack on.

Willi Lanig, the driver of the *Muli*, organized the troubleshooters in the woods; Helmut Scheuermann took care of that from the edge of the woods back to Saschtschebje. I drilled it into those remaining behind—no, I implored them—to keep the line going under all circumstances, since the fate of our division was completely dependent upon it. We took leave of one another with a handshake.

"Do well!"

"Cross your fingers for us!"

"*Horrido!*"[6]

We gave some clearance with the line around the terrible corner of the woods, from which the road emptied into the clearing. We waited for a break in the firing and then took off with a jump.

Blub—blub—blub. The sound came from the vegetation. *Ratsch—bummm. Ratsch—bummm.* That was the sound we heard at our location. We hit the deck and the heavy back racks smacked us in the back. It was a feat of pure acrobatics each time to go from the vertical to the horizontal with the wire on the play-out, the bag of tools, the grounding plug and field telephone on the belly, the carbine in your paw. We were not spared crawling through the soft marshland of the pasture, either, since the road embankment was only about a meter high and only offered us protection against direct fire. Our "friends" in the bushes were quite nice to provide us with all sorts of things.

Once the engineers set out to conduct another immediate counterattack, we hopped behind the embankment like rabbits. The height of the road base was stupid. We had no other choice but to crawl along on all fours in the marshland past the Russians. Unfortunately, the back rack, from which the wire was being paid out, made a racket that could be heard at some distance. And the Russians listened well.

Blub—blub—blub. That was the response we heard from over there. They weren't aiming too badly based just on hearing! We were moving forward damned slowly. It was only when the firing started up that we could take off in a trot. If the helmet only went a little bit above the edge of the road, then Ivan's machine guns started rattling. We hoped they wouldn't try to cut off our route. But I was thinking that the mechanized infantry at the edge of the woods were paying damned close attention. They kept on giving us comradely covering fire. They fired whenever we took off, so that Ivan didn't hear the rattling of the back racks.

Gradually, we figured out that the mortar rounds, which only landed a few meters away, exploded in the marshland and could have little effect on us. They could only cover us with mud. Of the ones that landed on the street, the shrapnel could not reach us if we kept our heads tucked well in. It was only a very narrow section along the road embankment that could be life threatening to us.

---

[6] Translator's Note. Although this is more commonly considered to be the battle cry of fighter pilots, it was also used in the army. It was used as both a greeting and a call for good luck. The term comes from hunting circles.

The connection worked. The operations officer spoke with the operations offi-
of the corps. He didn't say many nice things, and he also didn't send any compli-
s his way.

The hard-bitten conversation and the drastic portrayal of the situation moved the
s to have the relief attack of the *5. Panzer-Division* advance as far as our location.
We hoped they didn't blow us to smithereens, since the *5. Panzer-Division* was
zed that a little group of signaleers, of all people, had gotten out of the pocket.
Major von Gaudecker was also seriously concerned about us, since we were sit-
all alone between the fronts, with the Russians right at our nose. He advised me
ave the connection on and establish security or disappear into the bushes.

After thirty minutes, nine German tanks worked their way carefully towards us.
crews looked at us in amazement. I grabbed the leader of the *Kampfgruppe* and
him on the telephone so that he could establish contact with the other side of
clearing. *Major* von Gaudecker ordered him to screen to the north. The tanks
us from being surprised in no-man's-land, but we also paid for it with a few
tar barrages.

I listened in to the conversation with division. Everything was switched to a
e line. *Panzergrenadier-Regiment 33* complained bitterly that it had not succeeded
lentifying and eliminating the antitank gun and mortar positions in the moor.
y had to be somewhere between the edge of the woods and the improved road.
It was our youngest man, milk-face Benjamin, of all people, who gave me a
l idea: "There was a water culvert in the middle of the clearing, through which
could see really well to the north, without being seen." That was true. But did
really matter to us at all?

Poldi and I slung on a field telephone and the tool bag and wanted to go get
bearings. Benjamin snapped. He asked me for permission to go along in such an
ting military fashion that I had to laugh. Poldi was happy to remain behind. I
ked my way along the embankment to the middle of the clearing. The little one
right behind me. There was a concrete pipe there that was right across form the
e in the moor, where the Russians had to have a heavily manned strongpoint,
e there was constant firing from the bushes in the direction of the woodline.

Barely 100 meters in front of our noses, I saw the Russians busy running back
forth. Unaided, I could see four antitank guns and a whole slew of mortars and
hine guns. We entered the line, and I reported my observations to *Major* von
decker, who reacted I a flash: "I'll get the forward observer on the line. He'll
l a little light on the subject."

A few minutes later, he was there.

"There, where the two tall pines jut out of the moor . . . that's right where the
sians are."

"Identified!" he said. "We'll fire a spotting round. Tell me where it lands." A few
utes later: "Did you see anything?"

We maintained an interval of 200 meters between us and cro
rain in front of the noses of the Russians without incident. At that
cal to watch like crazy to make sure the Russians didn't come a
grab us. By then, we were already about 1,000 meters from th
woodline.

The attentiveness of the Russians was diverted at that point,
appeared to have arrived. A few of them came out of the woo
immediately engaged by antitank guns. The island on the moor
tanks under fire.

Thick vegetation started to appear on both sides of the road. V
the Russians? I carefully spied over the embankment, but I did no
raced off. Wire out! A blind knot in the wire, and the next man ra
man, who had just been freed from his burden, patched the wires t

Benjamin never left my side. He acted like my shadow. Whene
he also took a dive; whenever I jumped, he hopped along, light
when I stumbled, he promptly fell on his nose. Despite the seriou
unable to stifle a slight smile. He no longer showed inordinate fear,
took his entire attention. It was only for the two old *Obergefreite*
didn't take him seriously or had even harassed him, that he got
much as possible.

After three kilometers of fighting the mud and doing up
shadow of the road, we reached a bunker—exhausted—at the e
"Strongpoint 139.1" was written on it. We found telephone wir
completely intact. At the far end, a switchboard reported with a co
recognize. My God! Were we really going to be that lucky and
connection to the rear?

"Tell me who you are?"

Icy silence.

"This is the *4. Panzer-Division.*"

Nothing, just a rush.

Damned secrecy requirements!

"This is *Leutnant* Schäufler from *Panzernachrichten-Abteilung*
corps signal officer, please!"

"This is *Oberstleutnant* so and so."

I didn't understand his name. It didn't matter.

"Stay on the line!" I yelled at him. It was something that seem
most in the military: "I'll connect you with our operations officer!"

Damn it! The line was disrupted. Poldi and Peronnje headed ou
utes, the connection was back. I discovered that the division con
under heavy artillery and mortar fire and was being constantly at
sides.

"Are you still there? Our ops officer would like to speak to you

"No . . . because of the culvert, I only have a small field of vision. Besides, there's firing everywhere. Many the round landed too far to the north in the woods."

"We'll adjust. The next round is smoke."

Wummmm. There was an impact behind me. The black muck slammed into my back. Benjamin also churned his way out of the peat porridge, disgusted and disappointed. A cloud of smoke grew from the gigantic crater behind us. So that was the spotting round. The distance was exactly right; only the impacts needed to be adjusted 100 meters north. You had to be an artilleryman in order to direct the guns properly. But that was of no consequence at the moment, since the line was gone. Benjamin took off. I crawled a bit further into the culvert. You never know?

Blubbb—blubbb—blubbb. That came from the island on the moor.

Wubbb—wubbb—wubbb. That was from behind the woods at the location of our artillery. I could not differentiate between German shells and Russian mortar rounds. As I said, I am no artilleryman. All of the impacts were in the vicinity of the road, and Benjamin was off by himself. The poor guy was probably sweating blood! Then the line was back again. Bravo, Benjamin!

"As thanks for our help, you're shooting us to bits. You need to fire 100 meters further north, you amateurs!" I screamed to the artillery *Leutnant.*

"Thank you! Tuck in your heads. It's starting up!"

Benjamin crept into the culvert with me. There was a rushing, a howling a cracking—it didn't seem to ever want to stop. Around fifty shells landed among the bushes between the pines. A few landed close to the road.

Then there was a howling behind us in the woods. There was a rattling and a rumbling. The tanks broke through the woods. The Russian antitank guns fired like crazy. It was terrible to have to watch and not be able to do anything about it. The artillery started firing smoke. The engineers stormed the woods across from us with the German battle cry of "Hurra." The 33rd followed the tanks. The artillery fired again for all it was worth. It was all over quickly. The Russians scrammed to get out of there, heading west. They ran right into the guns of the *5. Panzer-Division.* The 33rd stormed the moor island. Ivan started to cover the road with artillery fire. Cobblestones flew through the air, and fountains of peat sprang out of the moor. We hope not to get a direct hit on our heads! All of a sudden, the fireworks stopped. The line was gone; both of us scrambled off.

The sound of fighting coming from the woods gradually moved north. The wire from Strongpoint 139.1 to the division command post was under artillery and mortar fire again. The Russians wanted to block the road with their fireworks. Connections lasted for only a matter of seconds. I got on the line again, since there was little happening on the wire at the moment. Willi Dierl was working with his people between the strongpoint and the culvert; Benjamin ran from the culvert to the edge of the woods; Willi Lanig and his two men patched continuously in the woods; and Helmut Scheuermann between the edge of the woods and Saschtschebje.

A dark cloud of smoke arose from behind the woods. The Russian machine guns hacked in the vegetation. The tanks and the engineers pushed north, but there were Russians behind them again already. From my position, I had a marvelous viewpoint. The devil was on the loose behind us . . . or was that in front of us? What was the front or the rear in this case?

At that point, the road to the rear was clear. The first armored personnel carriers bounced along through the shell craters and past burning armored vehicles to the west with hundreds of wounded. Ivan threw another tantrum. The firing slowly ebbed. The first trucks and field kitchens jangled past us. The line was patched again. Benjamin and I jumped on the running board of a truck going past. All of us rallied at the strongpoint. Willi Lanig then came with his *Muli*. It started to turn dusk.

The division rolled westward for hours. There were no hold-ups, since there was no oncoming traffic. Benjamin slept the sleep of the just in a dark corner.

Toward midnight, *General* von Saucken came to our location. I had never seen him so relaxed and, at the same time, relieved. He thanked all of my men with a handshake. I also woke up Benjamin.

"Well, kid, your *Leutnant* says you were terrific."

He didn't quite understand what was going on, he was so sleepy. It was not until he saw the general's boards that he slowly woke up.

The *General* then called the field army, cursing a blue streak. The army reacted sheepishly.

"The last vehicle of my division will get out of this goat screw you directed me into around 0200 hours. Until then, I can be reached at Strongpoint 139.1." *Bang!* He slammed the handset on the receiver.

Against all expectations, everything worked out without a hitch. To the east of us, there was a rumbling everywhere. Our artillery fired to all sides from within the army ammunition dump until the barrels started glowing. The vehicles continued rolling past us to the west and out of this mousetrap. They were rolling to the rear and behind the Wit Canal. The next day, we assembled in Glinaja Ssoboda.

It was there that my fellow traveler, Willi Dierl, received a well-earned Iron Cross, First Class. Benjamin received the Iron Cross, Second Class for his very first operation at the front, although a few of the old *Obergefreite* reacted poorly: "We needed three years for that, and the little snot nose gets it on the first day!" I offered him my heartfelt congratulations, since he had really earned it.

I was allowed to ask for something special. And I did. A few days later, I departed Mosyr on four weeks of special leave. For the first time since 1940, I was able to celebrate Christmas with my young wife back home. Another pleasant surprise awaited me, as well. A friend of mine from my youth, Schorsch, whom I hadn't seen for years, was on the same train as I was.

Artillery during the counterattack on Seredina Buda, 15 March 1943.

Assault guns of Panzer-Regiment 35 *with winter camouflage, 13 March 1943. The vehicles also have winter track extenders—the so-called* Ostketten—*mounted on the regular track.*

He no longer had the strength to dismount—a Soviet tanker burned to death in his knocked-out T-34, 19 March 1943.

Battlefield communications on Hill 238.1 at Teploje, 12 July 1943. From left to right: Obergefreiter *Klippel,* Unteroffizier *Scheuermann,* Leutnant *Schäufler, and* Hauptmann *Berger.*

A knocked-out German tank—in this case, a Panzer III—*at Teploje, 10 July 1943. It was but one of many.*

Chapter 8

EGG DIVING AT SLONIM

Robert Poensgen, war correspondent with *Panzer-Regiment 35*

That took place during those hot July days of 1944, when the combat elements of our *4. Panzer-Division* were employed to block the Russian breakthrough from the area of Minsk-Baranowitschi. I had participated in the operations of the *Panther* battalion and was on the way to the division command post with a vehicle that had weapons problems to write down what I had heard and seen for German newspapers.

It was a truly hot day. Although we did not have a thermometer on board, it must have been 30 in the shade [86 Fahrenheit] and you could have cooked an egg on the armor plating of our tank. If we had only had some . . . eggs that is.

We did have cognac, however, the real French stuff. *Schoka-Cola*,[1] cigarettes all types of magnificent things that we had taken as we passed by from a large rations dump that was being prepared for demolition, since Ivan was rolling and rolling. When we entered the town of Slonim, we made an interesting discovery. Initially, we saw a *Landser* running along with a mess tin full of eggs. Then another . . . and then yet another. Two approached us with an entire bathtub full of them. Eggs, eggs, eggs . . . the things we had just been dreaming about. There must have been a considerable source somewhere in the town. But where? We stopped, asked and discovered that there was a large storehouse of eggs in the middle of the town, which had been cleared for free issue. We needed to hurry up, however, since there were not too many left of the original large amount.

And so we hurried up, and not just because of the eggs. We wanted and needed to get to the armaments facility to get the main gun of our *Panther* repaired. We were soon in front of the building, from which civilian and soldiers were taking egg after egg . . . in bags, in crates, in cans, and in tubs.

---

[1] Translator's Note. A type of chocolate intended for soldiers in the field that had caffeine added to it.

It was pleasantly cool in the building. Bewildered, we stood in front of gigantic concrete vats, which were halfway filled with a cloudy brew. Bent far over the edge we egg fishermen, who were looking for the fragile oval things. God knows how many—eggs, of course—had already suffered as a result of those coarse fishing methods. The original solution—no doubt, clean—had become practically saturated with slippery egg white and creamy egg yolks. The pails, which were pulled up from the bottom, were barely a quarter full with eggs. Of those, nearly half were broken due to the brutal evacuation method and, as a result, flew back in the brew.

It would have been a tiresome and prolonged operation to fill up the two water buckets we had brought along by using that method. We couldn't allow ourselves that much time. We thought about an alternate way.

I had been treated in such a comradely way by the crew the many days I had been with it and had been taken care of in every which way that I was practically happy to show my appreciation in some way. Therefore, I volunteered for a frogman operation. I pulled off my denims, slid off the underwear and slipped over the thick concrete edge, the way nature had created me, held by the outstretched arms of my comrades.

Brrrr! The water was cold. After the heat outside, it was a shock. My legs went deeper and deeper, and then my stomach in the horrible, slimy brew. In desperation, I fished for the bottom with my toes, but the only thing I felt with my toes was eggs and eggshells.

It was not until the "water" was around my throat that I felt the concrete basin under me. There were only a few eggs still hopping around on the bottom. All of the rest had already been fished out. There wasn't a whole lot to be had with the pails that were handed down to me. There was only one way to get to my objective quickly and with certainty. I had to get over the nausea rising in me and dive.

With one hand holding a pail and the other pressing my mouth and nose, I disappeared into the depths. I moved the pail flat along the bottom and quickly rose again. A great success! The pail was more than half full, although it also had a lot of "defects." I passed up the quick selection, before going back down in the scary depths. Then a third time followed by a fourth time. I was halfway blue from cold and covered from head to foot with solution, egg whites, yolks and eggshells when my comrades pulled me back up "on land." The cleaning bucket of water might have been cold, but compared to the polar temperature in the egg container, it seemed luke warm to me.

We didn't count how good our catch was. Two water buckets full of eggs—no doubt a couple of hundred. That would mean a feast for the entire maintenance facility.

I sat on the back deck of the tank and shivered with cold in the blazing heat. It was only after I had taken a couple of cognacs—without egg—that I started to feel better again. Dinner was magnificent: scrambled eggs with tinned meat and an egg liquor as dessert.

I then got on to the division command post. My mess tin was full of eggs, as well as my gasmask container. My bread bag was full of chocolate.

I had rarely been greeted so well by my comrades. No one could understand why I was so generous: "Here are some eggs . . . eggs . . . take all of them."

I no longer wanted to see eggs or to smell them, let alone talk about eating them.

A SHORT LOVE STORY

Leutnant **Rudolf Meckel,** *Panzer-Regiment 35, 4. Panzer-Division*
Late summer, 1944. I saw the movie *Maske in Blau*[2] eight times. One time in my hometown and seven times in Radom. What I remember nowadays about that once famous but none-the-less inconsequential film goes back to vague memories of my seeing it in my hometown. Nothing has remained of the seven *Maske in Blau* showings in the military movie theater in Radom.

There was a girl sitting at the box office in Radom, however. She pushed the tickets to the soldiers across the counter silently and with a deadpan expression. The flirty banter of the Landser quickly died under the gaze of those cool, gray eyes. The girl openly showed that she did not like the Germans.

I never did discover why she was selling tickets at the military movie theater. Perhaps she was one of those informants of the partisans, who had the area around Radom firmly in their hands and also commanded large portions of the city. Perhaps she also sat that the box office in order not to starve, since things were not good for the Poles in the cities at the time.

While seeing *Maske in Blau* for the second time, I discovered that the wonderfully pretty, slim-faced Polish girl still maintained the box office a half hour after the start of the film to take care of latecomers.

For *Maske in Blau*, I was a straggler. It was not possible to establish contact with the exciting unapproachable one. There was still that hostile shaking of the head. That meant I could write off the attempts at irony.

Since the German armed forces had achieved their greatest successes with agile combat leadership, I decided to use that tactic. As a straggler for *Maske in Blau* number four, I stuck my head through the door marked "Entrance for Armed Forces Personnel Strictly Forbidden!" with a masterfully shy smile: "Would it be possible to come in?" It was not possible.

With *Maske in Blau* five, I was allowed in, but I had to sit silently and motionless in the corner, which could not be seen from the outside.

Moreover, I discovered that for Tanuta—that was her name, the stuff of fairy tales and legends—no tricks nor even the dashing black *Panzer* uniform would work

---

[2] Translator's Note. *Mask in Blue* was a musical directed by Paul Martin in 1943. It makes reference to the operetta of the same name by Fred Raymond, but it has nothing to do with the operetta.

for that gentle and blooming creature. It resulted in red-faced embarrassment and the fatal feeling that the impression of an awkward school kid had been created.

With *Maske in Blau* six, it appeared that all previously gained successes, no matter how meager they may have been, were scattered to the wind. The usherette was sitting at the box office. She immediately received the persistent straggler and directed him resolutely into the pitch-black movie hall. All efforts to intercept at least a comforting gaze from Tanuta's gray eyes ended in failure. And so I sat at the best seat in the house—it was all the way to the rear—angry, desperate and sheepish, all at once. I was disgusted with the limitless kitsch of the movie plot and decided to evacuate the scene of the tragedy and initiate a tactical retreat.

Suddenly, she was there. A shadow, but warm and soft with hot lips. With a touchingly tender grasping of her slender hands, she pulled my head to her face. "You, dear one!" she whispered. Once again: "You, dear one!" I felt tears on her cheeks, salty and cool.

We sat there not moving in the dark, coated over by the flickering light of the film—and saw nothing at all.

Shortly before the end of the movie, she slipped away before I could even think of a word or gesture of goodbye.

I stumbled across the legs of soldiers and looked for the exit, accompanied by cursing and hissing. All at once, the usherette was standing in front of me. She pressed her hand on my arm, beseechingly: "Tanuta already gone! You may not look for her, please!" The harsh Polish accent underscored the hopelessness of any type of questions concerning Tanuta's whereabouts.

On the next evening, I didn't see *Maske in Blau*, but I did post myself in time by the movie exit. Just before the end of the film. The door opened. And who shipped out? The usherette! She looked at me in a distressed manner and with a face that showed no limit of disappointment: "Why you not come? Tanuta has waited the entire film!"

That's right, the entire film! My stomach was turning over.

The next day, I received marching orders from the adjutant's office of the *LVI. Panzer-Korps*. I had been reporting directly to it with my special company, which was in the process of being disbanded in Radom. I was ordered to the Army Movement Center at Lodz, called Litzmannstadt back then, and ordered back to *Panzer-Regiment 35*, which was en route to Kurland.[3]

I had one more evening left in Radom. I attended *Maske in Blau* seven. We sat one more time in the film-flickered darkness and her whispering was like a faint birdsong to my ear. Even though it was Polish and Tanuta's vocabulary of tender German consisted of "You, dear one!" my heart understood every word. I almost wanted to bawl.

---

[3] Translator's Note. Courland in English. A region of western Latvia with strong historical ties to Germany because of settlements formed there by the Teutonic Knights.

Before she was able to flee in the darkness, I bravely said: "Tanuta, Tanuta . . . today's the last day. I have to go tomorrow!" Tense and fearful, I awaited her reaction. She remained still. After a short while, she stood up, grabbed me by the hand and pulled me along hurriedly to an exit, which I had not noticed before. On the street, she said to me: "Come!"

We walked slowly in the cool late summer night and through streets unfamiliar to me. There was hardly a word between us. What were we to say?

We wandered through Radom, visibly void of people: a *Panzer Leutnant* and a young Polish woman. We didn't think that we were playing with our lives. Radom was full of partisans. Every day, German soldiers disappeared. They were snapped up outside of the secured portions of the city and silently dispatched around the corner.

Incomprehensible heart: it scorns death only to drink in the pain of an unavoidable parting.

The minutes passed in the slow measure of our steps. They led us to a small plaza in which several streets emptied. Tanuta remained standing there, kissed me, pulling my head to her face with both hands. Before she disappeared with swift steps into the nighttime shadows of the houses, she looked at me silently for a long time with a penetrating, transfixed gaze, with eyes that were terrible in their lack of tears.

Don't days like those—in the middle of a terrible war—weigh more than years nowadays?

WOUNDED IN KURLAND

Leutnant **Rudolf Meckel,** *Panzer-Regiment 35, 4. Panzer-Division*
Fall 1944. With the war coming to a close and the front moving backwards at an ever-increasing tempo, it turned out that former rear-area military hospitals turned into collection points in the blink of an eye for the wounded streaming in almost directly from the battlefield. Doctors, medics and nurses, who once enjoyed the pleasant quietness of the rear, saw themselves facing the horrors and uncertainties of the front. A sterile hospital atmosphere yielded to a hectic unrest, a sedate conservativeness to a desperate struggle with death hovering over shattered bodies.

That was also the case at the naval hospital in Libau, which housed more soldiers of the Kurland field army than naval heroes at the time.

Fate washed me ashore at that building on the sea, which resembled a palace, after the cannoneers of a Russian 122-millimeter mortar battery had managed to fire on my tank after a lot of exacting work. Our efforts to patch together our tracks and put them back on our tank were prematurely interrupted by that.

Nurse Alla, an energetic East Prussian, later told me that I had not been a pretty picture when I was admitted. They didn't operate a lot on me, since they were directed to avoid vivisections.

As a result, I was sent to a large hall, which was divided into sections by portable walls made out of cloth. In my "department" were the unpleasant matters, such as those torn apart, ripped apart, or burned and for whom not a lot could be done. Almost all of them died—it was around forty of them—as I vaguely remember. *Leutnant* Hänsgen and I were left. But then, I'm getting ahead of myself.

In a practically miraculous manner, I had an unexpected healing, in which the aforementioned *Leutnant* Hänsgen had his part. His childlike sensibility got me all riled up all the time, which made it impossible for me to sink into that lethargy with which most of the comrades around us quietly faced the end.

You should know that *Leutnant* Hänsgen—six feet, two inches tall—was restrained to the bed due to a nailed heel and a stretching apparatus and bemoaned his status in a variety of ways. On the other hand, Hänsgen was the only lightly wounded man in our section. After the fact, the way he reacted may appear understandable since no healthy person, who is afflicted with a fractured lower thigh, wants to be hitched up to a procrustean bed. At the time, however, his lamentations were a source to me of grim embitterment.

It was said that Hänsgen was the acting commander of an antitank company, and his wounding was a direct consequence of that. Whoever remembers the narrow roads in Kurland, which were always accompanied by deep ditches to both the left and the right, knows that the opportunity to escape the sudden appearance of fighter-bomber attacks was slim and the insufficient training of the Russian pilots was sometimes your only salvation.

But Hänsgen had not thought about that. When he was riding along one such road in the commander's staff car and he suddenly took notice of the scampering shadow of an aircraft above him, he took a flying leap out of the vehicle and into the ditch. Prior to that, he had forgotten to turn of the engine and pull the hand brake, as the regulation required. His vehicle, irritated by that fact, promptly followed him into the ditch. The results were a complicated lower thigh fracture and admittance into the naval hospital at Libau.

The greatest military doctor I ever encountered was the head doctor and chief surgeon of the naval hospital at Libau. He was *Marineoberstabsarzt* Dr. Steinbrücker. That *vir vere humanus* was a man who incorporated goodness, humor and level headedness in one person. When Hänsgen portrayed the anguish of his situation to the doctor for the umpteenth time during the latter's rounds, Dr. Steinbrücker said in a friendly manner: "You see, my dear Hänsgen, that's why you are a patient!"

As it turned out, fighter-bombers appeared occasionally and circled over the city. They were predatory birds, which the naval *Flak* engaged. Accompanied by the metallic call of the sirens, the bombs landed in the palace park near the hospital. What good did it do that a Red Cross was painted on the roof. The gigantic windows rang and the baroque stucco ceiling bore down on us like a threatening cloud.

With every impact, mortar and plaster drizzled down on the beds. We were fettered to our beds, however, as the result of our wounds and falling victim to the wretched fear of the defenseless. Panic lurked in the corners. But it did not break out, not even when a hissing concussive wave shattered the windows in the hall, sweeping glass shrapnel over the beds . . .

It was three Red Cross nurses who prevented the torch of blind self-destruction from flaming up out of paralyzing horror. If you thought that the strict and unbending East Prussian Alla could look terror coolly in the face, then it was a sheer miracle in the case of the other two: They were youthful things, who had just come from the homeland. One was a blonde; the other had black hair and possessed a Madonna-like beauty.

Like the personification of angels, they stood between the rows of beds. Their calm, alert gazes wandered from face to face. Whenever one of the helpless bodies threatened to rear up under the unbearable stress and fear, they placed a cool, gentle hand on a forehead dripping with sweat. By doing so, it remained still in the ante-room of death.

And so I learned from the wordless courage of those young women, who voluntarily forewent the protection of the bunker in order to help the wounded through the hell of fear, that the unreflected bravery of a man is nothing compared to the merciful love of a woman.

One night, while fever kept me awake, I discovered that a hospital train was supposed to be going to the homeland within the next twenty-four hours. The Russians were already almost to the sea at Memel.

When Dr. Steinbrücker saw my hesitation—it was more an uncomprehending joy than any conscious deliberation—he said to me with a very kindly, fatherly smile: Of course, you can stay here with us."

Then it was difficult for me to show any happiness about the upcoming departure. I had that doctor to thank for my life and didn't know what to say. And so I kept quiet and attempted a thankful smile under my thick dressings. Dr. Steinbrücker seemed to understand me. He placed his hand on my arm, a heavy, large and almost farmer-like hand. It was a farewell at midnight without sentimentality; it was almost without a word.

Very early in the morning, Nurse Alla was in front of my bed.

"How did you want to get out of here?"

"Well, with the train, of course!" I said in bewilderment.

Have you thought about what you wanted to wear?" I initially thought it was a dumb question. I felt perfectly fine in my armed forces nightgown.

She then said scornfully: "You have to leave your gown here. It belongs to the hospital. I had to sign for it."

"Yes . . . and where are my things?"

"Your things?" Boundless surprise registered in the icy gray eyes of the nurse. "Didn't you know that that's all there is?"

And she held up a brownish red iridescent scrap of cloth. It was only with a great deal of imagination that you could see that it was once a bluish gray *Panzer* shirt. It had been shredded by a lot of shrapnel and stained by dried blood.

She eyeballed my perplexed embarrassment with reproachful severity and let me lay there in doubt and the fatalistic expectation that I would have to go "home to the *Reich*" in nothing more than my Adam and Eve outfit.

The day passed slowly by. No one looked after me. Only my friend, the smart but childlike medical corps cadet Henning slowed down a bit by my bed. Gradually, evening crawled through the window, and the crows assembled on the bald branches of the leafless park trees. The stretcher-bearers came into the hall. The picked up this man and that out of bed and carted them out into the night. I started to panic. Was I really going to have to drift out of there like Lazarus, "wearing" only my dressings?

All of a sudden, Nurse Alla appeared in the uncertain light of the bluish night lamp. She speedily unfolded a set of regulation armed forces underwear. They were white, long, repaired, and clean to the point of being sterile. She looked around carefully and whispered: "Quick, put them on. I just stole them for you!"

And so I discovered that all male logic is nothing in comparison to the tricky heart of a woman . . .

DANGEROUS "SLEEPWALKING" IN KURLAND

Leutnant **Hans Schäufler, regimental signals officer of** *Panzer-Regiment 35,*
4. *Panzer-Division*

26 December 1944. The Battle of Kurland was in full swing. After hours of barrage fire, the Russians had been charging our bled-white positions again and again for four days. They had all of the advantages of the attacker. The front lines on both sides had been decimated. The snow-covered terrain was saturated with dead. The Russian tank concentrations had thrust through our lines while the artillery fire was still raging. No one knew where they were at that point.

All of a sudden, an uncanny silence descended, since there was no longer anyone there who could fight. Here and there, a wounded man cried out in a bone-chilling way for a medic. A lonely machine gun bellowed eerily into the silence.

Our regimental command vehicle, the *RN 1*, was located behind a group of trees. The commander, *Oberst* Christern, had taken the radio *SPW* to the division command post in Ozolini, to get a better feeling for the confusing situation.

Since there was not a whole lot for us to do at the moment, we dozed off apathetically, since we had been on the go constantly for four days and three nights—no sleep, no warm rations. There was a whistling in the headphones: "Meet to discuss operations at the XYZ farmstead!"

I pressed the binoculars to my tired eyes and observed the foreground. In the approaching darkness, I recognized a group of houses off to the left of us, which were being approached by individual armored vehicles. Exhausted as I was, I didn't think about it too long: "Crank it up . . . direction of march is the farmstead off to the left!"

We plodded on over shot-up tree trunks, mounds of earth and ditches to the collection of tanks. We set up in the shadow of a tree and turned of the short-wave radio. We then allowed ourselves to take a nap. They would call us when everyone was here.

It was pitch black when I woke up with a startle. That's taking a long time, I thought to myself, and I took a look at my watch. We'd been there for two hours. Need to take a look to see what's going on! I struggled out of the hatch and knocked on the tank next to us. Nothing stirred. A transformer was humming inside. What were the guys radioing? No one's monitoring the radio. Everyone's here, aren't they? I climbed up on the tank to set the guys straight.

Even though I knew every handhold, I kept missing them. The step from the roadwheel to the track guard was enormous. I practically dislocated my legs. My hands couldn't find any handles, where they knew they had to be. What was wrong with me today?

"What company is this?" I yelled into the turret. A completely foreign face looked up at me. On top of that, the face was framed by a Russian tanker's cap. I felt a massive turret with coarsely welded seams under my groping hands. A gun as big as a tree jutted out of the turret.

That couldn't be possible! There I was, completely stunned, standing on top of a Josef Stalin tank! And there was a Russian crew inside. And all of the tanks around me, engulfed by the darkness, were all Russian tanks. If it doesn't exist in wartime, it doesn't exist!

In a flash, I was wide-awake. I took a headfirst dive into the darkness. While still in the air, I yelled out: "Crank it up!"

Oberfeldwebel Schmidt grabbed me by the collar and pulled me into the hatch. *Feldwebel* Eichhorn rushed out into the night with the *RN 1*. After about 300 meters, we bogged down in a clay pit. The engine choked out. All of the radios had been turned on "receive" for some time. We tensely listened into the ether and gazed out into a night pregnant with misfortune. Behind us, we heard the "sneezing" of the traversing gears of the Russian tank turrets. They must have heard something. Thank God that the earth had literally swallowed us up.

From the edge of the clay pit, I could count the number of Russian tanks by the milky light of the signal flares. There were twenty of them. An ice-cold chill went down my spine whenever I thought we had spent two hours sleeping among them without a worry in the world, with a fake barrel made of aluminum and a raft of classified documents on board.

"Alpine rose . . . alpine rose . . . alpine rose . . . over!" it croaked desperately out of the headphones.

Initially, we only radioed our location to the regiment.

"Are you crazy?" it croaked back.

I could almost see old Christern standing in front of me. Now he was probably angrily but also worriedly slipping the throat mike over his massive head. And I wasn't wrong. I soon heard his rumbling bass voice: "What's going on? Alpine rose? What are you doing there?"

I outlined our awkward situation.

"Stay where you are! We'll get you!" he blasted.

In the distance, we heard the heavy tank engines turn over. We heard the tanks coming, casting shadows along the woodline.

We directed them over the radio, based on the noise. When they were close enough, we lit up the haystacks at the farmstead with signal flares. The Russian tanks stood out as if on a platter. Nine of them were set alight; the rest escaped into the night.

A sympathetic *Panther* drug us out of the clay soup. In low spirits, we steamed away with Tautorus's company to the north, awaiting our ass chewing.

The Beginning of the End: A Portrait of West Prussia

End of January 1945. Head over tails, we were withdrawn from the Kurland bridge-head and out of the fight. It was rumored that everything was topsy-turvy on the east German frontier. We transferred our tanks, heavy weapons and vehicles to the combat elements of the *14. Panzer-Division*.

At the Libau harbor, they pressed and penned us into battle-ready transporters and naval ferries. For our departure, the Russians dropped all the bombs they could spare on our heads so that we would keep them in our memories.

And then we headed out into the storm-tossed Baltic.

Air alert! But where could you go? There was no running away there. There were no foxholes on the Goddamned water. The only thing that helped was to pray that the on-board *Flak* fired well, since the German fighters had long since checked out.

Submarine alert! For land warriors, that was something completely new that slammed home in the pit of your stomach. Escort boats dropped depth charges. The underwater detonations hit the sides of the ships hard. The pitching and canting caused by the constant zigzag course was unbearable. It was enough to make you puke, quite literally. There was no demand for food on the ship.

Finally, finally . . . after a long day and a longer night, we saw the piers of Danzig. Thank God! Solid ground under our feet again!

It was like peacetime everywhere. We had a short break in a hotel in Zoppot, with everything you could imagine. The unaccustomed comfort seemed somewhat strange to us hard-bitten frontline soldiers, what with soft feather beds in well-maintained rooms. But it was bearable. But just as we gradually got used to the new lifestyle, we also slowly learned about the entire tragedy of the military situation.

It was said that the Russians had already crossed the Vistula at Bromberg. They were marching in a broad attack wedge to the west. They were supposed to have reached the Vistula Lagoon at Elbing with a battle group that had branched north. That meant they weren't so far from our own front door.

And we had to wait around there without doing anything. We had no vehicles, no heavy weapons.

We were cynically informed: "There are enough tanks, assault guns, armored personnel carriers, armored cars, self-propelled artillery, and combat vehicles at the

Gruppe training area, about 100 kilometers south of the Russian-besieged Elbing. You can have them! Go get them, if Ivan lets you, and you have the courage to do so!"

Might as well before someone tries to stupidly use us here as infantry! Without delay, we raced off to the south with tractor trailers, prime movers and trucks that we "procured" and stole from supply units. We moved through muck and snow, by day and by night, without stopping and without rest and past an endless snake line of refugees fleeing north. For the first time, we saw Germans taking flight. Our hearts were broken: caravans of children, led by young girls, nuns, and Red Cross nurses. Horse carts with the old and infirm, wrapped in blankets and overcoats, covered with snow and frost. Wounded and more wounded. Misery after misery!

All of them looked at us with reproachful eyes, begging us to keep the Russians off of them. Not leave them in the lurch.

Tattered and fought-out German soldiers blocked our path and clenched their fists: "Stupid bastards . . . keeping the war going!"

We started to doubt whether we were doing the right thing, if we put ourselves in the path of the Russians one more time. Then we would run into individual German *Kampfgruppen*, which tried to occupy defensive positions as well as they could with their weak forces and paucity of weapons. More and more columns of refugees, wounded, children, women, old people. They were the ones who obligated us to wager everything. The villages were abandoned, dead. Everyone was moving and wanted to head north to the salvation of the sea. They wanted to be helped by the German forces still fighting.

Fools like us were swimming against the tide, against those mighty floodwaters. We wanted to, had to protect the escape route of the procession of misery.

We actually did make it to the training area before the Russians. But what a disappointment! There were only *Panzer III's* and assault guns there, most of them with Africa camouflage. And a whole lot less than we had been led to believe. There was enough, at most, for two companies.

A pair of ancient *Obergefreite* "managed" the arsenal. The finer folks apparently had found more important missions to do at more valuable places—where there wasn't firing going on.

We took everything without any formalities. The ancient warriors scrammed as quickly as they could. Understandably, they were happy to be done with their final mission. One disaster after the other! The tanks had no transformers; most of the vehicles had no receivers. The combat vehicles had to be sent into battle without radios. We were just barely able to outfit the company commander tanks with a complete radio set. But that wasn't the worst of it. The bitterly needed fuel was missing. Our tried and true "procurers" had to prove what they were worth. *Hauptmann* Bruno Schalmat got enough fuel at the last minute to make us mobile for thirty kilometers. It was poor consolation, but at least it was something.

Then the heavy motors were fired up. We didn't need to move very far. The Russians did us the favor of driving up to our main guns. The ones so used to victory got a cold shower. After the very first encounter, a good dozen T-34's were burning without any friendly losses. That gave us some self-confidence back, and it reminded the Russians, who had grown careless, to be more careful. It was only against the Josef Stalins that we couldn't do anything. Even at the shortest distances, the rounds ricocheted off. *Hauptmann* Kästner was given the mission of finding some Panthers for the 1st Battalion.

A wide screen was established; there was no point in describing it as a front. We didn't imagine that we were going to turn the wheels of history. With our weak forces, we only wanted to—all that we could do—was somewhat delay the unimpeded and fierce advance of the Red Army to the north to give the columns of wounded and refugees a chance to reach the saving Baltic before the Russians.

Our attacks were only a wasp's sting in the body of the Red Army. Despite that, we were able to ensure that the Russians only advanced at a walking pace wherever we were.

Rearguard reporting center at the end of a balka *near Nowgorod-Sserwersk, September 1943.*

Commander's conference at Major *Schultz's vehicle, summer 1944. From left to right:* Stabsarzt *Schulz-Merkel, the "*Panzer Doctor"; Major *Schultz;* Hauptmann *Möller; and* Hauptmann *Grohe (who was killed a short while later).*

Major *Fritz-Rudolf Schultz takes leave of his battalion, the* II./Panzer-Regiment 35. *In 1972, he became the ombudsman of the German parliament for the military.*

Tankers cross the sea from Courland (Kurland) to Danzig, 22 January 1945. From left to right: Oberleutnant *Peters,* Leutnant *Finkelmann, and* Hauptmann *Prast.*

A command-and-control tank of the I./Panzer-Regiment 35, *the* Befehlspanther, *March 1945.*

All escape routes are clogged by refugees.

Chapter 9

TANK ATTACK ON BLONDMIN

Unteroffizier **Robert Poensgen, war correspondent with** *Panzer-Regiment 35*

1 February 1945. I discovered that a counterattack on Blondmin was to start at 1600 hours. I wanted to be part of it. A *Kettenkrad*[1] was to take me to the front. The road we moved on headed towards Lake Eben. We had pulled back through there several days ago. It was said that our forward positions were at Bislau. After about ten kilometers, my ride broke down—engine problems.

I continued on by foot and reached Bislau around 1730 hours in the muck and the mud and the snow. It was quiet there. No trace of the war.

I encountered an *SPW* of our signals battalion. It was a telephone section that had the mission of laying wire as far as the command post of *Hauptmann* Küspert. That was where I want to go, and so I was taken along.

From wounded humping back, I discovered our tanks attacked with mounted grenadiers and that Ivan had fled as fast as his feet could fly. I was angry that I had missed that. The line trip was only moving slowly, since it had to drop wire, after all.

Up front, only an occasional shot could be heard. It was turning dark and the shimmer of many fires could be seen on the horizon. We got ever closer to the light and the sound of fighting that had flared up started coming ever closer. A farmstead was burning to the right of the road. In the light of the flames, two wildly firing assault guns were maneuvering through the snow. A pocket of resistance was being smoked out. A few mortar rounds smacked down on the road, with the result that we had to move more carefully. Grenadiers told us that the tanks had already crossed the railway line.

We reached the railway crossing and burning houses were crackling off to the left. At that point, things started getting critical. It was imperative to find out where the

---

[1] Translator's Note. The *Kettenkrad* was a small utility vehicle that had a motorcycle-like front end and a tracked cargo compartment. It saw widespread employment in the East and was popular because of its cross-country mobility, even though it had only a small payload.

forward lines were so that we didn't rattle into the Russians. At the forestry depart-ment building ahead, where the road disappeared into the woods, were a few tanks.

The wire *SPW* snuck forward with a low throttled engine. There was only infrequent firing in the village, which was ablaze, off to the right.

On the edge of the road was the first tank. It was securing to the left. I went to it and discovered that it was another 600 meters to Küspert's command post. But we needed to be careful.

The road showed unmistakable signs of fighting. The trees were shot up. Shred-ded limbs were lying on the road that had been torn down by artillery impacts.

Off to the left, in the bottomland, two tanks had sunk up to their mudguards in the soft ground. Bogged down. Most of the combat vehicles were gathered around the forestry building. Two tanks were another 100 meters to the front, where they screened the road with grenadiers. It wasn't so simple to get into the building. The Russians had barricaded the door and our *Landser* had not taken the time to remove the beams. The leader of the tanks, *Leutnant* Nieder-Schabbehard, was sitting in a tiny room. The company commander of the mechanized infantry company, *Haupt-mann* Küspert, who was leading the attack, had gone back to the rear to report to *Oberst* Christern. He was able to report success. The Russians had been pushed back twelve kilometers. It was not until the rail line had been crossed that the tanks started receiving strong antitank fire from the village in front of us, Blondmin. When they tried to swing out to the left, they ran into the treacherous marshland. Since it was dark by then, the attack could only be continued in the morning. In the course of the night, another tank company and a second mechanized infantry company were to be brought us as reinforcements in order to take Blondmin, which was heavily fortified, and then advance on to the crossroads at Lake Eben.

The wire *SPW* had also arrived in the meantime. The telephone line to the rear worked and the halftrack rumbled off. Occasionally, there was firing outside. All at once, there was a horrific crash. Antitank guns! Then another and another. We ran to the door to check out the situation. There was another crash and, at the same moment, a red tracer flitted past our noses going down the road. It was coming from the rear. We initially thought it was one of our tanks that had gotten misoriented. A patrol was sent out. In the meantime, it continued to crash and boom. Could that be Ivan?

All of a sudden, there was the sound of engines—howling wildly. The wire *SPW* came racing up. A tracer hissed right above us, only a hand's breadth away. The halftrack rattled into the courtyard to take cover. The signaleers jumped out, sup-ported two wounded and reported: Ivan was at the railway crossing with antitank guns and machine guns. That was all they were capable of initially getting out.

The wounded were then taken care of; blood was running across their faces—hit in the head. But it wasn't all that bad, since both of them could still walk and had already recovered a bit from the initial shock.

Had Ivan really set up some antitank guns to our rear at the railway crossing? On top of that, secured by machine guns? The signaleers had recognized the roadblock in the nick of time and were able to turn around. Thank God, the first round was not a direct hit.

Leutnant Nieder-Schabbehard employed three tanks against the antitank gun position. After a short firefight, the nightmare was over. The antitank guns and machine guns had been overrun.

2 February 1945. It was hazy outside at night. A patrol moved out in the direction of the Blondmin cemetery and identified a Russian assault detachment, without being seen itself. The patrol worked its way back carefully and was able to warn our outposts. Everyone was outside at that point. Nothing could be heard. The Russians were sneaking up carefully! All of a sudden, there was a rattling off to the left. You could hear the unmistakable dull hammering of heavy Russian machine guns firing. An antitank gun bellowed. Mortar rounds fell. The clattering lasted five minutes, and then there was a deathly silence.

A messenger came gasping: Enemy assault detachment turned back; one prisoner. The Russian was brought to the command post. He was wounded and his wounds were properly dressed. He was hungry. We gave him some bread, a cigarette and a cup with Schnapps. He became lively and started talking a lot, which we didn't understand. He was taken back with the vehicle that brought warm coffee forward.

A couple of wounded came hobbling up. They were followed by a young kid, who was putting all of his weight on a stick. He fell heavily into the straw in the room, which was lit up by a couple of Hindenburg lights. You could see him grinding his teeth, and he pointed to his pants, which were drenched in blood. We carefully undressed him. There was a gaping hole on the right upper thigh below the groin. You could easily put your fist in it. Ricochet! He must have lost a lot of blood. But he was amazingly brave. While the others applied dressings, I held his head and talked to him to divert his attention. He was definitely no more than 18, and it had been his first operation.

"That it would all happen so fast . . . I couldn't believe it. I haven't seen anything of the war yet!" That appeared to be his biggest worry. Poor kid! He asked whether the wound was bad. He really wanted to see it. We diverted him, since it was so frightful that he probably would have keeled over.

After they finished dressing him, he complained about pain in his left leg. We looked further and a second deep wound on the left side of the lower body, but it did not appear to be life threatening. Just a chunk of regular flesh was missing. Despite all the bad luck, the kid had a streak of tremendously good luck, and we told him that. We gave him some greetings to take with him back home. He was from Ingolstadt.

I then slept some while sitting on some junk. My head was against a large earthenware pot with salted meat that had gone bad and stunk terribly. I was so tired, however, that I missed the return of *Hauptmann* Küspert and did not wake up until everyone was going outside. It was already starting to get light. It was intended for the attack to start in half an hour.

I reported to *Hauptmann* Küspert as a war correspondent and asked his permission to ride along on his command tank. It was an old *Panzer IV* without a traversable turret and a fake main gun.[2]

I had a bad feeling and was unable to eat anything, despite the best of intentions. The tanks slowly pushed through the garden to get ready to move out. Right at eight, the vehicles that had gone into position the night before in the woodline along the rail line broke out in the direction of Blondmin. They rolled like the devil across the snowy fields. Heavy firing started coming from out of the village. We observed the attack through binoculars while standing concealed by a bush. *Hauptmann* Küspert sat on the edge of his turret and radioed fire commands, since we were able to identify several antitank gun positions by their muzzle flashes. Our tanks started firing wildly into the village, which started to burn in a number of places. There was one black dot after the other on the field. Those were the impacts of the mortar rounds from the Russians. They sprinkled the ground with black gunpowder residue.

There was a thick fog of gunpowder smoke over the field, and the brilliant red muzzle flashes twitched through it. The mechanized infantry followed in a thin wave behind the advancing tanks. Here and there, you saw one or two men jump up, hop a few steps and then throw themselves down in the snow again. A couple of them remained where they were.

When the our left wing had reached the village, *Hauptmann* Küspert issued orders for the right wing to attack. The tanks pushed forwards out of their covered positions; the mechanized infantry advanced.

I had the secret wish that the captain would remain where he was with his command vehicle, since we had good cover between the houses. But he was no "remote control" commander. I was standing on the rear deck of our vehicle. It pushed forward with a rocking motion and a drone as far as the furthest edge of the vegetation. There was a small chapel behind us. We then started to receive heavy fire as well. You could hear it by the crack of the antitank gun, whether it was firing at you or had another target in its sights. Heavy mortar rounds rumbled in the houses behind us. The bricks flew and the reddish dust was thrown around the area.

A friendly tank fifty meters in front of us was hit in the side. All of a sudden, an ear-deafening roar. I had long since crawled behind the turret; at that point, I pressed myself as flat as a bug on the rear deck.

Hauptmann Küspert, who had been observing with his upper body out of the commander's cupola, disappeared as fast as lightning. Only an arm remained jutting out of the cupola. For a moment, everything turned dark around me. Clumps of snow and earth rained down on me, as thick as hail. Shrapnel smashed against steel;

---

[2] Editor's Note. This vehicle may have been a field conversion, as the standard command version of the *Panzer IV*, the *Panzerbefehlswagen mit 7.5-cm KwK L/48*, retained the 7.5-centimeter main armament. The author may also be mistaken, and this was actually the *Panzerbefehlswagen III*.

one piece went though my gloves, missing my index finger by a millimeter. It had been the impact of a 12.2 half a meter away from our right drive sprocket.

We pulled back and set up next to the chapel. Once again, there was a harsh blow, a pelting and a rumbling. Ten meters away, an impact in the church. I was showered with bits of red brick. The adjutant was standing in the commander's cupola at that point. *Hauptmann* Küspert had been wounded. Even though he had dropped down quickly, his arm had remained outside and it had gotten hit by a couple of terrible things.

Our tanks continued to roll forward. The left wing was involved in intense street fighting. The Soviets were firing from out of all the houses. The right wing also pushed its way closer and closer to the village through the raging fire. Flames were shooting out of the roofs; black banks of smoke rose above the village.

Our command vehicle followed the tanks. We rocked our way forward to the cemetery, which had been churned up by the impacting rounds. Not a single tank track was seen over the graves. That was striking, since the land had been torn up everywhere else by tank tracks.

The artillery fire started abating all at once. The Russian batteries at the edge of the village had been silenced. There was only artillery and antitank gunfire coming from farther to the rear. But the fire control of the Russians seemed to be in a state of chaos, since the impacting rounds landed arbitrarily in the area.

At that point, we were at the entrance to Blondmin. The lead tanks appeared at the far side of the village. We could see the abandoned Russian guns, antitank guns and infantry guns with our naked eyes.

We moved closely past one such position. The ground was churned up by impacts; the edge of the woods behind it shredded. A lot of dead were lying around; the guns had been shot to pieces. Not too far away were the ammunition trucks, nothing but American Studebakers.

The sound of fighting in the village died down. We moved a bit farther forward until we could see Lake Eben. On the far side of it was the estate, where the division command post had been set up a few days previously. At regular intervals, a heavy hitter, a Josef Stalin, fired over at us. Our tanks could not reach it with their main guns.

At that point, there was a wild hunt for Soviets in progress. They were trying to flee the far side of the village. A number of trucks and guns had bogged down in the snow, since the road was no longer trafficable. The Russians fled individually like black dots across the white snow—on foot and in sleds.

Three tanks, which had been along the road at the forestry building, then joined the attack as well, rolling through the woods. At 1100 hours, the important crossroads was attacked concentrically from three sides. From where we were, we could no longer observe, since a curtain of woods pushed its way in between from the right. So we moved back. Past the cemetery one more time and then got to the main route.

The mechanized infantry had already got a couple of the Russian trucks running again. The valuable fuel was siphoned out of the remaining ones. We then went into the village. There was a rich bounty there, nothing but good things that Ivan had to leave behind. Most of it was captured German comfort items. There was huge amounts of fruit conserves, tinned meat, cans of fish, smoking items—everything the heart could desire. In the houses, the cooked chickens were still on the tables, since the comrades had slaughtered all of the poultry. Although it probably never would have crossed their minds in a million years that we would come and consume it.

The fires crackled outside. We sat in front of steaming pots and ate ourselves full. It didn't bother us at all that there were piles of shit in the corners that stank. After that "snack," we rolled back to the main road in our tanks and raced through the woods at high speed towards the crossroads. About 100 meters in front of it, we encountered the lead vehicles.

Two farmsteads were burning brightly off to the left. The Soviets had dug in there and received our tanks with heavy fire. We saw the wrecks of two T-34's and an assault gun, which gave off pitch-black smoke.

Hauptmann Küspert briefed the tank commanders on the situation and issued his attack orders.

One of our *Kampfgruppen* moved out on the left, while the vehicles in our vicinity observed the edges of the woods and provided immediate fire support in the event resistance flared up. The tanks rolled forward as if on a parade ground. Fire and movement alternated. They then crossed the road that came from Lake Eben. While three vehicles went into position and screened from there to the left, the remaining vehicles swung out wide to the right towards the burning farmsteads. We saw the mounted grenadiers dismount and clear the buildings, while the tanks, smashing down fences and vegetation, followed slowly. But it appeared that the enemy had already pulled back. We crossed the crossroads and moved past the other vehicles through the curtain of woods. At that point, the formation was reorganized. Outposts were directed to be established after the mechanized infantry determined that the woods were clear of the enemy.

For me, it was time to return to Tuchel if I wanted to turn in my articles in a timely manner. There was certainly nothing more to be expected that day.

Later on, I regretted that decision, since our tanks turned back a strong Soviet flank attack supported by tanks and threw Ivan an additional five kilometers back in the direction of Haselmühl. In addition to a number of T-34's, they also rendered two Josef Stalins immobile after an intense firefight.

A LOT OF LUCK AND A *JAGDPANTHER*

Oberfeldwebel Hermann Bix, tank commander in *Panzer-Regiment 35*

We were really upset when we did not receive the accustomed and promised *Panzer V's* and were issued instead the *Jagdpanther*, which could not be sent to an assault-gun battalion as a result of the general chaos.

Out of necessity, we then took a closer look at the new gear. The crates did not have a turret. You had to roughly aim the entire vehicle, which meant you were sort of exposed. But looked at in another light, the steel colossus had a pronounced low silhouette, which housed an excellent 8.8-centimeter main gun. The cannon had enormous penetrating ability, a legendary range and a captivating hit probability.

As a result, we quickly forgot about the unaccustomed lack of a turret on the vehicle and familiarized ourselves intensively with its advantages. We soon had opportunity enough to test that out completely.

End of February 1945. I was east of Preußisch-Stargard with three *Jagdpanther*. I was screening the withdrawal of our grenadiers and the establishment of a new defensive front further to the rear. Everything was moving back. The only thing that remained were dark mounds of dirt, the abandoned field positions. I was in a small locality with my vehicle, located behind a pile of manure. It was in such a manner that I could still observe and the main gun was above the pile. The flat superstructure of the vehicle only jutted a small amount above our cover.

Oberfeldwebel Dehm was behind me with one other *Jagdpanther*. The two of them had hardly any ammunition left. Without rounds, the two vehicles were only a burden to me. I therefore directed them to pull back a bit.

As the fog slowly started to lift, two Russian tanks appeared very, very carefully on the hill in front of us and felt their way closer slowly. When they arrived to within about 1,200 meters, I determined that they were neither T-34's nor KV-I's. Instead, they were combat vehicle of an American type. From experience, I knew that they could be knocked out at that distance relatively easily. We lit up both of them, and Ivan didn't stick his nose out any more for some time.

A group of tankers, who had lost their tanks, were screening in the village. That meant that I was safe against surprises to either the right or the left, since there was only a limited field of vision from the vehicle proper. Besides, you can't have eyes everywhere.

About a half an hour after knocking out the two tanks, I heard tank noises off to the right and identified two Russian tanks that wanted to bypass our village. My 8.8-centimeter main gun fired so accurately at that distance that there was hardly any such thing as a near miss. In short order, the two tanks were burning. At that point, I knew the Russians were feverishly trying to find a "weak spot" to be able to thrust through. It was imperative that I was attentive to the entire sector, since I was the only one in the area. The two remaining vehicles had taken off with my permission, since they had expended all of their ammunition.

My gunner reported to me that we only had five high-explosive and twenty antitank rounds left.

Leutnant Tautorus had to be out there somewhere, since he was screening in a neighboring sector. I reported to him by radio that I was being constantly attacked by enemy tanks, that I was all by myself and that I had little ammunition left. I received orders to hold up the Russians for as long as possible, since the infantry behind us had not yet finished establishing its positions.

In the meantime, my security on the ground also had to depart so as not to lose contact to the rear. That meant I could no longer observe what was going on to the right or left. Ivan could march there in parade formation and three across, and we would not see him.

I then observed the slope in front of me more exactly and determined that the Russians were openly bringing two antitank guns into position there. What was that supposed to mean? Were they trying to grab me by the collar? I had high-explosive rounds loaded and gave a fire command. *Rums!* Well lookie there! Bits of wood and fabric were flying through the air. The bastards had pulled a fast one and brought fake guns into position to get us to fire and determine where we were positioned. Pretty clever! And we fell right into their trap. I wasn't going to be the butt of a joke a second time. I wasn't going to expend any more of our valuable ammunition, if more wooden antitank guns showed up on the slope.

I kept as quiet as a church mouse. I even had the vehicle pull back a bit so that there was no way I could be seen from the front. It was only when I stuck my head out of the fighting compartment that I could see over our cover. I couldn't believe my eyes. I saw a long column moving at speed directly towards my position. The lead vehicles were 1,200 meters away. Tanks in front and supply vehicles behind them.

I had surveyed the terrain in front of me and divided it into certain sectors with the ranges carefully determined. That meant I could afford to wait until the lead tank was 800 meters from me before firing an antitank round.

I don't know why, but my great gunner did not hit the tank with his first round. Instead, he got a big tree on the edge of the road. The trunk broke in the middle and the crown collapsed on the lead tank with its thick branches. The tank then careened into the roadside ditch, since it had lost its ability to see. It remained there, immobilized.

The tanks that followed closed up and halted, but they did not identify me. One after the other, they all traversed their turrets to the right and fired like the fire department into the dark mounds of the abandoned infantry positions.

At that point, it was easy pickings, since the sides of the turrets were facing my direction of fire. But we also had to take careful aim, since we only had a few rounds. And if one of the tanks was left after we fired all of our ammunition, things could turn ugly for us.

Correspondingly, I had the middle tank in the column engaged first. It immediately went up in flames after the first round. The next one was the tank at the end of the column. Rums! It was also burning. Then we shot up the rest effortlessly, one after the other, since all of them were positioned there as if on a gunnery range.

We knocked out eleven Russian tanks in the column in ten minutes. The rest of them got bogged down in the ditch after attempting to turn around in a panic. They were then covered by the flames and smoke of the tanks burning in a long column.

The "Water" Front, April 1945. The dikes in the Danziger Werder have been blown up.

The Grove of Honor for the Panzertruppe *at Lüneburg Heath—memorial stones for all forty-nine of the German armored divisions.*

All praise for the ferry at Schiewenhorst! It transported day and night and took the last load to Kiel.

Chapter 10

ALPINE ROSE, OVER!

Leutnant **Hans Schäufler, regimental signals officer with** *Panzer-Regiment* **35, 4.** *Panzer-Division*

Beginning of February to the middle of March 1945. Fuel for our tanks—that was problem number one at the time. They devoured fuel in huge quantities when conducting combat operations of this nature. We were supposed to be everywhere at the same time, but our fuel tanks were usually empty. The combat strength of our mechanized infantry had shrunk so much that sometimes fifteen men had to cover a frontage of two kilometers. We avoided the term "front" as much as possible. We invented the term "observation veil." Our artillery had no ammunition. Whenever the Russian attacked somewhere, it was up to the tanks to take care of the penetration.

Correspondingly, out of the need for sheer self-preservation, we hunted for columns of Russian trucks whenever there was a chance they might be loaded with fuel. The report went from vehicle to vehicle whenever one believed it had made a "find."

With regard to radios—that was the second rubbing point, for which only the regimental signals officer bore responsibility. Although all of the vehicles had received a complete radio complement, Ivan was jamming our radio traffic day and night with strong transmitters on all frequencies, as well as eavesdropping on all traffic and attempting to mislead crews with false orders and break down morale with propaganda.

I had to be very creative so that we could be heard by the opposite station among the stew of frequencies and, moreover, so that the comrades did not get wind of whatever we were thinking of doing.

The secret signals operating instructions, which had been worked out with great precision at the highest command levels had long since been in Russian hands. There was no relying on them any more—we discovered that daily. As a result of the necessary and single-handed improvisations that were bitterly necessary, we were always walking on the edge of court-martial proceedings. Effectiveness trumps secrecy. That was an old military saying, and the courts-martial were far to the rear.

My regimental commander, *Oberst* Christern, insisted on a well-organized and always functioning radio network. Given the situation, that was more than understandable. For me, however, it meant that I had to go from company to company each night on a motorcycle and coordinate the radio instructions with the head radio operators.

The 1st Battalion was still waiting for its *Panthers*, which were supposed to come from Kurland or God knew where else. As a result, I had the frequencies allocated to the 1st Battalion at my disposal as well. As a result, we often changed frequencies from message to message by the use of a code word so as to be able to get our traffic through at all. Up to that point, the system had worked terrifically and until such point as Ivan found our frequency again and attempted to disrupt or eavesdrop we had completed our traffic. As a safety precaution, we had an emergency frequency in case radio contact was lost in some manner due to a misunderstanding. That was not to be found in any manual, but nothing could have been worse in our situation that to be left hanging in the air. The success of these measures—in contravention of army procedures—justified them, even if the division signals officer did not approve of them, at least officially. But what he did not know did not hurt him, and the end justified the means.

Using that concept, we successfully conducted armor operations in the Tuchel Heath. We advanced in the direction of Bromberg and Nackel, then towards Kamin and then far to the west as far as Konitz. We chased the nonplussed Russians back everywhere, captured a bit of fuel here and there and, above all, won some time—since time was the most important thing in that hopeless struggle.

We heard the Russian "morning prayers" in our receivers everywhere: "Put an end to the war!" "You are encircled!" "You have no fuel and no ammunition!" "Stop resisting, if you want to see your homeland again!" Always the same old story. Although we didn't imagine things and knew that the war could no longer be won, we had to do our part to hold open the route to the saving banks of the Baltic for the desperate people.

On 15 February, Tuchel had to be handed over to the Russians. We pulled out of the town during the night to keep it from being destroyed even more. We established a new blocking position at Heiderode. Then, on 24 February, the long-awaited *Panthers* of the 1st Battalion came to us.

The new signals situation demanded new thought. Usually, during operations, the two battalions were far apart from one another; the short-wave radios did not cover such long distances. As a result, the two regimental command vehicles, which both had medium-wave radios, were detached to the battalions and the signals battalion made a "goat," that is, a radio *SPW*, available to the regiment. *Oberst* Christern, who always gave me free reign in signals matters, agreed to the solution.

Hopefully, he would also consider in the future the fact that he no longer had eight centimeters of armored plate in front of his head.[1]

February passed with armored thrusts, fuel worries and problems with radio traffic. We went tank hunting to the west, to the south and, in the end, also to the north. We were always close to being cut off and cashiered. The columns of refugees to our rear often advanced very slowly due to the congested roads; the Russian aircraft dominated the refugee routes. In addition, we needed the roads ourselves for our supplies. As a result, little ammunition, fuel and rations came forward.

Hold tough and fight for time—that was and remained the slogan. We accomplished more than we should have been able to. We put ourselves in the way of the advancing Russians again and again. The tank crews performed miracles, since the mechanized infantry had been bled white.

Our "Russian counterparts" attempted to break us down and intimidate us with all the means at their disposal. Day-in, day-out, the same old broken record. Beyond that, however, there were personally directed messages: "You won't have anything to radio tomorrow, since we'll be cashiering you tomorrow! . . . We'll give you three more days, then the devil take the hindmost!"

We gradually figured out that we could get all sorts of information from those attempts to intimidate us. As a result, we listened to even the worst of the abuse without so much as batting an eye. And the bastard with the slight Saxony accent grew ever more venomous, since we never reacted, no matter how much he called us out and tempted us.

On 8 March, the Russians advanced with strong forces to the west of us all the way to the Baltic. Stolp fell into their hands. We had been cut off from every land connection. The *2. Armee*, that is, what was left of it, had to be supplied in the future from the sea and the refugees had to be taken to safety by boat. It was going to get interesting!

An armored *Kampfgruppe* under *Oberst* Christern was sent as expeditiously as possible to Bütow to be loaded on trains, since there wasn't enough fuel for the road march to the new area of operations around Neustadt. The deep flank had been torn wide open. The situation there was completely uncertain. We moved at almost a walking pace for hours on end on flat cars to the north. The train stations had no personnel. There were no German forces to be seen. But also no Russian. It was only the Russian fighter-bombers that laid into us. Then it started to snow, and we were happy as could be to get rid of the bastards.

Strict radio silence was ordered. As a result, we discovered nothing and were left up to our own devices and our lack of knowledge. It was like a dance on the volcano

---

[1] Translator's Note. The author is referring to the fact that *Oberst* Christern normally had a *Panther* as his command vehicle. Because of the slope of the armor in the turret, Christern had the equivalent of eight centimeters of steel protection.

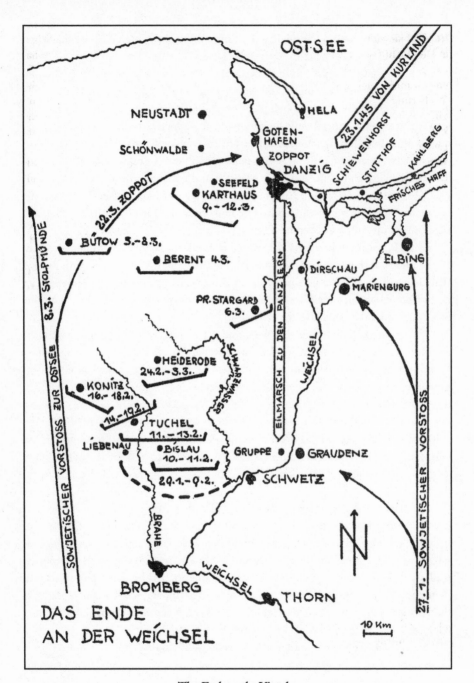

The End on the Vistula.

(Sowjetischer Vorstoß zur Ostsee = *Soviet advance to the Baltic;* 21.1. Sowjetischer
Vorstoß = *Soviet advance on 21 January;* Eilmarsch zu den Panzern = *forced march to
the armor;* 23.1.45 von Kurland = *from Courland on 23 January 1945)*

that could erupt at any moment. The troops were informed to be prepared for operations right off the transport train. That didn't sound very promising.

All of a sudden, we halted on an open stretch. *Oberst* Christern was uninformed of what was happening, as we all were. I had no idea where we were at the time when we threw the "goat" off the train. "Throw" is not an exaggeration. We literally had to toss it off the car because there were no offload facilities.

Oberst Christern intended to personally reconnoiter to find out where the forward German lines were so that the combat vehicles would have the shortest route to the area of operations, thus saving the few liters of fuel in the tanks for fighting. We took off on a broad asphalt road, about a kilometer west of the tracks. It was intended for the train to slowly follow. I had everyone prepared to use their radios, just in case.

We kept going and going. No German soldiers, no German vehicles, no humans far and wide. I had never seen a section of land so dead. But, there also wasn't any firing. Nothing at all. The environment there was eerie.

I uttered my doubts: "Something's not right here. There's no more German forces coming, otherwise you'd see trains and supply elements." The *Oberst*, who was always brisk, sometimes too much so for my taste, waved me off.

We moved fifteen or twenty kilometers. Always the same picture. No signs of life to be seen anywhere.

Then I thought I saw well-camouflaged and fresh mounds of dirt, as well as vegetation, that did not seem right for the area.

"*Herr Oberst*, take a look through the binoculars over there!"

"What are you, Schäufler, afraid?"

I am not particularly sensitive, but even my commander was not allowed to say that to me. I replied, more drastically and loudly, than I intended: "No, by God no, but I'm still fed up from the last time!"

During a similar "excursion" about six weeks previously, *Oberwachtmeister* Wegener was killed and I still had shrapnel in my chin and a hole in my eardrum.

The *Oberst*, a tough warrior, who led his tank regiment from the front lines and who used the coarse language of a soldier, looked at me horrified. But I no longer had any time for an apology or my derailment, since I then saw Russian helmets flashing through the thin branches . . . there . . . there . . . there. And I also saw the barrel of an antitank gun that was directed toward us.

"We're right in the middle of the Russians," I yelled into the ears of the *Oberst*. But he still had his doubts, the perpetual optimist. I kicked the driver in the back: "There's a gravel pit off to the left. Get in there as fast as you can!"

The *Oberst* yelled at me, but his ass chewing got stuck in his throat as the first antitank round whizzed just above our heads. The driver put the pedal to the metal and raced across the snow-covered field and then braked with a jerk. We slid down the steep gradient of the gravel pit. Above us, a hurricane of fire stormed past. *Oberst* Christern, no friend of overly hasty improvisation, looked at me for a moment with uncertainty before life came back to his massive figure. He indicated the radio set with his eyes and then looked at me questioningly. I understand his silent directive. I put on the headphones and switch to "transmit." At the same time, under the direction of the commander, the crew ripped the machine gun out of its mount, grabbed submachine guns and hand grenades, occupied the edge of the gravel pit and let loose with everything they had. Everyone knew that seconds could decide our lives, which were not worth very much at all at the moment.

Damn it! No one answered.

"Alpine Rose . . . Alpine Rose . . . Alpine Rose . . . this is urgent, over!"

Finally, there was a crackle in my headset: "This is Alpine Rose . . . what's going on?"

"We've been encircled by the Russians and can only hold out for five minutes. Urgently need help. Get here immediately."

"This is Alpine Rose . . . understood . . . what's your location? . . . we're coming with three tanks."

"We're in a gravel pit in a heavy firefight with Russians attacking on all sides. Move along the road. Move now! Come quickly!"

Up top, they were already throwing hand grenades. Russian machine guns and submachine guns were rattling, and they were getting closer and closer. Antitank round flung stones against the armor plating of the vehicle.

"Alpine Rose . . . where are you? . . . I'm firing white signal flares . . . can you see them?"

Then the diabolic laugh of our "Ivan Saxon" entered the net: "Alpine Rose . . . now we have you . . . you won't get away this time!"

No, they won't take us alive! That was the only thought I had.

I yelled to the *Oberst*: "Three tanks are en route . . . they have to be here any minute!"

He raised his hand casually in acknowledgement and continued to fire. I wished I had his calmness!

"Alpine Rose . . . move as fast as your crates will fly . . . and fire with everything you have so that our friends forget about us for a moment!"

High-explosive rounds raced down the roadway. The firing of our crew picked up. I counted them. Everyone was still there. The firing by the Russians stopped all of a sudden. I tossed down the headset and crept up to the edge of the pit.

Good God! What a picture! Our three tanks were moving for all they were worth across the open field and fired with everything they had. The descended on the surprised Russian antitank-gun positions and overran them. The Russians were running en masse. They had identified the tanks too late and were barely able to get a round off.

I ran back to the radio set. Ivan was still crowing: "Is it all over for you? . . . Have we already finished you off?"

"You're in a world of shit!" I was barely able to suppress the temptation to yell into the microphone.

The two radio operators came back to the vehicle with pale faces and retook their duty stations at the equipment. I was then able to observe the magic topside at my leisure. The three tanks were cleaning up and had advanced another 300 meters. They were able to knock out a few more antitank guns. And the crews ran as if the devil himself were behind them.

The *Oberst* sauntered up to me in a leisurely fashion. He laughed a bit, embarrassed, and called me a crude Bavarian, but he didn't hold a grudge against me for my outburst.

Hauptmann Petrelli, the regimental adjutant, then reported that all of the vehicles had detrained. The *Oberst* gave orders to move out, and we awaited the main body of tanks. While waiting, we set off a situation report to the division.

It was pretty rare for a gigantic antitank-gun blocking position to be forced so easily. Even the Russians couldn't believe it, since they offered very little resistance. We then received orders from the division to call off the attack, which was still going well.

No, there were no more German soldiers there. Even the *Oberst* was completely convinced of that.

"You were right once again, Schäufler!"

Nothing could shake up old Christern, neither masses of Russian antitank guns nor a signals officer who didn't know his place. You had to give him that.

The "Ivan Saxon" kept silent for hours, embarrassed. I had the feeling that he had to change positions.

Urgent radio traffic from the division: "New situation. Russian tanks attacking Karthaus and Seefeld. Get ready to move immediately. Fight your way through to Karthaus as soon as possible!" Karthaus was way to our rear just outside the gates of Danzig. That couldn't be true!

We assembled and moved along the main road back to the northeast. The closer we got to Karthaus, the more the streets were jammed with refugees, trains vehicles, horse-drawn conveyances. Some wanted to get into Karthaus, other out. It was impossible to get through on roads like that when there was so much chaos. Two tanks were given the mission of remaining behind to protect the refugees and look for an escape route to Gotenhafen. We then moved cross-country.

In Karthaus, we reported in to the local area commander. The old *Oberst*, who was sitting there, was in a state of panic and jittery. He was in no way up to the confusing situation. By order of the division, *Oberst* Christern assumed command.

He immediately had some of the tanks move southeast to screen. Almost half of the vehicles had to be towed into position, due to a lack of fuel. It was chaotic in and around the village. The access roads were completely overwhelmed with refugee vehicles. The distraught people ran around aimlessly since they did not know the situation. Vehicles without fuel hindered the flow of traffic.

The *Oberst* employed all of his soldiers, who were not essential for the fighting, as traffic regulators. The route to the Baltic for the refugees were reconnoitered, and the columns rerouted in those directions. The routes were screened by a few tanks.

It appeared that a dramatic competition was in progress between the German and Russian forces to see who could get to Danzig and its all-important Baltic harbor.

A few kilometers from us, strong Russian armored formations were marching in the direction of Seefeld, and we could not prevent them or join in the fight, since we did not have a single liter of fuel in our tanks.

Tank drivers and loaders, even noncommissioned officers and company-grade officers with Knight's Crosses ran around with fuel canisters in their hands in an effort to beg a few liters of fuel so that they could at least move their tanks under their own power into a firing position. It was a portrait of unspeakable misery. No one wanted to sacrifice his vehicle, since everyone knew that every tank was urgently needed.

A route to the north, to Gotenhafen, was found and cleared. On 8 March, the village of Karthaus was cleared of all vehicles. It was only south of the town that columns still jammed up. They were increasingly becoming the targets of Russian aircraft. That only served to increase the confusion.

The situation around Seefeld gradually grew desperate. Correspondingly, the division ordered: "All available elements of the *4. Panzer-Division*, are to assemble in the area around Karthaus as soon as possible, by foot march, if necessary."

All of us were employed in clearing the roads. Disabled trucks were tipped over into the ditches without a second thought. Every liter of fuel was collected with a fine-tooth comb. We found a few hidden canisters of fuel of some trains vehicles. The horse-drawn vehicles were sent cross-country. Gradually, the chaos abated. A sort of "might makes right" ruled the roads. But there was no looking back. Even the stupidest or most stubborn of men could easily see that the Russians were using every means possible to cut us off. Rumors made the threatening situation even more uncertain. It was whispered from mouth to mouth that Ivan was already in Danzig.

In a last effort, our grenadiers descended one more time on the enemy; meter-by-meter, they fought themselves and the pitiful refugees clear. They had to fight to clear the essential roads not only against the Russians, but also against our own failures and against laggards and dawdlers. They sacrificed their own trains vehicles, so that the combat vehicles would get a few liters of fuel. Despite promises, no fuel arrived.

A friendly attack to open the road to Danzig bogged down. The Russians were already too strong there. The very last fuel from the trains vehicles was also used up. That meant that we were completely immobilized in Karthaus. We then heard that fuel had been set aside for us, but that it could not reach us, since it was not possible to bring it in from Danzig.

On 9 March, orders were received: "Keep only the valuable combat vehicles. All remaining vehicles are to be blown up immediately."

We held the area around Karthaus for two more days and defended against fairly weak Russian attacks, and, for the first time, against a slowly mounting despair. Russian aircraft dropped clouds of propaganda leaflets on us; Ivan attempted to wear us down with loudspeaker propaganda. We waited hour-by-hour for the promised fuel, since the division had ordered that all operational tanks were to be preserved.

In bitter fighting with a few combat vehicles, *Hauptmann* Lange held the withdrawal route to Zoppot open for us at Schönwalde.

I don't know how they did it, but two prime movers arrived on 12 March after moving through woods and open fields and brought the promised fuel. By then, Karthaus was devoid of civilians.

On back roads and through morass and bush country, we snaked our way with cunning and cleverness—and some luck—to the north past the Russians. We bogged down again due to a lack of fuel, but more was brought to us at nighttime. Through circuitous routes, we reached the large, but also abandoned *Adlerhorst Flak*[2] position at Zoppot. We were able to get a full night's sleep there in the bunkers.

It was only later that we discovered that our commander had had to fight higher headquarters for that few hours of sleep, since we were already expected for new operations at Oliva.

---

[2] Translator's Note: *Adlerhorst* = "eagle's nest."

Early-model Panzer IV's *advance along the ubiquitous dirt roads of the Eastern Front. For obvious reasons, the roads became nearly impassible to armored vehicles during the so-called "mud seasons" in the spring and fall.*

An officer in an Sd.Kfz. 250—a light half-track—confers with infantry. The tactical symbol indicates a 7.5-centimeter antitank gun towed by a half-track.

Panzer III Ausf. J's *and* Panzer II's *of* Panzer-Regiment 24 *of the* 24. Panzer-Division *during a halt on the Eastern Front. This image was most likely taken during the drive on Stalingrad, which saw the subsequent destruction of the division.*

Commander's conference in the field. The officers are in early-model Panzer III's *with a short 3.7-centimeter main gun. To augment their relatively thin armor, track links have been mounted along the front hull and slope of the tanks.*

The old and the new. A late-model Panzer IV passes a horse-drawn wagon on its way to the front. The Panzer IV has been outfitted with Ostketten—"Eastern tracks"—which were track extensions intended to lower the ground pressure of German tanks. Up through the Panzer IV, German tanks had high ground pressure because of the narrowness of the tracks, making them less maneuverable on snowy or very muddy ground.

Chapter 11

WRITE YOUR WILLS, COMRADES!

***Unteroffizier* Robert Poensgen, war correspondent with the**
4. Panzer-Division

15 March 1945. Together with other elements and the courage of desperation, our *4. Panzer-Division*, bled white and emaciated, conducted an unequal fight against time and Russian superiority for the Baltic still-free ports of Danzig and Gotenhafen.

Streams of refugees rolled in from all directions of the compass: Down from East Prussia across the sand spit along the outer edge of the Vistula lagoon; up from West Prussia from the south; from Pomerania from the southwest. It was a grim picture of misery. Mothers carried dead children in limp arms. Dead people lay on the ox carts next to hastily assembled personal items, the wounded and the sick.

They had arrived through snow squalls and ice storms...across ice bursting under Russian artillery fire in the lagoon. Many died en route. They had been decimated by Russian aircraft and plundered by Polish partisans. Their eyes mirrored terror, sometimes insanity.

And the Russians, confident of victory and their numerical superiority, marched irresistibly north and west in the direction of Berlin. Their attack waves surged mercilessly; they had the leaflet from Ilja Rosenberg in their pockets, which had been countersigned by Stalin: "Kill the Germans, wherever you meet them! Kill! Kill! Kill!"

Who would want to remain there; who would want to be at the mercy of the Red Army?

That the war was lost was a fact known then by even the dumbest person. There was nothing to be picked up: No decorations, no promotions, just a dead, cold ass. That was the general take on the situation.

It was a merciless struggle for survival—for your own and for the hundreds of thousands who were placing their trust in us, who were begging us with their eyes, who looked at us accusingly, who were being chased along the roads to the sea, and who squatted and waited and waited for ships that would take them west and away from the hell around them.

Kill! Kill! Kill! The Russian tank tidal wave came rolling at us with that thought in mind: From the south, from the southeast, from the southwest. Everything was headed for Danzig. In fairness to the Soviet fighting forces, it must be said that most of them were more humane than that most inhumane order of that horrible war.

That was the situation on 15 March 1945, when *Oberleutnant* Gerlach was issued orders by *Oberst* Christern to move to the Oliva–Neue Welt[1] area with the five remaining operational *Panthers* of his company. They were to hinder an impending Russian armored assault in the sector of the *389. Infanterie-Division*.

Shortly before departure, one of the *Panthers* had to be detached to another *Kampfgruppe* of the regiment, which only had *Panzer III's* and in whose sector Josef Stalins had been reported as approaching.

During the movement, two additional *Panthers* were lost to mechanical problems, because the fuel that had been used contained too much water. Shortly before the onset of darkness, Gerlach reached the new area of operations with two *Panthers* and received orders to support the night attack of the fusilier battalion[2] on Neue Welt. After destroying the reported enemy tanks, he was to block the narrows between the bodies of water at Neue Welt.

The fusiliers moved out around 2000 hours. It was already pitch black. The attackers were received by heavy fire. You could clearly make out the sounds of a lot of tank main guns firing.

By then, it had also been determined that there were no fewer than twenty-four Russian tanks in the village of Neue Welt, including eight Josef Stalins. It had been directed for Gerlach to attack against that oppressive numerical superiority with his two *Panthers*! He tried to get the unequal operation scratched, since it would probably end in the Russian's favor with about a 95 percent probability, no matter how much courage was shown. But the attack had to be conducted, no matter the cost. The overall situation required it.

"Write your wills, comrades!" That was the only advice Gerlach could give his tankers. There was no way you could call him a pessimist or a laggard, either. He had already participated in some 150 tank engagements. But this operation seemed to be a suicide mission to him. There were no beginners in the two *Panthers*. They were battle-seasoned pros. They had all decided to exercise their duty to the bitter end, but to also make their lives cost as much as possible in the process. They did not feel they were heroes ...

The fusiliers had approached to the village outskirts. They knocked out an enemy tank and an antitank gun with *Panzerfäuste*. They received such heavy fire,

---

[1] Translator's Note. Neue Welt was essentially a suburb of Danzig. It translates as "New World," but since it is a place name, it has been retained in the original German.

[2] Translator's Note. In 1944, many of the infantry divisions redesignated and reorganized their reconnaissance battalions (*Aufklärungs-Abteilung*) into so-called *Füsilier* battalions. In essence, they remained reconnaissance battalions, but they were frequently augmented with additional firepower and mobility.

however, that they had to pull back some. Of all times, Gerlach's vehicle then suffered a mechanical problem. He had to send it back with its crew. He only took his proven radio operator, *Unteroffizier* Kupfer, with him, since there was a less experienced soldier in the vehicle he boarded. Otherwise, a bunch of old hands in the vehicle: The gunner, *Unteroffizier* Lang; the loader, Oberschütze Heinrich; and the driver, *Obergefreiter* Bauer.

The vehicle snuck up along the rail line all by itself toward the village. The motor was throttled down, so as not to draw attention to the vehicle.

As an experienced tanker, Gerlach knew that he had to get a good start on things, if he wanted to survive the unequal engagement. He was protected from enemy view by a snow fence. On the railway tracks to his left, there were freight cars. Even if it turned light, the shadow cast by his tank would not stand out on the horizon.

About 400 meters from the village, the tank bogged down in the soft earth. It took all of the driver's skills to get the vehicle out again. As a result of the unavoidably louder engine noises, the Russians had been alerted. They fired blind in the suspected direction, but they were unable to see or hit the well-concealed *Panther*.

Gunner Lang fired. Taking up a sight picture on the muzzle flash, and got an assault gun with his first round. It and the house immediately behind it caught fire and illuminated the surrounding terrain for some distance. Three more tanks were identified within the area of the illumination. They had been posted at the edge of the village to screen.

Since the *Panther* started to receive heavy and aimed fire, it pulled back a few hundred meters to a better hull-down position. Gerlach's crew succeeded in knocking out three tanks and two antitank guns, whose rounds had been passing uncomfortably close over the *Panther*.

As it started to turn light, Gerlach moved his vehicle further back into the hull-down opposition. He then observed the village through the scissors scope he had. The Russian tanks were clumped together between the houses. Heavy artillery and mortar fire commenced.

Toward noon, a second vehicle arrived. It was under the command of *Oberfeldwebel* Palm, a long-time "tank cracker." Palm's crew set two enemy tanks on fire in the course of the afternoon, including one Josef Stalin. Gerlach was able to put another Josef Stalin out of commission and completely knocked out an assault gun. A few antitank guns also paid the ultimate price.

The rest of the day passed, as well as the second night. The Russians did not dare to venture out. It was not until the next day that the Soviets attempted to attack further to the right with infantry. Gerlach immediately moved to the threatened sector.

While he took charge of engaging the enemy tanks that appeared, his radio operator, *Unteroffizier* Kupfer, directed the fires against the Russian infantry. Not only did the two German tanks completely eliminate a Russian rifle company during this engagement, they also knocked out another five Stalin tanks, an additional heavy tank of another type, three assault guns, and a heavy antitank gun.

On the following day, Gerlach was employed in the same sector with both *Panthers*. From a good high-ground position, another two Stalin tanks, two assault guns and two antitank guns were knocked out in bitter duels. Three more Stalin tanks were set on fire.

The degree of the physical strain and demands that can be placed on someone who is involved with life-and-death fighting for days on end, can be gauged by the fact that *Oberleutnant* Gerlach fell fast asleep during a conference at an infantry command post.

The "kills" registered during the three days of fighting: twenty-one heavy and super-heavy enemy tanks without a single friendly loss. One should also not lose sight of the fact that most of those combat vehicles were superior to the *Panther* in weaponry, armor and range. The more skillful leadership and the seamless teamwork among all of the old tankers had prevailed. What had really counted most, however, was the iron will of the five men behind the armored plate to hold open the path to salvation for the children, the women and the wounded.

THE BOULDER

Oberleutnant **Hans Schäufler and regimental signals officer in** *Panzer-Regiment 35, 4. Panzer-Division*

In Fritz Brustal-Navel's excellent book, *Unternehmen Rettung*,[3] one reads the following: "At the edge of the bridgehead of Danzig/Gotenhafen, the remnants of the *2. Armee* established a defensive ring. In front of it, some ten kilometers southwest of Danzig, was the *4. Panzer-Division*, like a huge boulder. They all fought with their backs to the harbors in which the most terrible of scenes were repeated. The people raced to the water and to the ships in deathly fear." What the famous "boulder" actually looked like at the time can be found in my diaries, which are paraphrased here.

Danzig, end of March 1945. The Russians were attempting with all means available and their concentrated power to take Danzig. The rounds from their enormous amount of artillery crashed almost ceaseless into our thin ranks. Rockets from Stalin organs hissed through the smoke-filled air. Mortar rounds of all calibers crumbled the already weakened walls of the suburbs of Oliva and Langfuhr. Bombers and fighter-bombers dropped their pernicious loads over us. We only took in what was happening around us in our sub-conscious. The dulled senses no longer registered the details. The measure of what was bearable had long since been reached. The Russian tanks advanced over and over again through the yellowish gray smoke. Protected by them, the Red infantry attempted to establish itself in the ruins.

---

[3] Translator's Note. The title translates as *Operation Rescue*. There is no record of an English translation of this book.

Panzergrenadier-Regiment 33 no longer existed. The few survivors had been transferred to *Panzergrenadier-Regiment 12*, which continued to be led by *Oberst* Hoffmann.

The headquarters of *Panzer-Regiment 35* was dissolved. It was no longer needed. The handful of operational tanks were consolidated into the 1st Battalion, which was led by Hauptmann Kästner. The battalion adjutant was *Oberleutnant* Grigat, the liaison officer *Leutnant* Badekow, the leader of the light platoon *Leutnant* Fintelmann and the battalion surgeon Dr. Rathke.

A tank destroyer company was formed out of the crews who no longer had tanks due to being knocked out or mechanically disabled. It was equipped with *Panzerfäuste* and pistols. *Leutnant* Schiller, who had only one arm left, led it.

Many of the rear-area services and command elements of the *4. Panzer-Division* were dissolved or reduced in size. The men were fighting in the companies of *Oberst* Hoffmann.

Likewise, the cannoneers of *Panzer-Artillerie-Regiment 103*, who no longer had guns, and the combat engineers of Panzer-Pionier-Bataillon 79, who no longer had vehicles, fought among the thinned ranks of the 12th. Stragglers from all branches were collected and continuously fed to Hoffmann's regiment. Despite that, it was not unusual to see companies with a trench strength of fifteen to twenty men.

So that was our "boulder": a colorfully patched-together *Panzergrenadier-Regiment 12* and a single tank battalion that had only a few operational vehicles and little ammunition.

But that cobbled-together bunch, that final offering, dug into the ruins of the dying city and defended every house like a fortress. The Russians assaulted, over and over again, and laid down barrage fires with heavy weapons. So much so, that none of the men had any time to think about it all.

The indigestible portion of this "crumb"[4] was the unbroken will to deny the overwhelming enemy the way to the harbors and the docking points of the ferries, where thousands upon thousands waited, for as long as possible.

A defensive line had been established around the former regimental command post. We were in holes on a rise, which might have been the Zigankenberg, like the name of the locality below us.

Hauptmann Kahle and *Hauptmann* Scalmat, the always happy East Prussian, were killed in the houses of the command post.

Leutnant Graf[5] von Moltke was a few hundred meters in front of us with his grouping of tanks, not allowing Ivan to approach by a single meter.

---

[4] Translator's Note. The original German uses *Brocken*, which has two meanings. In the first instance, it is the "boulder" described at the beginning of the passage. In the second, it is the "crumb" mentioned here. Thus, the usage in the original German is ironic.

[5] Translator's Note. *Graf* = count.

Oberst Christern prepared to depart; he was entrusted with the *Kampfgruppe* in Gotenhafen. The Russians had broken through as far as the Baltic on 22 March at Zappot. They had separated Gotenhafen from the rest of the defenses.

The commander said a hearty goodbye to each of the men, since he knew it was a permanent departure.

A yellow sulphuric smoke cloud hung over the roofs of the inner city. It kept turning darker and even more threatening. *Oberst* Christern left it up to me, whether I wanted to go to Gotenhafen with him or remain with the 1st Battalion as its signals officer. I could not make up my mind. In the end, however, I decided to remain with my comrades.

"But you'll come with me a little way?"

I couldn't turn him down, even though I had no great desire to go to the harbor through the hail of Russian shells raining down on Danzig. There were too many powerful experiences that bound us together. We had had our moments but, in the end, we had gotten along tremendously.

The commander mounted his radio vehicle for the last time. The radio remained shut off. Who were supposed to speak with, anyway? There was no longer a *Panzer-Regiment 35*.

There was rubble on the road. It was burning everywhere. The city was almost devoid of humans. The façade of an unscathed church rose in front of us. The *Oberst* asked for us to stop. He dismounted and asked the driver and me to accompany him into the church. That, too! What, after all, did he want there?

We walked into the semidarkness of a nave, which still had not suffered much from the war. The *Oberst* looked around him, searching. Then there was a subtle smile on his face. Gazing at me silently, he indicated I should sit on a pew. He then went with the driver and climbed the spiral staircase to the gallery.

I sat somewhat ill-at-ease on the heavy, brown-with-age oak pew and heard the seething of the war outside. All of a sudden, I was startled. The organ boomed, overpowered the melody of murder, and let me completely forget the war. A strange mood overcame me. The gloomy church appeared bright all of a sudden. I knew that the *Oberst* was a masterful and passionate musician, but I was hearing him play the organ for the first time. And how he played! From the melodic rush of the battle he transitioned slowly to more playful strains, which allowed me to remember the carefree days of peacetime. All of the misery around me sank: war and death; destruction and horror. The awe-inspiring melodies allowed me to believe in a future again.

Could there be a tomorrow for the War Damned? Would we experience a time when we no longer had to kill in order not to be killed ourselves?

I don't know how look I listened and dreamed. The *Oberst* tapped me on the shoulder and brought me back to a rough reality. His face looked transformed.

We mounted the *SPW* without saying a word. Gradually, I started to hear the shooting again.

At the harbor, the *Oberst* said a short good-bye, turned away rapidly, and boarded the motorboat waiting for him. He didn't wave, either. And I forgot to salute. He was looking straight ahead. In his thoughts, he was probably already contemplating his new mission.

The booming of the organ echoed in me for a long time. It drowned out the war and the suffering and the despair as we moved back by ourselves to our comrades in the *SPW*. Who of the two of us had drawn the better lot: the *Oberst* or me?

Command and control as practiced from up front in an armored vehicle—in this case, an Sd.Kfz 251 SPW.

As the Allies gained air superiority on all fronts—air supremacy in the West after June 1944—close-in air defense became increasingly important. Here is a half-tracked prime mover, well camouflaged and mounting a quad 20-millimeter rapid-fire cannon.

The tank commander of a Panzer V "Panther" observes his sector from a well-camouflaged vehicle.

A platoon of Panthers Ausf. G's on the move. These are very late-production vehicles as indicated by the reinforced straight bottom section of the gun mantlet. This modification prevented shells from deflecting into the thinner armor of the top of the hull.

Despite the overall superiority of the Panther—some observers consider it the best medium tank of the war—the vehicle was not produced fast enough to keep up with attrition on all the fronts. In addition, chronic fuel and other logistical shortages toward the end of the war often forced the Germans to blow up their own vehicles rather than let them be captured by the Allies. Although this photograph was not originally captioned, the type of destruction sustained to the vehicle—splayed gun tube and tremendous damage in the engine compartment— indicates that it might have been demolished by its own crew.

Chapter 12

***Unteroffizier* Robert Poensgen, war correspondent with the
*4. Panzer-Division***

Tuesday, 27 March 1945. Our division command post was in Langfuhr. There was an alert at 0200 hours. Be prepared to move out immediately: Enemy penetration on the east side of Langfuhr. We scurried about like ants, since our nerves were no longer the best. Somehow, we always had to be on guard.

The night was eerie, spooky. You couldn't see your hand in front of your face; despite that, the darkness was illuminated with a milky yellow. That stemmed from the many fires everywhere. You could perceive the stars and the moon above the roofs, but you could not see them. The heavy smoke, which bit into the eyes and lay heavy on the lungs, flowed like a heavy fog through the streets.

You only heard a shot occasionally; then, all of a sudden, one close by. Right behind our houses, there was a Russian machine gun hacking away. A tank was firing somewhere.

All of a sudden a strange sound, a scratching and a grating, then a march, a German military march: Russian loudspeaker propaganda. The music broke off abruptly, followed by a voice egging us on in the night:

German officers and soldiers! Lay down your arms! All resistance is pointless! You are completely surrounded! You ammunition and fuel are running out! Once more, the commander in chief of the Russian forces, Marshal Rokossowski, is giving you a chance. Whoever surrenders now will be treated well and send back home immediately after the war ends.

It was the standard record. It was only . . . well, the loudspeaker had to be damned close. Moreover, it had to be somewhat to the northeast of us, down in Langfuhr.

It seemed to be high time for us if we intended to change positions. Or was the command post to be defended, as we had already occasionally heard? But it appeared that someone had found yet another place that could be defended.

The *Spieß* moved out with a sidecar motorcycle. I was directed to ride along as a messenger so as to report the location of the new division command post to the rear-area elements. A Volkswagen also went along, as well as the signals vehicle.

We moved down Heiligbrunner Road, past burning houses and then onto the main road. It turned out that the *Spieß* was right: there weren't any Ivans on the main road yet. But the broad road was completely full of forces of all types, who were marching in the direction of the inner city. Among them were horse-drawn conveyances.

There was the sporadic sound of fighting coming from behind us in the direction of the market place. The tank obstacles had not yet been closed. Would someone remember to close them in time? Civilians were scurrying along in the mighty stream: Women, children . . . bundles on their backs . . . blankets and coats in their hands. Everything seemed to be moving along so eerily quietly. There really wasn't a single word to be heard; just the crackling of the flames, the crunching of the wheels and the sliding of the skids. Or did it only appear to be that way?

And then some soldiers appeared on the street corners. They were attempting to direct the traffic into an orderly flow. The directed the horse-drawn conveyances off into the alleys and side roads.

We were moving along fairly quickly, despite the numerous obstacles. The asphalt had been torn up from bombs and artillery shells; tree trunks and branches lay on the road surface; the electrical lines of the streetcar system formed knots and snake-like entanglements, which flapped and rattled, whenever you moved over them. Streetcars were stationary on the lines with shattered windows and frames that were peppered with holes. They had derailed and tipped over. In certain areas, the roadway was impassable. The wheeled vehicles then bounced along the tracks. I was always able to snake my way through on the motorcycle.

A few times, the tracks were ripped apart in such a way by direct hits that they spread out like the ends of a moustache and you had to bend over low to ride under them.

The closer we got to the city center, the thicker the smoke that was spilling out of the ruins. A military police traffic control point from our division was there. It directed us to turn off to the left. The route led over a bridge. The *Spieß* stopped briefly to put up a "Betzel" sign.[1] We then moved along the Neufahrwasser road to the Petri School.[2] We turned off again, and moved through a wide gate, which had the words "Schichau Shipyards" above it.

---

[1] Translator's Note. *Generalleutnant* Clemens Betzel, the next-to-last commander of the division. He was killed in action on 27 March 1945. An artillery officer, he commanded the divisional artillery before assuming command in May 1944. His highest award was the Oak Leaves to the Knight's Cross.

[2] Translator's Note. The Petri School, or *Petrischule*, was one of the oldest schools in Danzig, essentially a college-preparatory academy.

Large basement rooms, weakly illuminated, which smelled of iodine and ether. A main clearing station had evacuated the place a few hours earlier. It was the new division command post at that point.

I dozed a little bit and then rattled off to tell the logistics officer and the division support commander of the new location of the command element.

It slowly turned light. The streets were littered with shards of glass and brick-work. Despite that, it was possible to make better progress during the day, since the streets were completely devoid of people.

When I got to the first intersection, I saw a gigantic explosion out of the corner of my eye off to the left. It was in the roof of a multi-storied building. I involuntarily ducked and then it started spraying around me, just like tossing a handful of stones in a puddle. But, man, did it ever! Cobblestones, bricks and clumps of earth were sky-ward, almost as high as a house. They were mixed with black fumes. Stalin organs! Because of the rumbling of the motorcycle, I hadn't heard anything, of course.

I stepped on the brake with everything I had, threw the bike on the street and, before it could even stop, I was pressing myself flat in the corner of a wall.

All around me, hell had broken loose. Impact after impact of heavy and super-heavy calibers were churning up the entire quarter of the city. Houses collapsed like matchboxes; roof beams were flung high; pieces of stonewalls clattered onto the street. In the blink of an eye, everything was covered in red brick dust. In between, there were the constant yellowish red flashes and flames. Columns of flames from impacts arose out of the dust. It was like the end of the world.

I didn't want to leave the spot. Shrapnel smashed against the pavement, and brick shingles crashed and thundered down from the roofs. They shattered close by, and the shards of brick hit my skin like needles.

I thought I recognized a break in the fires. I made it to the next house door with a few leaps. I shook it. It was locked. Across the street to the next one! No, flames were shooting out of the shattered windows. On to the third house! I attempted to rip open the door. Rubble crashed down on me. Can't get through!

Then I heard the scary howling again. The *huiii—huiii—huiii* of the Stalin organs was spill chilling. The next salvo could be there any second. Artillery rounds hissed directly over the roofs, impacting with a burst. They were big boys and with delayed fuses to boot. The residences would burst open like ripe plums.

When I got to the fourth house, I was lucky. Like a panther, I hurried to the imagined protection of a house wall. With a second leap, I made it into a tile-lined entryway. There was a stairwell to the basement ahead of me. Outside, there was an ear-deafening din; the house was shaking in its foundation. At the entrance to the basement, there was a man in a gray-blue coverall of an air warden, a steel helmet on his head. He asked me what it was like outside; he then pressed me into the shelter. I was through; my knees were shaking. I felt me way through the semi-darkness. Women, children, and soldiers were interspersed, listening fearfully to the powerful crashing outside.

I must have looked "finished," since they immediately made an area available to me to sit down and they handed me a cup of hot coffee.

After I had smoked a cigarette and had calmed down a bit, I went up again. The barrage continued with undiminished ferocity. I had to wait another half hour before I dared to move on.

At that point, it looked even more desolate than it had previously. Flames were leaping out many houses, with burning curtains jutting out of windows. There were flames coming out of the rubble on the street.

I looked for my bike. A miracle—it was unscathed and also started up immediately. I rumbled off to get out of that inferno as quickly as possible. I rode some of the way and pushed some of the way across the rubble and debris, which was often up to a meter high on the roadway.

After the Petri School, there were no houses that were intact. And the street, over which I had driven or walked so many times: rubble, debris, craters, fire. The pavement could only be seen infrequently. I was amazed that I had not gotten a flat tire. But I also encountered other motorcycle messengers, who also had to fight their way through with great effort. Otherwise, you hardly saw anyone. One time, a Hitler Youth with a steel helmet and protective clothing. And then a couple of air defense men, who were attempting to put out a fire. There was even a work section that was trying to clear the road.

In front of me, the street was a valley of fire. The houses were burning to the left and the right as far as I could see. An air-raid warden turned me in another direction towards the ferry over the Mottlau. So I turned around and scrammed. How long would it be before the next barrage started?

On the ferry, I met a couple of *Landser* who were also waiting to be transported across. But a ferry operator was nowhere to be seen. It appeared that they had switched over to self-service at that location. So we fished a boat towards us. On the other side, others were also waiting to cross, including *Oberleutnant* Greiner from the division headquarters.

While we pushed ourselves meter by meter across the Mottlau, it was eerily quiet everywhere. Off to the right, I saw a gantry. How long would it remain up? The houses around that location showed relatively little signs of the fighting. I got to a wide road that led to Heubude and took off at a fast clip. There was little going on, but the air was filled with aircraft. Off in some pastureland, a smoke generator kept on spewing smoke quietly.

Just outside of Heubude—I was crossing completely open terrain—I suddenly saw dark objects fall from the sky. I looked to the heavens: Aircraft above me! I braked, let the machine fall into the roadside ditch with me and pressed myself as flat as a flounder. They must have been bombers, since what was left to fall from the sky today? Right! Half a minute later, the earth trembled under me from dull detonations. Each of the delayed-action fuses caused tidal waves of earth and stones to shoot high in the air. It rained down on me like hail.

I wanted to keep moving, but the machine did not want to start. Probably flooded. I pushed and pushed for all I was worth, but the stubborn goat wouldn't cooperate. And I had no tools with me—a punishable offense!

A 500cc *DKW* was leaned up against a fence. The driver was next to it; it appeared he was sleeping. I looked at him more closely, and his strange position caught my attention. I carefully turned his head. A piece of shrapnel was located right above his nasal cavity. He was dead, without a doubt. But his *DKW* didn't want to cooperate, either. It had been struck by something. I fetched the tools. While I was cleaning the spark plug, I had to seek cover again. High-altitude bombers, then close-air support, the cycle repeating itself. The main objective seemed to be the woods ahead of me.

Finally, the motorcycle started up, and I was soon in Heubude. It looked terrible. A horse-drawn column had apparently been caught up in a carpet-bombing attack. Hundreds of horses were lying around with shredded stomachs and ripped open legs. Among them was a hopeless entanglement of demolished vehicles. It was a complete portrait of destruction, 500 meters wide. Dante himself could not have portrayed hell more gruesomely.

When I reached the intersection, I saw everyone start to run: eighteen bombers were headed straight towards us. I turned at full speed, flew through a garden gate, went down a few steps, then moved along a concrete path to end up around the corner of a house. At the point, the aircraft were directly above us. And things smoked and hissed and howled and yelped as if Satan himself were there. With a single jump, I landed down a set of basement steps. There was a colorful mix of soldiers and civilians there. The air was terrible. Wounded were lying in a corner, poor bastards waiting to be evacuated. Outside, the bombs impacted. The floor of the basement shook.

When it turned quiet again, I forced my way out. I got my motorcycle fired up and continued on.

After a hundred meters, I saw something that surpassed what I had just seen. The road and the entire surrounding area was littered with the wrecks of all types of vehicles. I was informed that the main effort of the Soviet attack was there yesterday. The road had been completely jammed for kilometers on end—three, four vehicles abreast, fuel trucks, ammunition vehicles, horse-drawn conveyances, vehicles with wounded. There was no going forward or backward. And it was into that exposed, trapped concentration that the bombs of the Russian combat aircraft slammed. They attacked in wave after wave. It must have been hell! Ammunition exploded, burning fuel sprayed over the dead, the wounded and those still alive, over humans and animals. All of it had the effect of a burned-out trash heap of monstrous dimensions. It was the most horrific portrait of destruction I had seen in all of the years of war—and I had seen a lot.

I made my way with some difficulty past the entanglement of rubble. It smelled intensely of fire and carbonized flesh. The heat of the gigantic conflagration still emanated from annealed bits of iron.

Occasionally, I saw vehicles with the tactical sign of our division.

After a while, everything grew so thick that I was unable to get through with my motorcycle any more. That had to mean something. I turned off with other vehicles into a side road.

This is where the previous lot of bombs had fallen. Fresh fires were crackling in the timbers of collapsed houses. Yellow gunpowder smoke still rose from the craters. Here and there, there were some soldiers trying to free buried persons.

Three wounded—a civilian and two soldiers—were lying in the shadow of a fence right next to the road. They had torn the clothing away from their shredded limbs and dressed each other the best they could. It looked pretty bad. They were so pale from the loss of blood, that I would have thought them dead, if one of them hadn't lifted his arm with great effort.

They were almost crying with joy that someone had come by who was going to look after them. They had been lying helplessly there since the morning. They had had to endure the latest bombing helplessly. For hours, they had watched vehicles pass by them in long columns. No a single person had offered to help. War turns people hard!

I yanked out my first-aid packet and dressed them as well as I could. But I was unable to do a whole lot, since both of my packets were soon used up.

One of the men had a completely smashed leg. The second man, with a severe head wound, was already unconscious. The third man had a whole in his back that was almost as big as a fist. In addition, all of them had a series of smaller wounds distributed all over their bodies. Medical assistance was urgently needed.

All the while I was being the Good Samaritan, I had to seek cover again and again due to air attacks. I then saw a bus from our maintenance company moving its way slowly in the long snake line of vehicles. I asked the driver to take the wounded with him. Initially, he did not want to stop at that dangerous spot. It was understandable that everyone wanted to get out of that Hellhole as soon as possible. He also pointed out the refugees who filled his vehicle down to the last seat with their bundles and suitcases. The women started to cry hysterically, when they heard that they were going to stop there.

At that point, I lost my patience and got rough. I threatened to report the driver and put the women out into the fresh air. That helped. A few *Landser* assisted me in getting the three wounded men, who were shrieking in pain, into the vehicle. There was another aerial attack. The panicky turmoil in the bus is something I'll never forget.

I moved on and saw unattended wounded at different places. At that point, I also turned hard. After all, I had a completely different mission from that of collecting the wounded in Heubude. I did allow myself the time to request help for them at the next aid station, however.

I then arrived at an extensive patch of pinewoods, whose dark outline extended all the way to the Vistula Spit. There was vehicle after vehicle in those woods. Thousands upon thousands laid about, fearful and apathetic, like sardines in a can. The population of Danzig and Zoppot, apparently from half of West Prussia, had fled there to wait for ships after all land communication had been lost. Some of those pitiful people, for whom we were fighting for time, attempted to dig foxholes in the soft dirt with their bare hands. The woods appeared to be the focal point of the Russian aerial attacks. I had to "go underwater" every few hundred meters.

Finally, I ran into the trains of our armored reconnaissance battalion. They offered me a warm lunch. Then I continued looking for the directional signs to our rear-area services. There was another rushing sound. I took a headfirst dive form the bike, but this time the well-practiced routine did not work out so well. I felt a sting to my hand. It was bleeding. I didn't have any more field bandages, but it also appeared not to be too bad.

Two hundred meters farther: main aid station. A piece of shrapnel was taken out; I was given a tetanus shot and a simple dressing. "Don't forget the wounded on the way here!" I told the *Oberarzt*. He said he intended to send a medical vehicle there. I continued on.

There was another Russian fighter-bomber attack right in the middle of a traffic jam. Horses reared up, high on their back legs, intestines hanging out, striking out madly with their hooves, neighing in deathly fear. People yelled, vehicles turned over. In a circle about 100 meters across, I counted thirty-eight dead. Gradually, you started to lose your feelings. But what could I have done, anyway? I made my way on. Column after column. Everything was pressing to get out of that combat-enflamed city, get out of that hell of fire and smoke. But the route led over ferries and military bridges, narrow streets and restraining sand paths that could not accept this flood of vehicles that was bubbling over—and those collections of vehicles were naturally the targets of the Russian aircraft.

There was another snake line of vehicles at a bottleneck that could not be bypassed: Military police control point. Everyone, who really didn't have a mission to move to the rear was held. An *Oberleutnant* checked me out. I ventured a shy question. Then he yelled at me: "How interesting, a war correspondent! Why don't you come with me? I want to show you something!"

He grabbed me roughly by the sleeve and dragged me to long, long pits, which were covered with branches. Under them were fuel canisters in ungodly amounts, barrel after barrel, 200 liters in each of them.

"Take a good look at that! That's our army's fuel depot, Mr. War Correspondent! There are thousands of liters of regular fuel, diesel fuel and motor oil here…and up front the tanks don't have any fuel, not a single drop . . . and have to be blown up as a result. And where are the guys who issue this stuff? What do you think, Mr. War Correspondent? They've fled . . . simply taken off, because they've shit their pants full!"

He screamed it with a high voice that had gone bonkers. I had the impression that he was not in full control of himself. Who could blame him in that inferno?

I was allowed to pass after he once more urgently pressed upon me that I was to inform he division that there was fuel here.

At the next crossing, I saw the sign for our logistics officer. I went in that direction and, ten minutes later, I was at my objective. I accomplished my mission and went to sleep for a couple of hours.

Then I was told to get back to Danzig. A mighty cloud of smoke hung over the dying city, which had put itself in the way of the frenziedly assaulting Russians with its old walls and venerable structures, with its bridges and water courses. Russians who were attacking with the slogan: "Kill the Germans, wherever you meet them! Kill! Kill! Kill!"

For a limited time, the city provided the desperate defenders with protection and a backstop until its populace and refugees from the surrounding areas could be brought to safety.

Danzig had to die so that the hundreds of thousands in the Vistula lowlands could survive.

The horrible fate of a German city!

Two Panthers *provide all-round security in an assembly or holding area. Both are well camouflaged to diminish the possibility of detection from the air, and the* Panther *on the left has one of its machine guns mounted for engaging aircraft. The fact that one of the vehicles has a tow cable already mounted indicates that it might have already towed the other vehicle into position since one of the crew members appears to be performing some kind of repair or maintenance.*

Sd.Kfz. 250 *half-tracks, probably from a reconnaissance unit, staged for a move or operation.*

Crew members of late-model Panzer IV Ausf. H's *prepare for an operation as infantry (possibly mountain troops) file past in the wintry terrain.*

Infantry—some in snow suits—move along a roadside ditch past late-model Panzer IV Ausf. H's. *The trail vehicle features a full complement of sideskirts although these were usually quickly lost in the field as a result of maneuvering or battle damage.*

Chapter 13

THE GENERAL

***Unteroffizier* Robert Poensgen, war correspondent with the
*4. Panzer-Division***

27 March 1945. What can words say when the heart wants to speak? It was an oppressive weight that bore down on all of us: the *General* is dead!

You back home also grew to know what war is. You cowered unsettled in bunkers and basements. Bombs burst above and around you, and you waded through sprays of fire. The cold monsters of enemy tanks rolled past you in the streets, and the march of foreign soldiers echoed in the ashes of the razed cities. You fled in endless columns in the face of the waves of the enemy. Perhaps you understand what our mood was like at the front when the war robbed us of our leader. After death took the *General* from us, it grasped for the very last thing we had—the courage of desperation.

You don't understand why I say so much about the death of a single man, when thousands gave their lives daily? Because this one man was the last thing we—the 5,000 soldiers of the *4. Panzer-Division* in the Danzig bridgehead—had to hold on to in the raging, unleashed Hell. If you attempt to understand, then you will be able to grasp why the effort was made to hide the death from 5,000 soldiers. But it was in vain. No measures could prevent the horrible news of his death from filtering through. You have to understand why that news had, as a consequence, the fact that groups of fighting men, who had previously held out bitterly, suddenly turned weak and important positions were lost. It is only then that you will understand that in hours such as those in that unparalleled battle of attrition that it is not materiel that dominates, but men.

I knew the *General* for nearly a year. It was the same amount of time that he led our *4. Panzer-Division*.

It was in May 1944. The days of Kovel were already behind us, and the glasses in the bunkers of the division staff clinked in honor of the departing commander, who had been summoned to a higher position. Next to *Generalleutnant* von Saucken, whose Oak Leaves and Swords glittered between his gold-embroidered collar tabs, was his successor, *Oberst* Betzel, the former commander of our artillery regiment, *Panzer-Artillerie-Regiment 103*.

The cool gray eyes almost looked a little cold looking into the festive surroundings. It might have been that he was thinking of the great responsibility that lay ahead of him or the fact that he was sad to see the *General* go.

He was certainly well aware that he would have a damned difficult time in being a worthy successor to an armored commander, who was well known throughout the army.

At first, things were quiet. For an entire month, the vehicle of the *Oberst*, which then bore the black-white-red triangular pennant of the division commander, rolled through peaceful countryside. He saw soldiers training and firing at targets; he saw tanks, which had every bolt gleaming; and guns that seem to have already forgotten the roar of battle.

But then, in the last days of June, the radio sets crackled and the motorcycle messengers stirred up the dust along the roads. Time to move! *Herr Oberst*, show us what you can do!

On 1 July, at the same time that the division was rolling towards the great summer fighting in White Russia, the division tailor was sewing the collar tabs and shoulder boards of a general officer on the uniform of the commander.

There was no toast, no ceremonial formation . . . hardly anyone among the troops in the field heard about the promotion. They were decisively engaged in the fight against the gigantic approaching enemy.

The forces were not familiar with the actual orders that they carried out, but the simple soldier, the man who doubted, questioned and was always ready to complain, knew that it was a firm hand that led him.

The simple soldier did not spend a lot of time thinking about the how and the why. It was simply something that was. But he also went into battle with confidence that someone was there who thought and ordered with him in mind. It was no different with the officers. In their case, however, their knowledge was based more on facts. Every day, they read the orders in their entirety or in excerpts that the newly promoted *General* had signed in his clear and firm signature.

His deep bass voice was a lubricant against the rough waves of excitement. As a result, there was an over-all satisfaction with him that settled in.

July was a difficult month for everyone. Pull back . . . halt . . . pull back . . . halt! Every day, ten to twenty kilometers back. In the morning, there was a cohesive front. In the evening, the division jutted into the assaulting mass of the enemy. Graves and destroyed vehicles marked the path of the division. Despite that, it remained a cohesive whole, both to the outside and on the inside. At no time did the *General* lose control. That was saying something in that July 1944 in the center of the Eastern Front, when regiments, divisions, corps, and even entire field armies were shattered under the vicious blows of the enemy.

An offensive operation, carefully planned and executed with aplomb, restored the ripped-apart front. Then there was a single jump more than 100 kilometers to the rear. Swinging out widely, the division hit the Soviet III Tank Corps outside of Warsaw with a deadly blow.

The location of the fighting changed; the men remained the same. Latvia then became the ground, across which the tanks of the division rolled. Attack on Autz; opening of the supply routes to Riga; establishment of a cohesive front. The large-scale Russian offensive in the north came to a standstill.

During those days, *General* von Saucken met up with Betzel again. The commanding general presented his successor with the Knight's Cross on 7 September 1944.

The men thought: Now we have a proper *General*. Ever since Poland, there had not been a commander of the division, who had not received the prestigious award. And they were proud of it, since they knew that they had contributed their part in his getting the award.

Fall passed. A Soviet breakthrough to the Baltic cut the Latvian front off from the territory of the *Reich*. The "Kurland bridgehead" developed. Operation followed operation. The *4. Panzer-Division* was always and everywhere in the thick of things. Maintain composure—that was the highest imperative at the time.

The third Kurland battle was raging. The ranks of the old fighters had been thinned. A young crop took its place. Like thunder, the bellowing bass of the *General* could be heard: "Here, boy, get down here . . . you have cover here!"

The bursts of the Russian machine guns and the earth fountains from the impacting rounds crashed down on the lightly armored and shaking vehicle, where the erect *General* stood erect.

At the end of January, the *4. Panzer-Division* was moved to the highly threatened homeland by ship. Offering tough and bitter resistance, coupled with thousands of tricks, the division stood in the path of the advancing Russians in the Tuchel Heath and in East Pomerania. Betzel's tactic of forming points of main effort proved itself over and over again.

On 12 March, a telegram from the Army High Command arrived at the command post in Zappot: "In recognition of his service and his heroic devotion to duty, I award *General* Betzel the Oak Leaves to the Knight's Cross."

The division was overjoyed, but it had to be celebrated quietly, since it was once again fighting with an enemy, who was superior in terms of numbers of men and materiel. The fighting was for Danzig this time, a city for which the disastrous war had started and around which the final main effort would be formed. Once again, the commander was Betzel; this time, the commander in chief of the field army was *Panzer General* von Saucken, who had entrusted the command of the division to Betzel ten months earlier.

Danzig was hell on earth. A city that had previously shown no signs of war had been transformed in the space of a week into a field of rubble. The remnants of three divisions dug into that rubble. They knew there were hundreds of thousands of refugees to their rear and still among them. The soldiers had to protect them with their bodies from the flood of the surging Russian waves. They knew that for every hour they offered resistance, hundreds would find their way into ships and to safety. And the divisions fought and held. All contact with the corps and the field army was lost. With a single voice, the division commanders named *General* Betzel as the leader of *Kampfgruppe Danzig* and voluntarily placed themselves under his command.

The pile of rubble called Danzig lay under a fearful hail of bombs and heavy-caliber artillery. Untold numbers of Russian tanks ground their way through the streets with clattering tracks and against the German defenders, who had to pull back, step-by-step, against the oppressive numbers as the result of a lack of fuel and ammunition.

General Betzel went from regiment to regiment, battalion to battalion, all the time in order to take the necessary steps at the spot they were required. He had his vehicle halt in the vicinity of the freight yards. He jumped like a grenadier from cover to cover through the inferno of the barrage. There was a command post in the basement of a shattered house, an outpost at the door.

"Come on, go down a few steps towards the basement. The air's too iron rich up here!" the *General* muttered.

"*Herr General*, you're outside, too!" the man replied.

A few minutes later, the *General* left the command post and was springing back towards his SPW. He had almost reached it, when the horrified outpost soldier, who had returned to his duty station and was looking back towards the *General*, saw the broad-shouldered figure in the colorfully camouflaged jacket collapse under a pitch-black, flame-spewing cloud that came from the impact of a heavy shell.

The *General* was lying close to his vehicle. A large piece of shrapnel had hit his head. The life of a great troop leader was suddenly extinguished. It was 1600 hours on 27 March 1945.

The grief for our commander, our comrade, and our friend choked us. Despondency descended on all who heard the news. A heavy burden fell on all of us. What can words say when the heart wants to speak?

THE WITHDRAWAL FROM DANZIG

Unteroffizier Robert Poensgen, war correspondent with the
4. Panzer-Division
28 March 1945. Midnight had already passed. The vehicles of the command group rolled out onto the road and took up positions behind one another. I rode on the running board of the general's *Kübelwagen*. *Feldwebel* Lemm was at the wheel. He had been Betzel's long-time driver. Next to him was Hans Putz, Betzel's enlisted aide.

The death of the *General* had affected these two the most. They had been with him for years, had accompanied him on all official duty trips and leaves, had been with him at his home. For them, he was their superior, their comrade and their friend—more than for anyone else.

The armored radio vehicle of the commander moved ahead of us, a few vehicle ahead in the line. The modest wooden casket, covered by the Reich war flag, had been placed on the rear deck.

That march through nighttime Danzig, a city of ruins, a march through rubble and smoke, accompanied by the howling and bursting of shells and from the cracking of collapsing houses, was the last march of the *General*. It was a funeral procession that choked the breath out of you. The entire headquarters rode behind the dead division commander; no one formed a cordon. Occasionally, a *Landser* from another formation tossed a shy glance at the covered coffin—and the Russians also fired a salute.

The procession moved past the Petri School, along the railway, across the train station plaza; we moved one more time through the streets that were so familiar to me. But the picture of the city had changed so fundamentally the last seven days! Wherever the eye looked: ruins, ruins, ruins. The city seemed lifeless and empty. It hearts had stopped beating. The burned-out facades, with pale moonlight falling through the empty windows, jutted towards the smoke-filled heavens like unearthly theater backdrops. The streets were barely passable: shell craters, shattered trees, rubble from concrete walls, shredded streetcar tracks.

There appeared to be something going on up ahead. The sound of fighting flared up. Antitank-gun rounds whipped through the night . . . machine-gun fire . . . detonations. Muzzle flashes blazed here and there. Correspondingly, we turned off to the left into *Hundegasse*.[1]

How often had I been there during better times? Had watched peaceful people engaged in hard work? I knew just about every house there—knew them once. At that point, *Hundegasse* was nothing but a row of ruins, just like all the other streets.

We had to stop, since a column of infantry was blocking the route. In front of us, standing at the spot where they had always been riding, were the motorcycle messengers of the individual troop elements. There were girls from Zappot and Danzig riding in some of the sidecars. They had been doing that for several days, and no one said anything about it. The cute little railway conductor was also there. The messenger for the engineers was in love with her and wanted to marry her as soon as the opportunity presented itself.

Eerily, the narrow gables of the old houses jutted into the heavens. There were only thin walls left, which appeared to waver in the wind. Before I could think things through to the end, a warning sounded up front: "Watch out! The gable's coming down!" In a fraction of a second, I saw the motorcycles whiz past one

---

[1] Translator's Note: *Hundegasse* = "Dog Alley."

another. The wall collapsed on the knot of people, breaking apart in the air several times. A crashing . . . a cracking . . . a strong blast of air . . . then an impenetrable cloud of dust. I remained on the running board, as if paralyzed.

All of us then ran to the unfortunate spot. The rubble was piled almost a meter high above the motorcycles. The soldiers were all there. They had grown accustomed to reacting in a flash and had been able to jump to the side. But the girls were not able to get out of the sidecars. All of them were buried. Cold sweat ran down our backs, as we started digging like wild men. We knew from the very beginning that it would all be in vain, but nevertheless, we did it anyway. We tore away at the rubble with our bare hands. Hardly a word was spoken. Then we let our hands sink. I had to turn away. I could not look—and I had already seen so much suffering. The small engineer messenger almost went crazy. We helped him lift his dead bride from the sidecar. He cleared off her face gently; it had been covered in a thick coat of dust. Her head hung far forward. The collapsing mass of wall must have snapped her neck. She had probably not felt a thing, since her face was so peaceful. There was still a slight smile on her lips. The engineer found her cap under some brickwork. He carefully tapped off the dust and placed it on the dark-blonde locks of the girl. Then he kissed her gently on the forehead. The gesture had something so touching about it that all of us were deeply moved.

The column started moving again up front. We hastily gathered the belongings out of the completely destroyed machines. The engineer told us with a tear-choked voice that he had wanted to send his bride-to-be away so many times, but that she always remained with him. She had always said that if they were to die, then they would die together. She was dead now, and he had to live on all by himself. A terrible fate! He had attempted to pull her out of the sidecar as the gable started sagging, but it was already too late. At the very last moment, a comrade had yanked him back by the arm.

The column moved on. We stole out like thieves in the night. We had no time to recover the other corpses. But we had turned a little bit more taciturn and contemplative.

We moved through the city gate and onto the Mottlau Bridge. It had been hit hard. The roadway had been cobbled together with beams and planks. It was the last passable crossing from out of the city to the east.

Above us, there were a number of harassment aircraft. The houses were aflame to the right and the left. The night bombers continued dropping their bombs on that brightly lit corner at the bridge. It was high time to get out of there! Widely dispersed, we crossed the bridge over the Vistula and then headed with full speed on the open highway to the irrigation fields.

A couple of *Tigers* were screening along the road. There was an antitank gun firing behind us. Rounds whipped down the road, impacting near the Tigers. A wounded man cried out harshly, stretching his syllables. His voice slowly died.

BABYLON IN THE VISTULA LOWLANDS

Leutnant **Hans Schäufler, signals officer of the *I./Panzer-Regiment 35*,**
4. Panzer-Division

It must have been 29 March 1945, but I do not know for sure. The Russians were infiltrating slowly but surely into Oliva and pressing towards the inner city. Ivan was advancing step by step from the direction of Langfuhr. At the Oliva city gate, the 12th stood like a bulwark with a few of our tanks and defended their lives and our lives. But it could not escape your notice, despite all of the desperate defending: The front was breaking apart here and there, like the rectangular patrician houses of the Hansa city. It was no longer so clear, where there were still German forces standing and where the Russians already were.

During the night of 29–30 March, it was rumored that the city of Danzig was to be evacuated. No one knew anything more exact than that. It was burning and crackling everywhere. One thing was certain: Our tanks could not all disengage from the enemy at the same time. Each tank had find its own way through the inferno, along with its troop of grenadiers, as long as the single bridge at Heubude was still passable. But how long would that remain the case? The Russian bombers were flying sortie after sortie against that eye of the needle.

According to my orders, I took off in my *SPW* with my radio crew in the early afternoon. The battalion adjutant, *Oberleutnant* Grigat, had already gone ahead and was looking for a new command post.

The tracks churned their way through the rubble on the roadway that had once been a street. There were dead lying about everywhere. Given the situation, it would have been madness to recover them. We only made sure that we did not run over any corpses. We could not render any more service for our dead comrades.

The route to the Heubude Bridge had to be about three kilometers. I had memorized the way on the map. But the reality was something quite different. We occasionally encountered a group of completely distraught *Landser*, who were closer to being driven crazy than exhibiting cool reasoning. They asked us—if they addressed us at all—what was going on? I could only tell them that Danzig was probably going to be evacuated that night by all forces.

After being chased by aircraft, Stalin Organ salvoes and artillery fire that seemed to last an eternity, we reached the end of a vehicle snake line.

Initially, we waited a while, like good soldiers do. But it was so unpleasant there. A Russian antitank gun was firing into the intersection from a cross street. Vehicles were burning and ammunition detonated, but no one ran out of them. That seemed very strange to me. I went to take a look on foot; the effort was risky and onerous. I then discovered to my amazement, that almost all of the vehicles in front of us were unmanned. The gentlemen apparently continued the pilgrimage on foot, and they left their vehicles behind on the street. I also discovered that it was another 300 meters to the bridge, 300 meters of incomprehensible horror: rotting horse cadavers; glowing wrecks of trucks; meter-deep bomb craters; burning houses; and smoking vehicles.

And in the midst of all that were still some distraught patient men who stared at the man in front of them and waited until he drove on. But it was a dead man who was crouching behind the wheel up ahead.

We climbed over blocks of rubble in our cross-country half-track. We moved through gardens and courtyards, and we reached the bridge right at the moment that a large Russian bomber formation was approaching it. What to do? Where to go? Well, we could get hit anywhere and anytime, and we had already become inured against everything. The main thing was to get over the bridge. Who knew how long it would continue standing? So we raced off; it was wonderfully empty at that point. And that was what saved us. We plopped into shell holes; we rumbled across clumps of concrete walls. The bombs hissed to the right and the left. They burst with an ear-deafening crash. They shook the vehicle so much that there was a grating noise everywhere and the springs broke off. Shrapnel rained against the armor plating, and fountains of water rose towards the heavens. It was a fearful journey! I saw through my vision port that the bridge had been ripped open along the edge from a bomb impact. It was wavering, but it held. Everyone outside took cover as best they could, pressing their noses into the muck. But we rattled on, only looking up fearfully towards the bomb-bay doors.

On the far side, there were more burning vehicles, horse bodies, destroyed trucks and the detritus of war—as far as the eye could see. We rumbled through a roadside ditch—God help our cross-country goat—and knocked over a tree. We pushed a vehicle in front of us until it tipped over and reached an open field.

It was there that we discovered that the bridge had been "off limits" for hours due to a bomb hit. The engineers and the military police had been taking cover. That's why we had been able to cross unimpeded.

A new pack of bombers approached and strafed us. They apparently had dropped their bombs somewhere else already; most likely in the woods that were filled to the brim with refugees.

Where were we supposed to establish a new defensive line here after the evacuation of Danzig? There were women, children, the elderly, horses and carts everywhere. And the graves of those who had died during the continuous bombing attacks. It was impossible for the Russian aircraft to miss, given those concentrations of people in the sparse pine forest. But many people seemed to have already learned their lesson—or there was no more room in the woods—and shrapnel trenches had been dug all over the place in the open fields.

As had been discussed in advance, we rallied behind an embankment that offered cover toward the south in the direction of Danzig. The night seemed relatively quiet to us; with the exception of the radio watch, we slept like bears after the craziness of the last few weeks. In the morning, we did not wake up until an artillery salvo covered us with muck. We then dug tunnels into the embankment and took it easy for a while. There were infantry outposts in front of us.

In the course of the night, all of the tanks had trundled up. It appeared that there had been no difficulties. I could only assume that, since the crews slept the sleep of the dead. The radios were turned off. Slowly, we tried to collect our thoughts and get back to normal. We were in the second defensive line as the ready reserve. At the moment, the water formed the front all the way around us. That served to calm us down. I heard that the dikes had been opened and broad areas flooded, making them impassable. The concentration of people had been considerably reduced during the night. Many probably thought that wherever tanks showed up, the Russians could not be far behind. Under the cover of darkness, they sought protection by heading in the direction of the Baltic. It was also possible that they had been moved on by higher command. I don't know; I never did hear anything in that regard.

A warm soup with a lot of meat helped restore us. I took a closer look at the area we were in, since I had to locate the companies. Moreover, it was never a bad thing to know what was out front and behind in such situations.

The throngs here reminded me of the construction of the Tower of babel. Not only because we were between two bodies of water and everyone was digging and shoveling, but also because all of the peoples of Europe and all languages were represented.

I once again encountered the twenty-three prisoner-of-war British officers who had appeared in front of us four weeks ago in fantasy uniforms and, in accordance with the law of war, sending a white flag and an emissary ahead of them. The told us that they had been liberated by the Russians at Schloßberg—abandoned there by the Germans—and then had been shipped off to the east. But they didn't quite trust what was going on and took off on their own at the first opportunity, working their way through woods and marshland back to the German lines in the west. They asked us in a proper and formal manner, as is the English way, whether they could join us and remain with us. If necessary, they were prepared to fight on the German side. We overcame our resistance to the idea and took them in. We shared our rations and cigarettes with them. The situation required that they stayed with us at the regimental command post for three days before they could be sent off to the division headquarters. During those three days, we befriended several of them. In conversation, it turned out that four of them had been taken prisoner in 1940 in Bethune in our division's sector. And so they waited there, like hundreds of thousands of others, to be shipped off to the west.

It also occurred to me that there were French prisoners of war with practically every farm family in East and West Prussia, who scrupulously ensured that they were not separated from "their" family. They were usually the only man in the family, excepting, of course, the feeble elderly. They were very concerned about the children—it was very moving—and the children clung to "their" Jean, it was plain to see. Some of them had been with those families since 1940.

Somewhat offset from the "simple folk" were the reserved well-to-do from Reval and Riga in their fur coats with heavy crates and steamer trunks. They argued with their former manual laborers, who no longer put up with things in light of the completely changed social situation.

In a defile, there was a group of Poles. They also wanted to go with us, perhaps because they were fearful of the wrath of their fellow countrymen. I wasn't sure, I only saw that all of them were somewhat panicky. Among them were some Russian volunteers, who discussed things a lot, which was understandable, since they had to decide in which direction they wanted to head.

And then there were some 6,000 prisoners from concentration camps. Their SS guards had run away. The curious thing was that they were guarding themselves. I was told that they had been offered the chance of turning themselves over to the Russians. They had turned down the offer unanimously. They wanted to go to Schleswig-Holstein. They were also waiting to be shipped out.

It was truly confusion of Babylonian proportions, an international gibberish. I was able to understand a few things most places. It was only the East Prussians, whom I could not understand when they talked among themselves.

And those hundreds of thousands—soldiers and civilians, West Prussians, East Prussians, people from the Memelland,[2] Estonians, Lithuanians, Russians, Poles, people from Danzig, English, French, and the 6,000 former prisoners from all over the world—ate from our field kitchen. The astounding thing was that they all had their fill.

Of course, all of the military horse of the infantry as well as the cart mules of the refugees wandered into the pocket. We ate all of them in succession, from the tip of the nose to the end of the tail. The organization that remained despite that hodgepodge of terror and fear was masterful.

The second major achievement, which only registered slightly on our consciousness at the time, was the untiring, day-and-night efforts of the navy. The men in the blue uniforms took the people from there to Hela on ships and boats of all types. The large transports were at Hela. The woods and the dunes increasingly grew empty. There was never a true panic to be seen anywhere. After the hectic days spent in Danzig, that had a calming effect.

How long would it be before things got hot again? The Russians were still celebrating in Danzig. The noise of their victory rush carried over to us during the night.

---

[2] Translator's Note. A portion of Germany that was separated from East Prussia at the end of World War I and, after a period of French administration under the League of Nations, annexed by Lithuania. It was returned to Germany in 1939.

The often nightmarish road and weather conditions of the Eastern Front are well illustrated in this image: half-tracks and Panzer IV Ausf. H's *in a muddy assembly area prepare for another operation.*

Two paratroopers in a motorcycle sidecar combination pass a sign warning of the dangers of fighter-bombers: "Look right and left for aircraft and take cover in a foxhole."

The Jagdpanther *tank destroyer, based on the running gear of a* Panther Ausf. G *with a fixed superstructure mounting a high-velocity L/71 8.8-centimeter gun. A highly effective vehicle, it was probably the best tank destroyer of the war.*

A Panzer III Pz.Beob.Wg. *armored observation vehicle. A dummy main gun has been fitted. About 260 of these vehicles were produced using converted* Panzer III Ausf. E, F, G, *and* H *chassis.*

Chapter 14

RACE TO THE WATER

Leutnant **Hans Schäufler, battalion signals officer for the *I./Panzer-Regiment 35*, and Kurt Moser of the *I./Panzer-Regiment 35***

Beginning of April 1945. The Russians took Danzig, celebrating their victory loudly, with music and vodka. Marika Röck bellowed out *In der Nacht ist der Mensch nicht gern alleine*[1] night after night from loudspeakers in the harbor directed toward us.

We had a short break to catch our breath. It was used to reorganize the combat formations and to fill up the bled-white *Panzergrenadier* companies with combat-inexperienced soldiers from rear-area services and the various headquarters. It was a matter of life or death! There was no more demand for administration, filing, or repairing. There was no longer a "rear." The front was everywhere!

Our 1st Battalion had only twenty operational tanks left. The 2nd Battalion and the regimental headquarters had been dissolved for some time. The crews, who no longer had tanks, had fought in Danzig with submachine guns and *Panzerfäuste*.

All of the units of the tank regiment were combed through one more time. The soldiers of the maintenance facility, the recovery platoon, the maintenance sections and the regimental headquarters had to be detached to *Panzergrenadier-Regiment 12*. That was difficult, very difficult, since it practically was a death sentence for the men, who had had little training in infantry tactics and had no combat experience whatsoever. The only consolation was to get a "homeland wound" soon, before it was too late, since the evacuation of the wounded by waterway was still functioning.

Some of the men found a sympathetic ear with the military physicians, concerning heretofore "hidden issues." Occasionally, a medic would place a wound tag on an ancient *Obergefreiter* and tell him how he was to behave. It was well known that the only way out was with papers that were in order. The military police were strict. The set up control points at all bottlenecks and bridges. A few tried-and-true warriors

---

[1] Translator's Note: The title translates, *A Person Does Not Like to Be Alone at Night.*

who tried to make it out on their own—despite repeated warnings—were found dangling from a tree limb with a sign: "Condemned to death for desertion."

Suddenly, the rumor was making the rounds that 200 tankers were to be taken by ship to Schleswig-Holstein to be issued new tanks there. But no one knew what was to come after that. It didn't really matter: Just get out of here . . . out of this hell . . . out of this mousetrap, where you didn't really know when it was going to snap shut.

A race with fate had started; a courting of comrades and superiors for their favor. Who would be among the fortunate ones who would be allowed to leave that witches' cauldron? What would be the criteria?

A completely justified decision was very difficult, but it was demanded all of a sudden. What everyone hoped for and no one truly believed, suddenly became reality: 200 men from *Panzer-Regiment 35*, all experienced tank crewmembers, were to be nominated immediately and sent to Hela as quickly as possible, according to a division order. *Hauptmann* Küspert, the commander of the 2nd Battalion, was placed in charge of the group.

After some back-and-forth, one came to the wise decision that it was to be mainly fathers, married men and the only surviving sons, who were to be shipped home across the Baltic. Of course, that did not take place with some petty jealousies and scrambling on the part of those who did not make the list of the 200. There was just too much involved to expect otherwise. But the decision of the commander was generally accepted by everyone as a just one.

The fortunate ones, the saved ones—at least in our opinion—were given properly filled-out paperwork with signatures and seals and sent off. They took off in groups and handfuls of men, either on foot or in bicycles that had been "procured." A race to the coast ensued. No one wanted to miss what was perhaps the last ship to freedom and to life.

With a thousand hopes for the future and plans for a reclaimed life, our 200 comrades took off on 16 April 1945, along with 6,000 others on the transporter *Goya*. They were carried away from that merciless front and sailed in the direction of freedom.

They had our well wishes with them in their march luggage, as well as our last wishes for our loved ones. Bitter at heart and with little hope for the future, we remained behind. Death so close it was palpable.

They could stretch out their hands toward the homeland and life. Then they were struck down by a hard fate that was merciless. A Soviet submarine torpedoed the *Goya*. The powerful boat broke into two parts and yanked 6,000 people down with it to their deaths. Only about 250 could save themselves. Out of our comrades, 193 died out of 200.

✠

Kurt Moser, one of the seven rescued from *Panzer-Regiment 35*, made the following statement at the reception point at the Copenhagen Citadel to *Hauptmann* Stegmann:

I was an *Oberfeldwebel* with the 3rd Company and was with my unit on the Vistula Spit. We constructed bunkers there as protection against Russian bombers and fighter-bombers. We could no longer consider conducting operations, since we did not have any more tanks. Over time, the rumor went around that a *Kampfgruppe* was being formed that was supposed to be employed in the area around Berlin and which would be equipped with new tanks. The most-experienced people were selected from the companies and assembled for movement. The group was called *Gruppe Küspert*. I was part of it. We were indescribably happy.

After a while, things were ready to proceed. On 15 April, we marched to the beach. We were transported to the Hela Peninsula on military ferries. We waited there to be loaded out. We really wanted to get away from that hopeless witch's cauldron.

During the evening of 16 April, we were transported by means of small boats to the 7,000-ton *Goya* and loaded. With us were about 1,000 badly wounded and 3,000 to 4,000 women and children, all refugees. Along with the crew, there were well more than 6,000 people on board. There were other ships still in the harbor, including the cruiser *Prinz Eugen*. It was around 2000 hours. Then we got our first greetings from the enemy. The Russians must have noticed that something was going on, since they approached the harbor with some twenty-five or thirty bombers and arbitrarily dropped their bombs on the ships, but without scoring much success. We had a few wounded as the result of bomb shrapnel. The *Flak* put down a good curtain of fire, with the result that it was difficult for the Russians to drop their payloads with accuracy.

After the aerial attack, things did not take too long to get moving. The convoy was already assembled. We were allowed to steam out. We all breathed a sigh of relief, even though the *Goya* was completely overloaded. The many people on board were not registered. We were in a compartment amidship on a lower deck. It was about forty square meters. It was packed man to man in the passageways. It was difficult to get topside.

Around 2315 hours, I started to feel uncomfortable below deck. I was no longer able to bear the bad air and the unaccustomed heat. I told *Feldwebel* Hungerland: "Let's go up to get some fresh air." But he said to me sleepily: "You go . . . then I can stretch out." I forced my way topside by myself. It was pitch black up there. Suddenly, I heard a command: "Submarine danger! Everyone put on life vests!" Unfortunately, there were not enough available. I did not have one. We were still of the opinion that there were no submarines in the Baltic. Correspondingly, I was not too ruffled. But I was soon taught a lesson.

It was just before 2400 hours. A troop transport in our convoy had mechanical problems. It was directed to be towed. That was our fate. Our ship was very modern and had diesel engines and dual screws. The other one still had a boiler room. The *Goya* turned about to approach alongside the other ship. At that point, two mighty detonations shook the *Goya*. At first, I though we had hit a mine. By the time I recovered from the shock and looked around, the ship was already listing to one side. I had to hold on for dear life to keep from falling off the deck. A short while later, we were horizontal again, and I was hoping that everything would then go well. But, in the next moment, the deck was already flooding. I then realized the terrible seriousness of the situation. The ship was sinking. I then heard rounds being fired. There was no saving the comrades below deck. We wanted to release the lifeboats, but were unsuccessful. I climbed up to the bridge, but it only took a few seconds before I was surrounded by water there. The *Goya* had split in two. A lot of comrades jumped into the water. I remained on board; that was what saved me. When the water was up to my neck, I tried to get out of the suction, since I am not a half-bad swimmer. But no success. I was sucked into the depths.

I was still fully conscious and was fighting for my life. Suddenly, the mast of the sinking ship approached me. I grasped on to it. Then, the improbable happened. I assume it was a pocket of air from the ship that was shooting me to the top. I could breath again.

Light buoys lit up the night. I saw a lot of people treading water. In my need, I grabbed on to floating pieces of baggage. Then I reached a life raft. With all of my remaining strength, I was able to pull myself up into it. A sailor and a woman helped me get all the way in.

We floated around on the water for about two hours. All of a sudden, I heard: "Come over here *Panzer-Regiment 35*." But I could not see anything. A large shadow glided past us. It was a surfaced submarine. We kept very quiet. It did not notice us. Those were terrible hours.

Then we saw a black behemoth approach us, a German destroyer. We drew attention to ourselves by shouting and waving. Someone immediately threw us a line. We held on to it, and the crew pulled us up to the ship's hull. We were quickly pulled aboard. The destroyer was only able to pick up fifty survivors. It then had to quickly depart, since Russians submarines had been reported.

The next morning, German fast boats searched the area. I do not believe they found many survivors, since the water was very cold. The *Goya* sank fifty nautical miles from Hela. It would be impossible for even a single swimmer to have reached shore.

Only 250 people could be rescued from the 6,000. Seven were soldiers from *Panzer-Regiment 35*. When I was brought ashore at Copenhagen, I was afforded the opportunity to see all of them. Besides me, those rescued from the regiment were *Feldwebel* Hannemann, *Unteroffizier* Wehner, *Unteroffizier* Grohs, *Gefreiter* Jung, *Obergefreiter* Veit, and *Gefreiter* Burckhardt.

WHEN ALL HOPE DIED

Oberleutnant* Manfred Nase, regimental adjutant for *Panzergrenadier-Regiment 12, 4. Panzer-Division

The total collapse of the *4. Armee* in East Prussia brought with it a life-threatening situation for our *2. Armee* in the Vistula lowlands. After the fall of Königsberg on 26 April, the Russians took the city of Pillau and landed on the Vistula Spit, where we were fighting for our lives on the other end.

Correspondingly, an armored *Kampfgruppe* under the command of *Major* von Heyden was hastily formed. It consisted of *Panzergrenadier-Regiment 12*, the 2nd Battalion of *Panzer-Artillerie-Regiment 103*, and the remaining tanks of *Panzer-Regiment 35*. This field army reserve was sent as expeditiously as possible onto the Vistula Spit and committed against the Russians around the area of Kahlberg. The area of operations there was suited for everything but employment with armor.

The small strip of land, the Vistula Spit, was a wooded sector of dunes that sometimes was only 800 meters wide. It was completely churned up by auxiliary bunkers and field positions, all of which were directed towards the west. Pillau was to the east, however, and that was where the enemy was coming from. The unimproved sand roads had been torn up and made passable only by the use of corduroy-type replacement.

In January and February, thousands upon thousands of civilians and soldiers of the *4. Armee* had fled across the ice of the lagoon from the Heiligenbeil Pocket. They had moved by carts and sleds under a hail of artillery fire and bombs and had made their first stop in that area on their way to the rescuing harbors. We still encountered burned-out and shattered formations, which looked upon our intact columns with amazement.

We occupied a blocking position east of Kahlberg and stood by, since there were still forces fighting in front of us. Indeed, there was even a small airstrip in front of us, which was soon evacuated, however. Every day, blocking positions were lost; it didn't take to much effort to see when we would be "next."

As a result, the bivouac areas of the *Kampfgruppe* were soon drawn into the fighting before we could even realize it. At the beginning of May—Berlin had already fallen—the *Kampfgruppe* was involved in bitter fighting. The employment of the tanks and the *SPW's* turned out to be very difficult, since there was little opportunity for maneuver warfare in the narrow, thickly wooded area. Usually employed as tank destroyers, the friendly tanks often fell victim to the superior Russian assault guns, which had frontal armor up to twenty centimeters thick and a tree of a cannon for a main gun.

Constantly being attached and detached from different commands, we found ourselves in a merciless defensive struggle. We were numerically inferior and vastly outdone by the Russians in physical terms, who could constantly bring forward fresh units and pull back the burned-out ones.

During the day, there was little opportunity to conduct resupply, since fighter-bombers and bombers continued to churn up the "sandbox" and the tree bursts, which the Russians sent over the lagoon from the far side, caused a lot of casualties. Gunboats on the Baltic also ensured there was a constant surprise from that side, and we had to constantly be on the alert for a Russian landing to our rear.

On 4 and 5 May, the casualty-intensive fighting had already been pushed back to the area around Vogelsang, which was only ten kilometers from the start of the spit at the mainland.

Ever since 1 May, a deliberate evacuation of the bridgehead had been in progress, after all of the civilians had been taken to safety. Every night, about 25,000 men were taken to Hela on marine ferries for onward transport to Schleswig-Holstein.

On 6 May, *Kampfgruppe von Heyden* entered the sector of the 7. *Infanterie-Division*, which was defending the area between the lagoon and the Vistula. It was the so-called water main line of resistance, since considerable stretches of land were under water from demolitions of the embankments so as to save forces for a strong-point defense. That same evening, the regimental adjutant was sent to the commander in chief, *General der Panzertruppen* von Saucken, to receive orders for continued operations. The *General* stressed that it imperative at that point to make sure no German soldiers fell into Russian hands, now that all civilians had been evacuated form the mainland.

He additionally stressed that the time remaining for executing that plan was extremely short. The forces in the field knew nothing of the capitulation, which was just around the corner. The bridgehead at the mouth of the Vistula had become small, and the 7. *Infanterie-Division* was sufficient to maintain the defense there for the remaining short period. The 1st Battalion (Armored) of *Panzergrenadier-Regiment 12* and the last eight tanks of the 35th were attached to it. For most of *Panzergrenadier-Regiment 12*, 6 May was the last day of fighting of the war, even though we did not know it at the time. We moved to loading points on the Vistula at Nickelswalde. That was preceded by the destruction of the vehicles and the equipment. Personal belongings were reduced to the barest of essentials.

It was 7 May when our units approached the loading points, hoping that the coming night would mark the first stage in getting out of the hopeless situation. But it turned out that our departure was delayed. The ferries took off, but they were full with other units. We spent the night of 7–8 May in the wooded parts of the dunes near the Baltic.

The next day, a streaming sun appeared in the cloudless skies. It was exactly that type of weather that we did not want. The Russian fighter-bombers attacked the positions ceaselessly, as well as the rest of the area of the small bridgehead. Rockets hissed into the crowns of trees and the sand was raked by strafing runs. Here and there you cold heard a cry: Medic!

For the first time, there was talk of capitulation. We didn't want to believe it at first, since we wanted to get the sea journey behind us before the war was over.

Late that afternoon, a few overcrowded ferries left the tributary of the Vistula, followed by a couple of small boats. All at once, it grew still. The planed time for our departure had come. But there was no more to be seen of the Navy. We didn't have a good feeling.

After a telephone call with the acting regimental commander, it became clear what our situation was.

When *Major* von Heyden opened a sealed envelope at 2300 hours, our fate was finally sealed: For most of our men, it meant Russian captivity, if they didn't suffer a senseless death before then.

With luck and courage, a few might be able to escape the trap and make it back to their homeland. To the north was the Baltic and to the south a country where it was mostly Poles, who had remained behind, and which was thick with Russians. The chance of getting through here or there was pretty slim. The men in the black uniforms of the 35th under *Oberleutnant* Grigat wanted to try their luck and departed after reporting out to *Major* von Heyden.

In a depressed mood, we moved back into our patch of woods from the previous night, when we had still been full of hope. Parachute flares lit the way. The Russians did not trust us and wanted to prevent a flight across the Baltic.

That night, one question haunted all of those who leaned up against the pines: What was going to happen to us? And some of the old combat comrades of the *4. Panzer-Division* might have retraced in their minds the path that had led them here: The Bug, the Dnjepr, the Pripyet, the Oka, and the Suscha to just outside of Moscow. And then the even longer and bloodier way back here to the Vistula. It had truly been a long way. And all along that long way were the crosses of our comrades. Might it have been better to be with them, lying there? Despondency and doubt lay over that clear night. Only the rumbling of the nighttime aircraft interrupted it occasionally, making it even more depressing. One man watched the next to ensure that nothing stupid was done. There was a disturbance in one area. The former regimental adjutant, who was entrusted with the 2nd Battalion at that point, was reported as missing. We looked for him. But it wasn't what everyone had feared: A hundred meters away he was digging a hole in the soft sand to get rid of the remaining classified documents that had not been burned.

And so everyone had something to get in order before they marched out into that long, uncertain journey.

In the morning of 9 May, we saw the first Russians: officers and translators. They ordered us to march to Elbing. We were expressly promised a rapid return home—*scoro domoi.*

Well prepared for the march into captivity, equipped with horse-drawn wagons and rations, *Panzergrenadier-Regiment 12* and the units attached to it set off towards noon. Initially, we didn't see any guards. Our 1st Battalion joined us en route. We crossed a checkpoint, where any remaining weapons were taken away. We first headed in the direction of Fischerbabke; then detours were necessary, since most of the bridges had been blown in the watery area. We rested the first night at a rural estate.

We spent 10 May on marching on a road. We needed to be on the lookout for Russians looking for booty. But our internal and external cohesiveness offered little opportunity for them to relieve us of things.

We did not reach Elbing until early on 11 May. We marched singing into the city, which made a frightening impression. We didn't see any men, not even old ones.

The unprotected women and girls, who had lost everything they once had—the possessions, their men, their womanhood—clambered out of the burned-out ruin and told us of their misfortune. The Russians continuously attempted to take away the few horse-drawn wagons and goods we had left, which could only be prevented by energetic intervention on our part.

A prisoner collection point had been established at an athletic field. We were searched there one more time. We tossed our cameras, compasses, and binoculars into large containers. The columns that arrived were then separated into groups of about 1,000 men.

That same day, the march continued towards Braunsberg. The march out of Elbing turned into an emotional demonstration. We marched in step, singing loudly. The songs echoed back defiantly from the crumbled walls. Crying women and girls tossed us the first spring flowers, arranged in small bouquets. For the very last time, our regiment marched as one.

It helped us to forget our bleak situation when comrades in front of us, next to us and behind us got in step and sang the same song. Individuality had no place there!

We were constantly harassed. At that point, it was mostly supply personnel, who also wanted their part of us. Watches, boots, and decorations were the most sought-after souvenirs. We had to take the self-propelled artillerymen into the middle of the column, since they awakened the most interest with their black uniforms.

After two days of marching, we reached Braunsberg in East Prussia, which had been a rear-area city of the enemy for some time. As we discovered, there wasn't an intact rail line there that could take us on our promised journey home.

While the long column waited in front of the gate to the barracks that once housed *Infanterie-Regiment 21*, the officers were ordered up front. There was only time for a quick shaking of hands and well wishes. Later on, on the parade grounds, we had one more time to say good-bye from behind the wire fence and let it be known how firmly the difficult years had welded together the bonds between and among the officers, noncommissioned officers and enlisted personnel of the *4. Panzer-Division*.

Regardless of rank, everyone was obligated to loyalty and comradeship towards the other. That had never been so well understood as at that moment, when we had to separate at the enemy's behest.

We stayed in separate camps for a few days before our paths separated into different parts of the Russian interior.

When we reached the prisoner-of-war camp at Morschansk, about 450 kilometers southeast of Moscow, at the beginning of June—the first step among many—it was the beginning of a new chapter of our lives, a chapter filled with bitter suffering, occasional small joys, disappointed hopes, death, comradeship, and—not least of all—a hoard of life experience, expensively bought.

A TRIP INTO THE PAST

Oberleutnant Wilfreg Grigat, adjutant of the I. /Panzer-Regiment 35, 4. Panzer-Division

Wind south-southwest, speed three, good visibility. With a raw wind, we run toward the southern tip of Öland Island, coming from Christians-Ö. The first lights of evening shine in front of us on the island. The goal is the skerries outside of Stockholm. Therefore: port or starboard for Öland? We would try it portside. That way, we could be outside of Gräsgord around 2300 hours, the same time as back then. I had already dealt with the concept of "back then" two times on this trip: When we went under the bridge at Vordingborg and then outside of Mön. Three days ago, we had anchored for a night outside of Möns-Klint, the chalk cliffs, just like back then.

There are two of us in the cockpit, exactly like back then. Twenty-five years ago, *Leutnant* Finkelmann stood next to me at the wheel. Now, in 1970, it is my wife, who is manning the rudder. Back then, there were some forty soldiers in all corners of the boat, wrapped up in their overcoats. Today, it is our two children sleeping in the forepeak.

While I set the new course, the question came back, a question that had occupied me for days and which wouldn't let me go: What was it actually like back then?

Yes, what was it really like when the great Orlog[2] came to an end twenty-five years ago? Certainly, everyone had frequently thought about it . . . on this or that individual detail . . . on a certain face . . . whenever you had old photos in your hands or encountered a book about the period or encountered old comrades from the war.

Twenty-five years . . . that was a quarter of a century. That which has already occurred is recognized as a generation. That which is about to come seemed like a light year to us at the time. One could not conceive of it. In any event, the way it is recorded in accounts written later most likely cannot be the way it was, in all likelihood not the way it was.

Do you still remember the names of comrades, of locations? A few of them are still there in memory; the rest is a gaping hole. And how often has it occurred that you see young soldiers and think: What a greenhorn, still wet behind the ears. But we were also that young back then. We've also forgotten that; that's how old we've become.

---

[2] Translator's Note: Of course, he means the war, but defines it here in almost mythological overtones.

Of course, we know that the ability to forget is a true blessing. The psyche is not capable of limitless stress. And when it becomes too much for it, it either throws the ballast off in succession, with the heaviest going first, or it come to the aid with a benevolent trick, in which it takes the unpleasant, the especially stressful and changes it in the memory so much that it no longer exerts pressure.

Be that all as it may, the question remained. And ever since I had been preoccupied with it on this trip into the past, no answer has occurred to me. Individual events have come back to life, however.

While setting the course and looking at the maritime charts, for example, I remember how we navigated back then.

Late in the afternoon, 9 May 1945. We still heard cannon fire at Hela, which had just disappeared behind us. I called out the usual "Everyone here!" and explained the plan to initially sail to Bornholm.[3] When I received questioning glances, I explained that it was quite simple: We only had to sail west; initially at about 18 degrees east longitude to the north and then about 55 degrees north latitude to the west.

Our physician, *Assistenzarzt* Arthur Rathke, had opened up the stored inventory of a Danzig bookshop in the attic of a farmer's house in the Vistula lowlands some time ago. Out of the great items—there was really a little bit of everything there—I was able to get Knaur's *Pocket Atlas*, in addition to Morgenstern's *Mondschaf* with which I was able to convincingly put together the plan.

I was almost touching to watch our warriors from Franconia, whose familiarity with bodies of water from home were limited to the Main and the Regnitz, attempt to understand what everything meant. Trust is good, but one of them still summoned up the heart to ask how we actually knew when we were supposed to make a left turn.

That's where it started to get complicated. Although I had been to sea early in my childhood and had all sorts of relevant qualifications and had been preparing for days as a precautionary measure, I had yet to prove that I was a reliable sea captain. Quite the opposite.

We had set sail at 0230 hours at Nickelswalde. A mere ten minutes later, we had bottomed out on a sandbar just outside the mouth of the Vistula. There was, of course, an explanation for that. The normal sea traffic used the so-called "dead" Vistula, which led to Danzig. Our branch of the Vistula, the so-called Vistula cut-off of 1840, was correspondingly not dredged continuously and had become filled with sand. We just didn't know the location of the sandbars. Despite that, I thought a special lesson was in order to remove any doubts about the qualifications of the sea captain.

And so I started with the circumference of the earth of 40,000,000 meters; divided it by 360 degrees, which comes to 111,111; which, in turn, is further divided

---

[3] Translator's Note. Bornholm is a Danish island in the Baltic east of Denmark, southeast of Sweden and north of present-day Poland. It had a large German garrison during the war, which effectively blocked direct naval intervention against German coastal areas.

into sixty parts, which results in an arc minute or a nautical mile of 1,852 meters. This went on, since I then needed to prove that we could measure the speed of the boat by means of a clock with a second hand. I thought we were back in school when we calculated the following together: if a boat covered a nautical mile in an hour, it would cover 30.87 meters in a minute (1,852/60) and roughly half a meter in a second (30.87/60). Through group participation, we came up with the formula: movement in knots, that is, in nautical miles an hour, equaled twice the measured distance in meters, divided by the number of seconds.

After we had tested that—we threw a piece of wood overboard and determined how many seconds it took to pass a previously measured stretch as determined by the reading of several military watches—there was a considerable increase in trust for our continued operations.

With a speed estimated by us at between four and five knots—we had cleared the sandbar around 1400 hours—we had to establish a western course around midnight. The fact that we had headed northwest due to the wind was not noticed by anyone. Correspondingly, when land came into sight towards evening of the next day, a general outcry started: "Bornholm in sight!" We had no idea, where we actually were. Only this much was clear: It was not outside of Bornholm. By "we" I mean the leaders on the boat. Besides me, those were *Leutnant* Uli Fintelmann, who had developed into a reliable helmsman, and two navy *Obergefreite*, whom we had found on board. One manned the rudder and the other supervised the asthmatic hot-bulb engine.

We had set a course for Karlskrona, since no deviation had been built in and we were unable to measure for the deviation of the compass by the metal parts of the boat. Since the boat had apparently only been used in navigating the Vistula—perhaps having once gone to Hela—no one had ever adjusted the compass or established a deviation table. On top of that, the entire Baltic in our Knaur's Pocket Atlas was smaller than the width of a hand.

We had Sweden in front of us, that much was certain. But it could have been the southern portion of Öland just as easily as Hanö Bay. That we were at Karlskrona, almost right in the middle of that area, I had not counted on. It didn't really matter to us, however. We had the Russians and certain captivity far behind us; there was a peaceful country in front of us. What did it matter whether we were a few miles to the north or south?

By then, my boat was about three kilometers outside of Gräsgord. The wind had died down almost completely, and we gently bobbed up and down somewhat unpleasantly in the swells. With oilcloth over two pullovers against the moist night air and a mug of hot tea in my hand, my wife and I sat in the cockpit and looked at the lights on land and at the beacons whose labels we had identified in the beacon index.

It must have looked almost the same back then. How had it impressed us to see a peaceful village, not blacked out . . . to see cars with their headlights on! No one was sleeping on board. Everyone stood there and marveled as we secured the sail and chugged towards the harbor.

Of course, I was also happy to have the crossing of the Baltic behind me, but I wasn't as pleased as the others. I knew all too well how treacherous the Swedish coast is and how uncomfortable the many rocky cliffs right under the water could be.

About at the spot where we were presently located, we pulled around and discussed how we needed to establish contact with shore and how to ask for a guide. Since there was no flashlight to be found that had batteries strong enough to send out a readable Morse code signal, I gave the machinist orders: torchlight. Out of an old broom, some cotton rags, some diesel oil and some petroleum, we produced a terrific torch, which was quickly confirmed from shore. Not twenty minutes later, a launch from the Swedish Coast Guard chugged out towards us. The crew insisted on appearing in steel helmets and carrying submachine guns. We then sailed slowly into the tiny harbor behind the launch. It was truly tiny, inasmuch as we touched bottom as son as we tied up at the berth. We remained exactly four and a half hours in Gräsgord. Of that time, we had to struggle for three hours not to be interned. We didn't know at the time what a tragic fate awaited the German soldiers interned in Sweden, and the mood on board in this regard was not completely unanimous. Besides there were a number of soldiers, who were certainly good men on land but who had puked their guts out during the crossing, particularly during the stormy nighttime portion, and would have preferred not to continue the sea journey. Discipline, at least in the case of our people, was still completely intact, so that we did not have to take those voices into consideration. The man we were talking to, if I remember correctly, was a tenured instructor from Stockholm, who served as the harbor commander as a reserve captain. I had to sweet talk to him to convince him that we were not German soldiers who had been washed ashore along the Swedish coastline and he had to intern. Instead, we were simple mariners in a maritime emergency, who needed to be helped and had to be afforded the opportunity to continue their journey.

My arguments were not completely convincing. For one, we still wore uniforms and were armed. Moreover, I also had to ask that two badly wounded and three slightly wounded men be taken ashore, whereby the types of wounds were conspicuously not caused by an accident at sea.

Once again, I had the last few hours on the Vistula land spit before my eyes: How we had found the boat, the *Brunhilde*, and how we had taken it in a *coup de main* . . . how we then went on board and some two and a half hours after the capitulation were subjected to the bombs of a Russian night bomber.

I had formed two patrols. One of them had been sent north and the other south along the east bank of the Vistula to scout our suitable maritime capacity. We had arranged that a green signal flare would be used to indicate that something had been found. After twenty minutes, one went up.

The boat was a fifteen-meter-long former fishing cutter, which had been converted for passenger use, presumably for along the river, and still had all of its old sail-cloth as well as a powerful hot-bulb engine. The boat had a highly visible Red Cross painted on it; in the end, it had been used to transport wounded from the mouth of the Vistula to Hela. It was guarded by two grim-looking military policemen, who had announced in a decisive manner that the boat had been confiscated for a division headquarters. Since the military police had also heard talk that the war had been over for some two hours, it only took a question to get them to become members of the crew: Whether they wanted to go with us and stay behind. The patrol took the boat into its possession and a messenger was sent to the rest of us with orders for the rest to work their way to the boat, individually and unobtrusively, without haste or speed, and to only take the most necessary baggage. Unfortunately, I still had to think about the tens of thousands of soldiers, who were bivouacking at the edge of the woods, disciplined and quietly, and who had given up all hopes of escaping captivity. Any out-of-the-ordinary movement would have only led to a veritable assault on the boat. But to take all of them was impossible. At least our own people should go.

But at the last minute something happened that we had wanted to prevent. You know how that goes. All of a sudden, people started become uncertain. They didn't know whether they might be too late. A casual stroll soon became a forced march. In the end, it was a flat-out run, none of which remained unnoticed. Before our last few people were on board, a veritable flood of humanity descended on the boat, with the result that we had to cast off even before the engine had been started. It was right during that movement that a Russian bomber dropped an illumination bomb, followed by a sack full of small bombs. I personally was hit in the back with a small piece of shrapnel; two mechanized infantrymen, who had come aboard, were hit in the abdominal cavity; three more were hit in the legs. Other than the obligatory first-aid kit, we had no way to help the wounded.

All of this is to help set the stage. Of course, the two badly wounded men had to have medical attention. I left it up to the three slightly wounded as to what they wanted to do. All opted to remain in Sweden.

All this meant that my negotiating position was not the best. In discussions that lasted hours, which were alternately conducted by the tenured instructor in proper English and then broken German and during which he constantly pointed out how burdensome the entire matter was for him, since he had to produce a detailed written report concerning the incident, I succeeded in finding some understanding for our position from him and, above all, from his superior, with whom he was in telephonic contact several times.

The wounded were taken ashore and transported to the nearest hospital. We were allowed to fill our water tanks, and I received a maritime chart that went as far as beyond Mön. By then it was 0330 hours. We were thereupon instructed more or less to cast off and set sail in the direction of Karlskrona, lying at anchor in the roads. That meant that our further fate had not yet been completely decided.

On the way to Karlskrona, routine gradually settled in and we went over everything that we should have done before but had not done due to the excitement and the special situation. We determined how much we had in rations on board; we had sufficient water at least as far as Karlskrona. While taking inventory, it was determined that almost all of it was cans of fish. There was almost no bread. Uli Fintelmann was then given the mission of drawing up a list of all on board. It turned out, unfortunately, that a lot of our people were missing.

At this point, I need to flash back again: We had cast off with a completely overcrowded boat. There were so many people on deck that it was impossible to move from the rudder to the front of the boat. We moved very slowly downstream on the Vistula. One cannot forget that it was night, even though starry, and we were trying to keep in the navigation channel without a clear view. Barely 15 minutes had passed—we had just left the mouth behind us—when we ran aground with a loud scraping. It is hard to imagine the mood on board nowadays. Just a few minutes ago the men had been relieved to know that they had escaped captivity at the last possible moment only to then sit back in the mousetrap again. I must confess that my own mood was not much different. I had also received a fairly painful wound to my back as well.

After all of the attempts to free the boat with a reverse screw and heeling had failed, indifference set in along with an apathetic surrender to fate. I also lay down next to the rudder and caught a couple of hours of sleep. It was not until it had become light and we had a hasty breakfast that we started to consider the situation again. It became clear to me that we had to solve two problems.

On the one hand, we had to get free, which was obvious. On the other hand, we had to get rid of at least a third of the people on board, since we only had a chance to reach home on such an overcrowded boat if the seas remained as smooth as glass–and I knew the Baltic. By then, the number on board had increased by another twenty men. They were SS combat engineers, who had come aboard via inflatable craft. It was the inflatable craft, however, that offered me the solution. Even though it was very difficult for me, I had to point out that we were violating the terms of the capitulation by our attempt to flee and that we could count on being punished. That announcement had the desired effect in a very short time. Over the course of the next two hours, about half of those on board left on the rubber boats of the SS, which had been moving back and forth from the boat to the shore. As a result, the boat became a bit more seaworthy.

But when that relief did not suffice to free the boat, *Oberleutnant* Kolisch, *Leutnant* Fintelmann, and *Leutnant* Schulz, along with a few others from our group, went ashore to check out the situation. It was intended for contact to be maintained with the shore so as to be able to call back our people. Towards noon, a powerful wind from the northwest came in, with the result that the water rose somewhat and we were able to float free around 1400 hours. Although we fired the last two white signal flares we had, only Fintelmann came back. There was no trace of Kolisch, Schulz, and the other people. Correspondingly, we had to set sail to the open sea with a heavy heart with only a few of those from the 35th.

I thought of all of that as I took a look at the list drawn up by Fintelmann. Of the forty on board, only sixteen came from our bunch. Unfortunately, the list has been lost.

Toward noon, a Swedish Coast Guard ship coming from Karlskrona approached us. We had apparently been reported, and the ship ordered us to stop by means of signal flags. A naval lieutenant and four men came on board, reported properly to me and requested permission to search the ship. Somewhat horrified, they determined that we were armed to the teeth and asked for an explanation. I could only repeat my old, nice-sounding platitudes: We were poor, plagued mariners who were in a maritime emergency only insofar as we had no bread on board and that the weapons were meaningless, inasmuch as we didn't have any intention of attacking Sweden now that the war was ended. The lieutenant smiled understandingly, when I admitted to him, that we had been determined during the sea movement to sink any Russian naval units with *Panzerfäuste* that would have made any attempt to seize our boat. To my great surprise, I received as an answer the statement that we had only escaped that murderous act of heroism by a hair, because the entire Russian Baltic Fleet had set sail into the Baltic last night and occupied Bornholm. Bornholm, of all places. It was where I had intended to sail originally.

Without commenting, the Swedes left the boat, but they came back a short while later with large quantities of crisp bread and great powdered milk. They brought me a recent English newspaper with the compliments of the local commander. Not wanting to be outdone, we gave them two *Panzerfäuste* and an *MG 42*.

He had heard of those weapons before and he accepted both gifts with thanks. He asked whether there was something else he could do. Since the relationship between us had increasingly grown friendlier and more understanding, I told him that I had been hit in the back and thought a tetanus injection was in order. The good man promised immediate attention, and not thirty minutes later a doctor was on board. He regretted that he was unable to remove the shrapnel without an operation. Nevertheless, he gave me the tetanus and dressed the wound professionally. Once again, we could only pay with articles of war and handed over a submachine gun, an *08* pistol, a *P 38* and—what might be called the highlight—a hollow-charge demolition. Our newly won friends presented their calling cards with a slight bow. Our Swedish friends took their leave of us and promised to keep an eye on us at least as far as Karlskrona. In light of the Russian fleet, that helped calm our nerves considerably.

Around 1500 hours on 11 May, we arrived at Karlskrona and dropped anchor at the spot we had been directed to.

Once again, there was a lot of palaver with an officer from the harbor command, who had come alongside with his launch. There was more discussion about internment; that issue seemed to have been removed from the list of topics. On the contrary, they treated us like soldiers of a foreign power, whom they wished to get rid us as soon as possible. In plain English, we were irritating foreigners. Correspondingly, everything revolved around the practical question of what we needed to get out of the country as quickly as possible. For the Swedes, getting out of the country meant Denmark. By then, all of it had been occupied by the English, with the exception of Bornholm. We, on the other hand, were thinking of Germany and either Kiel or Flensburg as our target harbors. We therefore argued about two or three maritime charts and—what was certainly a greater cost factor for the Swedes—rations and possibly also fuel for one to three days, depending on the weather situation.

That the Swedes won the day is self-explanatory. We could even understand why, since we were also familiar with the mentality of the rear-area paymasters. The target port was originally Copenhagen, which I categorically said I would not do, after they had shown me the map of the minefields in the sound, which looked pretty miserable. In the end—the Swedes understood our navigational issues—we finally agreed on Klintholm on the island of Mön, and we were only given one and one half day's worth of bread, canned soup, powdered milk and fuel. My confirmation of receipt for those items has no doubt been sent to the Federal Republic of Germany in the meantime for payment. Regarding technical matters, the Swedes were more generous. We received maritime charts that went as far as Fünen, our compass was adjusted and, since our engine had stopped its benedictory duties two hours outside of Karlskrona, a mechanic came on board with the most important replacement parts. Almost as important was the fact that we received permission to anchor until the next day in the roads. Although the sailing from Öland had only been under a light wind—nowadays I would call it a gentle breeze—and had been quite pleasant, the *Landser* had been battered by the unaccustomed seafaring. The possibility of sleeping through the night while anchored in a calm sea was a pleasant prospect for everyone.

The first order of business was the compensation of the compass. While the Swedish mechanic and two of our maintenance people tinkered with the engine, *Leutnant* Fintelmann and a *Feldwebel* from the mechanized infantry established a meal plan for four days. We insisted on reaching Germany. Since we had even larger stocks of cans of meat on board that the Swedes did not know about, it was primarily a matter of rationing the bread and water.

At 1800 hours, the Swedish mechanic left without the engine running. It was the end of the day for him and, since he also took his tool along, it was also quitting time for us, as we referred to it in civilian terms.

Although everyone was dead tired, most stayed on deck in small groups until deep into the night. The men looked at the lights on land and at the stars above. Our thoughts wandered back to the Vistula Spit and to our comrades, who had not come along and who were then with Ivan.

We had been convinced almost to the end that we had a secure passage back for the remnants of the 1st Battalion. All of us had felt that the war coming to a close and, during the final days, there were concrete indications of capitulation negotiations, our source being the navy. It goes without saying that we prepared for that. It appeared to me to be a requirement as part of our obligation to take care of the men. On the other hand, there was no question that everyone would do his duty to the very end, but it was a bit easier to do, if you knew that the route back was open.

While our few remaining operational *Panthers* defended from the cuts in the woods along the spit, one blocking position at a time—a cat-and-mouse game with the Russians that was unusual for us, but which allowed us to backstop the 12th—a sort of crisis headquarters was established in Nickelswalde. Heading it was *Assistenz-arzt* Dr. Arthur Rathke. Good old Arturio, as we like to call him, was the man for the job. He was a real go-getter. He was a good battalion surgeon and, more importantly, an indispensible doctor of the mood and the soul. He was effectively a one-man-band, who sometimes played saxophone, sometimes the accordion. Whenever it was necessary, he could hold us in his spell with wild rhythms or move us to tears with melancholy notes. He also possessed the essential imagination and negotiating skills that were necessary for "chartering" the required maritime capacity for our transport to the rear.

The first mission of the crisis headquarters was "Operation Big Head," which was the dissolution of our rear-area services. The headquarters, maintenance services and supply elements were still set up for administering to an almost complete battalion. In actuality, during the previous two weeks, only three to eight vehicles were operational at any given time, depending on the spare parts and fuel situation. All of the vehicles could be manned several times over.

At first, the people were simply listed as sick. That was only a drop in the bucket, however. That didn't quite work, since we couldn't have a regular epidemic breaking out. As a result, our dear, meditative Dr. Vogel, another surgeon, went to the division surgeon to get his advice. Not only did the division surgeon show understanding for our situation, he also came up with a suitable illness, with the result that a fair-sized march serial of "sick" could be released back to the homeland under the supervision of Dr. Vogel. Arturio served as the sea transport officer.

Just two days after assuming his new job, Rathke had requisitioned a real recreational steamer upstream on the Vistula. He had it drop anchor in the roads outside of Nickelswalde. It was well equipped and would have been sufficient not only for the 35th but there would have also been space for the remnants of the mechanized infantry. The steamer tore loose in a storm, however, and went aground. We had no way of freeing it. So we had to stand by and watch as the navy hooked on to it, and it disappeared in the direction of Hela. That was the end of that.

For his next effort, Arturio had established contact with the naval ferries operating between Nickelswalde and Hela. We gave them diesel fuel that was no longer needed.

Another march serial, consisting primarily of superfluous tank crews, was dispatched under the command of *Leutnant* Tautorus. That brave and combat-experienced warrior reported out of the battalion with tears in his eyes. He had received orders, just like *Stabsarzt* Dr. Vogel, to report to *Hauptmann* Küspert of the 2nd Battalion in Schleswig-Holstein.

The fact that Küspert and almost 200 men of his battalion had gone down with the *Goya* was something we did not know at the time. Fortunately, I have to add. We also didn't know that elements of the maintenance company that had been sent back previously had been on the torpedoed *Wilhelm Gustav*.[4]

On the evening of 4 May, Rathke reported learning from the navy that a cease-fire was to go into effect at 0500 hours on 5 May across from the Montgomery's forces, which included Schleswig-Holstein and Denmark. The navy's orders read, however: "Transport movements of the navy at sea will continue to run."

Correspondingly, the final preparations for the end were discussed with Rathke. He made arrangements for a naval ferry to pick up what was left of the 1st Battalion just behind the main line of resistance shortly after the capitulation. In order to ensure that happened, Rathke was sent to board the ferry. Our signals officer, *Leutnant* Schäufler, sent a radio section along and established frequencies and transmittal times for "Operation Finale." The tank crews were briefed on the plan; I informed *Major* von Heyden, the acting commander of *Panzergrenadier-Regiment 12*, to which we were attached.

After the refugee camps in the Nickelswalde and Schwienhorst areas had been mostly evacuated and the end of the fighting could be foreseen, an increased tempo in the withdrawal of the forces was also stressed by the field-army command. Correspondingly, *Oberleutnant* Thiel, the commander of the Headquarters Company, *Oberleutnant* Bonfigt, the commander of the supply company, along with *Leutnant* Helmbrecht, and *Oberleutnant* Werner, the commander of the armored escort company, each left with a march serial.

As a result, we shrank to a small, manageable group. We comprised eight tank crews, along with a small maintenance section, a supply section and a signals "goat." It did not appear that it would be any problem to disengage from the enemy after the capitulation and take the boat "chartered" by Arturio back into the homeland.

But the shock didn't come until early in the afternoon of 8 May, when Arturio reported by radio from the naval ferry. At 2400 hours German summer time, the Eastern Front would also capitulate. The captain of the ferry refused to pick up our people after the capitulation as had been agreed upon, since that was contrary to his orders. I only had a single answer to this situation: "Thanks for everything. Have a nice trip home. Out."

---

[4] Editor's Note. The author is thinking of the *Wilhelm Gustloff*. The sinking of the former cruise ship on 30 January 1945 was the worst loss of lives in maritime history. Carrying more than 8,000 soldiers and refugees, the ship was torpedoed by the Soviet submarine *S-13*. More than 7,000 of the passengers died. However, as it was carrying military personnel, the ship was a legitimate military target.

We immediately withdrew the crews of the non-operational tanks, and *Leutnant* Schäufler received orders to work their way to the rear on their own along with the rest of the rear-area services. Despite everything else, they were fortunate and able to link up with the remnants of *Panzer-Aufklärungs-Abteilung 4.* As I later discovered, all of them reached the homeland, albeit under considerably adventurous circumstances.

At the mouth of the Vistula, there was no longer that much of the feverish activity of the last few days that had been seen when *Großadmiral* Dönitz ordered the Navy to transport away as many people as it could in one final push, with the water-craft taking on as many as they could.[5] There was only the occasional boat docking, including inflatable and outboard craft. There was no longer any organized evacuation. At that point, we really were alone: two *Oberleutnants*, two *Leutnants*, and approximately twenty men—what remained of the once so proud and powerful 1st Battalion of *Panzer-Regiment 35.*

The sound of fighting along the main line of resistance had abated, the war was dying. We slowly started to comprehend what that meant. The knowledge weighed down on us like lead: We were sitting in a mousetrap and Ivan was in front of it as the cat. Despite all that, there were no scenes, no regrets about not having quietly or otherwise having shirked one's duty under some pretext previously, which might have been possible. Although a few others had done that, we had only cursed them vociferously initially and then, later, just smiled wanly. Disgrace never digests in your stomach, the quiet Leutnant Schulz added.

That evening, I was at the last orders conference held by *General* von Saucken. Closely pressed together, we stood around him in his bunker. Everyone was somber, when he reminded us to keep fulfilling our duty in dignity in captivity as we had so well up to that point. He bade farewell to all with a handshake. I saw *General* von Saucken for the last time, when he spoke to soldiers at the mouth of the Vistula. His presence alone helped quell any unrest.

"The officers are to remain with the troops in the field." *Major* von Heyden reminded me of those words of the commander in chief when I reported out after the last orders conference. He could only shake his head when I replied that we wanted to try to somehow get through with our small group. Somehow.

We were thinking about that "somehow" while we lay on the deck of the *Brun-hilde* in the roads of Karlskrona. Someone threw out the question whether the comrades that had been left behind would still want to try to get through with us. Something like shame was part of that, since we were part of the very few who had escaped the fate that had been ordained for us by means of unvarnished luck.

---

[5] Editors Note. In the largest, most successful seaborne evacuation in history, more than two million German soldiers and refugees were evacuated from various areas along the Baltic from 23 January to 8 May 1945. The much-maligned German navy, the *Kriegsmarine*, performed magnificently and heroically.

We had often talked about how we would get home after the capitulation. If there had not been a way to go across the sea, then the only way left was walking. Although it would have been long and difficult, we thought that all of us could do it, since we were in the best of shape. I was the only one that didn't apply to, since my left leg was almost lame due to a wound. We had thoroughly discussed that option, which was located somewhere between the boy scouts and the *Wehrwolf*,[6] in our youthful naiveté. We had set aside field uniforms, compasses, assault packs, march rations and inner tubes for the crossing of rivers with our luggage. We assumed we would break out on the first night of the capitulation, since Ivan would first drink himself senselessly drunk in his joy and therefore not maintain any effective security along his lines.

The part about getting drunk was right on the money. During the night of the capitulation, we listened to his nerve-wracking bellowing and saw his fireworks, consisting of signal flares and tracer ammunition. It was just that almost all of us were still together that night, with the consequence that a breakout from the pocket could not take place until the following night. Whether it would still be possible then was something we didn't know.

The next day in Karlskrona, 12 May 1945, started with the usual routine on board: first call, washing by jumping overboard, a large breakfast with rationed tea, followed by maintenance. The latter because we intended to raise anchor that day, but we still had to get the engine running. When the engine finally turned over but then suddenly died, it could only be one thing: There was something in the screw. After several dives, it was *Leutnant* Fintelmann who removed a long piece of rope that had wrapped itself around the propeller.

We were ready to go then and raised anchor at 1600 hours. With western winds of medium strength, we sailed all the way across Hanö Bay. Toward evening, we held up close to land, since we had to run between Sweden and Bornholm during the night and didn't want to encounter any Russian ships. Although they had told us that there were Swedish warships in that area, we didn't want to take any risks. Unfortunately, the winds blew west the entire night, so we had to steam against them using the engine.

By the morning of 13 May, the dangerous island of Bornholm was backboard. A beaming green strip of land that was the Swedish coast surfaced starboard out of the morning haze. The winds continued from the west, that is, headwinds, and we continued to sail under power. In the course of the morning, the engine continued running ever more slowly, however; something wasn't right. We turned the engine off and raised sail as soon as we were in a possible to reach Mön. We were around Trelleborg at the time. In the afternoon, we sailed into Danish waters and, towards evening, Möns-Klint, the large chalk cliffs, surfaced in front of us. The winds continued to die

---

[6] Editor's Note. An abortive German attempt at a behind-the-lines resistance movement.

out and we approached the coast very slowly. At 2230 hours, in seven meters of water, we dropped anchor.

By then, it was our fifth night on board and everyone had made some sort of sleeping arrangements by then. There were only two bunks on board, which had been for the two men of the original crew. I commandeered one of them, since my back pain started to become unbearable. The wound channel was obviously festering, but the pus did not want to come out. The shrapnel was too deep. And there was no one on board whom I would happily entrust with a knife to cut it out. There was neither doctor nor medic far and wide. *Stabsarzt* Dr. Vogel had to be with out people in Schleswig Holstein, just like Arturio. If only I had good old *Oberfeldwebel* Schwalb, a senior medic, but he was dead. I can still see him before my eyes: The endearing humor in his elegant eyes and the wire-rimmed glasses on his nose, which he struggled with constantly. He had to try to restore them to reason with the middle finger of his right hand every few minutes and push them upwards, while they, the glasses, felt much better in the vicinity of the tip of his nose. He got it at Kahlberg-Liep, when he jumped out of a bunker, because a wounded man was calling for him. It was really terrible there.

At its widest, the Vistula Spit was only 800 meters wide in spots. Our last *Panthers* operated along the sandy and rolling road along the spit and in the cuts in the woods running parallel to the road. They hunkered down in hull-down positions along the blocking positions that had been established in the swells in the ground that ran all along the spit. They were the backstops for *Panzergrenadier-Regiment 12* and *Panzer-Aufklärungs-Abteilung 4*: Bix, Kolter, Hofknecht, Fintelmann, Igel, Eidloth, Schwaffers, Tautorus—the last tank commanders of *Panzer-Regiment 35*. All of it was under almost constant fire from the front and the sides. The light and medium artillery and the heavy mortars fired from the front; across the lagoon from the right came the heavy artillery. Occasionally, Russian light naval forces attacked from the sea or along the lagoon. The Vistula Spit was heavily wooded and you can imagine the fireworks that took place in the crowns of the trees. It was a tree burst that got our medic Schwalb.

✠

It was just a few days prior to that that I had dropped anchor in the *Moby Dick III* right at this spot by Möns-Klint. I had paddled ashore in our small rubber boat with my wife and two small ones. The children had found calcified snails, crayfish and thunder stones among the chalk deposits; we had watched thousands upon thousands of European swifts build their nests, one after the other, on the steeply falling chalk cliffs. Then we clambered up to the top along a narrow and slippery path and enjoyed the view of the water from above. Close to the coast, but very small nonetheless, was our boat as seen from a bird's perspective, something we had done for the first time. It was wonderfully beautiful in the thick woods and in the Liselund palace and its grounds. How different the landscape can look to a person based on his mood! What seemed to be the symbol of peace twenty-five years later seemed sinister, almost antagonistic to us in 1945. We saw moving lights everywhere along the coast; we heard voices and shouts. Car lights were directed on us from the high ground. They called out to us on loudspeakers, without us being able to understand it or feeling compelled to answer. But . . . to go on land, like we did twenty-five years later . . . no one had any desire to do that. The next day we discovered the reason for the unrest. Danish so-called "freedom fighters" had been the ones screening Möns-Klint. They were guarding against us, who were happy to have escaped the Russians and be in freedom.

Around 0400 hours on the morning of 14 May 1945, the engine ran after a fashion again, and we held a council of war, the first one since we had gotten the boat free outside of Nickelswalde. Where did we want to go? The harbor at Klintholm, which the Swedes had designated for us, was exactly four nautical miles away. No one wanted to go to Klintholm. The closest course to Germany went thirty-five nautical miles south-southwest to the southern tip of Falster and, from there, around thirty nautical miles west, then south to Fehmarn. From there, it was another forty nautical miles to Kiel.

The whole thing had a hitch, however, and a pretty big one. From the southern tip of Falster and running in a southeasterly direction was the feared Gedser Riff, which extended a good seven nautical miles. I had sailed there a lot in peacetime and, at the end of the riff, was the Gedser lightship. But that was only in peacetime. Even if you maneuvered well, which was possible with the engine, and found that spot, you were within ten nautical miles of the Russian-occupied Pomeranian coast. A bloodcurdling thought. If we waited until 1800 hours to sail out, I mentioned for consideration, then we would pass the critical spot around midnight, that is, while it was dark. And the weather was supposed to be good. That would put us in Kiel the next evening.

Even though I painted the docks at the Kiel Olympic harbor and the virtues of the Kiel Yacht Club—formerly the Kiel Imperial Yacht Club—in the most glowing terms, everyone had had a belly full of the Russians and no one want to take a risk after everything had good unexpectedly well.

That left one option: Sail through Grön Sound west of Mön and the Smaalands Channel. That meant going around Falster and Lolland from the north and into the Great Belt, sailing into Kiel Bay from there. There was a lot to be said for that, including the fact that the distance was not considerably greater. The only concern: Grön Sound and the Smaalands Channel were very narrow in spots, with the result that we would be reliant on our not-so-reliable engine for a good twenty nautical miles due to the predominant westerly winds. None of that had any effect; no one wanted to be anywhere near any Russian fast boats.

In short, I was outvoted.

When we hauled anchor at 0430 hours on 14 May—it was our sixth day at sea—and rounded Mön, taking up a course for Grön Sound, the narrows between

Mön and Falster, the weather was not cooperating. The skies had clouded over, and it began to drizzle. Although there was only a moderate wind, it blew more from the north than from the west. That meant that we would have to chug along under engine power until far outside of Vordingborg. We passed Stubbeköbing at 09000 hours; the island of Bogö was starboard. The rain stopped and it started to clear up, but the wind had also picked up in the meantime. It was probably a four on the Beaufort Scale.[7] In the choppy seas, the water occasionally sprayed up on deck. None of that was particularly worrisome, except for the fact that the engine started running noticeably slower again. Around 1000 hours, the large bridge that connected Falster and Seeland turned up. It was high enough to be able to pass, but the situation was becoming critical. In the maritime chart, the narrows were called *Storström*, which wasn't a bad name, since it had to mean something like large, strong current.

The northwest wind sprayed the water against us as if through a nozzle. Our hot-bulb engine increasingly grew more listless, not even reaching half of its power any more. When we reached the bridge, we were moving at a walking pace. As a precautionary measure, we didn't stop at the southern edge of the navigation channel. We didn't pick up any speed. Since a change in the situation was not expected, the wind was actually increasing somewhat and we would not be able to put up sail for at least another ten nautical miles in the navigation channel, we gave up on the enterprise. With some difficulty, we were able to turn around and reach the small harbor of Orehoved around 1100 hours.

We stepped on Danish soil for the first time, although I wish it had been a more exciting venue. Prior to the construction of the bridge, Orehoved had served as a ferry harbor and where the ferries had formerly docked was where we tied up. A few ugly shacks could be seen and, a little further, some houses. Our *Landser* were not all that disturbed, since they had not had land under their feet since Nickelswalde. Correspondingly, they enthusiastically reconnoitered the area. After about an hour, the results of the patrol were available: (1) The local populace was very nice and accommodating but apparently keen on getting weapons. For an *08* pistol, they had been offered a kilogram of bread, a kilogram of ham, and a pound of butter. For an egg, they wanted two *08* bullets. (2) Danish resistance fighters were in the process of sealing off the harbor. I immediately issued orders: remain close to the boat, empty all weapons, wear small arms conspicuously, emplace three machine guns on land and two on board where they were visible. Do not allow yourselves to be provoked.

Visibly impressed by our gleaming weaponry, the Danes carefully went into position at the edge of the village. Their leader came aboard and explained to me in a short but not unfriendly manner that the *Reich* had capitulated and he had to disarm us. We answered in a short but not unfriendly manner that we were aware of the

---

[7] Editor's Note. A measure of the wind speed in relation to conditions at sea or on land. A four on the scale is a moderate breeze of thirteen to seventeen miles per hour (twenty to twenty-eight kilometers per hour)—i.e., sea conditions of small waves and frequent whitecaps.

capitulation but that a disarming was only possible by the English. Moreover, we intended to set sail again the following morning. He didn't have to worry about us and could move his outposts to behind the village. He agreed. Of most concern to us was the last point. We would soon be getting rid of the weapons anyway, but it was a whole lot better to trade them for rations, for which we needed contact with the locals, that is, the village. A portion of the weapons was therefore released for sale—minus the bolts, of course—with minimum prices established to prevent being undersold.

While two tank drivers and the navy man worked on the engine on board, we opened up our arms market in Orehoved. The menu that night: tomato soup, Swedish style; eggs over easy or scrambled, Danish style, with bacon or ham; white bread; milk. The weather remained unchanged on the morning of 15 May: wind northwest, speed four. The navy man thought the engine would make it. Correspondingly, we set sail at 0900 hours. After we had covered barely four nautical miles after a good hour—that is, not far enough out of the narrow navigation channel in order to put up sail—the engine started its fainting spells again. It was really too dumb. With the boat I have today, it would have been child's play to sail out of the slight current. I would not even have needed to use my nine horsepower Wankel at all. But we were sitting on the weak-in-the-groins *Brunhilde*, and we had no other choice but to turn around for the second time and wait for better weather and winds from the south, north or, better yet, the east. At 1100 hours, we dropped tied up in Orehoved again. Lunch at noon followed by the arms market in the village.

In the afternoon, our Danish freedom fighters were back and announced they were going to get the English to disarm us. The arms sales took on new impetus. People came all the way form Vordingbord, on the other side of the island, to get their needs filled. By evening, we only had a machine gun, two assault rifles and a handful of pistols. Fintelmann and I still carried them openly, while others had sewn their *08's* into their backpacks.

Then 16 May arrived, the last day aboard the good *Brunhilde*. The Danes had reported us to the British that morning.

They arrived at 1100 hours. It was a jeep and a striking but unarmed English sergeant. While the last machine gun and assault rifles went overboard, he greeted us beamingly, shook all of our hands and distributed cigarettes. He explained that the Danes had complained about our invasion. We were directed to turn over the many weapons the Danes had talked about and put them in the back of his jeep. When we told him what had happened to our weapons and what the prices were, he started to laugh resoundingly.

The reaction of the Dane was quite different. He was the police chief there, and he told me the many German weapons lying around were already causing him concern. In that regard, I was able to calm him down when I told him our weapons were at best souvenirs. In the hands of the Danes, they most certainly would not shoot.

The German-Danish-English Peace of Orehoved was concluded with a final cognac. The *Brunhilde* was then ceremoniously transferred to the Danes. Fintelmann received orders to march off to a prisoner collection point. Together with two mechanized infantrymen, I wanted to go to the German military hospital in Vordingborg, which had been recommended to me by the Danes. Fintelmann had the men assemble. As we took leave of one another, the English sergeant saluted. That group marched off with a cheerful song.

No speech with fancy words for the history books was held; no one had spoken the motto of our former 2nd Battalion:

> *Ehre kannst du nirgends borgen,*
> *Dafür musst du selber sorgen!*
> You can't borrow honor anywhere;
> You have to provide for it yourself!

We had only said good-bye to one another, take care, and let me hear from you sometime.

APPENDIX A

Rank Table

U.S. Army	German Army	Waffen-SS	English Equivalent
Enlisted			
Private	*Schütze*	*SS-Schütze*[1]	Private
Private First Class	*Oberschütze*	*SS-Oberschütze*[2]	Private First Class
Corporal	*Gefreiter*	*SS-Sturmmann*	Acting Corporal
(Senior Corporal)	*Obergefreiter*	*SS-Rottenführer*	Corporal
(Staff Corporal)	*Stabsgefreiter*	*SS-Stabsrottenführer*[3]	
Noncommissioned Officers			
Sergeant	*Unteroffizier*	*SS-Unterscharführer*	Sergeant
(None)	*Unterfeldwebel*	*SS-Scharführer*	Staff Sergeant
Staff Sergeant	*Feldwebel*	*SS-Oberscharführer*	Technical Sergeant
Sergeant First Class	*Oberfeldwebel*	*SS-Hauptscharführer*	Master Sergeant
Master Sergeant	*Hauptfeldwebel*	*SS-Sturmscharführer*	Sergeant Major
Sergeant Major	*Stabsfeldwebel*		
Officers			
2nd Lieutenant	*Leutnant*	*SS-Untersturmführer*	2nd Lieutenant
1st Lieutenant	*Oberleutnant*	*SS-Obersturmführer*	1st Lieutenant
Captain	*Hauptmann*	*SS-Hauptsturmführer*	Captain
Major	*Major*	*SS-Sturmbannführer*	Major
Lieutenant Colonel	*Oberstleutnant*	*SS-Obersturmbannführer*	Lieutenant Colonel
Colonel	*Oberst*	*SS-Standartenführer*	Colonel
(None)	(None)	*SS-Oberführer*	(None)
Brigadier General	*Generalmajor*	*SS-Brigadeführer*	Brigadier General
Major General	*Generalleutnant*	*SS-Gruppenführer*	Major General
Lieutenant General	*General der Panzertruppen*, etc.	*SS-Obergruppenführer*	Lieutenant General
General	*Generaloberst*	*SS-Oberstgruppenführer*	General
General of the Army	*Feldmarschall*	*Reichsführer-SS*	Field Marshal

---

[1] *SS-Mann* before 1942.
[2] Not used before 1942.
[3] Rank did not officially exist but has been seen in written records.

APPENDIX B

4. *Panzer-Division* Order of Battle

ACTIVATION

The *4. Panzer-Division* was activated on 10 November 1938, with its headquarters in Würzburg. Other than the campaign in France in 1940, it fought exclusively on the Eastern Front. It surrendered to Soviet forces on the Frische Nehrung (around Danzig) in May 1945.[1]

COMMANDERS

10 November 1938: *Generaloberst* Georg-Hans Reinhardt[2]
15 February 1940: *Generalleutnant* Ludwig *Ritter* von Radlmaier
6 April 1940: *Generalleutnant* Johann-Joachim Stever
15 May 1940: *Oberst* Hans *Freiherr* von Boineburg-Lengsfeld
19 May 1940: *Generalleutnant* Johann-Joachim Stever
24 July 1940: *Oberst* Hans *Freiherr* von Boineburg-Lengsfeld
7 September 1940: *Generalmajor* Willibald *Freiherr* von Langermann und Erlencamp
24 December 1941: *General der Panzertruppen* Dietrich von Saucken
6 January 1942: *General der Panzertruppen* Heinrich Eberbach
2 March 1942: *Generalleutnant* Otto Heidkämper
4 April 1942: *General der Panzertruppen* Heinrich Eberbach
23 June 1942: *Oberstleutnant* (?) Edgar Hielscher

---

[1] Translator's Note. The information in this and subsequent orders of battle draws from Peter Schmitz et al., *Die Deutschen Divisionen* (Osnabrück: Biblio-Verlag) and *Lexikon der Wehrmacht* (www.lexikon-der-wehrmacht.de). In cases where there is a divergence, the work by Schmitz et al. is used for dates and information.

[2] Translator's Note. The highest rank achieved is listed. The dates indicate the date on which (acting) command of the division was assumed.

COMMANDERS *continued*

3 July 1942: *General der Panzertruppen* Heinrich Eberbach

24 November 1942: *General der Panzertruppen* Dr. Karl Mauss

28 November 1942: *Generalleutnant Dipl.-Ing.* Erich Schneider

7 January 1943: *General der Panzertruppen* Dr. Karl Mauss

29 January 1943: *Generalleutnant Dipl.-Ing.* Erich Schneider

15 May 1943: *General der Panzertruppen* Dietrich von Saucken

23 October 1943: *General der Panzertruppen* Dr. Karl Mauss

21 January 1944: *Generalleutnant Dipl.-Ing.* Hans Junck

7 February 1944: *Generalleutnant* Clemans Betzel

3 March 1944: *General der Panzertruppen* Dietrich von Saucken

6 May 1944: *Generalleutnant* Clemans Betzel

June 1944: *General der Panzertruppen* Dietrich von Saucken

21 December 1944: *Oberst* Hans Christern

28 December 1944: *Generalleutnant* Clemans Betzel

27 March 1945: *Oberst* Ernst-Wilhelm Hoffmann

1 April 1945: *Generalmajor* Hans Hecker

ORGANIZATION FOR BATTLE

Motorized/Mechanized Infantry

- *4. Schützen-Brigade.* Formed on 1 November 1939 in Bamberg as the headquarters for the two motorized rifle regiments of the division. On 5 July 1942, the brigade was redesignated as the *4. Panzergrenadier-Brigade.*

- *Schützen-Regiment 12.* Formed on 1 April 1938 from *Infanterie-Regiment Kaiser Franz Josef I Nr. 1* and *Kraftfahr-Jäger-Bataillon Nr. 1* of the Austrian Army. On 10 July 1942, redesignated as *Panzergrenadier-Regiment 12.* Dissolved on 4 January 1943 and never reformed.

- *Schützen-Regiment 33.* Formed on 1 April 1938 by reorganizing and redesignating *Infanterie-Regiment (mot) 33* of the *13. Infanterie-Division.* On 5 July 1942, redesignated as *Panzergrenadier-Regiment 33.* It underwent a (battlefield?) reconstitution in January 1945.

- *Grenadier-Regiment 1071.* Formed out of elements of the *154. Reserve-Division* on 1 July 1944. The regiment was disbanded on 5 August 1944, with the majority of its personnel and assets incorporated into the *4. Panzer-Division.* Some elements were transferred into the *129. Infanterie-Division.*

Armor

- *5. Panzer-Brigade.* Formed on 10 November 1938, with headquarters in Bamberg. In 1940, redesignated as the *3. Panzer-Brigade.* On 27 January 1941, transferred to the *3. Panzer-Division,* where it was disbanded on 21 February 1942.
- *Panzer-Regiment 35.* Formed on 10 November 1938, with headquarters in Bamberg. On 24 May 1943, the regimental headquarters provided cadre for the establishment of the headquarters of *schweres Heeres-Panzerjäger-Regiment 656* (two battalions of the *Ferdinand* tank destroyer and one battalion of the *Brummbär* assault tank). The regimental headquarters was reestablished on 5 June 1944. In January 1945, the regiment received a (battlefield?) reconstitution.
- *Panzer-Regiment 36.* Formed on 10 November 1938, with headquarters in Schweinfurt. On 11 November 1940, transferred to the *14. Panzer-Division,* where it was destroyed in February 1943 in Stalingrad. Reactivated on 25 April 1943.

Reconnaissance

- *Aufklärungs-Abteilung (mot) 7.* Formed on 15 October 1938 in Munich from *Kraftfahr-Abteilung München* (1 October 1934), which, in turn, was formed from the *7. (bayer.) Kraftfahr-Abteilung* (1 January 1921). Redesignated as *Panzer-Aufklärungs-Abteilung 7* on 1 February 1940. On 5 May 1942, the battalion was consolidated with *Kradschützen-Bataillon 34,* retaining the latter designation.
- *Kradschützen-Bataillon 34.* Formed on 7 January 1941 from the *III./Infanterie-Regiment 5.* On 5 May 1942, it consolidated with *Panzer-Aufklärungs-Abteilung 7* (see above). On 30 April 1943, reorganized and redesignated as *Panzer-Aufklärungs-Abteilung 4* (see below).
- *Panzer-Aufklärungs-Abteilung 4.* Formed on 30 April 1943 out of *Kradschützen-Bataillon 34* (see above). In January 1945, the battalion received a (battlefield?) reconstitution.

Artillery

- *Artillerie-Regiment 93.* Formed on 12 October 1937 in Würzburg with only the 2nd Battalion (Heavy). On 2 July 1940, it was attached to the division artillery, *Artillerie-Regiment 103.* On 7 January 1941, it was consolidated with the divisional artillery and redesignated as the *III./Artillerie-Regiment 103.*
- *Artillerie-Regiment 103.* Formed on 7 November 1938 in Meiningen (with the 1st Battalion coming from the *II./Niederösterreichisches leichtes Artillerie-Regiment Nr. 3* of the former Austrian Army). In June 1944, the regiment was redesignated as *Panzer-Artillerie-Regiment 103.* In January 1945, the regiment received a (battlefield?) reconstitution.

Air Defense Artillery

- *Heeres-Flak-Artillerie-Abteilung (mot) 290.* Formed on 1 November 1942 from *Fla-Bataillon 605.* In January 1945, the battalion received a (battlefield?) reconstitution.

Antitank

- *Panzerabwehr-Abteilung 49.* Formed on 1 August 1939 in Wöllersdorf out of the Austrian *Infanterie-Kanonen-Abteilung 1.* Redesignated as *Panzerjäger-Abteilung 49* on 16 March 1940. Reconstituted in January 1944 (assigned new field post numbers as well).

Combat Engineers

- *Pionier-Bataillon 79.* Formed on 1 November 1939. Redesignated as *Panzer-Pionier-Bataillon 79* on 15 April 1940. In January 1945, the battalion received a (battlefield?) reconstitution.

Divisional Troops

- *Nachrichten-Abteilung 79.* Formed on 1 March 1939 in Würzburg. In January 1945, the battalion received a (battlefield?) reconstitution.
- *Feld-Ersatz-Bataillon 84.* Formed for the division on 14 March 1941. Redesignated as *Feld-Ersatz-Bataillon 103.* on 1 September 1943.
- *Divisions-Nachschubführer (mot) 84.* The division support command. Divisional support elements not designated otherwise were given the numerical designator of 84.

9. *Panzer-Division* Order of Battle

ACTIVATION

The division was formed through the redesignation and reorganization of the *4. leichte Division* on 3 January 1940. The division fought in Poland and France and then on the Eastern Front until 1944, when it was pulled out of the line for reconstitution, which took place in southern France. It then fought on the Western Front until the end of the war. *Panzer-Brigade 105* was consolidated with the division in September 1944. The division surrendered to U.S. forces in the Ruhr Pocket in April 1945.

COMMANDERS (SCHMITZ)

1 September 1939: *Generalleutnant* Dr. Alfred *Ritter* von Hubicki (also commanded
    the *4. leichte Division*)
14 April 1942: *Generalleutnant* Johannes Baeßler
25 July 1942: *Generalmajor* Heinrich-Hermann von Hülsen
4 August 1942: *Generalleutnant* Walter Scheller
22 July 1943: *Generalleutnant* Erwin Jollasse
1 October 1943: *Generalmajor* Dr. Johannes Schulz
1 December 1943: Bömers
January 1944: *Generalleutnant* Erwin Jollasse
20 March 1944: *Generalleutnant* Clemens Betzel
15 August 1944: *Oberst* Max Sperling
2 September 1944: *Generalmajor* Gerhard Müller
6 September 1944: *Generalleutnant* Harald *Freiherr* von Everfeldt
6 March 1945: *Oberst* Helmut Zollenkopf

COMMANDERS (LEXIKON)[1]

Generalleutnant Alfred *Ritter* von Hubicki—until 14 April 1942
Generalleutnant Johannes Baeßler—15 April 1942
Generalmajor Heinrich-Hermann von Hülsen—27 July 1942
Generalleutnant Walter Scheller—4 August 1942
Generalleutnant Erwin Jollasse—22 July 1943
Generalmajor Dr. Johannes Schulz—20 October 1943
Oberst Max Sperling—27 November 1943
Generalleutnant Erwin Jollasse—28 November 1943
Oberst Max Sperling—10 August 1944
Generalmajor Gerhard Müller—3 September 1944
Generalleutnant Harald *Freiherr* von Everfeldt—16 September 1944
Generalleutnant Friedrich Wilhelm von Mellenthin—28 December 1944
Generalleutnant Harald *Freiherr* von Everfeldt—February 1945
Oberst Helmut Zollenkopf—6 March 1945.

ORGANIZATION FOR BATTLE

Motorized/Mechanized Infantry

- *9. Schützen-Brigade*. Formed on 16 February 1940 as the headquarters for the division's two motorized rifle regiments. Redesignated as the *9. Panzergrenadier-Brigade* on 5 July 1942. Disbanded on 15 December 1942.
- *Kavallerie-Schützen-Regiment 10*. Formed on 1 August 1938 from the former Austrian Army *Kraftfahrjäger-Bataillon 3 "Kopal"* and *Infanterie-Regiment 6*. Redesignated as *Schützen-Regiment 10* on 18 March 1940 and further redesignated as *Panzergrenadier-Regiment 10* on 7 May 1942. Reconstituted in France in June 1944, with personnel and cadre coming from *Reserve-Grenadier-Regiment 5*, along with *Panzergrenadier-Regiment 56* and *Reserve-Grenadier-Bataillon (mot) 35 (155. Reserve-Division)*.
- *Kavallerie-Schützen-Regiment 11*. Formed on 1 August 1938 from the former Austrian Army *Kraftfahrjäger-Bataillon 2 "Feldmarschall Radetzky"* and *Feldjäger-Bataillon 2*. Redesignated as *Schützen-Regiment 11* on 19 March 1940 and further redesignated as *Panzergrenadier-Regiment 10* on 7 May 1942. Reconstituted in France in June 1944, with personnel and cadre coming from *Reserve-Grenadier-Regiment 25*, along with *Reserve-Panzergrenadier-Bataillon 25* and *Reserve-Grenadier-Bataillon (mot) 119 (155. Reserve-Division)*.

---

[1] Translator's Note. Since there is considerable disparity between Schmitz and the Lexikon concerning dates and commanders, both are given here.

Reconnaissance

- *Aufklärungs-Regiment 9.* Formed on 1 August 1938 from the former Austrian Army *Kraftfahrjäger-Bataillon 4.* Disbanded on 1 August 1940, with the first battalion used to form *Kradschützen-Bataillon 59* and the second battalion for *Aufklärungs-Abteilung 9.*
- *Aufklärungs-Abteilung (mot) 9.* Activated on 1 August 1940 from the *II./Aufklärungs-Regiment 9* (see above). Disbanded on 14 March 1942 and consolidated with *Kradschützen-Bataillon 59,* retaining the later designation.
- *Kradschützen-Bataillon 59.* Formed on 1 August 1940 from the *I./Aufklärungs-Regiment 9* (see above). Consolidated with *Aufklärungs-Abteilung 9* on 14 March 1942, retaining the original designation. Reorganized and redesignated as *Panzer-Aufklärungs-Abteilung 9* on 13 April 1943 (with an effective date of 17 March 1943).
- *Panzer-Aufklärungs-Abteilung 9.* Formed by the reorganization and redesignation of *Kradschützen-Bataillon 59* (see above). Reconstituted in France in June 1944, using assets from *Reserve-Panzer-Aufklärungs-Abteilung 9* (Krems).

Armor

- *Panzer-Abteilung 33.* Formed on 1 July 1938 from the former Austrian Army *Panzerwagen-Abteilung.* On 2 February 1940, it became the *II./Panzer-Regiment 33.*
- *Panzer-Regiment 33.* Formed on 2 February 1940 from the headquarters of *Panzer-Regiment Conze* (*Panzer-Lehr-Regiment*), the reinforced *Panzer-Lehr-Abteilung* and *Panzer-Abteilung 33* (see above). Reconstituted in southern France in June 1944; received a battlefield reconstitution in October 1944 near Arnheim.

Artillery

- *Artillerie-Regiment 102.* Formed on 1 September 1938 from the former Austrian Army *Artillerie-Regiment 9* and the *II./leichte Artillerie-Regiment 1.* Redesignated as *Panzer-Artillerie-Regiment 102* on 12 December 1942. Reconstituted in southern France in April 1944, using assets from *Reserve-Artillerie-Abteilung (mot) 260* of the *155. Reserve-Panzer-Division.*

Air Defense Artillery

- *Heeres-Flak-Artillerie-Abteilung 287.* Formed on 16 March 1942 (effective 7 February 1942), using assets from the *1./Heeres-Flak-Artillerie-Abteilung 277.* On 2 June 1942, it was consolidated with the divisional artillery, receiving the designation *IV./Panzer-Artillerie-Regiment 192.* On 1 May 1943, it was released from assignment and reconstituted as *Heeres-Flak-Artillerie-Abteilung 287.*

Antitank

- *Panzerabwehr-Abteilung 50.* Formed on 1 August 1938 from the former Austrian Army *Infanterie-Kanonen-Abteilung 3.* Redesignated as *Panzerjäger-Abteilung 50* on 1 January 1940. Reconstituted in southern France in early 1944 from assets of *Reserve-Panzerjäger-Abteilung 5.*

Combat Engineers

- *Pionier-Bataillon 86.* Formed on 10 November 1938; redesignated as *Panzer-Pionier-Bataillon 86* on 22 April 1940. Reconstituted in France in April 1944.

Divisional Troops

- *Panzer-Nachrichten-Abteilung 85.* Formed on 15 February 1940.
- *Feld-Ersatz-Bataillon 60.* Formed for the division in the spring of 1940. Redesignated as *Feldersatz-Bataillon 102* on 1 September 1943.
- *Panzer-Divisions-Nachschubführer 60.* The division support command. Divisional support elements not designated otherwise were given the numerical designator of 60.

11. *Panzer-Division* Order of Battle

ACTIVATION

The division was activated on 1 August 1940 by reorganizing and redesignating the *11. Schützen-Brigade*, which had been formed on 1 December 1939. The division fought primarily on the Eastern Front until the beginning of 1944, when it was pulled out of the line to be reconstituted, primarily through cadre and equipment of the *273. Reserve-Panzer-Division*. It then fought in the west for the remainder of the war, surrendering to U.S. forces in the Bavarian Woods in 1945.

COMMANDERS

1 August 1940: *General der Panzertruppen* Ludwig Crüwell
15 August 1940: *Generalleutnant* Günther Angern
20 August 1940: *General der Panzertruppen* Hans-Karl *Freiherr* von Esebeck
20 October 1940: *Generalleutnant* Walter Scheller
16 May 1942: *General der Panzertruppen* Hermann Balck
5 March 1943: *General der Infanterie* Dietrich von Choltitz
15 May 1943: *Generalleutnant* Johannes Mickl
10 August 1943: *Generalleutnant* Wend von Wietersheim
7 May 1944: von Hake
1 January 1945: *Generalmajor* Horst *Freiherr* Treusch von Buttlar-Brandenfels
3 May 1945: *Generalleutnant* Wend von Wietersheim

ORGANIZATION FOR BATTLE

Motorized/Mechanized Infantry

- *11. Schützen-Brigade.* Formed on 8 December 1939 as a separate motorized rifle brigade with *Schützen-Regiment 110* and *Schützen-Regiment 111.* Cornerstone for the formation of the division. Redesignated as the *11. Panzergrenadier-Brigade* on 5 July 1942. Disbanded sometime in 1943.

- *Schützen-Regiment 110.* Formed on 7 December 1939, with cadre for the headquarters coming from *Infanterie-Ersatz-Regiment (mot) 20.* Redesignated as *Panzergrenadier-Regiment 110* on 7 May 1942. Reconstituted in France in May 1944, with personnel and cadre coming from *Reserve-Panzergrenadier-Regiment 92,* along with *Reserve-Panzergrenadier-Regiment 12* and *Reserve-Grenadier-Bataillon (mot) 20.*

- *Schützen-Regiment 111.* Formed on 7 December 1939, with cadre coming from *Infanterie-Ersatz-Regiment 29* and *Infanterie-Ersatz-Regiment 2.* Redesignated as *Panzergrenadier-Regiment 111* on 7 May 1942. Reconstituted in France in May 1944, with personnel and cadre coming from *Reserve-Grenadier-Regiment (mot) 73,* along with *Reserve-Panzergrenadier-Bataillon 40* and *Reserve-Grenadier-Bataillon (mot) 41.*

- *Panzergrenadier-Regiment 2111.* Formed on 4 September 1944 as a Valkyrie unit.[1] The regiment was intended for incorporation into the *15. Panzer-Grenadier-Division,* but it was diverted to the *11. Panzer-Division* by orders dated 25 September 1944.[2]

Armor

- *Panzer-Regiment 15.* Formed on 12 October 1937. The regiment was employed as a field army asset in Poland and then attached to the *5. Panzer-Division* for the campaign in France. In September 1940, it was ordered to the *11. Panzer-Division* as the divisional armor regiment. In May 1944, replacement personnel and equipment for the reconstitution came from *Reserve-Panzer-Abteilung 25* and *Reserve-Panzer-Abteilung 35.*

- *Panzer-Abteilung 52.* Formed on 15 March 1943 as a *Panther* battalion from personnel detachments from the *I./Panzer-Regiment 15.* On 21 August 1943, it reverted to its original designation and rejoined *Panzer-Regiment 15.*

Reconnaissance

- *Aufklärungs-Abteilung 231.* Formed on 26 August 1939 in Bamberg and attached to the division on 1 August 1940. On 5 September 1940, it was redesignated as *Panzer-Aufklärungs-Abteilung 231.* On 1 December 1941, it was consolidated into *Kradschützen-Bataillon 61.*

---

[1] Translator's Note. Despite extensive research, the exact meaning is unclear in force-structure terms, although it has nothing to do with the attempted assassination attempt on Hitler.

[2] Translator's Note. The Lexikon mentions nothing about this regiment.

- *Kradschützen-Bataillon 61.* Formed on 6 August 1940 from assets supplied by *Schützen-Regiment 110* and *Schützen-Regiment 111.* On 1 December 1941, it was consolidated with *Panzer-Aufklärungs-Abteilung 231,* retaining its original designation (see above). On 27 April 1943, it was reorganized and redesignated as *Panzer-Aufklärungs-Abteilung 11* (see below).
- *Panzer-Aufklärungs-Abteilung 11.* Formed by the reorganization and redesignation of *Kradschützen-Bataillon 61* (see above). Reconstituted in France in May 1944, using assets from *Reserve-Panzer-Aufklärungs-Abteilung 7* (Munich).

Artillery

- *Artillerie-Regiment 231.* Formed on 14 May 1940 for the *231. Division,* with assets (headquarters and 1st and 2nd Battalions) coming from *Artillerie-Regiment 746.* Disbanded as a regiment on 1 August 1940, being redesignated as *Artillerie-Regiment 119* on 10 October 1940. Redesignated as *Panzer-Artillerie-Regiment 119* in May 1942. Reconstituted in France in May 1944, with assets coming from *Reserve-Artillerie-Abteilung 167.*

Air Defense Artillery

- *Heeres-Flak-Artillerie-Abteilung (mot) 277.* Formed on 22 February 1941. Reformed in Munich on 18 March 1942. Temporarily designated as the *IV. (Flak)/Artillerie-Regiment 119* on 24 June 1942. Reverted to original designation on 1 May 1943. On 8 June 1944, reconstituted with three batteries.

Antitank

- *Panzerjäger-Abteilung 61.* Formed on 1 August 1940, with assets coming from the headquarters and 1st Company of Panzerjäger-Abteilung 222. Reconstituted in France in May 1944, with assets coming from *Reserve-Panzer-Jäger-Abteilung 10.*

Combat Engineers

- *Pionier-Bataillon 209.* Formed on 26 August 1939; redesignated as *Panzer-Pionier-Bataillon 209* on 8 August 1940. Reconstituted in France on 12 May 1944, with assets from *Reserve-Panzer-Pionier-Bataillon 19.*

Divisional Troops

- *Nachrichten-Abteilung 341.* Formed on 8 March 1940. Redesignated as *Panzer-Nachrichten-Abteilung 341* on 1 August 1940 and further redesignated as *Panzer-Nachrichten-Abteilung 89* on 1 June 1943. Reconstituted in France in May 1944.
- *Feld-Ersatz-Bataillon 61.* Formed for the division in the spring of 1941. Disbanded that winter and reformed in the summer of 1942. Redesignated as *Feldersatz-Bataillon 119* on 1 September 1943.
- *Panzer-Divisions-Nachschubführer 61.* The division support command. Divisional support elements not designated otherwise were given the numerical designator of 61.

16. Panzer-Division Order of Battle

ACTIVATION

The *4. Panzer-Division* was activated on 1 November 1940 from the *16. Infanterie-Division*. It was effectively destroyed in the Battle of Stalingrad. The division was reconstituted in March 1943 under the supervision of the commander in chief, West. By May 1943, it was considered operational again. In December 1944, the division was assigned to the *XXIV. Panzer-Korps* as part of the recently introduced fixed corps structure. In February 1945, the remnants of the division were consolidated with *Panzer-Division Jüterbog*, effectively reforming the division. Elements of the division surrendered to both Soviet and U.S. forces.

COMMANDERS

August 1940: *Generaloberst* Hans–Valentin Hube
15 September 1942: *Generalleutnant* Günther Angern
5 March 1943: *Generalmajor* Rudolf Sieckenius[1]
8 November 1943: *Generalmajor* Hans-Ulrich Back
August 1944: *Generalleutnant* Dietrich von Müller
1 December 1944: *Oberst* Theodor Kretschmer (acting commander)
28 February 1945: *Generalleutnant* Dietrich von Müller
1 April 1945: Dr. Aschoff
19 April 1945: *Oberst* Kurt Treuhaupt

---

[1] Translator's Note. The Lexikon lists the commander at this time as *Generalmajor* Burkhart Müller-Hillebrand, with Sieckenius not assuming command until May 1943.

ORGANIZATION FOR BATTLE

Motorized/Mechanized Infantry

- *16. Schützen-Brigade.* Formed on 3 August 1940 from the deactivated Headquarters of the *III./Schützen-Regiment 4* as the headquarters for the two motorized rifle regiments of the division. On 5 July 1942, the brigade was redesignated as the *16. Panzergrenadier-Brigade.* The brigade headquarters element was deactivated in November 1942.
- *Schützen-Regiment 64.* Formed on 3 August 1940 from *Infanterie-Regiment 64 (16. Infanterie-Division).* On 5 July 1942, redesignated as *Panzergrenadier-Regiment 64.* Destroyed in Stalingrad in January 1943. Reconstituted in northwest France starting in March 1943. In December 1944 brought up to three battalions by consolidating with the *II./Panzergrenadier-Regiment 79.* Reconstituted by elements of *Panzer-Division Jüterbog* in February 1945.
- *Schützen-Regiment 79.* Formed on 3 August 1940 from *Infanterie-Regiment 79 (16. Infanterie-Division).* On 5 July 1942, redesignated as *Panzergrenadier-Regiment 79.* Destroyed in Stalingrad in January 1943. Reconstituted in northwest France starting in March 1943. In December 1944, reorganized and redesignated as *Panzer-Füsilier-Regiment 79* as a corps troop of the *XXIV. Panzer-Korps.* For the reorganization, *Panzergrenadier-Regiment 79* provided its 1st Battalion, while an additional battalion came from *Panzergrenadier-Regiment 63.* The regiment provided its 3rd Battalion to *Panzergrenadier-Regiment 64* (see above).

Armor

- *Panzer-Regiment 2.* Formed on 15 October 1935, originally serving with the *1. Panzer-Division.* The regiment joined the *16. Panzer-Division* on 20 October 1940. On 28 May 1942, the regiment received a 3rd Battalion, provided by the *II./Panzer-Regiment 10 (8. Panzer-Division).* Destroyed in the Battle of Stalingrad in January 1943. Reconstituted in France starting in March 1943 and reformed with three battalions. Reconstituted by elements of *Panzer-Division Jüterbog* in February 1945.

Reconnaissance

- *Kradschützen-Bataillon 16.* Formed on 2 August 1940 through a reorganization and redesignation of *Maschinen-Gewehr-Bataillon 1.* Consolidated with *Panzer-Aufklärungs-Abteilung 16* on 1 August 1941 (see below). Reconstituted starting on 1 May 1942 in Artemowsk. Destroyed in Stalingrad. Reconstituted in March 1943, using cadre from *Kradschützen-Grenadier-Regiment 890 (mot.).* Reorganized and redesignated as *Panzer-Aufklärungs-Abteilung 16* in April 1943.
- *Panzer-Aufklärungs-Abteilung 16.* Formed on 2 August 1940. Consolidated with *Kradschützen-Bataillon 16* on 1 September 1941 after the fighting for Uman (see above). Reorganized and redesignated as *Panzer-Aufklärungs-Abteilung 16* in April 1943 out of *Kradschützen-Bataillon 16* (see above).

Artillery

- *Artillerie-Regiment 16.* Divisional artillery of the *16. Infanterie-Division.* Reorganized and redesignated as *Artillerie-Regiment 16 (mot.)* on 3 August 1940. Redesignated as *Panzer-Artillerie-Regiment 16* on 1 July 1942. Consolidated with *Heeres-Flak-Artillerie-Abteilung 274,* retaining its original designation and incorporating the *Flak* battalion as its 4th Battalion. Destroyed in Stalingrad in January 1943. Reconstituted in France starting in March 1943. The *Flak* battalion was reconstituted as a separate battalion and redesignated as *Heeres-Flak-Artillerie-Abteilung 274* on 22 April 1943.

Air Defense Artillery

- *Heeres-Flak-Artillerie-Abteilung 274.* Formed on 22 February 1941. Temporarily redesignated and consolidated with the divisional artillery in 1942 and 1943 (see above). The *Flak* battalion was reconstituted as a separate battalion and redesignated as *Heeres-Flak-Artillerie-Abteilung 274* on 22 April 1943.

Antitank

- *Panzerjäger-Abteilung 16.* Formed on 16 March 1940. Destroyed in Stalingrad. Reconstituted in France starting in March 1943. Apparently inactivated on 6 May 1943 (see below).

Combat Engineers

- *Panzer-Pionier-Bataillon 16.* Formed on 20 August 1940. Served as an instructional battalion for Rumanian forces from January to March 1941. Destroyed in Stalingrad. Reconstituted in France starting in April 1943, with cadre coming from the engineer battalion of the reinforced *Grenadier-Regiment (mot) 890.*

Divisional Troops

- *Panzer-Divisions-Nachrichten-Abteilung 16.* Formed on 3 August 1940. Destroyed in Stalingrad. Reconstituted in France starting in March 1943, with some cadre coming from *Panzer-Nachrichten-Abteilung 127.*
- *Feld-Ersatz-Bataillon 16.* Formed for the division on 1 March 1941, only to be quickly deactivated. Reconstituted on 6 May 1943, using cadre from the dissolved *Panzerjäger-Abteilung 16* (see above). Redesignated (and reorganized?) as the *I./Panzer-Feld-Ersatz-Regiment 63.*
- *Panzer-Divisions-Nachschubführer 16.* The division support command. Divisional support elements not designated otherwise were given the numerical designator of 16.

18. Panzer-Division Order of Battle

ACTIVATION

The *18. Panzer-Division* was activated on 26 October 1940, with its headquarters in Chemnitz. Its cadre was taken from elements of the *4. Infanterie-Division* and the *14. Infanterie-Division*. The division completed its activation on 1 May 1941.

COMMANDERS

25 October 1940: *General der Panzertruppen* Walther K. Nehring
26 January 1942: *Generalleutnant* Karl *Freiherr* von Thüngen
25 April 1942: *General der Nachrichtentruppen* Albert Praun
May 1942: *Generalleutnant* Karl *Freiherr* von Thüngen
15 August 1942: *General der Nachrichtentruppen* Albert Praun
21 August 1942: *Oberst* Walter Gleininger
15 September 1942: *Generalleutnant* Erwin Menny
25 December 1942: *Generalleutnant* Karl *Freiherr* von Thüngen
1 April 1943: *Generalleutnant* Karl-Wilhelm von Schlieben

ORGANIZATION FOR BATTLE

Motorized/Mechanized Infantry
- *18. Schützen-Brigade.* Formed on 26 October 1940 as the headquarters for the two motorized rifle regiments of the division. On 5 July 1942, the brigade was redesignated as the *18. Panzergrenadier-Brigade.* The brigade was dissolved in 1944 and became *Radfahrjäger-Brigade 10.*
- *Schützen-Regiment 52.* Formed on 15 October 1940 by reorganizing and redesignating *Infanterie-Regiment 52* of the *4. Infanterie-Division.* On 5 July 1942, redesignated as *Panzergrenadier-Regiment 52.* Dissolved on 4 January 1943 and never reformed.

- *Schützen-Regiment 101.* Formed on 15 October 1940 by reorganizing and redesignated *Infanterie-Regiment 101* of the *14. Infanterie-Division.* On 5 July 1942, redesignated as *Panzergrenadier-Regiment 101.* When the division was dissolved on 29 September 1943, the regimental headquarters and the 1st Battalion were used to form the *II./Grenadier-Regiment 101* of the *14. Infanterie-Division.*

Armor

- *Panzer-Brigade 18.* Formed on 15 May 1942 out of the headquarters of *Panzer-Regiment 18.* Dissolved on 4 January 1943.
- *Panzer-Regiment 18.* Formed on 6 December 1940 from *Panzer-Abteilung A* and *Panzer-Abteilung B.* Dissolved on 15 May 1942 to form the brigade headquarters (see above).
- *Panzer-Regiment 28.* Formed on 6 December 1940 from *Panzer-Abteilung C* and *Panzer-Abteilung D.* Dissolved on 1 March 1941. The 2nd Battalion was used to form the *III./Panzer-Regiment 18.*
- *Panzer-Abteilung 18.* Formed on 15 May 1942 from the headquarters of the *III./Panzer-Regiment 18* and its 6th, 7th, and 11th Companies. In December 1943, the battalion was used to form *schwere Panzer-Abteilung 504 (Tiger).*

Reconnaissance

- *Panzer-Aufklärungs-Abteilung 88.* Formed on 15 October 1940 from *Aufklärungs-Abteilung Werder* (which, in turn, had been formed on 30 August 1940 from the *Kavallerie-Lehr- und Ersatz-Abteilung* of the Cavalry School in Potsdam-Krampnitz). On 10 November 1991, it was consolidated with *Kradschützen-Bataillon 18* to form the reinforced *Panzer-Aufklärungs-Abteilung 88.* Barely six weeks later, on 21 December 1941, the formation was redesignated again as *Kradschützen-Bataillon 18.*
- *Kradschützen-Bataillon 18.* Formed on 15 October 1940 from the *I./Infanterie-Regiment 52 (mot)* of the *14. Panzer-Division.* On 10 November 1991, it was consolidated with *Panzer-Aufklärungs-Abteilung 88* and then redesignated as *Kradschützen-Bataillon 18* again on 21 December 1941 (see above).
- *Panzer-Aufklärungs-Abteilung 18.* Formed on 1 April 1943. When the division was disbanded, the battalion was consolidated with *Schützen-Regiment 88* of the *18. Artillerie-Division.*

Artillery

- *Artillerie-Regiment (mot) 88.* Formed on 15 October 1940 from the headquarters of *Artillerie-Regiment 209.* The regiment was redesignated as *Panzer-Artillerie-Regiment 88* on 18 May 1942 and redesignated again on 16 October 1943 as *Artillerie-Regiment 88 (mot).* After the *18. Artillerie-Division* was disbanded on 25 July 1944, the regiment was redesignated as *Heeres-Artillerie-Regiment 88 (mot)* (reinforced by elements of *Artillerie-Abteilung 854*).

Air Defense Artillery

• *Heeres-Flak-Artillerie-Abteilung 292.* Formed on 1 November 1942.

Antitank

• *Panzerjäger-Abteilung 88.* Formed on 29 October 1940 from cadre from *Panzerjäger-Ersatz-Abteilung 4* in Borna. When the division was disbanded, the battalion became a separate formation and was redesignated as *schwere Heeres-Panzerjäger-Abteilung 88* and equipped with the *Nashorn* self-propelled antitank gun.

Combat Engineers

• *Panzer-Pionier-Bataillon 98.* Formed on 15 October 1940 from elements of *Pionier-Ersatz-Bataillon 24* in Riesa. Disbanded in October 1943 after the division was reorganized as an artillery division.

Divisional Troops

• *Nachrichten-Abteilung 88.* Formed on 15 October 1940 as the divisional signals battalion from *Infanterie-Division-Nachrichten-Abteilung 209.* Reorganized and redesignated as *Divisions-Nachrichten-Abteilung (mot) 88* of the *18. Artillerie-Division* when the division was disbanded. Completely disbanded on 22 October 1944.

• *Feld-Ersatz-Bataillon 88.* Formed for the division in Freiburg on 18 April 1941. Formed the cadre for the *II./Schützen-Regiment 52* on 23 January 1942 and the reformed. Disbanded with the division in the fall of 1942.

• *Panzer-Division-Nachschubführer 88.* The division support command. Divisional support elements not designated otherwise were given the numerical designator of 88.